The Third Industrial Revolution in Global Business

The essays in this volume probe the impact the digital revolution has had, or sometimes failed to have, on global business. Has digital technology, the authors ask, led to structural changes and greater efficiency and innovation? Although most of the essays support the idea that the information age has increased productivity in global business, the evidence of a "revolution" in the ways industries are organized is somewhat more blurred, with both significant discontinuities and features that persist from the second industrial revolution.

Giovanni Dosi is professor of economics at the Sant'Anna School of Advanced Studies in Pisa, Italy, where he directs the Institute of Economics. He is co-director of the task forces on Industrial Policy and on Intellectual Property Rights at the Initiative for Policy Dialogue, Columbia University, and Continental European editor of *Industrial and Corporate Change*.

Louis Galambos is professor of history and codirector of the Institute of Applied Economics, Global Health, and the Study of Business Enterprise at Johns Hopkins University. His most recent book is *The Creative Society – And the Price Americans Paid for It* (Cambridge, 2012).

COMPARATIVE PERSPECTIVES IN BUSINESS HISTORY

In the early decades of the twenty-first century, the world economy is experiencing its most profound transformation since the industrial revolution. Firms, communications systems, and markets for products, services, labor, and currencies are all breaking out of national boundaries. Business enterprises today must negotiate a global environment in order to innovate and to compete in ways that will protect or enhance their market shares. Governments must respond in new ways to the periodic crises that occur in all market-centered systems. At the same time, governments and firms find it essential to understand the different perspectives growing out of local, regional, and national experiences with business and economic development. This has become a crucial competitive advantage to companies and a vital skill for those who study them. *Comparative Perspectives in Business History* explores these developments in a series of volumes that draw on the best work of scholars from a variety of nations writing on the history of enterprise, public and private. The series encourages the use of new styles of analysis and seeks to enhance understanding of modern enterprise and its social and political relations, leaders, cultures, economic strategies, accomplishments, and failures.

Series Editors
Franco Amatori, *Bocconi University*
Louis Galambos, *The Johns Hopkins University*

Sponsors
Associazione per gli Studi Storici sull'Impresa (ASSI), Milan
Istituto di Storia Economic, Bocconi University, Milan
The Institute for Applied Economics, Global Health, and the Study of Business Enterprise, The Johns Hopkins University

Previously Published
The Rise and Fall of State-Owned Enterprise in the Western World, edited by Pier Angelo Toninelli
Business History Around the World, edited by Franco Amatori and Geoffrey Jones
The Global Chemical Industry in the Age of the Petrochemical Revolution, edited by Louis Galambos, Takashi Hikino, and Vera Zamagni
The Cooperative Business Movement, 1950 to the Present, edited by Patrizia Battilani and Harm G. Schröter

The Third Industrial Revolution in Global Business

Edited by

GIOVANNI DOSI

Scuola Superiore Sant'Anna

LOUIS GALAMBOS

Johns Hopkins University

CAMBRIDGE
UNIVERSITY PRESS

University Printing House, Cambridge CB2 8BS, United Kingdom

Published in the United States of America by Cambridge University Press, New York

Cambridge University Press is part of the University of Cambridge.

It furthers the University's mission by disseminating knowledge in the pursuit of education, learning and research at the highest international levels of excellence.

www.cambridge.org
Information on this title: www.cambridge.org/9781107028616

© Cambridge University Press 2013

First published 2013

A catalogue record for this publication is available from the British Library

Library of Congress Cataloguing in Publication data

The third industrial revolution in global business / [edited by] Giovanni Dosi, Scuola Superiore Sant'Anna, Louis Galambos, Johns Hopkins University.
pages cm. – (Comparative perspectives in business history)
Includes bibliographical references and index.
ISBN 978-1-107-02861-6
1. Internet – Social aspects.   2. Information technology – Social aspects.   3. Industrial revolution.   I. Dosi, Giovanni, 1953– editor of compilation.   II. Galambos, Louis, editor of compilation.
HM851.T525   2012
302.23′1–dc23   2012031956

ISBN 978-1-107-02861-6 Hardback

Contents

List of Figures

List of Tables

List of Tables

List of Contributors

Pamela Adams, Franklin College

Stefano Brusoni, ETH Zentrum

Andrea Colli, Bucconi University

Nicoletta Corrocher, Bucconi University

Giovanni Dosi, Sant'Anna School of Advanced Studies

Martin Fiedler, Bielefeld University

Louis Galambos, Johns Hopkins University

Alfonso Gambardella, Bucconi University

Howard Gospel, King's College London

Margaret Graham, McGill University

Marco Grazzi, University of Bologna

Richard N. Langlois, University of Connecticut

Franco Malerba, Bucconi University

Stefano Musso, University of Turin

Luigi Orsenigo, Bucconi University

Mary A. O'Sullivan, University of Geneva

Andrea Prencipe, University G. d'Annunzio

Introduction

LOUIS GALAMBOS

The information age is all around us. Our children and grandchildren text messages to each other at a frantic pace. They listen to music and play obscure games on their computers and cell phones; most of them seem far more comfortable with the new age than their parents will ever be. At work, we nevertheless plug away at our word processors and regularly tap the deep oceans of information instantly available on the world wide web. For many, the Blackberry has become a way of life, an electronic companion that ensures us that we never will be very far away from our work. It's apparent every day that our lives have been transformed by the electronic marvels of the third industrial revolution.

This may prompt us to jump to the conclusion that business, like our personal lives, has been reshaped by the invention of the transistor, the integrated circuit, the computer, microwave transmission and the Internet. I had already set forth my own position in 2005: "The third industrial revolution," I wrote, "is barreling with hurricane force across national boundaries. The new technology, which has been applied most widely in the United States, has spread throughout the world and continues to reverberate in the developed and developing nations. This revolution is grounded in new information technologies (IT) that have transformed most of our institutions and the way they function. The resulting changes – like those of the first and second industrial revolutions – are occurring across a very broad front and appear to be deep, ongoing, and irreversible" (Galambos, 2005).

There already existed a broad range of publications, academic and journalistic, that guided one toward that conclusion. The attention focused on this subject has been truly awesome. A Goggle check on "the third industrial revolution" produces more than five million entries. The "information age" does even better with more than 150 million items, ranging from the inevitable Wikipedia articles to analyses of the privacy issue and explanations of how to wire your home for new-age electronics.

Closer to home for our concerns here are the serious academic books and articles on the history of the third industrial revolution. One of the most important is by the distinguished historical sociologist Manuel Castells, who developed a grand synthesis that emphasizes the sharp break in history created by *The Information Age*. According to Castells, *The Rise of the Network Society* (the title of volume one in his trilogy) decisively altered global economies, societies, and cultures (his subtitle). "The new economy emerged in the last quarter of the twentieth century," Castells said, "because the information technology revolution provided the indispensable, material basis for its creation." The new economy was global and "*networked* because, under the new historical conditions, productivity is generated through and competition is played out in a global network of interaction between business networks." The ability 'to generate, process, and apply efficiently knowledge-based information" was the vital determinant of the competitiveness of firms (Castells, 2000, 2004).

Numerous other scholars began to add work on a broad historical context for this late twentieth-century technological breakthrough in information processing and transmission. Their efforts were handicapped by the fact that aggregate IT statistics are not available, as such; so the IT sector could not be studied in the same manner as other industries. Undeterred, Moses Abramovitz and Paul David charted "American Macroeconomic Growth in the Era of Knowledge-Based Progress: The Long-Run Perspective." Their analysis placed IT in a framework that stressed a first transition in knowledge-based productivity gains near the beginning of the twentieth century and a second after World War II, as the information age began to have an impact on the United States (Abramovitz and David, 2000). David Mowery and Nathan Rosenberg filled out more of the context of that second transition in their study of "Twentieth-Century Technological Change." As they noted: "The development of the U.S. electronics industry complex illustrates a fundamental change in the nature of the U.S. 'resource endowment' and its relationship to technological innovation." Now the key variable was "the abundance of scientific and engineering human capital . . . , as well as an unusual mix of public and private demand for electronics technology" (Mowery and Rosenberg, 2000).

Naomi R. Lamoreaux, Daniel M. G. Raff, and Peter Temin developed a complementary but different context for the impact of IT on the American business system. Taking a long view, they concludedthat the new information age had called forth different strategies and structures in the corporate world. No longer, they said, was the vertically integrated business of the second industrial revolution the dominant business form. Now firms were frequently purchasing components instead of making them in-house. They were looking more to networks of suppliers, service firms, and business partners in foreign and domestic markets than to their own internal capabilities in dealing with those markets (Lamoreaux, Raff, and Temin, 2003).

All of these attempts to set the IT transition in its proper historical context emphasized the broad, deep impact and largely positive results of the electronic innovations, but there were challenges to this literature and its evaluations. Frank Webster chipped away at one aspect of Castells' paradigm, challenging the fundamental concept of a new age, an information society (Webster, 2002). Others – including the eminent business and economic historian Geoffrey G. Jones – were skeptical about the claims for a decisive historical watershed as a result of the electronic breakthroughs. There was, after all, considerable, carefully documented information on IT firms but less evidence for the businesses in significant commodity industries like those in aluminum and oil. Economist Robert J. Gordon asked, "Does the "New Economy' Measure up to the Great Inventions of the Past?" He concluded that the answer was "No:" "The New Economy, defined as the post-1995 acceleration in the rate of technical change in information technology together with the development of the Internet, has been both a great success and a profound disappointment . . . [T]he New Economy has meant little to the 88 percent of the economy outside of durable manufacturing; in that part of the economy, trend growth in multifactor productivity has actually *decelerated*, despite a massive investment boom in computers and related equipment." The information age, Gordon said, did not measure up to the revolutionary innovations of the second industrial revolution (Gordon, 2000).

The *Journal of Economic Perspectives* symposium in which Gordon's article appeared left the central issue in controversy (see also Oliner and Sichel; and Brynjolfsson and Hitt, in the same issue), and these questions prompted the Bocconi University in Milan, Italy, to collaborate with Johns Hopkins University in Baltimore, USA, in hosting an international colloquium (November 2006) to explore the impact of IT on business. The colloquium asked "Has There Been a Third Industrial Revolution in Global Business?" Professor Franco Amatori and his colleagues at Bocconi brought together a number of distinguished scholars who had written or were researching subjects that promised to improve our understanding of the direct and indirect effects of IT on global business. The essays that follow were chosen from among the papers presented at that conference.

Giovanni Dosi, Alfonso Gambardella, Marco Grazzi and Luigi Orsenigo combine forces to answer the colloquium's central question with a decisive "No." In Chapter one, they focus on "Technological revolutions and the evolution of industrial structures: Assessing the impact of new technologies upon the size, pattern of growth and boundaries of firms." They began by conceding that IT has given "rise to new industries but, even more importantly, deeply transformed incumbent industries (and for that matter also service activities), their organizational patterns, and their drivers of competitive success." But then they use firm-level data to examine the size of firms, their patterns of growth and industrial concentration. They find that "the evidence... does not support any notion of revolution...." There is, they find, "hardly any sign of a 'third industrial revolution,' at least if by the latter one means a revolution in the role of the 'visible hand' of organizations (as distinct from market exchanges) and in the relative competitive advantage of size such as compared to previous phases of capitalist development." Their global "map," with its emphasis on structural continuity, supports the general perspective developed by the late Alfred D. Chandler and challenges the other authors contributing to this volume to explore the balance between continuity and change from different perspectives.

Howard Gospel and Martin Fiedler take on this task in Chapter two. They describe and analyze "The Long-run Dynamics of Big Firms: The One Hundred Largest Employers from the United States, the United Kingdom, Germany, France and Japan: 1907–2002." They too bring into focus the Chandlerian paradigm with its emphasis on structural continuity and the powerful competitive advantages of first-movers. Unlike Dosi, et al., however, Gospel and Fiedler bridge the first, second and third industrial revolutions, include state-owned enterprises (SOEs) in their data-base, and use employment as their measure of firm size. After tightening the focus in this manner, they find evidence that the rate of growth is increasing, with the fastest growth rate in the era of the third industrial revolution. The rate of new entrants has also gone up. Along other dimensions, they find additional signs that the IT transformation has shifted the focus in their population of giant enterprises: retailing, services and communications have pushed to the top, while SOEs have decline in importance. Contra Chandler, they conclude that "death was more common than survival." Around the end of the twentieth century, they find a phase of high turbulence, "with a large number of exits and new entrants, major compositional change, and major changes in country contributions."

Pamela Adams, Stefano Brusoni, and Franco Malerba introduce even more complications in their chapter on "Knowledge and the Changing Boundaries of Firms and Industries." They step back from the firm and the industry and adopt a perspective that emphasizes the knowledge base of an economic activity, the resulting division of labor, and the sector in which the base is applied to innovation and production. In this paradigm, IT is a "pervasive technology" that cuts across boundaries and makes it difficult to use traditional measures of economic activity (such as those using SIC categories). Employed over a span of two centuries and three industrial revolutions, this framework relates structural change to the several transformations that have taken place in technology and science in the modern era.

The authors find "new forces" related to "increased specialization in knowledge production" emerging in the last two decades. The structural responses include the growing importance of outsourcing, vertical disintegration, differentiated knowledge sources and modular design. By cutting the costs of handling information, IT fosters network evolution. Some of the networks are tightly coupled, some loosely coupled and others modular and hence decoupled. In a non-revolutionary way, "knowledge integration" has gradually become "the core competence of . . . large, post industrialist firms. . . . " Part of the knowledge increasingly comes from users and consumers, and here too, IT accelerated a secular process of change. Control has, meanwhile, remained in the hands of the large firms, the system integrators and network firms.

The knowledge base of sectoral development also attracts the attention of Richard N. Langlois in chapter four, "Organizing the Electronic Century." His richly detailed and documented essay spans the sweeping timeframe from the beginning of electronic innovation to the major developments of this century. He challenges Alfred Chandler's excessive emphasis upon very large firms that build their activities upon an "integrated knowledge base." Langlois concludes that "the most recent manifestations of the electronic revolution . . . are notable precisely for the ways in which they have diminished the role of the large multi-divisional firm as a generator of innovation and a repository of economic capabilities." Large firms like Intel, he finds, have a "supporting nexus" that plays a crucial role in developing the sector's knowledge base. Langlois keeps the multinational firms in his history but emphasizes their "deverticalization" and links to external institutions. Here in the heart of the new era, he finds more structural change than Dosi, et al., could document in their much broader data base.

A different angle on change is provided by aircraft production, which helps us understand the impact of IT on the complex products as well as the processes in a large, batch-production setting. As Andrea Prencipe establishes in chapter five, "Aircraft and the Third Industrial Revolution," this industry can be seen as a "meso-system" that brings together an innovation superstructure, manufacturers who are the integrators, an innovation infrastructure and government interveners. There is a significant flow of innovations between electronics and aircraft production/operation, one of the several networks shaping change in this industry. The integrators, manufacturing firms, have considerable power to shape outcomes by governing learning and the diffusion of knowledge. Meanwhile, "the use of information and communication technology-based tools has enormously improved the management . . . " of the production interfaces. Both cost and risk dictate a network, rather than an integrated firm approach, to the supply of components. So much so that Prencipe envisions the process as "cascade of hierarchical contracting relationships. . . . " The most important contracts are of course those with customers, especially the airlines, and they have a decisive impact on technical development in this industry. The author concludes that in aircraft production and in air carriers, the impact of the third revolution can be seen – but only weakly.

The information age is even less likely to show up as a decisive break in a commodity industry like aluminum. Margaret Graham places the changes that took place since the 1970s in a broad sketch of the industry's history since its inception in the late nineteenth century. The era of regional oligopolies gave way, Graham says, to global concentration and then to an industry sharply divided between the developed and the developing nations. Applying ideas from the work of Manuel Castells, Graham surveys the aluminum networks and their efforts to recast an industry increasingly dominated by Russian output and Chinese demand. Drawn always to cheap power, new firms continued to emerge in the developing countries. Many of them are encouraged and supported by their governments. The Russian firm Rusal, she says, is becoming the Alcoa of the twenty-first century. "Mastery of information technology, and access to technological expertise through networks of associations certainly are helping it to achieve unprecedented scale in plant-size. . . . " Graham sees "information-sharing and networks" as a response to technological change: "Information technology has clearly been a combinatorial factor in this mix. It was also been a powerful enabler." The "turbulent times," she suggests, and the major dislocations they induce, are likely to continue: "In this sense, the aluminum industry may well be the canary in the mine."

The role of government is discussed in several of the chapters and Andrea Colli and Nicoletta Corrocher deal systematically with this subject in chapter seven, "The Role of the State in the Third Industrial Revolution: Continuity and Change." Using state activity in the second industrial revolution as their benchmark, the authors explore the complex networks of public, private and nonprofit actors that have fostered innovation in the electronic age. They highlight the characteristics of state involvement: With information and general purpose technologies at its core, the new paradigm employs highly flexible, shifting networks that make for convergence, technologically and organizationally, in the "knowledge bases and research activities in different domains." In the information/communications and biotechnology sectors, they find substantial evidence of the new patterns of state activity. Public technology procurement and standard setting, as well as a massive international deregulation drive, have transformed telecommunications. The state has been less active in biotechnology except in the shaping of intellectual property rights and, in Europe, in controlling prices. But overall, the authors conclude, state involvement has "profoundly changed" in form as a result of the third industrial revolution and changed in intensity in some sectors. As a result, the economically active state has remained a vigorous and significant participant – directly and indirectly – in the political economy of the electronic era.

Mary O'Sullivan's history of the U.S. stock market's "appetite for young firms" is perforce optimistic about change. She finds a decisive transformation taking place in the post-World War II years: "Particularly notable was the development of a cluster of industries which constituted the electronics sector." When that happened – and continued to happen into the latter years of the twentieth century – the market was already differentiated and the institutions of investment banking and venture capital were well established. NASDAQ, which completed a transition that was well underway by 1971, provided "a vibrant outlet for the stocks of promising new entrants. . . . " As the development of NASDAQ illustrates, the market for new stock markets was open to entry, and from World War II to the present, the newer markets were the most responsive to the demand for capital coming from startups and young firms in electronics. That was also the case with the growing Over-The-Counter (OTC) market and for investment banking. The electronic age was thus contributing significantly to the reshaping of the financial markets and the institutional setting for entrepreneurial ventures in America.

The final chapter is on labor and labor institutions, subjects that all too often are ignored by business historians. Indeed, for the late Al Chandler, the world's leading historian of business, labor was acted upon by business but was never a primary causal factor in the evolution of modern capitalism. Stefano Musso sets out to correct this imbalance in chapter nine on "Labor in the Third Industrial Revolution: A Tentative Synthesis." The information age, Musso concludes, accelerated the transition from manufacturing to services and began to undercut the economy of mass-produced, standardized goods made on rigid, dedicated machines and assembly lines. The so-called high performance work systems reduced the organizational layers in business and pressed employees "for active cooperation in reducing costs and enhancing quality." Musso's careful comparison of the employment conditions in the developed economies indicates that there is substantial variability in the different labor systems despite the globalization of the past half-century. Throughout most of the world, however, global competition has increased the sense of job insecurity, put downward pressure on wages, and weakened labor union. The trade-off was increasing employment – although not always the best kind of employment – in the developing world.

Musso's chapter is followed by a brief conclusion in which I attempt to pull these various strands of evidence and analysis into an answer to the question posed by the original colloquium: "Has There Been a Third Industrial Revolution in Global Business?" If my answer seems mixed, hesitant, too tentative, I hope our readers will bear in mind that we are still living through the dramatic economic, technological, political, social and cultural changes of the information age. Moreover, a tentative conclusion is an invitation for the reader to add his or her voice to an ongoing debate. We hope that will be the case.

REFERENCES

Abramovitz, Moses and Paul David. 2000. "American Macroeconomic Growth in the Era of Knowledge-Based Progress: The Long-Run Perspective," in Stanley L. Engerman and Robert E. Gallman, eds., *The Cambridge Economic History of the United States*, III, *The Twentieth Century*. New York: Cambridge University Press, 1-92.

Brynjolfsson, Erik and Lorin M. Hitt. 2000. "Beyond Computation: Information Technology, Organizational Transformation and Business Performance," *Journal of Economic Perspectives*, 14, 4, 23-48.

Castells, Manuel. 2000 and 2004. *The Rise of the Network Society*. 3 volumes. Malden, Mass: Blackwell Publishing.

Galambos, Louis. 2005. "Recasting the Organizational Synthesis: Structure and Process in the Twentieth and Twenty-First Centuries." *Business History Review*, 79, 5, 1-38.

Gordon, Robert J. 2000. "Does the 'New Economy' Measure up to the Great Inventions of the Past?" *Journal of Economic Perspectives*, 14, 4, 49-74.

Lamoreaux, Naomi R., Daniel M. G. Raff, and Peter Temin. 2003. "Beyond Markets and Hierarchies: Toward a New Synthesis of American Business History." *American Historical Review*, 108, 2, 404-33.

Oliner, Stephen D. and Daniel E. Sichel. 2000. "The Resurgence of Growth in the Late 1990s: Is Information Technology the Story?" *Journal of Economic Perspectives*, 14, 4, 3-22.

Webster, Frank. 2002. *Theories of the Information Society*. London: Psychological Press.

1

Technological Revolutions and the Evolution of Industrial Structures

Assessing the Impact of New Technologies on the Size, Pattern of Growth, and Boundaries of Firms[1]

GIOVANNI DOSI, ALFONSO GAMBARDELLA, MARCO GRAZZI, AND LUIGI ORSENIGO

INTRODUCTION

There is little doubt that over the last three decades the world economy has witnessed the emergence of a cluster of new technologies – that is, a new broad techno-economic paradigm in the sense of Freeman and Perez (1988) – centered on electronic-based information and communication technologies. Such information and communication technologies (ICTs) gave rise not only to new industries but, even more important, to deeply transformed incumbent industries (and for that matter also service activities), their organizational patterns, and their drivers of competitive success.

Granted such "revolutionary" features of the emerging ICT-based (and possibly life-science-based) technologies in manufacturing and services, what has been their impact on the vertical and horizontal boundaries of

[1] The statistical exercises that follow would not have been possible without the valuable help of the Italian Statistical Office (ISTAT) and in particular of Roberto Monducci and Andrea Mancini and of the French Statistical Office (INSEE). The data have been elaborated by one of the authors (G.D.) in collaboration with M.G. on Italian data and Nadia Jacoby on French data (fulfilling all the obligation on nondiffusion of the data involved in the agreement of access). We are grateful to several participants to the Sixth International Colloquium in Business History, Bocconi University, and to the conference Innovation and Competition in the New Economy, University of Milan Bicocca for useful comments.

firms? What is the evidence supporting the view according to which the new techno-economic paradigm is conducive to a progressive fading away of the Chandlerian multidivisional corporation, which was at the center of the previous techno-economic paradigm, in favor of more specialized, less vertically integrated structures? Is it true that large firms are generally losing their advantage in favor of smaller ones? More generally, how strong is the evidence of a "vanishing visible hand" (Langlois, 2003) in favor of a more market-centered organization of economic activities?

In this chapter we address these issues drawing on several pieces of circumstantial evidence and on firm-level statistical data. If the sources of competitive advantage conditional on firm size have significantly changed, this should reflect also on changes in the size distribution of firms, on their growth profiles, and on the degrees of concentration of industries. These are the variables we analyze, together with some evidence on the relationship between size and innovation, on entry and exit, and on job creation in different size classes. Because, plausibly, the mark of a hypothetical "revolution" in the forms of economic organization should be found quite universally, when possible we try to disentangle those properties that are country and industry specific and others that robustly apply across national borders and at different levels of aggregation.

In a nutshell, the evidence that we analyze does not support any notion of revolution, but merely hints at detectable but incremental changes in the size distribution in favor of smaller-size classes, which might have already ceased in some countries. Size distributions are, of course, a very rough indicator of underlying patterns of competitive advantage and of interorganizational division of labor. In the third section, we present a theoretical framework able to capture such underlying dynamics in terms of processes of market selection and of vertical integration (disintegration). Such an exercise also allows the identification of different types of firms even of a similar size (Figure 1.1).

Building on the foregoing statistical evidence and on an evolutionary conceptual framework on size dynamics, we turn to a "qualitative" discussion of change in the organization of industries associated with the new techno-economic paradigm and discuss the relationship among changing industrial structures, the dynamics of horizontal and vertical boundaries of firms, and the patterns of division of labor in general and of innovative labor in particular. The bottom line is that the new paradigm has significantly influenced both firm boundaries and patterns of interorganizational division of labor. However, there is hardly any

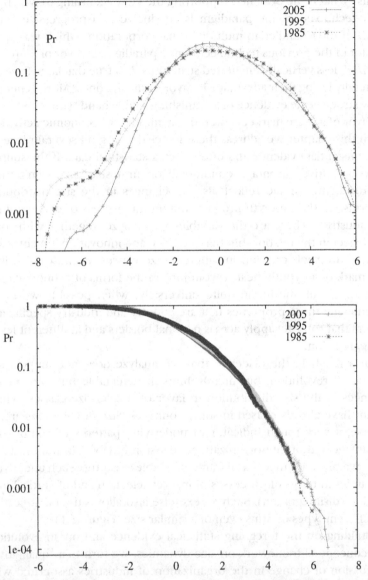

Figure 1.1. (Top) Size distribution of "world" largest firms (sales measures). (Bottom) Right-cumulated distribution. All publicly quoted firms with more than 500 employees from the Osiris databank (log scale).

sign of a "third industrial revolution," at least if by the latter one means a revolution in the role of the "visible hand" of organizations (as distinct from market exchanges) and in the relative competitive advantages of size such as compared to previous phases of capitalist development (Figure 1.2).

STRUCTURE AND DYNAMICS OF INDUSTRIES: "STYLIZED FACTS" AND LONG-TERM TRENDS

Let us begin by focusing on the invariances and changes in the structure of industries and growth processes,[2] trying to distinguish among those regularities that are common to all industrial sectors and those that reveal high degrees of sectoral or national specificities.

Size Distributions

The skewing of size distributions, over an impressively wide support, is probably the most known "stylized fact" concerning industrial structures. The principle holds true independently of the unit of observation (be it the firm or the establishment) and of the chosen proxy for size (be it sales, value added, or number of employees). In fact, at a first approximation and at the *aggregate* manufacturing level, the distribution of a firm's size is well described by a Pareto distribution.[3]

The (cumulative) probability density function of a Pareto distribution of discrete random variables is

$$\Pr[s \geq s_i] = \left(\frac{s_0}{s_i}\right)^{\alpha}, \tag{1}$$

where s_0 is the smallest firm size and $s_i \geq s_0$ is the size of the ith firm, as increasingly ranked. In the following discussion, one of the statistics that we show is the right-cumulated function (Figure 1.3).

These statistics are the first way to characterize the density in the population of different size classes. Pareto law [Eq. (1)] under the restriction

---

[2] Part of this section borrows from Dosi et al. (1995) and Dosi (2006). See also the special issues of *Industrial and Corporate Change*, 1997, and *International Journal of Industrial Organization*, 1997.

[3] For a classical discussion, see Ijiri and Simon (1997). More recent evidence is in Axtell (2001) and Marsili (2005).

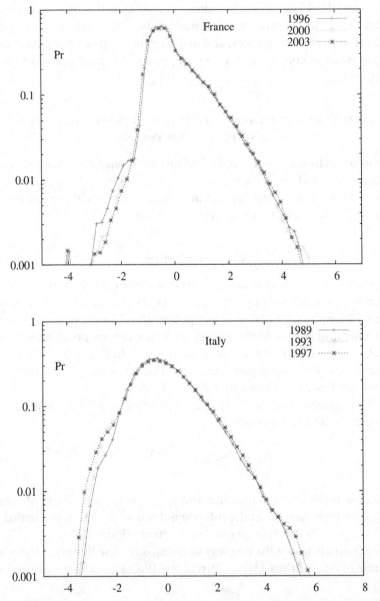

Figure 1.2. Size distribution (employment measures) of firms with more than 20 employees (log scale): (Top) France, (bottom) Italy.

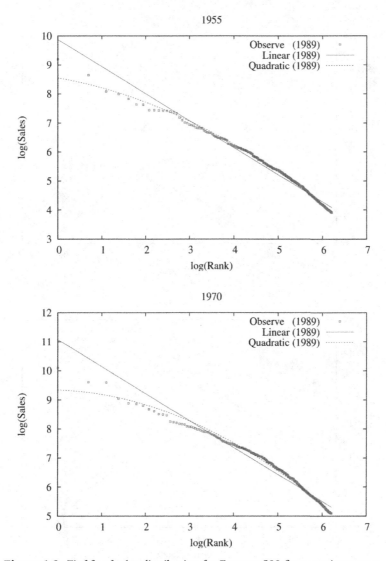

Figure 1.3. Zipf fit of sales distribution for Fortune 500 firms, various years.

that a $= 1$, reduces to the so-called Zipf law,[4] linking the log of the rank and log of the variable being analyzed:

$$sr^\beta = A, \tag{2}$$

---

[4] The Zipf distribution is a discrete, one-parameter, univariate distribution that has been used to describe various physical and social phenomena that are highly skewed (Axtell, 2001; Newman, 2005).

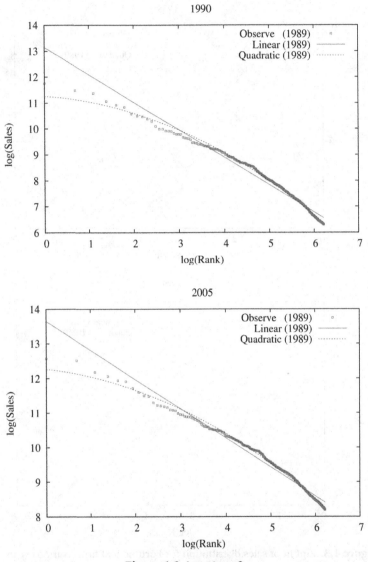

Figure 1.3 (*continued*)

where r is the rank and s, in our case, is a proxy for size [choosing sales, value added, or employees do not significantly affect the analysis: see Bottazzi et al. (2007)]. The largest firm is assigned rank 1. β and A are parameters, the former being an indicator of the degree of concentration of whatever measure in the population. Zipf plots are the other statistics that we use to characterize firm size distribution.

Figures 1.1 and 1.2 display the kernel estimates of the density of firm size for the world's medium–large publicly quoted companies and for France and Italy.[5] (The reader should not pay too much attention to the smaller-size densities that are affected by the truncation of the observation at a given threshold 20 employees in these samples.[6])

The evidence shows that the skewness in the distribution is very robust and quite invariant over time. Also note that skewness and the width of the support are not results of an ad hoc choice of the proxy for size (recall for example that Figure 1.1 is based on sales measures and Figure 1.2 on employment).[7]

The relative stability of the (nearly) Pareto upper tail of the distribution is confirmed by the Fortune 500 evidence since 1955, over which we estimate both the linear and quadratic form of Eq. (2), that is,

$$\log s_i = \alpha - \beta \log r_i + \varepsilon_i \tag{3}$$

and

$$\log s_i = \alpha - \gamma (\log r_i)^2 + \varepsilon_i, \tag{4}$$

where $\alpha = \log A$. The estimates (see Figure 1.3 and Table 1.1), while highlighting the (rough) fit of the Zipf relation in its canonic (linear) form, also reveal that if anything has changed in the size distribution of the top firms, this has been far from dramatic: Consider the coefficients b in the linear estimation (Table 1.2).

To repeat, although the approximation of the distribution with Pareto (Zipf) ones are highly imperfect ones, as discussed at greater length in Dosi et al. (1995), the skewness property is extremely robust. Further, the coefficients of the Pareto (Zipf) fits differ across countries but display similarity at the level of broadly defined manufacturing aggregates.

Sectoral Specificities

As conjectured on the ground of an evolutionary model in Dosi et al. (1995) and empirically shown in Bottazzi et al. (2007), working on Italian

---

[5] More detailed information on the database employed for the empirical analysis is provided in the Appendix.

[6] Plots are computed on the logarithms of normalized values, so that the distribution is centered to zero, with densities presented in sixty-four equispaced points using an Epanenchnikov kernel.

[7] On the stability over time of such asymmetric distributions, see also, among others, Armington (1986), Hall (1987), Storey (1994), and Bottazzi and Secchi (2003a).

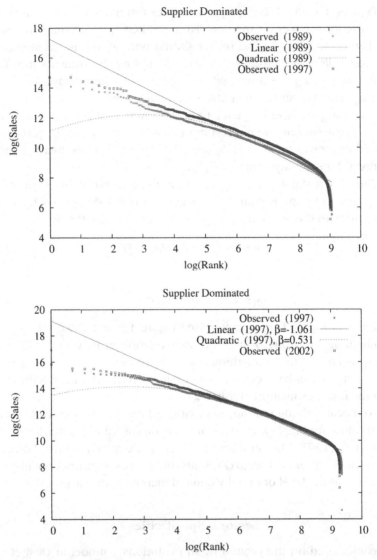

Figure 1.4. Zipf fit of sectors grouped according to Pavitt taxonomy, Italian and French manufacturing industry.

data, disaggregated size distributions continue to display skewness and a wide support for our hypotheses: that is, the coexistence of firms with very different sizes – even though the departures from a Pareto shape are often very wide (sometimes the distributions are even bimodal or trimodal). The structure of each industry is the outcome of its evolutionary

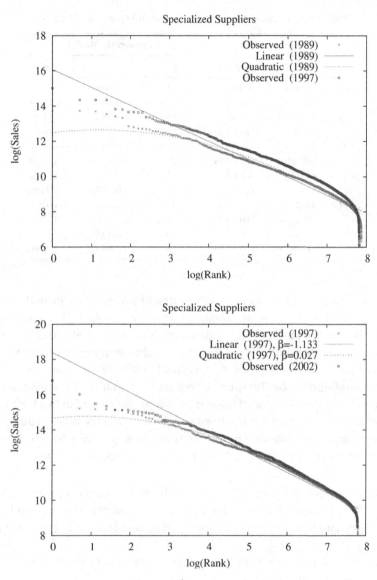

Figure 1.4 (*continued*)

history, in turn driven by the underlying patterns of technological and organizational learning and competitive interactions (see the next section). In particular, industries differ in terms of (a) intensity of innovative efforts and even more through the strategies they undertake (e.g., through formal R&D, learning by doing, learning by using); (b) their

Table 1.1. Fortune 500; Zipf fit. Linear and Quadratic Models

Year	Linear Model		Quadratic Model		
	α	β	α	β	γ
1955	9.871	−0.931	8.548	−0.263	−0.077
	(0.083)	(0.015)	(0.204)	(0.089)	(0.009)
1970	11.069	−0.928	9.342	−0.056	−0.100
	(0.103)	(0.019)	(0.249)	(0.124)	(0.011)
1980	12.506	−0.997	10.704	−0.087	−0.104
	(0.106)	(0.019)	(0.499)	(0.149)	(0.010)
1990	13.143	−1.059	11.254	−0.105	−0.109
	(0.119)	(0.118)	(0.181)	(0.077)	(0.008)
2000	13.254	−0.809	11.727	−0.038	−0.088
	(0.096)	(0.017)	(0.185)	(0.078)	(0.008)
2005	13.649	−0.843	12.264	−0.143	−0.080
	(0.087)	(0.016)	(0.130)	(0.056)	(0.005)

revealed rates of innovation; (c) the rates of productivity growth; and (d) the patterns of interorganizational division of labor. [For more on these issues, see Dosi (1988); Malerba and Orsenigo (1995, 1997); Dosi et al. (2005)]. Plausibly, such differences might entail size-biased capabilities of innovation. Together, they certainly yield different potentials to grow conditionally on the specific "regimes" of technological learning.[8] One of the aims of the well-known taxonomy by Keith Pavitt (1984) is precisely to capture such relations on maps: "industry types" (defined according to their learning modes) and firm size (Figure 1.5). To recap, Pavitt's taxonomy comprises four groups of sectors,[9] as follows:

1. "Supplier dominated," sectors whose innovative opportunities mostly come through the acquisition of new pieces of machinery and new intermediate inputs (e.g., textile, clothing, and metal products);
2. "specialized suppliers," including producers of industrial machinery and equipment;

---

[8] Here one should in fact distinguish between "discontinuous" complex-product industries such as automobiles, white goods, and other consumer durables vs. "continuous" flow industries such as refining or steel making.

[9] The Appendix reports an accurate description of the mapping we employed to relate a particular industrial activity, i.e., industrial classification code, into the corresponding "Pavitt's groups."

Table 1.2. Zipf fit. Linear and Quadratic Models. Our Elaboration on Micro.1 and EAE Databank

Sector	Year	Linear Model		Quadratic Model		
		α	β	α	β	γ
ITA - Supplier dominated	1989	17.263	− 1.058	11.131	0.743	− 0.127
		(0.065)	(0.008)	(0.399)	(0.110)	(0.007)
ITA - Supplier dominated	1997	18.028	− 1.122	11.264	0.878	− 0.142
		(0.074)	(0.009)	(0.447)	(0.124)	(0.008)
FRA - Supplier dominated	1997	19.134	− 1.061	13.477	0.531	− 0.108
		(0.022)	(0.002)	(0.053)	(0.014)	(0.001)
FRA - Supplier dominated	2002	19.297	− 1.064	13.714	0.524	− 0.108
		(0.023)	(0.003)	(0.053)	(0.014)	(0.001)
ITA - Scale intensive	1989	19.223	− 1.310	13.833	0.418	− 0.132
		(0.080)	(0.010)	(0.499)	(0.149)	(0.010)
ITA - Scale intensive	1997	19.861	− 1.370	14.313	0.479	− 0.146
		(0.092)	(0.012)	(0.551)	(0.170)	(0.012)
FRA - Scale intensive	1997	21.201	− 1.418	16.807	0.026	− 0.113
		(0.027)	(0.003)	(0.040)	(0.012)	(0.001)
FRA - Scale intensive	2002	21.273	− 1.402	16.234	0.252	− 0.129
		(0.030)	(0.004)	(0.039)	(0.012)	(0.001)
ITA -Specialized suppliers	1989	16.068	− 1.017	12.505	0.254	− 0.107
		(0.081)	(0.011)	(0.271)	(0.088)	(0.007)
ITA -Specialized suppliers	1997	17.137	− 1.120	13.048	0.353	− 0.125
		(0.095)	(0.013)	(0.364)	(0.121)	(0.009)
FRA -Specialized suppliers	1997	18.381	− 1.133	14.673	0.207	− 0.114
		(0.033)	(0.004)	(0.045)	(0.015)	(0.001)
FRA -Specialized suppliers	2002	18.821	− 1.177	15.376	0.071	− 0.107
		(0.031)	(0.004)	(0.042)	(0.014)	(0.001)
ITA − Science based	1989	17.777	− 1.458	13.578	0.428	− 0.195
		(0.195)	(0.033)	(0.549)	(0.220)	(0.021)
ITA − Science based	1997	18.405	− 1.547	14.745	0.171	− 0.185
		(0.195)	(0.035)	(0.360)	(0.151)	(0.015)
FRA − Science based	1997	10.502	− 0.654	3.339	2.169	− 0.260
		(0.123)	(0.019)	(0.254)	(0.093)	(0.008)
FRA − Science based	2002	10.557	− 0.653	3.332	2.175	− 0.259
		(0.012)	(0.019)	(0.252)	(0.092)	(0.008)
ITA - All manufacturing	1989	19.430	− 1.188	12.683	0.604	− 0.115
		(0.047)	(0.005)	(0.393)	(0.099)	(0.006)
ITA - All manufacturing	1997	20.305	− 1.267	12.915	0.732	− 0.131
		(0.054)	(0.006)	(0.444)	(0.114)	(0.007)
FRA - All manufacturing	1997	21.354	− 1.219	15.788	0.232	− 0.091
		(0.015)	(0.002)	(0.040)	(0.010)	(0.001)
FRA - All manufacturing	2002	21.536	− 1.222	15.718	0.299	− 0.096
		(0.018)	(0.002)	(0.039)	(0.010)	(0.006)

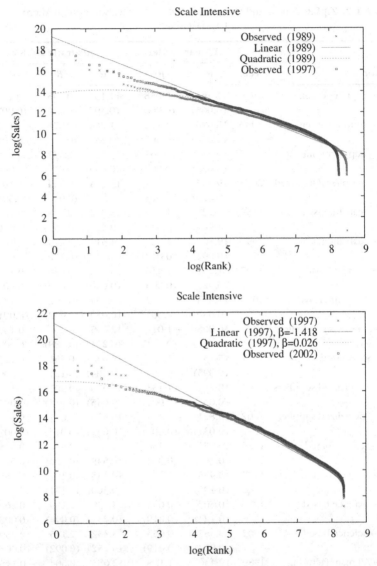

Figure 1.5. Zipf fit of sectors grouped according to Pavitt taxonomy, Italian and French manufacturing industry.

3. "scale-intensive" sectors, whose sheer scale of production influences the ability to exploit innovative opportunities partly endogenously generated and partly stemming from science-based inputs (see final group);

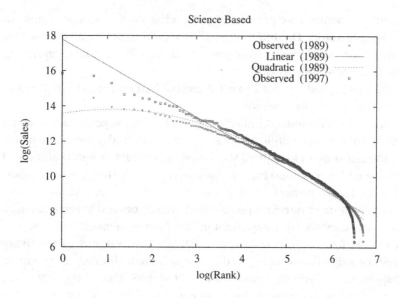

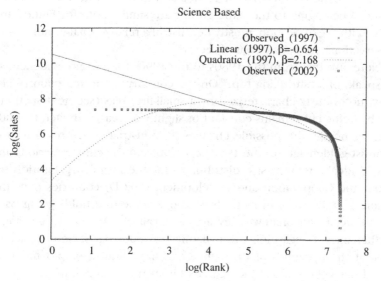

Figure 1.5 (*continued*)

4. "science-based" industries, whose innovative opportunities coevolve, especially in the early stages of their lives with advances in pure and applied sciences (e.g., microelectronics, informatics, drugs, and bioengineering).

Pavitt's evidence was provided by the characteristics of a sample of British innovators. Do different families of industries display diverse size distribution profiles also over greater samples,[10] including innovating and non-innovating firms?

Figures 1.4 and 1.5 and Table 1.2 present Zipf estimates on Italian and French manufacturing sectors.

The results do indeed indicate that technology-specific facts exert a significant influence on industry structures.[11] Consider again in particular the linear model (with all the foregoing caveats in mind) and recall that, roughly speaking, a higher absolute value of the b coefficient means a higher size advantage of the biggest firms. Of course, size advantages are relatively more important in scale-intensive sectors and in science-based ones, and they are least important in "supplier-dominated" sectors.

Results for the French case interestingly lend support to the hypothesis of a significant role played by the specific technological regime in shaping the industry structure of different sectors. This is apparent when comparing the coefficients for France and Italy in Table 1.2. Estimated α and β belonging to the same groups are similar both for France and Italy, with the exception, mostly because of a relative smaller number of observations, for science-based sectors.

Note also that from the 1980s to the 1990s there is no evidence, so to speak, of a "shrinking top." On the contrary, even in a country like Italy, notoriously characterized by a small-firm bias (see next section), the b coefficient remains constant or slightly increases. In fact, to study more generally the possible changes in industrial structures from the "Fordist golden age" of the 1950s and 1960s to the current period, one would ideally require size distribution for the major Organisation for Economic Cooperation and Development (OECD) countries over the whole population of firms (at least above some threshold) going back over time. Unfortunately, they are not available. Hence, to get some further insight regarding the dynamics of industrial structures, let us look at the dynamics of the number of firms and of employment by broad size cohort and at the degree of industrial concentration.

Number of Firms and Employment by Size Classes

Tables 1.3 and 1.4 report the distribution of the number of firms and of employment by size cohorts. The length of the footnotes to the tables,

---

[10] In fact, the universe of all firms responding to the Central Statistical Office survey.
[11] Similar evidence on The Netherlands is discussed in Marsili (2005).

Table 1.3. Distribution of Firms Per Size, Percentages

Country	Year	0–9	10–19	20–49	50–99	50–250	100–499	250+	500+
France	1962[a]	. . .	36.9[1]	34.1	13.6	. . .	12.8	. . .	2.7
	1977[a]	. . .	28.4[1]	38.3	14.6	. . .	15.1	. . .	3.6
	1990[a]	. . .	34.9[1]	37.8	13.4	. . .	11.5	. . .	2.5
	1996[b]	82.7	7.2	6.0	2.0	. . .	1.8	. . .	0.3
	1997[b]	82.4	7.3	6.2	2.0	. . .	1.8	. . .	0.3
	2000[b]	82.1	7.3	6.4	1.9	. . .	1.9	. . .	0.4
	2001[b]	81.8	7.5	6.4	2.0	. . .	1.9	. . .	0.4
	2003[b]	82.8	7.2	6.0	. . .	3.2	. . .	0.8	. . .
Germany	1967[a]	58.9[2]	. . .	17.9[3]	9.8	. . .	11.0	. . .	2.5
	1977[a]	56.6[2]	. . .	20.2[3]	10.2	. . .	10.3	. . .	2.6
	1990[a]	60.3[2]	. . .	17.7[3]	9.6	. . .	10.0	. . .	2.4
	2000[b]	67.3	16.3	7.4	4.1	. . .	4.1	. . .	0.8
	2001[b]	64.0	18.8	7.7	4.3	. . .	4.3	. . .	0.9
	2002[b]	62.1	18.4	8.9	. . .	8.4	. . .	2.2	. . .
	2004[b]	59.9	21.4	8.4	. . .	8.2	. . .	2.1	. . .
UK	1968[a]	62.5[2]	. . .	10.3[3]	10.4	. . .	13.4	. . .	3.4
	1977[a]	54.3	15.0	13.6	6.8	. . .	8.1	. . .	2.3
	1990[a]	66.2	13.3	10.2	4.5	. . .	4.8	. . .	1.0
	1996[b]	71.5	12.1	8.8	3.4	. . .	3.5	. . .	0.7
	1997[b]	72.0	12.1	8.4	3.3	. . .	3.5	. . .	0.7
	2000[b]	70.7	13.4	8.3	3.6	. . .	3.4	. . .	0.6
	2001[b]	71.7	12.2	8.8	3.5	. . .	3.2	. . .	0.6
	2002[b]	71.2	12.5	9.0	. . .	5.9	. . .	1.4	. . .
	2003[b]	72.9	11.8	8.5	. . .	5.5	. . .	1.3	. . .
Italy	1971[a]	. . .	48.0[1]	31.4	11.2	. . .	8.2	. . .	1.3
	1981[a]	. . .	57.3[1]	27.4	8.4	. . .	6.2	. . .	0.9
	1991[a]	. . .	59.0[1]	28.5	7.0	. . .	4.8	. . .	0.7
	1996[b]	83.7	9.5	4.8	1.1	. . .	0.8	. . .	0.1
	1997[b]	83.1	9.7	5.1	1.2	. . .	0.8	. . .	0.1
	1998[b]	83.5	9.6	4.8	1.2	. . .	0.8	. . .	0.1
	1999[b]	83.5	9.6	4.8	1.1	. . .	0.8	. . .	0.1
	2000[b]	83.5	9.6	4.7	1.2	. . .	0.8	. . .	0.1
	2001[b]	83.3	9.8	4.8	1.2	. . .	0.8	. . .	0.1
	2002[b]	83.4	9.7	4.7	. . .	1.9	. . .	0.3	. . .
	2004[b]	82.8	10.1	4.8	. . .	2.0	. . .	0.3	. . .
Japan	1967[a]	72.7	13.9	8.1	2.9	. . .	2.0	. . .	0.3
	1975[a]	76.2	12.3	7.0	2.5	. . .	1.7	. . .	0.3
	1990[a]	73.7	11.9	9.4	2.9	. . .	2.0	. . .	0.3
	1999[c]	71.6	13.5	9.2	3.0	. . .	2.5[8]	. . .	0.2[9]
	2001[c]	71.6	13.5	9.2	3.0	. . .	2.5[8]	. . .	0.2[9]
	2004[c]	72.1	13.2	9.0	3.0	. . .	2.5[8]	. . .	0.2[9]
USA	1972[d]	88.8	5.9	4.6[5]	. . .	. . .	0.6	. . .	0.1
	1977[d]	89.4	5.6	4.3[5]	. . .	. . .	0.6	. . .	0.1

(*continued*)

GIOVANNI DOSI ET AL.

Table 1.3 (*continued*)

Country	Year	0–9	10–19	20–49	50–99	50–250	100–499	250+	500+
	1982[d]	80.9	10.4	7.5[5]	...	...	1.0	...	0.2
	1988[e]	78.8	10.9	8.7[5]	...	...	1.3	...	0.3
	1992[e]	78.9	10.8	8.6[5]	...	...	1.4	...	0.3
	1997[e]	78.8	10.7	8.8[5]	...	...	1.4	...	0.3
	1999[e]	78.5	10.8	8.9[5]	...	...	1.5	...	0.3
	2000[e]	78.2	10.9	9.1[5]	...	...	1.5	...	0.3
	2003[e]	78.6	10.8	8.9[5]	...	...	1.5	...	0.3

[a] *Source:* OECD.

[b] *Source:* EUROSTAT.

[c] *Source:* Japan; Incorporated firms, all private sectors.

[d] *Source:* U.S. Census Bureau.

[e] *Source:* U.S. Census Bureau; Incorporated firms, all private sectors.

[o] *Source:* OECD; Manufacturing sectors only.

(1) Only firms with more than 10 employees are reported.
(2) The smallest size cohort has the range 0–24.
(3) Cohort of range 25–49.
(4) Establishments, rather than firms, are considered.
(5) Size cohort 20–99.
(6) 100–249.
(7) 250–499.
(8) 100–999.
(9) 1000+.

flagging differences in sources, coverage, and cohort breakdown, should warn the reader about too strong inferences from such data. With that in mind, the data do not seem to reveal anything reminding one of a revolution either with respect to the percentage distribution of firms or their employment share. At a first look, Germany, France, the United States. and the United Kingdom (in terms of employment share only) do appear to conform to the story of a growing hegemony of bigger firms up until the 1970s, with a turning point thereafter. However, in some countries like the United Kingdom, Germany, and Italy, the share of employment in the bigger size cohort continues to fall (and less so in Japan, too, with a corresponding growth in the medium–large share).[12] Conversely, evidence from the United States appears to suggest a *reversal* of such a trend, with a growing share in the number of big firms in manufacturing and a growing share in big-size employment in both manufacturing and the overall economy.

Industrial Concentration

Next, let us consider in turn proxies for industrial and geographical concentration, starting from the former. Ideally, the measure ought to be calculated on the universe of firms in a given sector. Short of that, and

Table 1.4. Employment Share Per Size Cohort, Percentages

Country	Year	1–9	10–19	20–49	50–99	50–250	100–499	250+	500+
France	1962[a]	...	4.7[1]	10.0	8.8	...	24.5	...	51.9
	1977[a]	...	3.1[1]	9.3	7.9	...	24.4	...	55.3
	1990[a]	...	5.7[1]	13.4	10.4	...	25.7	...	44.7
	1996[b]	13.0	6.3	13.1	8.4	...	23.5	...	35.7
	1997[b]	13.1	6.2	13.4	8.4	...	23.7	...	35.2
	2000[b]	12.2	6.2	12.9	8.5	...	24.3	...	35.9
	2001[b]	11.8	6.3	12.7	8.5	...	24.5	...	36.2
	2003	12.1	6.5	12.5	...	22.1	...	46.9	...
Germany	1967[a]	3.9[2]	...	6.2[3]	7.5	...	25.2	...	57.2
	1977[a]	3.9[2]	...	6.9[3]	7.7	...	23.5	...	58.0
	1990[a]	4.7[2]	...	6.8[3]	7.8	...	24.1	...	56.6
	1996[b]	...	...	8.3	10.0	...	29.3	...	52.4
	2000[b]	7.2	7.1	7.5	8.8	...	25.8	...	43.6
	2001[b]	7.0	7.7	7.4	8.7	...	25.8	...	43.4
	2002[b]	6.7	6.7	7.8	...	23.7	.	55.1	...
	2004[b]	6.6	8.5	7.7	...	23.6	...	53.6	...
UK	1968[a]	6.8[2]	...	4.2[3]	8.0	...	31.6	...	49.5
	1977[a]	3.8	3.2	6.2	7.1	...	25.6	...	54.3
	1990[a]	5.8	4.4	9.6	9.3	...	30.0	...	40.9
	1996[b]	11.4	6.8	11.2	9.7	...	28.1	...	32.8
	1997[b]	9.4	7.1	10.9	9.5	...	29.5	...	33.6
	2000[b]	10.0	7.6	10.5	10.0	...	28.3	...	33.6
	2001[b]	10.1	7.2	11.7	10.4	...	28.0	...	32.6
	2002[b]	10.5	7.5	12.1	...	26.0	...	43.9	...
	2003[b]	10.9	7.4	12.0	...	25.4	...	44.3	...
Italy	1971[a]	...	9.8[1]	14.6	11.8		24.1	...	39.7
	1981[a]	...	15.1[1]	16.2	11.6		23.8	...	33.4
	1991[a]	...	19.5[1]	20.2	11.8		22.3	...	26.2
	1995[a]	24.1	14.7	25.5[5]	...	10.0[6]	6.2[7]	...	19.4
	1996[b]	24.7	15.1	16.3	9.2	...	16.8	...	17.9
	1997[b]	24.4	15.1	16.6	9.7	...	17.1	...	17.1
	1999[b]	25.3	15.1	16.6	9.5	...	17.1	...	16.4
	2000[b]	25.1	15.1	16.2	9.6	...	17.5	...	16.5
	2001[b]	25.1	15.2	16.0	9.9	...	17.4	...	16.4
	2002[b]	25.5	15.1	15.9	...	20.7	...	22.8	16.4
	2004[b]	25.5	15.3	16.1	...	21.0	...	22.1	...
Japan	1967[a]	16.4	11.2	14.3	11.3	...	22.1	...	24.8
	1975[a]	19.1	11.3	14.1	11.1	...	21.2	...	23.1
	1990[a]	17.6	10.1	17.0	12.2	...	23.1	...	20.0
	1999[c]	10.6	8.6	13.2	9.8	...	28.4[8]	...	29.5[9]
	2001[c]	10.8	8.7	13.1	9.7	...	28.3[8]	...	29.4[9]
	2004[c]	11.0	8.6	13.0	9.9	...	29.3[8]	...	28.2[9]

(continued)

Table 1.4 (*continued*)

Country	Year	1–9	10–19	20–49	50–99	50–250	100–499	250+	500+
USA	1972^d	13.4	8.6	19.3^5	...	...	12.2	...	46.5
	1977^d	13.2	8.4	18.5^5	...	...	12.4	...	47.5
	1982^d	16.5	9.5	19.8^5	...	...	13.0	...	41.3
	1988^e	12.6	8.3	19.2^5	...	...	14.5	...	45.5
	1992^e	12.3	8.0	18.4^5	...	...	14.3	...	47.0
	1997^e	11.6	7.6	18.1^5	...	...	14.5	...	48.2
	1999^e	11.1	7.3	17.8^5	...	...	14.1	...	49.7
	2000^e	10.8	7.3	17.8^5	...	...	14.3	...	49.9
	2003^e	11.0	7.3	17.8^5	...	...	14.5	...	49.3

^{a} *Source:* OECD.

^{b} *Source:* EUROSTAT.
^{c} *Source:* Japan; Incorporated firms, all private sectors.
^{d} *Source:* CENSUS.

^{e} *Source:* CENSUS; Incorporated firms, all private sectors.
^{o} *Source:* OECD; Manufacturing sectors only.

(1) Only firms bigger than 10 employees are reported.
(2) The smallest size cohort has the range 0–24.
(3) Cohort of range 25–49.
(4) Establishments, rather than firms are considered.
(5) Size cohort 20–99.
(6) 100–249.
(7) 250–499.
(8) 100–999.
(9) 1000+.

given the biases associated with the lower size bound in the Osiris (2005) databank,[12] we feel safer in considering concentration in the *upper tail* of the distribution (Figure 1.6, Table 1.4).

$$D_{20}^4(t) = \frac{C_4}{C_{20}}, t = 1982 - 2005, \qquad (5)$$

where C_4 and C_{20} are the sums of the market shares of the top-four and top-twenty firms in each sector, respectively. If a sector is highly concentrated, D_{20}^4 would be near to 1, whereas it would be 1/5 if all firms were identical.

Figure 1.6 displays the densities of the concentration measure over the last two decades for all three-digit sectors with more than forty-five observations. Interestingly, the *shapes* of the distributions change a good deal, whereas the *means* of the distributions vary much less. The modal value of the concentration rates falls from the mid-1980s to the mid-1990s (remaining roughly stable thereafter). At the same time, the upper

---

[12] Note that the percentage of publicly quoted companies over the total of the size cohort tends to fall with the latter. However, in recent years, an increasing but indeterminate percentage also of small companies went public.

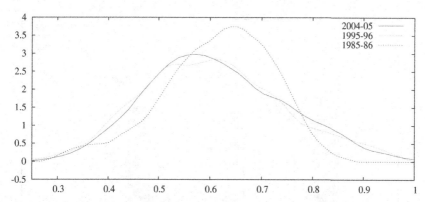

Figure 1.6. Probability densities of the sectoral concentration index D_4^{20} in terms of total sales, different years (kernel estimates). The support of these densities is [0.3,0.95]. World's largest firms from the Osiris database.

tail gets fatter. An increasing number of sectors display $D_{20}^4(t)$ statistics above 0.7, meaning that the first four firms in the "world," as defined in the Osiris dataset, in a particular sector, account for more than 70 percent of the top-twenty firms in the same sectoral data record. Note also that the lower tail seems to be remarkably stable over the last two decades.

This body of evidence, in principle, is not at all in conflict with the evidence put forward by Ghemawat and Ghadar (2006), suggesting that market globalization *has not in general* carried along an increasing industrial concentration (under all the ambiguities of measurement of corporate sales vs. production, etc.). Our somewhat similar point is that the new techno-economic paradigm has not brought along either flattening and shrinking size distributions and, with those, generally falling measures of industrial concentration across sectors and across countries.

A quite distinct issue concerns the geographical concentration (across countries) of industrial activities. Of course, the original legal location of any one firm is a very noisy indication for the location of the overall activities of each large firm (most likely multinational companies (MNCs)). Still, the national origins of world top-size firms are informative in their own right. Moreover, it continues to hold true that core activities such as strategic management and R&D are mostly performed in the country of origin (Cantwell and Iammarino, 2001). At this level of analysis, *first*, the evidence on the (Fortune 500) upper tail of the size distribution displays a persistent dominance of U.S.-based firms (see Figure 1.7). However, *second*, the relative balance among big firms[13] has shifted from the 1980s to the 1990s in favor of non-U.S. firms. It is a decline

---

[13] With "bigness" defined on the much larger meter of Osiris firms.

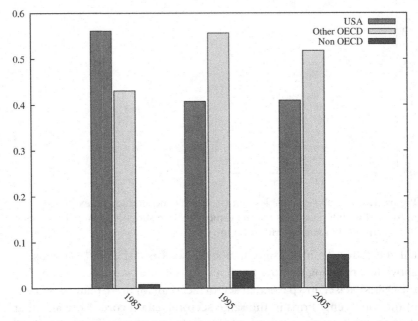

Figure 1.7. Histogram of the distribution of sales for biggest firms worldwide per geographic location. Our elaboration on Osiris.

that operated mostly in favor of Japan and to a lesser extent of European firms in the last part of the twentieth century. It slowed over the latest period, statistically highlighting a European and Japanese slowdown vis-à-vis non-OECD countries, together with the emergence of newer players (e.g. Korean and Chinese oligopolists) (Table 1.5).

The Dynamics of Corporate Growth

Clearly, the observed industrial structures – including size distributions and degrees of concentration – are the outcome of the underlying processes of growth of incumbent firms, together with the processes of entry and exit.

Concerning the former, a common starting point in the literature, and also a handy instrument to assess if and how size influences growth, is the so-called *Gibrat law* [for a discussion, see Dosi (2006); reviews of the literature are in Sutton (1997) and Lotti et al. (2003)].

Let

$$s_i(t + 1) = \alpha + \theta_i s_i(t) + \varepsilon_i(t), \tag{6}$$

Table 1.5. Total Sales and Number of Firms for Each Country. Fortune Global 500 (2003). Sales are in Billions of U.S. Dollars.

Country	Total Sales	Number of Firms	Country	Total Sales	Number of firms
United States	5841	189	Russia	62	3
Japan	2181	82	Brazil	61	3
Germany	1363	34	Belgium	60	3
France	1246	37	Norway	60	2
United Kingdom	1079	35	India	60	4
The Netherlands	388	12	Belgium/The Netherlands	57	1
Switzerland	382	12	Mexico	49	1
China	358	15	Venezuela	46	1
Italy	300	8	Denmark	35	2
South Korea	266	11	Luxembourg	29	1
United Kingdom/ The Netherlands	250	2	Malaysia	26	1
Canada	185	13	Singapore	15	1
Spain	162	7	Taiwan	14	1
Australia	107	7	Ireland	12	1
Sweden	96	6	Thailand	12	1
Finland	71	4			
			Total	14,873	500

where $s_i(.)$ are the log sizes of firm i at times t, $t + 1$, and α is the sector-wide (both nominal and real) component of growth.

Gibrat law in its strong form suggests that

1. $\theta_i = 1$ for every i,
2. $\varepsilon_i(t)$ is an independent identically and normally distributed random variable with zero mean.

Hypothesis 1 states the "law of proportionate effect": growth is a *multiplicative* process independent of initial conditions. In other words, there are no systematic scale effects.

Note that were one to find $\theta_i > 1$, one ought to observe a persistent tendency toward monopoly. Conversely, $\theta_i < 1$ would be evidence corroborating regression-to-the-mean, and, indirectly, witness of some underlying "optimal-size" attractor.

Overall, hypothesis 1, which is indeed the object of most inquiries, gets mixed support:

1. Most often, smaller firms – on average – grow faster (under the caveat that one generally considers small *surviving* firms);
2. otherwise, no strikingly robust relationship appears between size and average rates of growth [see Mansfield (1962), Kumar (1985), Hall (1987), Bottazzi et al. (2002), and Bottazzi and Secchi (2003b), among others], but the coefficient θ_i is generally quite close to one;
3. the relationship between size and growth is modulated by the age of firms themselves – broadly speaking, with age exerting *negative* effects on growth rates, but *positive* effects on survival probabilities, at least after some post-infancy threshold (Evans, 1987a, 1987b).[14]

(Recent works have also highlighted a rich, non-Gaussian structure in the shocks $\varepsilon_i(t)$: see Bottazzi and Secchi, 2006, on U.S. firms and Bottazzi et al., 2007, on Italy. The discussion of this property would, however, take us too far away from the thrust of this chapter.)

For our purposes, let us assume that corporate growth is (and has always been, as far back as our statistics go) a multiplicative process driven by factors that on average have little to do with size either way. That is, size does not seem – now as well as forty years ago – either to foster or to hinder growth, at least above a certain threshold, with faster growth and higher mortality rates in the smaller cohorts.

Size, Innovativeness, and Efficiency

The influence of size on innovative capabilities and/or revealed rates of innovation has long been debated in the literature, often under the misplaced heading of the so-called "Schumpeterian hypothesis" according to which size as such would confer an innovative advantage (for discussions, see Kamien and Schwartz, 1982; Baldwin and Scott, 1987; Cohen and Levin, 1989; Cohen, 1995; Symeonidis, 1996).

The evidence, again, does not seem to support any strong relation between size and innovativeness. So, for example, Scherer (1965), well before the current technological revolution, analyzes the relation among sales, R&D employment, and patents over a few hundred big firms and finds an inverted U-shaped relation between sales and R&D intensities.

---

[14] Moreover, the relationship between size and growth appears to be influenced by the stage of development of particular industries along their life cycles (Geroski and Mazzucato, 2002).

However, on quite similar data, Soete (1979) identifies strong intersectoral differences, with several sectors displaying "increasing returns" in the relation between size and innovativeness. Yet later, Bound et al. (1984), on a larger sample, find again the inverted U, with the peak of innovativeness in the medium-size cohorts. The sectoral specificities of the revealed correlation between innovativeness and size is explicitly addressed in Acs and Audretsch (1987, 1990), which find a positive correlation in 156 industrial sectors, a negative one in 122, and negligible rates of innovation – as they measure them – irrespectively of size in 170 sectors. Pavitt et al. (1987) analyzed innovativeness – using a discrete innovation count from the SPRU database – and found a U relation (not an inverted one!) with small–medium and very big firms displaying the highest propensity to innovate. Such a relation, however, shows strong sectoral specificities (see the taxonomy in Pavitt, 1984). So, for instance, innovative firms are likely to be rather small in industrial machinery; big firms prevail in chemicals, metal working, aerospace, and electrical equipment; and many science-based sectors (such as electronics and pharmaceuticals) tend to display a bimodal distribution with high rates of innovation of small and very large firms.

The bottom line, in agreement with Cohen and Levin (1989), is that the results on the relation between size and innovativeness are "inconclusive" and "fragile." And, in fact, a good deal of the evidence on such a relationship is further weakened, first, by endemic sample selection biases; quite often one compares the universe of medium–large firms with a biased sample of small ones (indeed, those that innovate). Second, even when one finds size–innovativeness correlations, one should be extremely careful in offering any causal interpretation. It could well be, for example, that in some circumstances being bigger is conducive to innovation (aerospace is a good example), but the opposite direction of causation is generally at work too: A firm is big today precisely because it has been innovative in the past (consider Intel, for example).

What about the relationship between size and production efficiency as measured by input productivity? We discuss the issue at greater length in Dosi and Grazzi (2006), in which we explore such a relation at disaggregated levels in the Italian case. Again, the data seem to suggest either, roughly, *constant returns to scale*, or a mild evidence of a continuing role of *economies of scale* (plausibly associated with scale-biased forms of mechanization or automation of production).

Entry, Exit, and Market Turbulence

The evidence discussed so far lends support to the existence of some powerful invariances in industrial structures (concerning size distribution and growth processes) that appear to hold throughout the current technological revolution. These persistent properties, however, should not be taken as evidence of "business as usual" and even less of any sort of long-term equilibrium.

On the contrary, underlying the foregoing statistical regularities one observes indeed the turbulent microeconomics that Metcalfe (2001) calls "restless capitalism." In fact, an extremely robust stylized fact that seems to apply irrespectively of periods of observation, of countries, and of sectors is the persistent turbulence in the profile of industrial evolution, which is due to persistent entry and exit flows and changes in the incumbents' market shares (see, among others, Acs and Audretsch, 1990, Beesley and Hamilton, 1984, Baldwin, 1998, Bartelsman and Doms, 2000, and the comprehensive comparative analysis on the patterns of entry and exit in Bartelsman et al. 2005).

Note that relatively high rates of entry are pervasive phenomena even in high capital intensity industries (Acs and Audretsch, 1989, 1991). The overwhelming majority of entrants are at first small (with the partial exception of those "entrants" that are actually new subsidiaries of incumbent, sometimes MNC, firms). Exit rates are quite high too, of the same order of magnitude of entry flows. Roughly, around half of the entrants are dead after seven years in all OECD countries (Bartelsman et al., 2005). The evidence on churning ("rubbish in, rubbish out" dynamics) is quite robust and apparently uncorrelated with the appearance of a new techno-economic paradigm.

Certainly, a phenomenon that distinguishes the last three decades from the previous period is the apparent increase in the rates of entry of new firms (generally, small start-ups). So, for example, *gross* entry flows in the United States were around 50,000 per year in the early 1950s and were around 500,000 in the last decade (with a peak of 700,000 in 1988). It is hard to disentangle the drivers of such a phenomenon. Circumstantial evidence suggests that a significant share of the new firms are in fact spin-offs from incumbent firms (on the characteristics of entrants, see also Bhidé, 2000). And, indeed, the emergence of a new technological paradigm is likely to have influenced entry dynamics (Table 1.6).

One should avoid any strict identification of entry with "innovative entrepreneurship," the latter being a small subset of the former.

Table 1.6. Average Percent Share[a] of Gross Job Gain and Gross Job Losses by Firm Size, 3rd Quarter 1992-1st Quarter 2005, in Thousands, Seasonally Adjusted

Category	Firm Size Class (Number of Employees)								
	1–4	5–9	10–19	20–49	50–99	100–249	250–499	500–999	1000+
Gross job gains	14.3	11.5	11.9	14.2	9.1	9.8	5.9	4.9	18.4
Expanding firms	7.0	10.6	12.0	15.1	10.0	11.1	6.8	5.7	21.7
Opening firms	51.8	16.0	11.6	9.8	4.3	3.1	1.3	0.9	1.2
Gross job losses	14.6	11.8	12.2	14.4	9.1	9.7	5.8	4.8	17.6
Contracting firms	7.5	11.1	12.3	15.2	10.0	10.8	6.7	5.5	20.9
Closing firms	49.2	15.5	11.7	10.3	4.8	3.9	1.8	1.2	1.6
Net change	9.9	6.6	8.1	12.1	9.2	11.5	7.3	6.0	29.3

[a] Share measures the percent of the category represented by each firm size class.
Source: Business Employment Dynamics, BLS (2005).

Less effort has gone into the investigation of the degree of turbulence *in the oligopolistic core of individual industries*. Rather old studies (e.g., Kaplan, 1954; Collins and Preston, 1961; Mermelstein, 1969; Bond, 1975) suggest a relatively high stability in the membership and rankings within such a core. Broadly, in the same vein, Chandler (1990) notes that 96 percent of the top 200 firms in 1924 were still present in 1958, albeit sometimes under different denominations. Louçã and Mendonça (2002) resort to the Fortune 500 to extend the work of Chandler. They emphasize the long-term turnover of the membership of the largest firms' group, which is probably attributable to change in the dominant techno-economic paradigm. Be that as it may, whatever measure of "turbulence" – including, of course, death rates – you use, it appears to be much higher among small firms as compared with that of bigger cohorts (see Acs and Audretsch, 1991; Geroski and Toker, 1996).

In any case, one has to carefully distinguish the relative stability of the oligopolistic core in many industries from the dynamics in the relative size rankings of top firms (see the next section for an interpretative framework). Anecdotal evidence goes both ways: Examples that come to mind are, on the "erosion of the oligopolistic leadership" side, General Motors or Westinghouse, and, on the "oligopolistic emergence" side, Microsoft or Nokia. No doubt, more than two-thirds of the first Fortune 500 firms (year 1954) do not appear in current statistics. However, it does not appear to be a sign of an "organizational revolution" specific to the currently emerging new techno-economic paradigm but rather a long-term feature of "restless capitalism," with its persistent emergence of new industrial activities and its changing weights among them.

36   GIOVANNI DOSI ET AL.

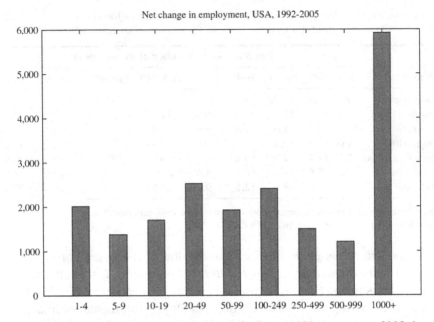

Figure 1.8. Net change in employment, 3rd quarter 1992–1st quarter 2005, in thousands, seasonally adjusted. *Source:* Business Employment Dynamics, BLS (2005).

A complementary angle from which to look at the organizational changes in contemporary industry is in terms of gross and net job flows conditional on firm size classes. In the "Fordist golden age," a good deal of employment creation occurred in medium–large companies. Over the last three decades, the contribution of small firms to job creation seems to have increased (for much more detailed analyses on the 1980s and early 1990s, see Boeri and Cramer, 1992, and Davis et al., 1996). This applies in different degrees to all OECD countries (OECD, 1994). For example, in the period 1990–5, new production units accounted in the United States for 69 percent of the total job creation (and 22 percent of the total was due to new start-ups).

Interestingly, however, the bias toward small firms in employment creation seems to have become less pronounced or even reversed in the most recent years, at least in the United States: Bigger firms (with more than 1,000 employees) in the new century are by far the biggest net source of employment (see Table 1.6 and Figure 1.8). Small firms (especially start-ups) continue to be a major source of *gross* employment creation, but this is matched by impressive rates of employment *destruction*, too (see again Table 1.6). This is in fact the employment facet of the "churning" discussed earlier in terms of entry and death of new firms.

Italy – a country characterized by high rates of new firm formation – is a good case in point: New firms are born mainly in rather traditional industries and often display very low degrees of innovativeness. More important, widespread entry is not a new phenomenon. As Chandler (1990) himself noted, large integrated firms were mostly concentrated in capital-intensive and technology-intensive industries, and in a handful of countries. Smaller firms have been the norm in labor-intensive activities and in many regions of the world. In both labor-intensive and capital-intensive industries, a good deal of entry and exit has always occurred. The novelty is the relative increase in turbulence.

Summary

Let us summarize the relevant stylized facts highlighted in the previous section:

1. A few OECD countries, especially European ones, displayed a decline in average firm size starting in the late 1970s and early 1980s. Yet the decline has not been dramatic. Large firms still play an important role, especially in terms of output and employment. And in fact the importance of the largest firms seems to have increased in the United States over the most recent period.
2. At the aggregate level, the size distribution of firms is still considerably skewed. In this respect, a well-established and persistent fact, which is robust across countries, is that the firm size distribution is close to a Pareto one. The picture is more blurred at a more disaggregate industry level, but the skewness of the distribution remains a robust property.
3. The science-based industries, and the scale-intensive ones according to the classification by Pavitt (1984), exhibit a more asymmetric distribution. Circumstantial evidence confirms Pavitt's findings that science-based industries display a higher share of both larger and smaller firms.
4. The most important change compared with that of the earlier decades has been the notable increase in the number of new firm entries, especially in the United States and partly in the United Kingdom. They are accounted for by start-ups and on many occasions by spin-offs from existing firms. The new firms account for

a significant share of the increase in gross job flows and a positive
but much lower share of net job gains.

5. Because the new entries are accompanied by corresponding high
exit rates, the recent decades have exhibited an increase in industrial turbulence.

6. Finally, although there has been a trend toward globalization, this
has not implied greater oligopolistic concentration worldwide or
a greater concentration of international production in the United
States. However, our elaboration shows that concentration has
not fallen systematically either, with the mode of concentration
measures falling from the 1980s to the 1990s (and remaining stable thereafter but also with an increase in the number of highly
concentrated sectors).

What does this evidence tell us about the possible emergence of a "new
regime" of industrial organization possibly based on a different balance
between small and big firms? To answer the question, let us first spell out
some elements of a theory of the processes of competition and division
of labor underlying the continuing coexistence of firms of different sizes
and different organizational and technological characteristics. To do that,
we ask the reader to bear with us through some formalism that will help
highlight the main process at work.

THEORETICAL MODELS AND OBSERVATIONAL IMPLICATIONS: LEARNING, COMPETITION, AND INDUSTRIAL ORGANIZATION

Firm Size: Some Introductory Remarks

As a starting point for our discussion, it might be useful to begin from
some simple identities. Let us consider an economy composed of m
productive activities which, in a first approximation, we assume to correspond to specific markets (M_j, where $j = 1, \ldots, m$). If the assumption
is added that each firm i ($i = 1, \ldots, n$) is active exclusively in a single
activity or market, its size in terms of output, S_i, is obviously equal to the
total size of the market multiplied by its market share, f_{ij}:

$$S_i \equiv f_{ij} M_j. \tag{7}$$

In the more empirically plausible case of firms characterized by varying degrees of diversification (among final products) and of vertical

integration (abstracting for the sake of simplicity from considering the input–output relations of the economy), the firm's size is

$$S_i \equiv \sum_j f_{ij} M_j. \tag{8}$$

Given these identities, each observed distribution in the S_i needs an interpretation of the distribution of the shares within each market and among markets, as well as of the dynamics of the shares themselves and of the total size of the markets.

Product Differentiation, Vertical Integration, and Diversification: The Boundaries of Firms

Start by noting that, rarely, each "market" could be simply identified and that it implies and corresponds to a univocal set of "productive activities." A first approximation to the first hypothesis is obviously a homogeneous good. Yet, in reality, each market usually involves a collection – changing over time – of imperfectly substitutable goods, even abstracting from the unavoidable statistical arbitrariness and the resulting aggregation problems. This applies to products that are (a) horizontally differentiated in their characteristics for the final consumer (Hotelling, 1929; Robinson, 1933; Chamberlin, 1962; Lancaster, 1979), (b) vertically differentiated in term of some ordering of quality (Shaked and Sutton, 1978), or (c) intermediate products and capital goods with different performances (see, among others, Freeman, 1982, and Dosi, 1988).

A fundamental result of this stream of literature is – as is well known – that many firms having a non-null measure can coexist, occupying different market niches. However, the simple observation of product differentiation or monopolistic competition as such does not suffice to support any prediction on the form of the firms' size distributions. Even (incorrectly) establishing a direct correlation between a firm's size and the size of the market, one may well observe that large firms horizontally diversify in many markets.

Consider next the "vertical measure" of firms. So far, we have been assuming that to each product or market was associated a characteristic set of productive activities. But ever since Adam Smith, it is well known that such activities are subject to varying degrees of decomposition, which change over time as a function of the size of the markets and of technical change. But each decomposition can in principle be associated with the existence of a corresponding "market" of the intermediate product. Thus, different decompositions – that is, different degrees of vertical integration or specialization – of productive processes may correspond to different sets of markets and in this way they can determine, *ceteris paribus*, different firms' size distributions. Thus, it is, of course, possible to think of a firm that is large in absolute terms because it is vertically integrated; but it is small with respect to the size of the final market in which it is active (i.e., with a small f_i over a large M_j).

In a fundamental sense, the "thickness" of each market is endogenous to the dynamics of technologies and institutions. Thus, in the former Soviet Union, the number of markets corresponded at the most to the number of final markets. Conversely, the Italian industrial districts are the examples that match more closely the ideal archetype in which to each technical task different firms and markets correspond, as in the Smithian parable of pin making. Finally, as already mentioned, size is influenced by the degree of horizontal diversification of firms across various markets.

In an extreme synthesis, size distributions depend tautologically – given the size of the markets – on (a) the distribution of market shares in each market, (b) the degree of integration among vertically related activities or markets, and (c) the degree of horizontal diversification on different markets.

The question then becomes this: What are the processes that generate those distributions? Ultimately, they concern (1) the dynamics of market shares in each market and (2) the determinants of the vertical and horizontal boundaries of firms (and their dynamics). Other works (Dosi, 1991; Dosi and Marengo, 1994; Teece et al., 1994; Dosi et al., 1995, 1997) discuss the comparative merits of competing theories as to which candidate gives an answer to at least one of these grand issues. For the purposes of this chapter, we propose succinctly only our interpretations and conjectures.

Let us start with the second set of issues concerning the vertical and horizontal boundaries of firms. This is a particularly delicate question because ultimately it has to do with the very problem of "what is a firm," jointly with an interpretation of its structure and behavior. Heroically reducing a particularly complicated object to a telegraphic discussion, we shall assume that each firm can be conceived as a relatively coherent behavioral entity that embodies (1) specific problem-solving procedures (i.e., competences concerning technologies, management of organizations, marketing, relationships with customers and suppliers, etc.); (2) specific mechanisms governing potentially conflicting interests within the organization itself and with the interacting entities; and (3) specific strategic orientations, concerning, for example, pricing policies, investments, R&D, and diversification (see Dosi and Marengo, 1994; Teece et al., 1994; Dosi and Coriat, 1998).

Coherent with this definition, our hypothesis is that the potential boundaries of the firms are approximately determined by their knowledge bases (i.e., by their technological, organizational, marketing, competences, productive capacity, and distribution networks) jointly with the complementary assets controlled by the firm itself (Teece et al., 1994). The word potential is crucial: A firm – or even entire systems of firms – can plausibly choose to explore a very small subset of this potential. On the contrary, one can historically observe firms that overstretch these boundaries in attempting to develop compensating factors for backwardness upstream and downstream, especially in technologically lagging countries.

These potential boundaries are highly conditioned by the sectors of principal activity of the firms. Various works have begun to provide taxonomies of these patterns. The basic intuitive idea is almost trivial for noneconomists (the competences needed for producing a car are useless for producing biscuits) but its operationalization is complex; it is not easy to find nontautological proxies of the very notion of "organizational competences."

Within these potential boundaries, we suggest, the actual patterns of vertical integration and diversification are modulated by factors pertaining to (1) alternative governance mechanisms of transactions, as in the Williamsonian tradition, and (2) processes of technical and organizational division of labor (*lato sensu*, "Smithian").

In synthesis: A first restriction on the "measure of firms" comes from the technological and organizational conditions that influence the non-null values of the summation in identity (9), even though these restrictions still leave ample degrees of behavioral freedom, as the comparative evidence from Italy, the United States, Japan, etc., shows.

Learning and Selection

Given whatever notion of market as the domain of competitive interactions, a fundamental question regards the dynamics in the shares in production and sales of individual firms. Following a large body of evolutionary-inspired works, we assume that a set of variables that approximates the specific capabilities of firms map – directly and indirectly - into their competitive performances (often, evolutionary models refer to a "fitness" variable, using a metaphor perhaps too close to the biological archetype). These variables include obviously the prices and the performance of products, but also other organizational and spatial dimensions, like localization of production, distribution channels, etc. Moreover, these characteristics of individual firms influence performances through their behavioral patterns: for example, price-cost margins, localization strategies, product positioning in niche versus mass markets, diversification versus specialization, etc. At a deeper level, these variables map onto underlying characteristic traits that constitute the firm itself, that is, their capabilities.

It is possible to heroically simplify and represent "reduced forms" of the competitive interactions, in which vectors of firm-specific characteristics influence the dynamics of their shares. Using a parsimonious representation, let us assume that

$$\Delta f = g(f, a), \tag{9}$$

where f is the vector of the firms' shares and the function $g(\dots)$ summarizes the interactions mapping the firms' specific technological, organizational, and behavioral characteristics on the dynamics of the shares. [In the jargon of many evolutionary models, function $g(\dots)$ defines the fitness landscape on which firms survive, grow, and die.] Even more parsimoniously, often the dynamic models sharing this inspiration collapse all the factors influencing the interactive dynamics in a "synthetic variable" - "competitiveness" $e(\dots)$ - and under further simplifications they study the properties of markets in which shares monotonically evolve in the differences between "average competitiveness" $\bar{e} = \Sigma_i f_i e_i$ and the specific competitiveness of each firm:

$$\Delta f = A[e_i(t) - \bar{e}(t)] f_i(t). \tag{10}$$

Let us discuss only some quite general considerations. First, notice that "space" - both literally and metaphorically referring to product characteristics - contributes to define the shape of the fitness landscape: *ceteris paribus*, a perfectly homogeneous market will tend to generate smooth (single-peaked) landscapes (lower prices attract more customers) whereas product differentiation will tend to produce many peaks (corresponding to market niches, etc.). Second, function $g(\dots)$ - when it is applied to economic domains - is inevitably influenced by behavioral factors. Approximately, the variables determine how much a firm's competitiveness can allow it to grow, but actual growth depends also on how much the firm wants to grow; that is, its expansion strategies, etc.

Function $g(\dots)$ captures then the "strength" of selection. In the linear form of Eq. (10), the parameter A determines the reactivity of shares to competitiveness differentials: The higher the A, the higher the prizes and the punishments that the market attributes to more or less competitive firms.

Third, technological and organizational innovation determines the dynamics of $\mathbf{a}_i$ for each firm. This is the essential link between the theory of firm growth on the one hand and the analysis of technological and organizational change on the other. The patterns of the latter determine the structure of the stochastic processes driving the dynamics of firm competitiveness. In this respect, a now considerable body of work has begun to explore both empirically and formally different learning regimes and their implications for industrial dynamics (for empirical analyses, see, among others, Malerba and Orsenigo, 1997, and Breschi et al., 2000; for formal models, see Winter, 1984; Dosi et al., 1995; Winter et al., 2000; Malerba et al., 1999; and Malerba and Orsenigo, 2002).

Let us come back to Eq. (9) (abstracting for a moment from the fact that growth can occur also through diversification and vertical integration): The dynamics observed on the firms' sizes – captured by $\theta_i(t)$ [see Eq. (6)] and by $\varepsilon_i(t)$ – is determined in this interpretation by the underlying dynamics of learning, that is, by the processes driving the dynamics of $\mathbf{a}_i$ in Eq. (9) or, in the simplified version, in e_i in Eq. (10) jointly with the mechanisms of competitive selection summarized in the function $g(\dots)$.

We can draw here a first general conclusion and, in our view, a challenging and still largely unexplored conjecture: the coexistence of firms with different sizes – more specifically, the form of the observed distributions – and their processes of growth can be interpreted on the basis of the underlying mechanisms of learning and selection. Thus, intersectoral, international, and intertemporal differences can in principle be determined in terms of differences (or changes over time) in such regimes (jointly with different behavioral patterns that modulate the differential effects of competitiveness on the propensity to grow, especially in intercountry comparisons).

Other works (Dosi et al., 1995; Malerba et al., 1999; Winter et al., 2000; Malerba and Orsenigo, 2002) have started to analyze the properties of alternative sectoral learning regimes, comparing, for example, the "Schumpeter I" archetype, in which innovation is essentially driven by new entrants, with the opposite "Schumpeter II" paradigm, in which incumbents learn in a cumulative way. More recent attempts include efforts to model industry evolution and firm growth considering also diversification and vertical integration–disintegration (Malerba et al., 2006). Here, the vertical structure of firms is critically affected by the actual distribution of capabilities across firms in upstream and downstream industries. For example, the decision to specialize is elicited from and critically depends on the actual existence of upstream suppliers at least as competent as the integrated firm itself. Moreover, when products are systems with various components and subsystems, the ability to coordinate and integrate the design of such systems and components may constitute an important competence in its own right and a significant source of competitive advantage (Robertson and Langlois, 1995). Such an advantage can be (more than) offset by considerations related to the risk of getting stuck in inferior technological trajectories, especially at times of rapid and uncertain technological change or when suppliers are able to offer significantly superior products.

In addition, the vertical scope of firms is influenced by the processes of market selection, which tends to promote the growth of more efficient firms and of the related organizational arrangements and to penalize the laggards. Thus, market selection amplifies the impact of differentiated capabilities on the vertical scope of firms. If specialized firms have superior capabilities, selection will push for greater specialization, and vice versa. Or, for instance, the growth of a competent supplier (or of a vibrant industry) is likely to induce processes of specialization of the downstream firms, as the supplier becomes able to offer increasingly better products. In turn, the process and the loci of capability development feed back on the conditions determining the entry of new firms.

It can be shown that if (1) learning is not too biased against incumbency, (2) the vertical boundaries of firms do not dramatically change, and (3) there are no "revolutions" in the balance between Schumpeter I and Schumpeter II regimes of industrial change, then the distribution of firm sizes in the aggregate turns out to be relatively close to a Pareto one (Dosi and Salvatore, 1992; Dosi et al., 1995).

Typologies of (Small) Firms

Up to this point, our discussion of industry structures and their dynamics has been conducted at a rather abstract level, attempting to identify some very general properties of the underlying evolutionary processes. More precise empirical characterizations of specific observed patterns in specific industries and countries require clearly detailed specifications of the learning regimes, of market interactions, and of institutional settings. In the next section, we try to use this simplified conceptual apparatus to discuss some of the main issues related to the existence of a third industrial revolution. However, it may be useful to begin linking the foregoing conceptual framework to the following more qualitative discussion by noting that beyond the analysis of firms' size distributions and the changing role of small and large companies, it is possible to identify different types of firms that can be small. Our previous discussion suggests indeed that small firms can be the outcome of quite different dynamic processes. In particular, we can make the following rough distinctions:

- "Marginal" firms, who manage to survive in local markets, often protected by the exercise of monopolistic power by larger and more efficient competitors or "simply" by the slowness and imperfections of market selection processes (see Steindl, 1945);
- "Chamberlin–Robinson–Hotelling" firms, i.e., small companies that survive and prosper in small niches of differentiated product markets;
- "Smithian" firms, i.e., firms based on processes of division of labor and specialized in the supply of intermediate products and components to other (often, larger) companies, often on the basis of organized subcontracting relations and hierarchies;
- "Marshallian" firms, i.e., companies that are active in a specific geographical area (clusters, districts, productive and innovation systems, etc.). They are typically extremely specialized at some stage of the value chain and/or in a product niche. They entertain close, often socially shaped, linkages with the other firms in the area;
- "Schumpeterian" firms, i.e., companies that are born on the basis of an innovation and try subsequently to develop it. In some cases, these firms grow or are acquired by larger companies. In most cases, these firms fail. However, these firms are small because they are young.

These distinctions are overly simplified, of course. For example, a new biotechnology firm may well be categorized as both a Schumpeterian and a Smithian firm; in some cases also as a Marshallian one. However, the distinction may remain useful as long as it forces us to distinguish among different processes and causes of the changes in the organization of productive activities and of large corporations in particular.

CONTINUITY AND CHANGES IN ORGANIZATIONAL FORMS, LEARNING PATTERNS, AND COMPETITIVE PROCESSES

The discussion so far has provided evidence and some general conceptualization to understand the observed changes in the firm size distribution and consequently in industry structure and the evolution of firms and industries. In this section, we move at an intermediate level of analysis and address the changes that appear to have indeed occurred in the most recent period. In particular, we ask the following questions. What can explain the greater importance of relatively smaller firms in firm size distributions? And at the same time, why have such processes of industrial reorganization in favor of smaller size seemed to have stopped? What are the underlying mechanisms explaining these patterns?

In the following discussion, first we argue that the role of smaller firms can be explained, in part, by the growth of product differentiation and variety. Following the argument in the subsection Learning and Selection, as the number of submarkets increases, it is more difficult for one firm to dominate a larger, fragmented market. The point is straightforward. If a market of size 100 is homogeneous, the assets that are necessary to gain market shares in that market are undifferentiated. Economies of scale and learning processes then might enable one firm to obtain an overall competitive advantage. By contrast, if the same market is divided into ten markets of size 10, the assets that are necessary to operate in each market are differentiated, learning across submarkets is more difficult, and the probability that different firms dominate the different niches is higher.

The second issue that we address is vertical specialization, the division of "innovative" labor following Arora et al. (2004), and the patterns of specialization and comparative advantages of firms of different size in this process. We point out the growing importance of these processes in high-tech industries, at least in some of them, and therefore suggest that some of the observed changes in the size distribution of firms that took place in the 1980s and the 1990s may be related to these phenomena. As a related point, we discuss the emergence of agglomeration of technology-based industries in geographical clusters. Silicon Valley is a prototypical example. At the same time, the Silicon Valley model, based on high rates of entry and exit and a high degree of technological exploration, has diffused in a few industries to other countries, including newly rising economies like those of Ireland, Israel, and India (Bresnahan and Gambardella, 2004; Arora and Gambardella, 2005). The growth of Silicon Valley models may then have given a new impetus to smaller firms associated with the processes of innovative exploration. Yet, it also produces a new role for the larger firms as they preserve a comparative advantage in the exploitation of innovative advances and in incremental innovation, which can even be enhanced by a more productive exploration process. Moreover, although Silicon Valley is the locus of smaller innovative firms, it is also the province of some rather large firms, whether established companies or start-ups that have grown considerably in the span of a few years. Third, we discuss the existing trends toward product modularity and the modularity of organizational processes. Once again, the separability in product components can give rise to specialization and smaller size because each individual firm can dominate a single module and does not need to control an entire product or process space. Yet, modularity requires coordination, and this calls for the role of larger firms as system integrators. In this respect, coordination is hard to achieve just through the market, and established corporations with the appropriate capabilities often dominate an entire process by mastering system integration.

Product Variety and Differentiation: The Horizontal Boundaries of Firms

A first reason for decreasing average firm sizes can be found in the opportunities for product differentiation. It is often suggested that increased product variety can be considered a natural trajectory of economic development, such as, as we discuss in the next section, division of labor. Moreover, it is frequently claimed that new technologies, *in primis* IT, and more generally post-Fordist patterns of production and demand make significant increases in product variety possible.

The laser is one example. As discussed by Klepper and Thompson (2007), laser products are differentiated. This is associated with several market niches. In turn, no firm has been able to cover a large set of such niches, which has kept the industry from consolidating into a tight oligopoly. Interestingly, this is the same process suggested by Sutton (1998) with his flowmeter example. In flowmeters, as in lasers, the lack of consolidation does not stem from the fragmented nature of the technology, whose basic features are common to the application sectors, but from the fragmentation of the industry downstream. That is, applications of the same technology are differentiated by the specific requirements of customers and uses. Sutton's point is simple. When an industry is not fragmented, economies of scale induce the more productive firms to cover larger shares of the market. Given that they are more productive, they can outcompete their rivals, and when they acquire the competitors' market share, economies of scale make them even more productive. But when a market of equal size is fragmented, such economies of scale are less prominent because the fixed costs have to be borne for each market niche, or at least learning or economies across niches are less pronounced than in a homogeneous market. As a result, companies can dominate only if they are better in each and every submarket or in a large number of them. This is unlikely in so far as different companies develop specific capabilities in different submarkets. As a result, a structure in which one firm covers the entire market – that is, the full set of submarkets or a large share thereof – is less likely than in the case of more homogeneous final products.

In a more dynamic, evolutionary perspective, this argument can be recast in terms of learning and capabilities. Take the example of pharmaceuticals. Here, research capabilities developed for one product – for example, a drug for the treatment of hypertension – might be of limited use for the search from, say, Parkinson treatments. In fact, capabilities are likely to be accumulated incrementally, and this is reflected also by the pace of diversification across submarkets.[15] That is, the horizontal boundaries of firms are defined by their capabilities in differentiated markets.

Smith, Marshall, and Schumpeter: The Vertical Boundaries of Firms

A second category of processes driving changes in firm sizes and firm boundaries involves changing patterns of division of labor. There is little question that division of labor and specialization constitute a fundamental secular tendency in economic activities. From Adam Smith to Allyn Young and Herbert Simon, the notion that division of labor is a crucial "natural" engine of productivity growth is probably one of the less disputed propositions in economics. Indeed, it is a major stylized fact in the history of industries, technologies, and business enterprises that progress

---

[15] In the case of the pharmaceutical industry, Bottazzi and Secchi (2006) show that the diversification patterns can be well described by a branching process.

occurs also through significant processes of specialization. The history of the mechanical and electromechanical industries are typical examples. In this respect, the birth and diffusion of specialized firms – what we have labeled "Smithian firms" – is by no means a new phenomenon (Pavitt, 1998). And, other things being equal, one would expect such processes to be favored by growing and more integrated markets (in line with the Smithian adage that the division of labor is limited by the extent of the market).

However, it is important to distinguish between drivers of processes of division of labor. One process concerns the "natural" tendency toward increasing specialization that occurs along an industry life cycle or a technological trajectory whereby, as a technological paradigm matures, intermediate inputs tend to become more standardized, economies of scale in production become more relevant, and the emergence of specialized producers gets easier. A significantly different question regards the extent to which specific new technologies tend intrinsically to favor more decentralized forms of organization as compared with more vertically integrated structures. In this respect, it has been suggested that the ICT revolution systematically favors vertical disintegration and arm's-length forms of coordination of what were previously integrated units (this is also part of Langlois's argument on the vanishing hand of big integrated corporations).

Certainly, in both scale-intensive and science-based sectors the application of information technologies to design and production has fostered concepts and practices like product modularity (since IBM's System 360), which has in turn affected organizational modularity (Sanchez and Mahoney, 1996; Brusoni and Prencipe, 2001).

Vertical specialization has become more prominent also in some high-tech industries (e.g., semiconductors, and even pharmaceuticals). In particular, as suggested by Arora et al. (2004), one observes a tendency toward an increasing division of "innovative" labor. The process is particularly evident in sectors like software, semiconductors – with the development of the fabless firms – and in the biopharmaceutical industry.

More generally, the advent of the ICT revolution has offered not only opportunities for the discovery and development of new products and processes, but has often entailed major organizational innovations. There is no need to emphasize how the diffusion of information technologies has made possible major organizational transformations, ranging from so-called "flexible automation" to modularization, to e-commerce, and in general to the possibility of decentralization of certain activities previously carried out within the boundaries of individual firms. The acknowledgment of the foregoing Smithian tendencies is sometimes complemented by a Marshallian argument. Not only has the large, vertically integrated corporation, it is argued, become less efficient than more decentralized and specialized structures interacting in the production process, but such collections of specialized firms have also specific spatial connotations; that is, spatial concentration of economic activities confers "externality" advantages to those firms. Despite their enormous differences, the emphasis on both Smithian and Marshallian tendencies is an ingredient of the argument, which would tend to suggest that a third industrial revolution did occur or is occurring involving the demise of the vertically and horizontally integrated corporation in favor of networks of small(er), highly specialized firms interacting together in the invention, development, production, and marketing of products. Although both the Smithian (vertical specialization) and the Marshallian (Silicon Valley) type processes would seem to have become more prominent than in the past, these points have to be qualified. First, as noted by our data, the trend toward smaller firm sizes is perceptible but not so dramatic as to constitute a revolution in the distribution of firm sizes. This observation is more consistent with secular Smithian processes of division of labor, rather than with the thesis of a drastic revolution favoring smaller sizes of firms.

Second, Marshallian clusters of small firms are certainly not a new phenomenon. Even assuming that Marshallian clusters have actually become increasingly important as compared with during the first and second industrial revolutions, it must be recognized that Silicon Valley itself is not simply a paradise of small entrepreneurs and small companies. It is also the locus of some of the largest firms worldwide in addition, of course, to many smaller ones.

A related but distinct question concerns whether a new model of organization of large corporations – loosely definable as the "network" form – is supplanting the Chandlerian–Fordist one. The statistical evidence discussed in the second section on the relative stickiness of size distributions throughout the current technological revolution throw doubts on such an hypothesis. If anything, as the data on the distribution of firms' sizes show, the ratio of what is produced within the boundaries of firms and what is exchanged via market transactions would appear to have remained fairly constant or only slightly decreasing.

Yet there is certainly ample evidence, both anecdotal and based on rigorous case studies of firms and industries, indicating that vertical disintegration, outsourcing, and deconglomeration are actually very important tendencies in the organization of innovative and productive activities in many industries, suggesting some discontinuity vis-á-vis the Chandlerian–Fordist past. Our interpretative suggestion is indeed that such discontinuity involves more the ways large firms are organized, managed, and interact with the environment that surrounds them than in the fact that they have been replaced by systems of smaller firms.

Once again, it could be argued that none of these processes is entirely new. As Langlois (2003) notes, the rise of the multidivisional firm was itself at one level a Smithian process, that is, an attempt at decoupling and separating vertically and horizontally related activities, through the professionalization of management and through the separation of strategy from day-to-day operations. Also, modularity and division of innovative labor are not completely new phenomena. Robertson and Langlois (1995) and Langlois (2002) have shown that in the PC as well as in the hi-fi industries, products evolved from unitary "blocks" to systems of thousands of components, which in turn yielded an increasing interorganizational division of labor across specialist firms. With regard to the distribution of innovative labor, Mueller noted that well inside the "Chandlerian era" most of the important innovations by DuPont originated outside DuPont: Ideas or early prototypes were often generated by others, typically smaller concerns. Likewise, Lamoreaux and Sokoloff (2007) have shown that vibrant markets for technology existed and prospered more than one century ago in the United States.

Yet, it can be legitimately argued that these tendencies have become more widespread than in the past and that their scale has increased so much as to raise the question as to whether they are manifestations of epochal changes in the organization of large firms, involving a greater reliance on outsourcing, a greater importance of markets for technology, and greater degrees of organizational decentralization. Let us start from outsourcing. Outsourcing is an increasingly important phenomenon, as epitomized by the growing fears of countries like the United States or even Europe for the movement of jobs outside their own national boundaries toward new locations in China, India, or Asia more generally. In fact, the concerns go beyond outsourcing in traditional sectors, experiencing "natural" industrial life cycles, and regarding outsourcing of jobs in more advanced industries in which the United States or other advanced countries could still retain comparative advantages when judged by the lens of the life-cycle story. At the same time, there is good evidence that licensing deals have increased significantly worldwide since 1990 and that markets for technology are rising (Arora et al., 2004; Athreye and Cantwell, 2007). Yet our point is that these very same processes have not pushed unilaterally toward a greater importance of smaller firms and decentralized networks as opposed to larger integrated firms.

Of course, outsourcing as such might not affect the "size" of firms when measured in terms of sales, but should do so when measured in terms of value added: Still there is no systematic evidence, to our knowledge, of a trend in this direction.

The Dynamics of Exploration and Exploitation

A particularly important issue regards the relationship between specialized (small) firms and integrated (plausibly bigger) ones with respect to the division of innovative labor. The tricky issue here can be read in terms of the trade-offs between exploration of new innovative knowledge and its exploitation on the one hand and between decentralization and coordination on the other. Start by noting that whenever the innovative process does not require significant complementary assets such as manufacturing facilities (Teece, 1986), Smithian vertical disintegration, Schumpeterian technology markets, and the Marshallian Silicon Valley are likely to enhance the degree of exploration. If the development of an innovation requires integration with downstream manufacturing or commercialization assets, only the firms owning these assets can innovate. But this sets an upper bound to the number of innovators. By contrast, as Arora et al. (2004) point out, if vertical specialization and related separation are possible in different organizations, between activities for producing innovations and activities for developing them, there are more innovation "trials." This is because "ideas" can be tried out at low fixed costs. Put simply, without separability, innovation producers have to have the downstream assets, and innovation users have to have the ability to produce innovations. Separation between these stages of the innovation process makes it possible for the "explorers" to pursue innovative searches even if they do not have the costly downstream assets. It is, of course, not at all clear *ex ante* whether new ideas will become profitable for someone else to buy and exploit. But the failure rates are limited to only the research assets and not to the downstream production or commercialization networks. In some cases – for example, new software programs – these innovation trial costs can be rather small. All this leads to more innovation trials, because it is less costly to do so, and hence there are lower barriers to entry in the exploration activities.

The obvious consequence of the higher degree of exploration and of the higher number of potential innovations is that technological opportunities are tapped more intensively. Under this scenario, the very process of vertical specialization means that the firms with the capabilities to develop new products downstream can access a wider set of the innovation inputs more productively. This makes them more productive and reinforces their comparative advantage and consequently their role in the vertical division of labor. In short, the very success of smaller decentralized firms ("upstream") and the very fact that these firms are part of a broader process that involves larger more integrated companies ("downstream") make the latter more effective. In sum, if anything, we ought to observe that larger firms become key agents downstream or in R&D activities that require large scale.

Clearly, under this scenario vertical disintegration of innovative labor does not necessarily involve a changing balance between small and big firms but just a different pattern of division of labor among them. There is, however, a downside to this setup.

In the vertical structure we described, even if more ideas are explored, one is bound to bear the costs of having a fragmented structure for innovation, as opposed to a more integrated one. More integrated structures may improve learning processes, which under vertical disintegration are harder to pursue because knowledge is dispersed in many different uncoordinated avenues, across many smaller independent firms. The point is made by Pisano (2006) with respect to biotech firms, but we think that such a trade-off – that is, greater exploration at the expense of better, more consolidated learning processes along fewer but well-defined trajectories – is an important one, which goes beyond the confines of the drug industry.

Indeed, the current technological revolution (as the other ones in the past; see Perez, 2007) has been associated with a surge of entry of small innovative companies that ultimately led to the dotcom bubble. There are signs of an increasing appreciation of the potential advantages from greater integration in recent years. For example, the nanotechnology business seems to be the province of firms that are still small compared with the larger established oligopolists of the world, but are also larger and more integrated than many biotech entities. To the extent that these tendencies are there to stay, they suggest that we ought to observe some reintegration in the near future. Our hunch is that again this will not make a revolution in the pattern of division of innovative labor. But the extent of exploration may cyclically leave room to a greater degree of exploitation, and this would resurrect the role of "exploitative vis-à-vis explorative firms." Once again, the trends of the past two decades are not likely to be the beginning of secular dynamics but rather part of repeated historical swings from excessive fragmentation – often associated with the decentralized activities of exploration typical of the emergence of new technological paradigms - to excessive integration, and thus the dominance of exploitation and incremental innovation, often characteristics of more mature technological paradigms.

Modularization and the Division of Innovative Labor: Integration and the Visible Hand

Another side of the specialization–integration trade-off has to do with the need for coordination, even in the presence of processes of modularization and of division of innovative labor. In this respect, it is often argued that, by adopting modular design strategies, firms can take responsibility for the design and development of separate modules. Thus, they can develop new products at a faster pace, as the integration of the final product is a matter of mix and match of "black boxes" (Sanchez and Mahoney, 1996; Baldwin and Clark, 2000, 2001). This is made possible by advanced technological knowledge about component interactions that can be used to fully specify and standardize component interfaces and therefore to decouple the design of the product architecture (i.e., arrangement of functional elements) from the design of each module. Modularity, by simplifying design and development processes, allows a greater division of labor across firms. As a consequence, firms can focus their capabilities on a few modules or on the architecture.

However, modularity implies a trade-off between the "speed" of search (enabled by modularity) and the "breadth" of search (enabled by nonmodular search strategies). Apparently, modular search strategies are indeed highly efficient in the short term (i.e., they provide "higher value"), enabling fast searches within a predefined search space. However, these gains might disappear in the long term, as "slower" (i.e., less modular) search strategies catch up and reach better solutions as they can explore wider search spaces, exactly because they rely on less tightly defined "design rules." Thus, in dynamic terms, modularity may entail some risks: Firms may miss value-generating alternatives because they cannot escape the boundaries set by the existing modular design strategies (Brusoni et al., 2001).[16]

In this respect, modularization, although "simplifying" the problem of searching for better design and fostering division of labor, calls at

---

[16] Some of these properties are formally explored and are corroborated in Marengo and Dosi (2005).

the same time for an increasing role played by systems integrators, who remain involved in exploratory research that looks beyond the boundaries set by current architectures in order to be able to lead the process of development of successive generations of systems. To put it another way, increasing specialization generated by modularity requires the development of more centralized agents who "coordinate" the integration of different modules and, even more important, the development of new systems.

We noted in the previous section that the greater opportunity to separate research from development and production and the possibility of defining specific intermediate research outputs to be transferred across organizations imply that the scale at which individuals can experiment with their innovations in the economy has increased. In turn, this explains some of the factors discussed earlier, specifically high-tech entrepreneurship, turbulence (higher entry and exit rates), and the higher rate of innovation, which is a natural outcome of the greater number of trials. Moreover, as noted, the picture that emerges from this dynamic process is one in which a balance is achieved over time between exploration and exploitation, especially in technology-based industries, with the smaller firms occupying a higher share of the domain of exploration.

However, in other respects, large corporations do not simply specialize in the development of innovations created by others. They perform at the same time the crucial role of integrators of fragments of specialized knowledge, building up architectures or frames that organize and structure the knowledge required to develop, produce, and sell new products. Even in the case of biotechnology, large firms appear as central nodes in a hierarchically structured network of relationships (Orsenigo et al., 2001), whose density remains practically stable. As the network grows bigger through the entry of new agents, other relationships consolidate and some agents increase their centrality.

Division of labor and decentralization (the expansion of the network) requires at the same time stronger integration and coordination within the nodes of the network. As some activities are outsourced, their coordination implies the development of highly structured functions dedicated to their management and to the achievement of coherence and integration. In other words, division of labor does not simply reduce the need for managerial control, but shifts it at different levels. Thus, the management of supply chains does not eliminate the need for hierarchical control. If anything, it changes its nature and its practices. But one could legitimately argue that the management of supply chains is a more organizationally complex activity than straightforward vertical integration.

In this perspective, the visible hand is not disappearing. Perhaps it is becoming smaller and the grip of its fist is relaxing. But its strength is not weakened: Its grip is perhaps smoother but firmer.

Innovation, Entrepreneurial Firms, and the Life Cycle of Industries

To conclude the analysis of this section, it is important to remark that the balance between exploration and exploitation, or decentralization and coordination, often depends on the stage of the industry life cycle, with the early stages favoring exploration and the production of many new technologies or ideas (Klepper, 1996, 2002). As shown by Klepper, even an industry as concentrated as that of automobiles was highly fragmented when it started, with a great deal of entry and exit. A shake-up then gradually reduced the number of suppliers. The Internet boom of the 1990s was a similar process. Many firms were created and the shake-up of early 2000 adjusted its industry structure. Even if the industry life-cycle model should not be taken as a model applicable to all industries or products (as Klepper, 1997, easily acknowledges,), technological revolutions open up rich technological opportunities to be explored and exploited by both small and large firms. The space of opportunities is often so wide and complex that no single organization can hope to be able to explore it extensively. Competing (and complementary) directions of search have to be tested and developed before, but, to a lesser extent, also after the establishment of specific paradigms and trajectories (Dosi, 1982). Thus, even without assuming any intrinsic advantage of size or age, periods of technological transitions are typically marked by entry of new firms and turbulence (Orsenigo et al., 2001). In addition, in many cases new companies are the carriers of new technologies precisely because incumbents embody old knowledge bases that make it harder for them to grasp and master the new ones (Christensen and Rosenbloom, 1995). Thus, some of the new firms are able to displace old leaders. The advantages of the new companies are not linked to their small size, though: Rather, they are small because they are young, and successful ones will grow larger. Thus, some of the large firms that have become prominent worldwide are new firms in a long-term perspective. This is especially true of the information technology (IT) firms, for example, Microsoft, Cisco, or Sun Microsystems.

Moreover, it is not always the case that new firms inevitably end up dominating the industry. In many instances, incumbents are able to survive technological disruptions and maintain their leadership: to a significant extent, for example, this is the case of pharmaceuticals after the biotechnology revolution (Henderson and Cockburn, 1994; Galambos and Sturchio, 1998; Henderson et al., 1999). In this respect, the increased entry of Schumpeterian, innovative firms is indeed likely to be linked to the advent of major technological revolutions like those occurring in ICT and life sciences. However, specifically with reference to the contemporary "technological revolution," this phenomenon is also likely to be linked to institutional changes that have little to do with technological change as such. For example, the diffusion of a tight intellectual property rights (IPR) regime especially in the United States has certainly favored the development of the biotechnology industry as an organizational solution alternative to more direct use of the knowledge created in universities by large corporations.[17]

It is worth noting that this outcome is not obviously and necessarily efficient (Pisano, 2006): very few of these companies are profitable, and most of them survive as specialized suppliers of a particular intermediate good – new promising molecules or research techniques – to large pharmaceutical corporations.

CONCLUSION

Long ago, Herbert Simon (1991, pp. 27-8) suggested the following thought experiment. Suppose that each interorganizational interaction is flagged with a green color and each market transaction with a red one. Allow some visitor from outer space to approach the earth. What will this visitor see? Simon's answer was this: a lot of continents and islands with the green color interlinked with many, thick and thin, red lines.

Has the picture changed since Simon's original answer? Our bird's-eye statistical answer is this: not too much, if at all. Hence, if the question of whether there has been a third industrial revolution is posed in terms of overall balances between the activities that are integrated within organizations and those that occur through market interactions, the answer is

---

[17] Likewise, entrepreneurship has been buttressed by a host of supporting policies ranging from public procurement to specific programs, e.g., SBIR in the United States. In other words, there may be institutional factors, fads, or simply path-dependent phenomena that may exacerbate problems of excessive exploration or, by the same token, of excessive exploitation at other moments in time.

largely negative. Of course, we do not know how to measure the types of interaction. However, if we reasonably assume that the bigger a firm, the higher the number of intraorganizational interactions it contains, then the evidence on the relative stability of size distributions offers a strong support to the point.

At a closer look, however, many things have changed, both as "normal" outcomes of the processes of creative destruction–creative accumulation and as specific features of the new techno-economic paradigm.

In the foregoing image, some continents have shrunk or even disappeared whereas some (old and new) islands have grown to the size of continents.

Hence, first, not too surprisingly, life-cycle phenomena imply that the seemingly dominant firms in 1900 (including, in the United States, some associated with the distribution of ice bars in New England!) are almost entirely different from those one observes in say, Fortune 500 today. At the same time, one observes the emergence of the Intel, Microsoft (and also Boeing and Airbus, etc.) firms of the current world.

Second, taking an even closer look at the image resolution of our outer-space observer, one sees significant, persistent, fluctuations in the location of innovative activities among "continents" and "islands" of different sizes and ages. Enough to corroborate the notion of a third industrial revolution? Certainly, the technological breakthroughs militate in favor of the "revolutionary" hypothesis. The organization picture is rather more blurred. Within the coevolutionary dynamics of technologies, sectors, and firms, revolutions are harder to see from the angle of the distribution of activities left to the visible hand of organizations and the invisible hand of market interactions.

TECHNICAL APPENDIX AND DATA DESCRIPTION

The analysis on Italian firms was performed on Micro.1 database.[18] Micro.1 contains longitudinal data on a panel of several thousands of Italian firms with employment of twenty units or more and covers the years 1989–97.

As reported in Bartelsman et al. (2004), the percentage of manufacturing firms with more than twenty employees is 12 percent of the

---

[18] The database has been made available to our team under the mandatory condition of censorship of any individual information. One of the authors gratefully acknowledges ISTAT for data provision.

total population. However, these relatively larger companies account for almost 70 percent in terms of employment. The empirical analysis performed in Figure 1.4 draws on firms in manufacturing sectors only.

Table 1.2 and Figures 1.4 and 1.5 report the Zipf fit of sectors grouped according to Pavitt taxonomy (Pavitt, 1984). The mapping of industrial activity to the corresponding "Pavitt sectors" has been adapted to the Italian standard ATECO, of whom NACE is an almost perfectly overlapping classification.[19] Table 1.7 reports such correspondence, which has been applied also to French data, because their standard [Nomenclature d'Activités Française (NAF)] perfectly maps the ATECO one at the three-digit level.

Results presented on French firms make use of the EAE databank collected by SESSI and provided by the French Statistical Office (INSEE). This database contains longitudinal data on a virtually exhaustive panel of French firms with twenty or more employees over the period 1989–2002. We restrict our analysis to the manufacturing sectors. For statistical consistency, we utilize only the period 1996–2003, and we consider only continuing firms over this period. Database characteristics are described in greater detail in Bottazzi et al. (2005).

The analysis of size distribution and concentration ratio of world's largest firms employed data collected in the database Osiris.[20]

Tables 1.3 and 1.4 report data on firm and employee distribution per size class as one might recover from publicly available statistics published by OECD, Eurostats, and some National Statistical Offices. Figures on earlier years for European countries and Japan have been retrieved from OECD sources (OECD, 1994, 1995). Data on more recent years have been collected for Europe from the "Industry, trade and services" statistics released yearly by Eurostat (EUROSTAT, 2006) and for Japan from the "Establishments and Enterprise Census" at the Statistics Bureau of Japan (Japan, 2006).

For the United States, it has been possible to access the "Enterprise statistics" of the U.S. Census Bureau starting from 1958 onward thanks to the access granted to their archives. After 1988, data are recovered from Statistics of U.S. Businesses (SUSB) (U.S. Census Bureau, 2006).

---

[19] International comparisons among various classification standards are permanently available from, in addition to national statistical offices, the United Nations Statistics Division at *http://unstats.un.org/unsd/*.

[20] Access to this database was kindly granted to one of the authors while visiting at the University of Pennsylvania.

Table 1.7. Mapping of Industrial Activities to the Corresponding Pavitt Sectors

ISIC	Sector	Supply Dominated	Scale Intensive	Special Suppliers	Science Based
151	Production, processing and preserving of meat		√		
155	Dairy products		√		
158	Production of other foodstuffs (bread, sugar, etc.)		√		
159	Production of beverages (alcoholic and nonalcoholic)		√		
171	Preparation and spinning of textiles	√			
172	Textiles weaving	√			
173	Finishing of textiles	√			
175	Carpets, rugs, and other textiles	√			
177	Knitted and crocheted articles	√			
182	Wearing apparel	√			
191	Tanning and dressing of leather	√			
193	Footwear	√			
202	Production of plywood and panels	√			
203	Wood products for construction	√			
205	Production of other wood products (cork, straw, etc.)	√			
211	Pulp, paper, and paperboard		√		
212	Articles of paper and paperboard	√			
221	Publishing	√			
222	Printing	√			
241	Production of basic chemicals		√		
243	Paints, varnishes, printing inks, and mastics		√		
244	Pharmaceutical, medicinal chemicals, and botanical products				√
245	Soap and detergents, cleaning and toilet preparations		√		
246	Other chemical products		√		
251	Rubber products	√			
252	Plastic products	√			
261	Glass and glass products		√		
262	Ceramic goods not for construction		√		
263	Ceramic goods for construction		√		

ISIC	Sector	Supply Dominated	Scale Intensive	Special Suppliers	Science Based
264	Bricks, tiles, and construction products in baked clay		√		
266	Articles in concrete, plaster, and cement	√			
267	Cutting, shaping, and finishing of stone	√			
273	First processing of iron and steel		√		
275	Casting of metals		√		
281	Structural metal products	√			
284	Forging, pressing, stamping, and roll forming of metal		√		
285	Treatment and coating of metals	√			
286	Cutlery, tools, and general hardware	√			
287	Other fabricated metal products				
291	Machinery for production and use of mechanical power			√	
292	Other general-purpose machinery			√	
293	Agricultural and forestry machinery		√		
294	Machine tools			√	
295	Other special-purpose machinery			√	
297	Domestic appliances not elsewhere classified		√		
311	Electric motors, generators, and transformers			√	
312	Manufacture of electricity distribution, control equipment			√	
316	Electrical equipment not elsewhere classified			√	
322	TV, radio transmitters, lines for telephony, telegraphy				√
332	Measure, control, and navigation instruments				√
342	Production of bodies for cars, trailers, semitrailers		√		
343	Production of spare parts and accessories for cars		√		
361	Furniture	√			

REFERENCES

Acs, Z. J., & Audretsch, D. B. (1987). *Innovation, market structure and firm size. Review of Economics and Statistics, 69*, 567-75.

Acs, Z. J., & Audretsch, D. B. (1989). Small-firm entry in U.S. manufacturing. *Economica, 56*, 255-65.

Acs, Z. J., & Audretsch, D. B. (1990). *Innovation and small firms.* Cambridge, MA: MIT Press.

Acs, Z. J., & D. B. Audretsch, D. B. (1991). R&D firm size and innovative activity. In Z. J. Acs & D. B. Audretsch (Eds.), *Innovation and technological change. An international comparison.* Ann Arbor, MI: University of Michigan Press.

Armington, C. (1986). *Entry and exit of firms: An international comparison.* Economic Council of Canada.

Arora, A., Fosfuri, A., & Gambardella, A. (2004). *Markets for technology: The economics of innovation and corporate strategy.* Cambridge, MA: MIT Press.

Arora, A., & Gambardella, A. (Eds.). (2005). *From underdogs to tigers: The rise and growth of the software industry in some emergent regions.* Oxford, UK: Oxford University Press.

Athreye, S., & Cantwell, J. (2007). Creating competition? : Globalisation and the emergence of new technology producers. *Research Policy, 36*(2), 209-26.

Axtell, R. L. (2001). Zipf distribution of US firm sizes. *Science, 293*, 1818-20.

Baldwin, C. Y., & Clark, K. B. (2000): *Design rules: The power of modularity.* Cambridge, MA: MIT Press.

Baldwin, C. Y., & Clark, K. B. (2001). *Modularity after the crash* (Working Paper No. 01-075). Cambridge, MA: Harvard Business School.

Baldwin, J. R. (1998). *The dynamics of industrial competition: A North American perspective.* New York: Cambridge University Press.

Baldwin, W. L., & Scott, J. T. (1987). *Market structure and technological change.* London: Harwood Academic.

Bartelsman, E. J., & Doms, M. (2000). Understanding productivity: Lessons from longitudinal microdata. *Journal of Economic Literature, 38*, 569-94.

Bartelsman, E. J., Haltiwanger, J., & Scarpetta, S. (2004). *Microeconomic evidence of creative destruction in industrial and developing countries* (Working Paper No. 04-114/3). Tinbergen Institute.

Bartelsman, E. J., Scarpetta, S., & and Schivardi, F. (2005). Comparative analysis of firm demographics and survival: Micro-level evidence for the OECD countries. *Industrial and Corporate Change, 14*, 365-91.

Beesley, M. E., & Hamilton, R. T. (1984). Small firms' seedbed role and the concept of turbulence. *Journal of Industrial Economics, 33*, 217-32.

Bhidé, A. V. (2000). *The origin and evolution of new businesses.* Oxford, UK: Oxford University Press.

Boeri, T., & Cramer, U. (1992). Employment growth, incumbents and entrants: Evidence from Germany. *International Journal of Industrial Organization, 10*(4), 545-65.

Bond, R. S. (1975). Mergers and mobility among largest corporations, 1948-68. *Antitrust Bulletin, 20*, 505-20.

Bottazzi, G., Cefis, E., & Dosi, G. (2002). Corporate growth and industrial structure. Some evidence from the Italian manufacturing industry. *Industrial and Corporate Change, 11*, 705-23.

Bottazzi, G., Cefis, E., Dosi, G., & Secchi, A. (2007). Invariances and diversities in the evolution of Italian manufacturing industry. *Small Business Economics, 29*(1-2), 137-59.

Bottazzi, G., Coad, A., Jacoby, N., & Secchi, A. (2005). Corporate growth and industrial dynamics: Evidence from French manufacturing (LEM Working Paper No. 21). S. Anna School of Advanced Studies, Pisa, Italy.

Bottazzi, G., & Secchi, A. (2003a). Properties and sectoral specificities in the dynamics of U.S. manufacturing companies. *Review of Industrial Organization, 23*, 217-32.

Bottazzi, G., & Secchi, A. (2003b). Why are distributions of firm growth rates tent-shaped? *Economics Letters, 80*, 415-20.

Bottazzi, G., & Secchi, A. (2006). Explaining the distribution of firms growth rates. RAND *Journal of Economics, 37*, 235-56.

Bound, J., Cummins, C., Griliches, Z., & Jaffe, A. (1984). Who does R&D and who patents? In Z. Griliches (Ed.), *R&D, patents, and productivity*. Chicago: University of Chicago Press.

Breschi, S., Malerba, F., & Orsenigo, L. (2000). Technological regimes and Schumpeterian patterns of innovation. *Economic Journal, 110*(463), 388-410.

Bresnahan, T., & Gambardella, A. (Eds.). (2004). *Building high-tech clusters: Silicon Valley and beyond*. Cambridge, UK: Cambridge University Press.

Brusoni, S., & Prencipe, A. (2001). Unpacking the black box of modularity: Technologies, products and organizations. *Industrial and Corporate Change, 10*, 179-205.

Brusoni, S., Prencipe, A., & Pavitt, K. (2001). Knowledge specialisation, organizational coupling and the boundaries of the firm: Why firms know more than they make?. *Administrative Science Quarterly, 46*(4), 597-621.

Cantwell, J., & Iammarino, S. (2001). EU regions and multinational corporations: Change, stability and strengthening of technological comparative advantages. *Industrial and Corporate Change, 10*, 1007-37.

Chamberlin, E. H. (1962). *The theory of monopolistic competition* (8th ed.). Cambridge, MA: Harvard University Press.

Chandler, A. D. J. (1990). *Scale and scope: The dynamics of industrial capitalism*. Cambridge, MA: Belknap.

Christensen, C. M., & Rosenbloom, R. S. (1995). Explaining the attacker's advantage: Technological paradigms, organizational dynamics, and the value network. *Research Policy, 24*(2), 233-57.

Cohen, W. M. (1995). Empirical studies of innovative activity. In P. Stoneman (Ed.), *Handbook of the Economics of Innovation and Technological Change* (Chap. 6, pp. 182-264). Oxford, UK: Blackwell.

Cohen, W. M., & Levin, R. C. (1989). Empirical studies of innovation and market structure. In R. Schmalensee & R. D. Willig (Eds.), *Handbook of Industrial Organization* (Vol. 2, pp. 1059-107). Amsterdam: North-Holland.

Collins, N. R., & Preston, L. E. (1961). The size structure of the largest industrial firms, 1909-58. *American Economic Review, 51*, 986-1011.

64 GIOVANNI DOSI ET AL.

Davis, S. J., Haltiwanger, J. C., & Schuh, S. (1996). *Job creation and destruction*. Cambridge, MA: MIT Press.

Dosi, G. (1982). Technological paradigms and technological trajectories: A suggested interpretation of the determinants and directions of technical change. *Research Policy, 11*, 147-62.

Dosi, G. (1988). Sources, procedures, and microeconomic effects of innovation. *Journal of Economic Literature, 26*, 1120-71.

Dosi, G. (1991). Perspectives on evolutionary theory. *Science and Public Policy*.

Dosi, G. (2006). Statistical regularities in the evolution of industries. A guide through some evidence and challenges for the theory. In S. Brusoni & F. Malerba (Eds.), *Perspectives on innovation*. New York: Cambridge University Press.

Dosi, G., & Coriat, B. (1998). Learning how to govern and learning how to solve problems. On the co-evolution of competences, conflicts and organizational routines. In A. D. Chandler & O. S. P. Hagström (Eds.), *The dynamic firm: The role of technology, strategy, organization, and regions*. New York: Oxford University Press.

Dosi, G., & Grazzi, M. (2006). Technologies as problem-solving procedures and technologies as input-output relations: Some perspectives on the theory of production. *Industrial and Corporate Change, 15*(1), 173-202.

Dosi, G., Malerba, F., Marsili, O., & Orsenigo, L. (1997). Industrial structures and dynamics: Evidence, interpretations and puzzles. *Industrial and Corporate Change, 6*(1), 3-24.

Dosi, G., & Marengo, L. (1994). Some elements of an evolutionary theory of organizational competence. In R. W. England (Ed.), *Evolutionary concepts in contemporary economics*. Ann Arbor, MI: University of Michigan Press.

Dosi, G., Marsili, O., Orsenigo, L., &Salvatore, R. (1995). Learning, market selection and evolution of industrial structures. *Small Business Economics, 7*, 411-36.

Dosi, G., Orsenigo, L., & Sylos-Labini, M. (2005). Technology and the economy. In J. Smelser & R. Swedberg (Eds.), *The handbook of economic sociology* (2nd ed.). Princeton, NJ: Princeton University Press.

Dosi, G., & Salvatore, R. (1992). The structure of industrial production and the boundaries between firms and markets. In M. Storper & A. J. Scott (Eds.), *Pathways to industrialization and regional development*. London: Routeledge.

EUROSTAT. (2006). *Industry, trade and services database*. Luxembourg: Author.

Evans, D. S. (1987a). The relationship between firm growth, size, and age: Estimates for 100 manufacturing industries. *Journal of Industrial Economics, 35*, 567-81.

Evans, D. S. (1987b). Tests of alternative theories of firm growth. *Journal of Political Economy, 95*, 657-74.

Freeman, C. (1982). *The economics of industrial innovation*. Cambridge, MA: MIT Press.

Freeman, C., & Perez, C. (1988). Structural crises of adjustment, business cycles and investment behaviour. In G. Dosi et al. (Eds.), *Technical change and economic theory*. London: Pinter.

Galambos, L., & Sturchio, J. L. (1998). Pharmaceutical firms and the transition to biotechnology: A study in strategic innovation. *Business History Review, 72*, 250-78.

Geroski, P. A., & Mazzucato, M. (2002). Learning and the sources of corporate growth. *Industrial and Corporate Change, 11*, 623-44.

Geroski, P. A., & Toker, S. (1996). The turnover of market leaders in UK manufacturing industry, 1979-86. *International Journal of Industrial Organization, 14*(2), 141-58.

Ghemawat, P., & Ghadar, F. (2006). Global integration, global concentration. *Industrial and Corporate Change, 15,* 595-623.

Hall, B. H. (1987). The relationship between firm size and firm growth in the US manufacturing sector. *Journal of Industrial Economics, 35,* 583-606.

Henderson, R., & Cockburn, I. (1994). Measuring competence? Exploring firm effects in pharmaceutical research. *Strategic Management Journal, 15,* 63-84.

Henderson, R., Orsenigo, L., & Pisano, G. (1999). The pharmaceutical industry and the revolution in molecular biology: Interactions among scientific, institutional, and organizational change. In D. Mowery & R. R. Nelson (Eds.), *Sources of industrial leadership: Studies of seven industries* (Chap. 13). Cambridge: Cambridge University Press.

Hotelling, H. (1929). Stability in competition. *Economic Journal, 39*(153), 41-57.

Ijiri, Y., & Simon, H. A. (1977). *Skew distributions and the sizes of business firms.* Amsterdam: North-Holland.

ISTAT. (1997). *Rapporto annuale 2004.* Rome: Istituto Nazionele di Statistica.

ISTAT. (2001). *Rapporto annuale 2004.* Rome: Istituto Nazionele di Statistica.

Japan, S. B. (2006). *Establishment and enterprise census.*

Kamien, M. I., &Schwartz, N. L. (1982). *Market structure and innovation.* Cambridge: Cambridge University Press.

Kaplan, A. D. (1954). *Big enterprise in a competitive system.* Washington, DC: Brookings Institution.

Klepper, S. (1996). Entry, exit, growth, and innovation over the product life cycle. *American Economic Review, 86,* 562-83.

Klepper, S. (1997). Industry life cycles. *Industrial and Corporate Change, 6*(1), 145-82.

Klepper, S. (2002). Firm survival and the evolution of oligopoly. *Rand Journal of Economics, 33*(1), 37-61.

Klepper, S. & Thompson, P. (2007). Submarkets and the evolution of market structure. *Rand Journal of Economics, 37*(4).

Kumar, M. S. (1985). Growth, acquisition activity and firm size: Evidence from the United Kingdom. *Journal of Industrial Economics, 33,* 327-38.

Lamoreaux, N. R., & Sokoloff, K. L. (Eds.). (2007). *Financing innovation in the United States, 1870 to present.* Cambridge, MA: MIT Press.

Lancaster, K. J. (1979). *Variety, equity and efficiency.* New York: Columbia University Press.

Langlois, R. N. (2002). Modularity in technology and organization. *Journal of Economic Behavior & Organization, 49*(1), 19-37.

Langlois, R. N. (2003). The vanishing hand: The changing dynamics of industrial capitalism. Industrial and Corporate Change, *12,* 351-85.

Lotti, F., Santarelli, E., & Vivarelli, M. (2003). Does Gibrat's Law hold among young, small firms? *Journal of Evolutionary Economics, 13,* 213-35.

Louçã, F., & Mendonça, S. (2002). Steady change: The 200 largest US manufacturing firms throughout the 20th century. *Industrial and Corporate Change, 11,* 817-45.

Malerba, F., Nelson, R., Orsenigo, L., & Winter, S. (2006). *Vertical integration and dis-integration of computer firms: A history friendly model of the co-evolution of the computer and semiconductor industries* (Papers on Economics and Evolution 2006-19). Munich: Evolutionary Economics Group, Max-Planck-Institute of Economics.

Malerba, F., Nelson, R. R., Winter, S. G., & Orsenigo, L. (1999). "History-friendly" models of industry evolution: The computer industry. Industrial and Corporate Change, 8(1), 3-40.

Malerba, F., & Orsenigo, L. (1995). Schumpeterian patterns of innovation. *Cambridge Journal of Economics, 19*(1), 47-65.

Malerba, F., & Orsenigo, L. (1997) Technological regimes and sectoral pattern of innovative activities. *Industrial and Corporate Change, 6*(1), 83-117.

Malerba, F., & Orsenigo, L. (2002). Innovation and market structure in the dynamics of the pharmaceutical industry and biotechnology: Towards a history-friendly model. *Industrial and Corporate Change, 11*, 667-703.

Mansfield, E. (1962). Entry, Gibrat's Law, innovation, and the growth of firms. *American Economic Review, 52*, 1023-51.

Marengo, L., & Dosi, G. (2005). Division of labor, organizational coordination and market mechanisms in collective problem-solving. *Journal of Economic Behavior and Organization, 58*, 303-26.

Marsili, O. (2005). Technology and the size distribution of firms: Evidence from Dutch manufacturing. *Review of Industrial Organization, 27*, 303-28.

Mermelstein, D. (1969). Large industrial corporations and asset shares. *American Economic Review, 59*, 531-41.

Metcalfe, S. J. (2001). Restless capitalism: Increasing returns and growth in enterprise economies. In *Industrial Structure and Innovation Dynamics*. London: Elgar.

Mueller, W. F. (1962). The origins of the basic inventions underlying DuPont's major product and process innovations, 1920 to 1950. In R. R. Nelson & K. J. Arrow (Eds.), *The rate and direction of inventive activity*. Princeton, NJ: Princeton University Press.

Newman, M. E. J. (2005). Power laws, Pareto distributions and Zipf's law. *Contemporary Physics, 46*, 323-51.

OECD. (1994). *Employment outlook*. Paris: Author.

OECD. (1995). *Industrial structure statistics*. Paris: Author.

OECD. (2006). *Structural demographic and business statistics 1996-2003*. Paris: Author.

Orsenigo, L., Pammolli, F., & Riccaboni, M. (2001). Technological change and network dynamics: Lessons from the pharmaceutical industry. Research Policy, 30, 485-508.

Osiris (2005). Bureau Van Dijk Electronic Publishing.

Pavitt, K. (1984). Sectoral pattern of technical change: Towards a taxonomy and a theory. *Research Policy, 13*, 343-73.

Pavitt, K. (1998). Technologies, products and organization in the innovating firm: What Adam Smith tells us and Joseph Schumpeter doesn't. Industrial and Corporate Change, 7, 433-52.

Pavitt, K., Robson, M., & Townsend, J. (1987). The size distribution of innovating firms in the UK: 1945-83. *Journal of Industrial Economics, 35*(3), 297-316.

Perez, C. (2007). Finance and technical change: A long-term view. In H. Hanusch & A. Pyka (Eds.), *The Elgar companion to neo-Schumpeterian economics.* Cheltenham, UK: Elgar.

Pisano, G. P. (2006). *Science business: The promise, the reality, and the future of biotech.* Cambridge, MA: Harvard Business School Press.

Robertson, P. L., & Langlois, R. N. (1995). Innovation, networks, and vertical integration. *Research Policy, 24,* 543-62.

Robinson, J. V. (1933). *Economic of imperfect competition.* London: Macmillan.

Sanchez, R., &Mahoney, J. T. (1996). Modularity, flexibility, and knowledge management in product and organization design. *Strategic Management Journal* (Special Issue: Knowledge and the firm), *17,* 63-76.

Scherer, F. M. (1965). Market structure, opportunity, and the output of patented inventions. *American Economic Review, 55,* 1097-125.

Shaked, A., & Sutton, J. (1978). Product differentiation and industrial structure. *Journal of Industrial Economics, 36*(2), 131-46.

Simon, H. A. (1991). Organizations and markets. *Journal of Economic Perspectives, 5*(2), 25-44.

Soete, L. L. G. (1979). Firm size and inventive activity : The evidence reconsidered. *European Economic Review, 12*(4), 319-40.

Steindl, J. (1945). *Small and big business: Economic problems of the size of firms.* Cambridge, MA: Blackwell.

Storey, D. J. (1994). *Understanding the small business sector.* London: Routeledge.

Sutton, J. (1997). Gibrat's legacy. *Journal of Economic Literature, 35*(1), 40-59.

Sutton, J. (1998). *Technology and market structure: Theory and evidence.* Cambridge, MA: MIT Press.

Symeonidis, G. (1996). *Innovation, firm size and market structure: Schumpeterian hypotheses and some new themes* (OECD Economics Department Working Papers 161). Paris: Economics Department, OECD.

Teece, D. J. (1986). Profiting from technological innovation: Implication for integration, collaboration, licensing and public policy. *Research Policy, 15,* 285-305.

Teece, D. J., Rumelt, R., Dosi, G., & Winter, S. (1994). Understanding corporate coherence: Theory and evidence. *Journal of Economic Behavior & Organization, 23*(1), 1-30.

U.S. Bureau of Labor Statistics. (2005). *Business employment dynamics.* Washington, DC: Author.

U.S. Census Bureau. (1972). *Enterprise statistics.* Washington, DC: Author.

U.S. Census Bureau. (1977). *Enterprise statistics.* Washington, DC: Author.

U.S. Census Bureau. (1982). *Enterprise statistics.* Washington, DC: Author.

U.S. Census Bureau. (2006). *Statistics of U.S. business.* Washington, DC: Author.

Winter, S. G. (1984). Schumpeterian competition under alternative technological regimes. *Journal of Economic Behavior and Organization, 5,* 287-320.

Winter, S. G., Kaniovski, Y. M., & Dosi, G. (2000). Modeling industrial dynamics with innovative entrants. *Structural Change and Economic Dynamics, 11,* 255-93.

2

The Long-Run Dynamics of Big Firms

The 100 Largest Employers from the United States, the United Kingdom, Germany, France, and Japan: 1907–2002[1]

HOWARD GOSPEL AND MARTIN FIEDLER

INTRODUCTION

The growth of large firms within national economies and in the global economy has long been of interest in economics and economic history. In *Principles of Economics* (1890 and 1910 editions), Marshall used an analogy of the "forest" for an industry or economy and suggested that, while the "trees" or firms in the forest would grow and die, the forest itself would be constantly renewed. However, he conceded that with the advent of the joint stock company, some firms might grow to very large sizes and be able to better survive. Later, Chandler (1977, 1990) suggested that large firms came into existence in certain industries for which there were advantages in internalizing market transactions. Some firms, he argued, used first-mover advantage, investing in production, distribution, and management, to grow in size and survive over the long term. In the terminology of Hannah (1999), such firms are the "giant redwoods" of the forest, surviving over a long period of time. However,

[1] We would like to thank the *Deutscher Akademischer Austauschdienst* and the *Centre for Economic Performance at London School of Economics* for their support with this research. We are indebted to Takashi Abe, Alfred Chandler, Youssef Cassis, Bruce Kogut, Les Hannah, Alison Sharp, Peter Wardley, Richard Whittington, and John Wilson, who helped us to detect some target firms or who provided comments.

using capitalization as the measure, the latter writer found deaths among the trees of the forest more common than survivals.

This chapter considers changes in the size, industrial composition, and survival of the major firms in major economies, from the beginning of the twentieth century to the beginning of the twenty-first century. It traces industries and firms that had their origin in the "first" industrial revolution, largely related to steam power (railways, coal mining, textiles, iron and steel, and heavy engineering), which dominated at the beginning of the twentieth century. It then charts the rise of industries and firms of the "second" industrial revolution, largely related to electricity, the internal combustion engine, and new chemical processes, which came to dominate the middle of the twentieth century. Finally, it examines the rise of firms and industry in large part related to the "third" industrial revolution of information and communications technology (ICT), many of which are firms in services and retail.

The chapter is based on two sets of interlinked analytical and theoretical considerations. The first concerns the pattern of change and continuity in a population of large firms as measured by employment. Here, the objective is to conceptualize, "dimensionalize," and analyze the pattern of change and continuity in this population of firms over time. For our sample of firms, the botanical analogy of the trees of the forest is not entirely appropriate because Marshall was referring to firms in a competitive market, especially in one industry. To date, most work of this kind has been done on manufacturing and mining companies that have existed in largely competitive markets (Chandler, 1990; Hannah 1999). By contrast, our population also includes service firms and state-owned enterprises that historically have been less subject to competition, especially from abroad, or that have enjoyed monopoly positions. Nevertheless, such organizations have played a very important role in the growth of the modern business enterprise and must be taken into account when considering whether there has been a "third" industrial revolution. The challenge is to map a pattern for all such enterprises in terms of size and composition while considering their survival over time and their country of origin. We also conceptualize and identify major periods of change in the population.

The second set of considerations relates to explanations of these same patterns of change and continuity. Three general sets of explanations are used to frame the analysis. These are not set out as hypotheses, because the variables are broad and interrelated and the data do not allow for statistical testing. The first set of explanations concerns the interaction between technology and markets. This was classically stated by Smith (1776), who analyzed the interaction between market size and competition and the division of labor in terms of the introduction of technological and organizational change. Schumpeter (1939, 1942) later developed an analysis in terms of periods of "creative destruction" when technology and markets interact to bring about major change. In this chapter, the advent of new technologies, in particular general-purpose technologies with broad applicability that facilitate organizational change (Helpman, 1998), are seen as interacting with periods of market growth and extension so as to stimulate new entrants into the population, some of which survive and others of which exit or die. The general proposition is that the advent of new technologies and the size and nature of markets have driven major changes in the pattern of large firms.

The second set of explanations concerns the influence of the state and the more or less supportive role it has played in creating and sustaining large firms. In his survey of the literature on the role of the state, Hancké (2002) suggested state-based explanations for big firm growth and survival. The general proposition is that a significant proportion of firms grew in size and survived under state support and that the withdrawal of such state support similarly has had an effect on the population of firms.

A third set of explanations relates to factors more internal to the firm and concerns strategy and structure in a broad Chandlerian sense (Chandler, 1962, 1977, 1990). Under this heading we include the adoption of strategies leading to internal growth (investment in production, distribution, and management), vertical or horizontal integration, diversification, multinationalization, the role of mergers and acquisitions, and the adaptation of organizational forms. The proposition is that large firms entered into our population and survived or declined over the course of a century mainly because of their own strategic and structural decisions.

The chapter proceeds as follows. The next section outlines the data available for the United States, the United Kingdom, Germany, France, and Japan on the basis of study design. The second section explores the size, composition, survival, national origin, and periods of change over time. Finally, explanations are offered for patterns, similarities, and differences with previous work, and possibilities for further research are suggested.

DATA, DESIGN, AND DEFINITIONS

Employment is used as the measure of firm size. Earlier studies have examined large firms using assets, turnover, or equity as measures (Chandler,

1990; Fruin, 1992; Schmitz, 1995; Hannah, 1999; *Fortune,* various). All measures entail certain disadvantages; for example, problems of asset and turnover valuation, the use of different national accounting practices and the existence of nonquoted companies. The use of employment also has some additional disadvantages; for example, part-time and temporary workers may be excluded from company figures or alternatively they may be counted as "whole" workers. An employment measure also obviously favors labor-intensive firms and industries that may not be asset rich or have high market valuations. Of course, similar objections about bias may be raised concerning capital-intensive or high-valuation firms. Thus, there is no "right" answer to the question of measurement, although value added would be highly desirable if it could be constructed. Our contention is that employment offers an alternative and important measure of how firms have changed over time. It also offers insight into firms for those interested in the human capital and labor relations aspects of business (Jeremy, 1991; Cassis, 1997; Fiedler, 1999; Wardley, 1991, 1999).

We examine firms from five countries: the United States, the United Kingdom, Germany, France, and Japan. These were chosen to represent five major capitalist economies of the twentieth century. The countries also were selected because lists already existed for the early years (for the United Kingdom, Germany, and Japan) or could be added to from various other sources (see Appendix). Of course, this provides "synthetic" top 100 firms and omits large firms in countries such as Italy, the Netherlands, Switzerland, Russia, China, and India. However, it is likely that we capture a significant portion of the top 100 global companies through the twentieth century. It should be noted here that, for all the organizations in this study, employment includes not just employment in the country of origin, but global employment throughout the world.

For the purposes of analysis, we examine the top 100 organizations at five periods in time, in part in line with earlier research, but also seeking relatively "normal" years about a quarter century apart. Thus, the years around 1907 provide our initial date before the First World War, by which time many giant firms had already come into existence. The period around 1935 reflects the era between the interwar depression and the outbreak of the Second World War. It should be noted that the data for Germany come from 1938 when that country was further into war production than the United States, the United Kingdom, or France. However, because the 1938 database for Germany (Fiedler, 1999) is particularly good, we decided to make use of it. A shorter time period, up to around 1955, is then reviewed, which provides a benchmark date following initial postwar reconstruction. The period around 1972 provides a date at the end of the postwar boom. We present data for 2002 as a terminal date. Again, we note that, depending on the availability of data, the exact dates may vary within a number of years, both within and between countries (see Appendix).

In terms of the coverage and reliability of the data, for the 1907 period, we are most confident about the German and French companies. We also have confidence that we have included most British companies, although there may be some underestimation. We are less confident that we have the full number of American firms, and, again, there may be a small underestimation. For 1935, the data may also miss some UK, American, and Japanese companies, although again the number is small. The post-Second World War data for the five countries are good, with the possible exception of Japan, for which the complexities of some group companies may lead to a small underestimation. We take the position that rather than wait to construct the perfect dataset, analysis of existing datasets is desirable to begin to understand patterns and to provide explanations for changes in big business (Jeremy and Farnie, 2001; Wardley, 2001).

The list of firms includes some organizations that to date have always been state concerns (e.g., national post offices). However, whereas in some countries the telephone system has always been private (the United States), in other countries it has been a part of the public postal service and/or has moved between the two sectors (the United Kingdom, Germany, Japan). Other firms, such as utilities, railways, and coal, have moved between the public and private sectors. This group also includes tobacco companies in France and Japan. However, we exclude from the analysis government departments, municipalities, and bodies such as the National Health Service in the United Kingdom; in other words, state organizations that do not operate for profit and for which output has not been charged or charged only at a nominal price.

In terms of ownership, we consider companies that are more than 50 percent owned by another firm to be part of the latter company. Firms such as Unilever and Shell that have joint nationality are attributed to one country, in these cases the United Kingdom. In the case of mergers, we identify the core or prime merging company and take it as a survivor and the other firms as deaths. Finally, firms are coded by standard industrial classification (SIC). For this, we use the British 1968 SIC that provides a roughly midcentury baseline. Where firms operate in a number of

Table 2.1. Size of Top 100 Firms (Number of Employees)

Size	1907	1935	1955	1972	2002
Minimum	18,996	30,000	49,188	82,000	113,000
Maximum	486,318	703,546	801,199	777,869	1,300,000
Mean	53,417	83,808	138,621	185,195	222,129
Median	33,650	49,685	79,575	122,800	183,819
Sum	5,341,747	8,380,811	13,862,142	18,519,530	22,212,911
Standard deviation	64,457	92,053	145,168	140,190	150,566
Coefficient of variation	1.21	1.10	1.05	0.76	0.68

industries, we have assigned them to what we consider to be their main area of activity.[2]

ANALYZING THE TOP 100

In terms of size, Table 2.1 shows that the minimum number for entry into the top 100 grew from 18,996 in the period around 1907 to 113,000 in 2002. This reflects an annual rate of growth of 2.1 percent over the period 1907-35, rising to 3.2 percent in 1935-55 and 3.9 percent in 1955-72. Thereafter, the annual rate of growth decelerated to 3.3 percent in the years 1972-2002. Over the entire time period, the mean rose from 53,417 to 222,129 and the median from 33,650 to 183,819. Over time, changes in the mean and median follow a broadly similar rising trend and a similar deceleration in the final period.

The maximum size grew from 486,318 in the period around 1907 to 1,300,000 in 2002. The maximum has been very much affected by large public concerns: Preußisch-Hessische Staatseisenbahn, Deutsche Reichsbahn, and the British Transport Commission, which took the top place in the first three observations. Only in the two later periods (1972 and 2002) have private-sector firms topped the list: AT&T and Wal-Mart. The coefficient of variation (the standard deviation expressed as a percentage of the mean) shows that the dispersion in the population has become less over time: In other words, these big firms have become more similar in size over the century.

Table 2.2 shows total employment of these giant firms as a percentage of the total labor force of the five countries. It can be seen that this more than doubled, from 4.1 percent in the period around 1907, to 8.4 percent

[2] The full dataset will be made available on the authors' website and direct from the authors on request.

Table 2.2. Number of Employees in Top 100 Firms as Percentage of Total
Employment in the United States, UK, Germany, France, and Japan

	1907	1935	1955	1972	2002
Employees top 100 (in millions)	5.342	8.381	13.862	18.520	22.213
Total labor force (in millions)	129.436	150.745	164.492	219.556	288.677
Employees top 100 as % of total labor force	4.1	5.6	8.4	8.4	7.7

Note: Global employment as sum of total labor force in the U.S., UK, Germany, France, and Japan, mainly based on Bairoch (1968); OECD (1995a, 1995b); ILO (2002).

in the mid-1950s, where it stabilized through to the 1970s. Thereafter, the number has fallen to 7.7 percent in 2002, a figure still significantly larger than at the start date. Thus, after a long period of increase, in the most recent period these giant firms have come to represent a reduced portion of total employment in these countries.

In terms of composition, Tables 2.3 and 2.4 show that the main sectors in the period around 1907 were railways and (albeit distantly behind) metals, mining, and food, drink, and tobacco. Table 2.3 shows the long-term decline in the number of large firms in railways, mining, textiles, mechanical engineering, and shipbuilding. The two periods, 1935–55 and 1955–72 were the "golden ages" of manufacturing, with around two-thirds of total firms for these years coming from the manufacturing sector. However, it should be noted that vehicles continued to rise over the whole period, from three at the beginning of the twentieth century to fifteen at the beginning of the twenty-first century. From the 1970s on, a significant change takes place with the rise of retailing and services. By 2002, the largest single group of firms comes from retailing, services, vehicles, and communications. Table 2.4 shows the significance of state enterprises until the 1970s (with around 20 in the top 100) and their subsequent decline (to fewer than 10). As an aside, it should be noted that we have no examples from certain SIC industry categories: agriculture, leather goods, timber and furniture, and professional services for which firms have not attained a large size by employment.

We turn next to survival and country of origin of firms. Here a caution is appropriate. Survival is not necessarily a good thing. It may reflect a successful firm, but it may also reflect inefficiency, protection, and the absence of competition. Also, a large portion of survivors in a country may reflect a healthy economy or represent a failure to develop big firms in new sectors. Similarly, a large number of big firms in a country may be a sign of state support and protection, which may have negative effects

Table 2.3. Industrial Composition of Top 100 Firms

Industry	1907	1935	1955	1972	2002
Mining	5	5	6	4	1
Food, drink, tobacco	8	7	4	5	5
Petroleum	1	6	7	3	3
Chemicals	0	3	4	9	1
Metal manufacture	11	16	12	7	1
Mechanical engineering	5	3	3	5	1
Instrument engineering	0	0	2	4	0
Electrical engineering	4	6	11	18	11
Shipbuilding	3	3	1	0	0
Vehicles	3	7	12	13	15
Other metal	0	1	1	0	0
Textiles	2	4	1	2	0
Brick, pottery, glass, cement	0	0	0	1	1
Paper, printing	0	1	1	0	0
Other manufacturing	0	3	4	4	1
Construction	0	0	0	0	2
Gas, electricity, water	0	2	4	4	4
Transport & communication	55	27	18	13	14
Retailing	1	5	7	8	26
Banking, insurance, finance	1	1	1	0	6
Miscellaneous services	0	0	1	0	8

Note: Firms are grouped by their main activity. We include military and defense organizations owned by government as either engineering or shipbuilding where they were organized as separate companies, for example, military and naval arsenals.

and may not be sustainable in the long term. Big enterprises are neither unambiguously good nor bad; it depends on why they are big and what they do with their resources. Having stated this caveat, the intrinsic interest of considering a population of large firms over time remains.

Table 2.4. Sectoral Composition of Top 100 Firms

Sector	1907	1935	1955	1972	2002
Mining	5	5	6	4	1
Manufacturing	38	60	63	71	39
Services	2	6	9	8	40
Transport, communications, public utilities, construction	55	29	22	17	20
Total	100	100	100	100	100
State	20	17	19	19	9

Table 2.5. Long-Run Dynamics of Top 100 Firms

	1907–35	1935–55	1955–72	1972–2002	1907–2002
New entrants in top 100	47	35	34	61	–
New entrants per year	1.7	1.8	1.9	2.0	1.9
Reentrants in top 100	–	1	5	3	–
Survivors in top 100	53	64	62	36	11
Survivors in any independent form outside top 100	30	49	63	38	25

In terms of entry, survival, and exit from the top 100, Table 2.5 shows that the number of entrants and exits has risen over time since the mid-1930s. Overall, looking at the entire period, death was more common than survival. In total, 11 firms survived over the long term, from 1907 to 2002. An additional 25 firms survived in an independent form outside the top 100. In total, therefore, over one-third of firms in the top 100 in the period around 1907 were still in business at the beginning of the next century. (A separate analysis, not reported in the table, shows that the top 25 firms had higher chances of survival than firms lower in the list had of surviving.)

Note, overall, the rising number of new entries and exits per annum since the mid-1930s. The final period, 1972–2002, has the highest number of new entrants, with an average of 2.0 per annum. The number of firms that reenter the top 100 over the period is small. Reentry is at its highest after the Second World War and reflects postwar reconstruction and restructuring in Germany and Japan, with the reentry of firms such as Thyssen, Gelsenkirchener Bergwerks-AG, Nippon Steel, and Mitsubishi Heavy Industry.

The 11 survivors over the century are the Preußisch-Hessische Staatseisenbahn (Deutsche Bundesbahn), Deutsche Reichspost (Deutsche Post), U.S. Post Office, General Post Office (Royal Mail), La Poste, National Post Office (Japan Post), Réseau de l´Etat (SNCF), Friedrich Krupp (Thyssen Krupp), General Electric, Siemens, and General Motors. It should be noted that 7 of these are state-owned enterprises. Some of the 25 survivors outside the top 100 are still very large companies, such as Exxon, VEBA (now E.ON), Mitsubishi Heavy Industry, and

Table 2.6. Country of Origin of Top 100 Firms

Country	1907	1935	1955	1972	2002
U.S.	40	45	50	42	47
UK	23	15	25	22	9
Germany	19	21	16	14	14
France	10	11	6	13	19
Japan	8	8	3	9	11

Prudential. Others are now much smaller companies, some of which have transformed their core activities. These include firms such as American Car & Foundry (which changed its name to ACF Industries and continues to exist as an independent specialist engineering firm), the German steel producer Gutehoffnungshütte-Haniel (successfully changing into a transport and logistics company), and the former French steel and mining company, de Wendel (today, a holding company in finance and real estate).

In terms of country of origin, Table 2.6 shows that the United States contributed the largest number of corporate giants through all years: between forty and fifty, around double that of the next country. The United Kingdom contributed the second largest number (twenty-three) at the beginning of the time period and sees fluctuation around this over the next two time periods. However, it has also seen the biggest decline, down to nine in 2002. Germany has consistently ranked either second or third, with a mean of seventeen companies. France has seen the largest decline and increase, from ten at the beginning of the period, down to six in the 1950s, but rising to nineteen in 2002. Japan had eight global giants before the First World War and the same number before the Second World War. Thereafter, the number fell back to three, but has since risen to nine and then eleven. However, it should be remembered that there may be some small understatement of Japanese figures because of the difficulty of measuring employment in prewar *zaibatsu* and postwar *keiretsu* companies. In summary, in terms of national contribution, the most striking features are the stability of the United States over the whole period, the relative decline in the number of UK companies, and the parallel rise of Japanese and especially French companies from 1955 onward.

We turn next to the timing of changes in size, composition, survival, and country of origin. In terms of size, the period with the highest growth was 1955–72, after postwar reconstruction and during the long postwar boom. Compositional change was highest in the years 1972–2002. This is reflected in the disappearance (see tables) of textile firms, the decline in the number of chemical, metal, mining, and engineering companies, the rise of retailing and financial services, and the appearance for the first time of firms in miscellaneous services. The period 1907–35 was also one of high compositional change, with the decline in the number of railways and mechanical engineering companies, the entry for the first time of electricity and chemical companies, and the rise of petroleum, vehicle, retailing, textile, electrical, and metal manufacturing firms. The least compositional change is seen during the two time periods 1935–55 and 1955–72. However, during those years, shipbuilding firms disappeared from the rankings, the number of textile, metal, railway, and petroleum companies declined, and electrical engineering, chemical, utilities, vehicles, and retailing firms grew.

Turning to timing by entry, exit, and survival, the periods with the largest number of new entrants per year are in the second half of the twentieth century. The annual average number of new entrants rises from 1.7 in 1907–35 to 2.0 in 1972–2002. A further breakdown of the figures (not reported in Table 2.5) suggests that much of the acceleration in the latter period was from the 1990s onward. The period when there is most change in country of origin is the final time period, with the decline in the number of British firms and the rise of French companies. The only comparable period in terms of change in country of origin is the post–Second World War years, with the more easily understandable decline and then revival of German and Japanese companies. In sum, in terms of the timing of change, the period of maximum change is at the end of the twentieth century, with a large number of exits and new entrants, major compositional change, and major changes in country contributions. The next most turbulent period is the beginning of the twentieth century, with significant changes in size, composition, and survival.

EXPLAINING LONG-RUN DYNAMICS

There are a number of patterns to be explained: changes in composition, size, entry, and exit, country of origin, and the timing of change. Each of these is addressed in turn, and we attempt to assess the effect of the three sets of explanations outlined at the beginning – changes in technologies and markets, the changing role of the state, and the effect of differences in corporate strategy and structure.

Compositional change in large part reflects major technological changes over the century, especially the impact of new general-purpose technologies. Industries of the first industrial revolution, largely related to steam power (railways, coal mining, textiles, iron and steel, and heavy engineering), dominate the list in the years around 1907. However, there are already a few firms from new sectors (electrical, telegraph, and telephone) that have entered the top 100 by this date. Over the next two periods, covering broadly 1935–55 and 1955–72, the industries of the second industrial revolution, largely related to electricity, the internal combustion engine, and new chemical processes, come to dominate the list. Thus, the number of railway and mining companies decline – in large part through the process of merger and acquisition and nationalization in Europe. During these years, new power generation, electrical, and chemical-related companies enter. The development of road transport is seen in the rise of vehicle and related firms (tires, other components, and petroleum). After the Second World War, these are joined by aircraft companies. Such firms, along with chemicals, grow steadily up to the 1970s. From then onward, the growth of the firms that enter the list is in large part related to the third industrial revolution of information and communications technology (ICT). These companies are not the manufacturers of such technologies, because such firms tend not to be labor intensive; nor are they manufacturers in general, because ICT in that sector tended to be labor saving. Rather, they are the users of these technologies in retail, distribution, and services that use information technology and modern transport and communications systems to obtain economies of scale and scope in areas where this was not previously possible (Freeman and Soete, 1997; David and Wright, 2005). By the beginning of the twenty-first century, ICT firms dominate the list.

There are a number of possible explanations for the increase in size. The rise in the size of state enterprises explains some of the overall increase, but mainly at the top end of the distribution. Given the decline in the number and size of such enterprises over time, this is not the major factor in driving the overall increase in size. A more important explanation again can be found in the progressive application of technologies that allowed firms to manage greater scale and scope of operations in particular industries, for example, vehicles, electricals, and food and drink. Also, we stress the progressive introduction of new business communications and processing technologies from the early twentieth century onward (Yates, 1989). Similarly, in recent decades, the introduction of

ICT has allowed the growth of new giants in retailing (Wal-Mart and Car-refour), distribution (FedEx and United Parcel Service), and in services such as catering (Compass and Sodexho). The rise in size has also been driven by the increase in effective demand in national markets and, in the post–Second World War period, the steady growth of international markets. Over the whole period, the processes of growth have been a product of a combination of both internal growth and growth by merger and acquisition. There has also been a growing multinationalization of these companies, including, increasingly, via cross-border acquisitions (Jones, 2005). Unfortunately, it is not possible to quantify and distinguish from the data available the relative contribution of these various determinants and processes.

As stated, the data show that a few giant firms have tended to pull out the distribution in the population. However, it should be remembered that the coefficient of variation has fallen over the long term, especially since the 1950s. In other words, overall, firms in the top 100 have tended to become more equal in size. Some of this decline in variation around the mean reflects the decline in the size of massive state enterprises (national postal and railway companies) and nonstate monopolies (AT&T). However, although there are signs that limits to growth in state firms and in manufacturing may have been reached, the phenomenon of Wal-Mart, with 1,300,000 employees and other large retailing and distribution companies, shows that this is not the case in all industries.

Turning to long-term entry, exit, and survival, entry and exit per year increased over time from the mid-1930s. Over the entire period, 11 firms in the top 100 survived, of which 7 were state-owned enterprises. An additional 25 firms survived outside the top 100, of which 5 were one-time state-owned enterprises (such as Veba in Germany and the former French and Japanese tobacco monopolies). There are therefore several tasks in terms of explaining the long-term story during the twentieth century. One is to explain why only 11 organizations survived within the top 100, with most of these being state-owned enterprises. A further task is to explain why a larger number, 36, survived over the whole period. In other words, it is necessary to explain why, of the top 100 population in 1907, 89 had exited the top 100 and 64 had died by 2002.

Of the 89 exits from the top 100, we have seen that 25 continued to exist in smaller size. This leaves 64 deaths to be explained. There are two main reasons for deaths. The first is technological change and the decline of certain sectors (railways, mining, and, later, manufacturing). The second is mergers and acquisitions, including government nationalization during the middle years of the twentieth century in Europe. In practice, these two factors have often been interrelated, though mergers and acquisitions have taken place in both technologically mature and new industries. It is notable that, overall, very few deaths have been caused by bankruptcies (Armstrong Whitworth and two U.S. railway companies). However, failing firms have usually been the target of acquisitions (as in the case of Republic Steel, Montgomery Ward, and Firestone in the United States, and AEG in Germany).

From this small sample of survivors, it is difficult to draw firm conclusions about causes of long-term survival over the whole period. Of the 11 long-term survivors, 7 are state-owned enterprises. However, none of the 25 that survived outside the top 100 was state-owned during the entire time period. On the other hand, 5 were state-owned enterprises over three of the four time periods. State ownership is undoubtedly one factor contributing to longevity, but it explains only a small number of survivors inside and outside the top 100.

Of the 4 private-sector firms that survived in the top 100 during the whole period, General Electric and Siemens were in expanding industries and managed over time to diversify successfully into newer and higher-value activities. General Motors was in an expanding industry, and, more recently, successfully expanded into financial services. Thyssen Krupp was in a sector that has not expanded continually, but has benefited from merger and progressive diversification into newer areas of its sector. All the companies have long been multinational. An additional 19 firms survived in the top 100 over three time periods – 13 between 1907 and 1972 and 6 between 1935 and 2002. No pattern emerges from this further group of survivors in terms of size, sector, or country. In the case of all these private-sector survivors, it would seem that a residual explanation in terms of corporate strategy and structure may be important. However, any fuller explanation would require a detailed analysis of the business histories of all the surviving firms.

Explanations of national contributions in part reflect the size of markets and national economies. To correct for this, we have calculated each country's gross domestic product (GDP) as a proportion of the total GDP of all five countries (actual figures not reported here). We then compare the percentages with each country's contribution of big firms. On this basis, it is not surprising that the United States has the largest number of big firms. However, it would seem that it always had fewer large firms than its size warrants, and this has been most marked in the post–Second World War period. By contrast, the United Kingdom has been overrepresented relative to its size, especially in 1955 and 1972; the present figure is roughly comparable with the relative size of its GDP. Before the Second World War, Germany had a number of large firms roughly commensurate with its size; since then it has been underrepresented. In the case of Japan, prior to the Second World War, it had a number of big firms roughly equivalent to its share of GDP; since that time, it has been significantly underrepresented. France was roughly proportionately represented up to the 1970s, but since then has come to be significantly overrepresented.

The size of national economies therefore cannot fully explain some of the relative positions of countries or changes over time. Other explanations must be sought, including conjectural ones. In the case of Japan, its fall from eight to three between 1935 and 1955 reflects the breakup of the *zaibatsu* companies and the effects of the postwar loss of foreign assets. In a parallel but smaller decrease, Germany moved from twenty-one to sixteen over the same period because of similar circumstances. From then onward, German numbers stagnate at fourteen. Japanese numbers grow from three to nine and to eleven by 2002, reflecting the postwar growth of the Japanese economy. However, as stated, Japan does not have the number of large global firms commensurate with the size of its national economy. This may in large part reflect the failure of Japanese financial and retailing firms to establish themselves as multinational giants.

One striking phenomenon to explain is the change in the fortunes of UK and French firms. The United Kingdom started the twentieth century with twice as many giants as France (22 as compared with 10), reflecting the earlier development and more international orientation of British companies and the slow growth in the big firm sector in France (Levy-Leboyer, 1980; Kogut, 1997; Fridenson, 1997; Smith 2006). The gap narrows in the interwar years (15 compared with 11) and widens again by 1955 (25 compared with 6). The size of the latter gap is striking. Thereafter, between 1972 and 2002, the two countries roughly change place: The United Kingdom falls from 22 to 9, and France rises from 13 to 19. In the case of the United Kingdom, this in part reflects the disappearance of the vehicle industry and electrical firms. However, it leaves Britain with about as many giant firms as the size of its economy warrants. Part of the explanation for the UK decline and the French increase may be the role of the state and national champions. As Hancké (2002) shows, through the 1980s, the French state helped preserve employment in a number of large firms, especially in vehicles, electricals, and related industries. By contrast, from the late 1970s onward, the British state eschewed such policies. However, this state-based explanation does not account so well for the entry of such French firms as Sodexho, Veolia, Bouygues, and major French retailers. Any further explanation would require a detailed analysis of the histories of these firms.

Finally, we turn to the main time periods of change. The period 1907–35 saw significant change in size, composition, and exits but less change in country rankings. This was the period of the rise of the new global corporate economy of the twentieth century, based on new manufacturing industries. The next two time periods, 1935–55 and 1955–72, saw more change in size and country of origin, but medium change in exits and less change in composition. The final time period saw big change on all measures – size, composition, exits, and country of origin. This period marks the remaking of the global corporate economy, with the decline of manufacturing and state enterprises and the rise of new retailing and service firms. The explanation for the two peak periods of change at the beginning and end of the twentieth century would seem to be twofold: the advent of new technologies, in particular general-purpose technologies and, especially for the latter period, relatively high levels of market competition as reflected in the greater openness of national economies. The greater stability in the mid-twentieth century likewise reflects the consolidation of technological innovation and lower product market competition, constrained by tariffs and cartel-type arrangements in some sectors and countries.

In summary, different sets of explanations seem better to account for different aspects of the changing pattern of large firms in our population. Size seems to be largely driven by technology and market interactions. Within this explanation, firm strategy and structure are important where policies of integration, diversification, multinationalization, and acquisitions have played an important role. The state influences size and survival mainly at the top end of the distribution. Composition is also largely driven by technology and market interactions. The roles of the state and the firm are of lesser importance in explaining compositional change. Technology and market interactions also have a significant effect on survival. Here, however, the state has played a role, albeit a declining one. Also, in terms of which specific firms in specific industries survive, company strategy and structure are clearly important factors but are difficult to determine. Country of origin is not much driven by technology, but market size plays a role. Once again, the state offers some explanation of survival, death, and entry by companies from different countries. Again, it is more difficult to determine the role played by corporate strategy and structure. The timing of change is best explained by waves of creative destruction as technologies and markets interact. The state plays a lesser role in the timing of change, except with the case of nationalizations midcentury and, to a lesser extent, privatizations at the end of the century. Corporate strategy and structure, especially mergers and acquisitions, may be important in explaining timing, but again it is difficult to determine the extent of this in the absence of detailed company histories.

To summarize by sets of explanations: Overall, interactions between technology and markets would seem to have the most effect on the population of firms. Next, corporate strategy and structure have a significant effect in terms of strategies of integration, diversification, multinationalization, and mergers and acquisitions. However, corporate strategy and structure remain something of a residual. Overall, state intervention and support have the least effect, and this declines over the century, although recent privatizations and possibly the French story are exceptions.

CONCLUSIONS

This chapter charted major changes in the population of the top 100 firms by employment, drawn from the five major industrial economies of the twentieth century. The size of these firms grew progressively over time, although with a deceleration in the final quarter of the twentieth century. This deceleration is also reflected in their smaller proportion of total employment in the countries concerned. Although the top organizations (often, state owned) have always been significantly larger than the rest, over time the firms have become more similar in size. Compositional changes show the following: the long-term decline of railways, mining, and metals; the rise and then decline of manufacturing industries, with the exception of vehicles, which rises throughout; and, in the final period, the rise of retailing and services of various kinds. Entry and exit increase progressively over time from the mid-1930s, and, overall, death is more common than survival. In every year, reflecting the size of its economy, the United States tops the list, with between 40 and 50 giant enterprises. The United Kingdom comes second or third in four time periods, but then falls dramatically. Japan and, to a greater degree, France gained the most in terms of catch-up over the long term. Finally, in terms of periods of change, the beginning and especially the end of the twentieth century witnessed the highest rate of change on most of the measures. The former period reflects the move from the industries and firms of the first industrial revolution to the second; the latter sees the move from the second to the third industrial revolution.

Various explanations are offered for these trends. It has been argued that size is mainly driven by a combination of technology and markets and, within that construct, by corporate strategy and structure, especially in terms of integration, diversification, multinationalization, and mergers and acquisitions. These factors also drive the timing of change and periods of greater turbulence in the population. Changes in composition are largely the result of technological and market developments, although mergers and acquisitions and nationalizations and privatizations play a part. The country of origin rankings broadly reflect the size of national economies and the catching up of Japan and France in the post–Second World War period. In the latter country in particular, national championship may have played some part in its recent increasing contribution. Entry and exit are largely phenomena of compositional and market change and mergers. Survival of particular private-sector firms is the most difficult to explain and remains as something of a residual factor. This chapter suggests similarities and differences with earlier findings with the caveat that earlier work has differed in terms of measurement criteria, time periods, and number of countries covered. We cannot consider these in detail in this chapter, but present a concluding overview.

In terms of size by employment, the chapter confirms earlier work by Fiedler (1999) on Germany, White (2001) on the United States, and Wardley (2005) and White (2003) on firms from a larger number of countries. These studies suggested a long-term increase in the size of firms by employment, but with a deceleration and fall relative to total employment in the final time period. Overall, big firms are getting bigger, but not in their contribution to total employment. The chapter might also lend some support to the Langlois (2003) "vanishing hand" argument in that the deceleration of growth in the final time period might indicate some vertical disintegration, divestiture, and outsourcing. However, we stress that in our population, size continues to increase. Clearly, no limits to size have been reached, at least in retail and services.

Looking at composition, the chapter has similarities with recent research that has gone beyond the Chandlerian emphasis on industrial firms in manufacturing and mining. Thus, it confirms work that stresses the early importance of large firms outside the industrial sector, the importance of state corporations, the rise and decline in the number of second industrial revolution manufacturing firms, and the later rise of retailing and services (Jeremy, 1991; Cassis, 1997; Fiedler, 1999; Wardley, 2005). The chapter also questions the appropriateness of the

Marshallian analogy, based on free competition between private-sector industrial firms, as a basis for comprehending the population of large twentieth-century employers.

In terms of periods of change, this chapter does not confirm Fiedler's suggestion of declining turbulence over time and greater stability in his population of German firms by employment. Nor does the chapter confirm the idea of Hannah (1998, 1999), who suggests roughly similar change over each of his time periods for large firms by capitalization. By contrast, our work shows that at the beginning and especially at the end of the twentieth century there was greater turbulence in the population than during other periods. This is more in line with the findings of Louca and Mendonca (2002), although their population is U.S. manufacturing firms by assets.

In the case of survival, Chandler posited first-mover advantage and continuity. Of course, he did not use employment as the basis of his analysis. Nevertheless, our findings question his emphasis on continuity. More specifically, they contradict Fiedler, who showed a rising survival over time for his population of large German firms by employment. By contrast, our work suggests survival decreased over time. Overall, death was much more common than survival, as suggested by Hannah (1998, 1999).

Survival also relates to country of origin. In recent years, a number of authors have contested comparative conclusions drawn by Chandler (1990). Thus, for the early period, Wardley (1999, 2005) suggested that top British firms were larger and more diverse than their U.S. and German counterparts. To understand this, Cassis (1997) and Hannah (1998, 1999) have suggested that, using capitalization over their time periods, Britain contributed a larger number of firms than its size would warrant and that British firms had higher survival rates than firms in other countries. Our data support this for all years up to the final period, when the number of British firms declined significantly. Our data also clearly show the rise in the number of French firms in a way that has been little remarked until now. White (2003), using employment, also suggested that in recent years the UK number has fallen and the U.S. and French numbers have risen. However, he also suggests that the German and Japanese numbers are falling.

Finally, by way of further research, there is room to improve the basic dataset and to include new firms. This includes improvement in the Japanese data, especially the data on group companies. Databases of the top 100 in the United Kingdom, Germany, and Japan already exist for these years. The completion of U.S. and French domestic lists will allow us to perform more detailed analyses of 500 firms. In addition, it is possible to construct a database that includes big firms from outside our five countries. Of course, it would be extremely useful (albeit also a major challenge) to complete the major task of bringing together the existing employment, asset, turnover, and capitalization data so as to better ascertain the links among the various aspects of the large business enterprise. Finally, more fine-tuned work on subperiods and, in particular, on the company histories of survivors, would provide more insight into the determinants of growth and survival.

APPENDIX: DATA SOURCES

United States

Pre–Second World War period: Wardley (1999), and our own unpublished research; 1955, 1972, and 2002: *Fortune 500* and our own research.

United Kingdom

1907, 1935, and 1955: Shaw (1983), Johnman (1986), Jeremy (1991); 1972 and 2002: *The Times 1000, Europe's 5000 Largest Companies*, Oslo 1975, and our research. We are kindly indebted to Les Hannah, Alison Sharp, and Peter Wardley for advice and data.

Germany

1907, 1938, and 1973: Fiedler (1999); 1955: our own unpublished research; 2002: *Fortune 500* and our own research.

France

For all years, Cassis (1997) and our own unpublished research.

Japan

We owe a considerable debt to Professor Takashi Abe, Osaka University, for making available his Japanese dataset and for explaining aspects of large firms in Japan. We have subsequently added to and reinterpreted his data, in particular by adding together the figures for *zaibatsu* companies for 1907 and the figures for military and naval arsenals for 1935. We are entirely responsible for these additions and reinterpretations.

In the case of twenty-four observations, estimates have been made, usually on the basis of interpolation between years. Requests for the datasets used to generate the results presented in this chapter should be made directly to the authors.

REFERENCES

Bairoch, P. (1968). *The working population and its structure*. Brussels: Université Libre.

Cassis, Y. (1997). *Big business: The European experience in the twentieth century*. Oxford, UK: Oxford University Press.

Chandler, A. D. (1962). *Strategy and structure: Chapters in the history of the American industrial enterprise*. Cambridge, MA: MIT Press.

Chandler, A. D. (1977). The *visible hand: The managerial revolution in American business*. Cambridge, MA: Harvard University Press.

Chandler, A. D. (1990). *Scale and scope: The dynamics of industrial capitalism*. Cambridge, MA: Harvard University Press.

David, P. A., & Wright, G. (2005). General purpose technologies and productivity stages: Historical reflection on the future of the ICT revolution (Mimeo). Oxford, UK: Oxford University.

Fiedler, M. (1999). Die 100 größten Unternehmen in Deutschland - nach der Zahl ihrer Beschäftigten - 1907, 1938, 1973 und 1995. *Zeitschrift für Unternehmensgeschichte, 44*, 32–66, 235–42.

Freeman, C., & Soete, L. (1997). *The economics of industrial innovation* (3rd ed.). London: Cassel.

Fridenson, P. (1997). The relatively slow development of big business in 20th century France. In A. Chandler, F. Amatori, & T. Hikino (Eds.), *Big business and the wealth of nations* (pp. 207–45). Cambridge: Cambridge University Press.

Fruin, M. (1992). *The Japanese enterprise system: Competitive strategies and cooperative structures*. Oxford, UK: Oxford University Press.

Hancké, B. (2002). *Large firms and institutional change: Industrial renewal and economic restructuring in France*. Oxford, UK: Oxford University Press.

Hannah, L. (1998). Survival and size mobility among the world's largest 100 industrial companies, 1912-95. *American Economic Review, 88*, 62–5.

Hannah, L. (1999). Marshall's "trees" and the global "forest": Were "giant redwoods" different? In N. Lamoreaux, D. Raff, and P. Temin (Eds.), *Learning by doing in markets, firms and countries* (pp. 253–86). Chicago: Chicago University Press.

Helpman, E. (Ed.). (1998). *General purpose technologies and economic growth*. Cambridge, MA: MIT Press.

International Labor Organisation (2002). Labor statistics data series. Available at http://laborsta.ilo.org.

Jeremy, D. J. (1991). The hundred largest employers in the United Kingdom, in manufacturing and non-manufacturing industries, in 1907, 1935 and 1955. *Business History, 33*, 93-111.

Jeremy, D. J., & Farnie, D. A. (2001). The ranking of firms, the counting of employees, and the classification of data: A cautionary note. *Business History, 43*, 105-18.

Johnman, L. (1986). The large manufacturing companies of 1935. *Business History, 28*, 226-37.

Jones, G. (2005). *Multinationals and global capitalism: From the nineteenth to the twenty-first century.* Oxford, UK: Oxford University Press.

Kogut, B. (1997). Evolution of the large firm in France in comparative perspective (manuscript). Wharton Business School and Insead published in Entreprises et Histoire, 1998, 19: 113-51.

Langlois, R. N. (2003). The vanishing hand: The changing dynamics of industrial capitalism. *Industrial and Corporate Change, 12*, 351-85.

Lévy-Leboyer, M. (1983). The large corporation in modern France. In A. D. Chandler & H. Daems (Eds.), *Managerial hierarchies: Comparative perspectives on the rise of the modern industrial enterprise* (pp. 117-60). Cambridge, MA: Harvard University Press.

Louca, F., & Mendonca, S. (2002). Steady change: The 200 largest US manufacturing firms throughout the twentieth century. *Industrial and Corporate Change, 11*, 817-45.

Marshall, A. (1920). *Principles of economics* (variorum ed.). London: Macmillan.

Organisation for Economic Cooperation and Development. (1995a). Historical statistics, 1960-93. Paris: Author.

Organisation for Economic Cooperation and Development. (1995b). *Labor force statistics.* Paris: Author.

Schmitz, C. (1995). The world´s largest industrial companies of 1912. *Business History, 37*, 85-96.

Schumpeter, J. A. (1939). *Business cycles: A theoretical, historical, and statistical analysis of the capitalist process.* New York: McGraw-Hill.

Schumpeter, J. A. (1942). *Capitalism, socialism, and democracy.* New York: Harper & Row.

Shaw, C. (1983). The largest manufacturing employers of 1907. *Business History, 25*, 42-59.

Smith, A. (1904). *An enquiry into the nature and causes of the wealth of nations.* London: Methuen. (Original work published 1776)

Smith, M. A. (2006). *The emergence of modern business enterprise in France.* Cambridge, MA: Harvard University Press.

Wardley, P. (1991). The anatomy of big business: Aspects of corporate development in the twentieth century. *Business History, 33*, 268-96.

Wardley, P. (1999). The emergence of big business: The largest corporate employers of labor in the United Kingdom, Germany and the United States c. 1907. *Business History, 41*, 88-116.

Wardley, P. (2001). On the ranking of firms: A response to Jeremy and Farnie. *Business History*, 43, 119-34.

Wardley, P. (2005). From industry to services; Or from services to industry, and back again? In A. Carreras (Ed.), *From industry to services*. Barcelona, Spain: EBHA and UPF.

White, L. J. (2002). Trends in aggregate concentration in the US. *Journal of Economic Perspectives*, 16, 4, 137-60.

White, L. J. (2003). *Aggregate concentration in the global economy: Issues and evidence* (Mimeo). Washington, DC: World Bank. New York University, Center for Law and Business Research.

Yates, J. (1989). *Control through communication: The rise of system in American management*. Baltimore, MD: Johns Hopkins University Press.

3

The Long-Term Evolution of the Knowledge Boundaries of Firms

Supply and Demand Perspectives

PAMELA ADAMS, STEFANO BRUSONI, AND
FRANCO MALERBA

INTRODUCTION

The central question posed in this chapter is whether there has been a long-term change in the knowledge boundaries of firms. To answer this question, we chose to analyze the whole set of activities in which firms and industries are engaged: innovation, production, and commercialization. Taking a supply and demand perspective, we focused on the boundaries of knowledge in terms of the content and the sources of knowledge for innovation and production, on the division of innovative and productive labor among actors on both sides, and on the governance of knowledge for innovation and production.

In this chapter, we take a broad and long-term perspective. We are convinced that when discussing the knowledge boundaries of firms it is necessary to associate a longer-term historical, dynamic, and system view with existing detailed and short-term analyses in order to shed light on broad trends, major shifts, and key links and interdependencies that unfold over time.

In the long run, the boundaries of innovation, production, and commercialization in terms of the content and the sources of relevant knowledge have greatly expanded, often to reach beyond the legal boundaries of firms or the conventional definition of industries. The division between production and innovative labor has also increased. At the same time, the role of customers as a source of useful knowledge has changed significantly. Yet, as many have argued, the governance of the knowledge that is relevant for innovation has remained in the hands of a relatively small number of firms within industries or in a few areas within firms. These actors may indeed decide how, where, and whose knowledge is used. Many of these observations (e.g., Prencipe, 1997; Brusoni et al., 2001; Orsenigo et al., 2001; Takeishi, 2001) stem from an analysis of the supply side: the dynamics of assembling organizations and their suppliers. In this chapter, we add the evolutionary dynamics on the demand side to the discussion. The extent and the means through which firms acquire and use customer knowledge has dramatically altered traditional distinctions between "demand" and "supply." More specifically, many have argued that customers are acquiring, and ought to acquire, a much more central role in the study of how innovation happens (e.g., Sawhney and Prandelli, 2001; Witt, 2001). Yet, relying on the concept of platform, we argue that, although important changes have occurred in terms of industry and firm boundaries, they do not represent a radical change from the past. Rather, they are a gradual transformation of the industrial system involving knowledge, technology, production, and demand.

After a general discussion about knowledge and its relevance for innovation and production and about the boundaries and governance of knowledge for firms and industries (second section), we concentrate on two key aspects: the recent transformation of the boundaries and governance of knowledge for production (third section) and the increasing role of demand and users in the innovation process (fourth section). In these latter two sections, we examine how the knowledge boundaries of firms and industries have changed and what consequences, if any, these changes have had on the governance of knowledge. In the last section, we draw some conclusions and indicate areas for further research.

KNOWLEDGE AND THE BOUNDARIES OF FIRMS AND INDUSTRIES: A CONCEPTUAL FRAMEWORK

Knowledge has become the driving force of transformation in economic systems. Learning and knowledge by individuals and organizations are at the base of innovation and the dynamics of firms and industries. It is therefore quite understandable that the focus of attention of economists, management scholars, and historians in this field has concentrated on the features, properties, and evolution of knowledge as they affect organizational change and industrial competition.

Knowledge affects and redefines the boundaries of firms and industries in various ways. First, knowledge differs in terms of sources (suppliers, universities, users, and so on), domains (e.g., the specific scientific and technological fields at the base of innovative activities in a sector), and applications (in terms of uses and demand). Knowledge may be more or less cumulative (i.e., the degree to which the generation of new knowledge builds on current knowledge) and may have different degrees of accessibility (i.e., opportunities of gaining knowledge that are external to firms and may be internal or external to the sector). Knowledge may also spread more or less intentionally across individuals and organizations, as the extensive literature on knowledge spillovers and the work on the effects of the mobility of inventors, managers, and skilled labor demonstrates.

The considerations of the boundaries of knowledge that are relevant for innovation and production have challenged the conventional view of firms and industries. According to this view, firms are often modeled in stylized ways as legal entities carrying out innovation and production, with more or less full information about the technologies to be used and the costs associated with that use. Firms are active in well-defined "industries." The traditional view sees industries as composed of the firms that share a similar technology, or address a similar demand, or are linked in terms of competitive dimensions (as is the case for the standard industrial statistical classifications). Within an industry, firms engage in strategic interaction, may face transaction costs in their activities, and are characterized by agency problems in their organization. The focus on knowledge has changed the traditional views of firms and industries by placing attention on the processes of learning and capability formation in firms. These processes may involve competition or cooperation in the development of products pertaining to a sector, the focus on a certain demand or application market, and the attempt to gain access to various sources of knowledge. Firms learn and accumulate knowledge through processes that involve interaction with several actors with heterogeneous knowledge and capabilities. These actors may be internal or external to the firms themselves. In this framework, organizational learning is the idiosyncratic way firms accumulate knowledge and develop capabilities. These capabilities may be seen as sets of skills, routines and complementary assets, partly tacit and not formalized, based on procedural knowledge linked to a specific application domain and not easily transferable among firms. In other words, firms become repositories of knowledge embodied in organizational routines, which may be only partly tacit. This knowledge evolves through a process of adaptation and search (Nelson and Winter, 1982; Malerba, 1992). In terms of knowledge, capabilities may be seen as the ability to match and integrate tacit and codified knowledge and to use it for specific functions, applications, and technological and productive transformations (Nelson, 1991; Malerba and Orsenigo, 2000; Dosi et al., 2004).

Within this new view of firms and industries, the "knowledge boundaries" of a firm become related to the use and creation of knowledge for innovation and production and therefore do not necessarily correspond to the legal boundaries of the firm. In their innovative activities, firms may access scientific knowledge in various ways and forms, including research and development (R&D) collaboration, informal networks, personnel mobility, and research contracts. In this respect, the knowledge boundaries of a firm may encompass links with universities, research centers, or even other firms involved in scientific activity. The same holds for the technological knowledge of firms. Here, the boundaries may reach suppliers from whom firms may get specialized specific knowledge. This is even more so for knowledge about applications and the needs of different market segments. Here, the knowledge boundaries may tap into consumers and users – such as lead users or experimental users – who have knowledge of a specific context related to a potential application. For understanding innovation, production, and commercialization, these networks of knowledge in terms of content and sources redefine the boundaries of firms in a more meaningful way than the traditional legal boundaries.

The same type of reasoning may be used for an industry. Pervasive technologies such as information and communications technologies (ICTs) cut across sectoral boundaries and make it rather difficult to adopt the concept of industry in a way that is conducive for understanding, for example, who the innovators versus who the adopters are. Along these lines, when dealing with issues such as the sources of knowledge, innovative ideas, and production feedbacks, the notion of "sectoral systems of innovation and production" becomes more meaningful (Malerba, 2002, 2004). A sectoral system is characterized by a knowledge base and technologies that may cut across conventional industry boundaries. Such systems are composed of heterogeneous organizations or individuals (e.g., consumers, entrepreneurs, or scientists) who may be sources of knowledge, ideas, and feedback for producers and innovators but who may not be part of "conventionally defined industries" in terms of both firms (e.g., users and suppliers) and other organizations (e.g., universities, financial institutions, government agencies, trade unions, or technical associations). These organizations are characterized by specific knowledge bases and learning processes. Thus, in a sectoral system framework, production and innovation are considered to be processes that involve systematic interactions among a wide variety of actors for the generation, use, and exchange of relevant knowledge. Interactions include market and nonmarket relations that are broader than the market for technological licensing and knowledge, interfirm alliances, and formal networks of firms. Often, their outcome is not adequately captured by our existing systems of measuring economic output.

According to this view, the structure of knowledge very often affects the type of actors who are present in a sector, as well as the relationships among these actors. For example, in pharmaceuticals and biotechnology, there is an isomorphism between the cognitive structures underlying the dynamics of knowledge and the structure of the network of innovators. The impact of science has created a proliferation of new and increasingly specialized hypotheses that have, in turn, generated new subdisciplines requiring new sets of search techniques, testing procedures, and skills. Over time, entrants have tended to be more specialized in terms of the scientific hypotheses that they are trying to test and in terms of the search techniques they are employing. The intrinsic characteristics of the search techniques and the patterns of learning in pharmaceutical R&D explain why the network has expanded over time to include different actors – some of whom are related to universities or research centers – that do not pertain to the pharmaceutical industry as traditionally defined. They also explain why the industry remains relatively stable in its core-periphery profile and why entrants make agreements with pharmaceutical incumbents, older new biotechnology firms (NBFs), or even university laboratories, rather than with firms of the same generation (Orsenigo et al., 2001).

In the traditional literature on sectoral systems, demand side considerations are not usually examined in depth. Yet, demand has become a very important part of the knowledge boundaries of a sectoral system. Individual consumers, user firms, and public agencies, each characterized by their own learning processes, competencies, and goals, provide relevant knowledge and feedbacks for innovation and production. In some cases, in fact, users participate intensively in the innovation process.

Their involvement may go beyond the simple transfer of information to include psychological and behavioral aspects.

A focus on knowledge boundaries, however, means that there are bounds to the expansion and use of knowledge and that these bounds are related to the specificity of the knowledge itself, as well as to the context in terms of technologies and sectors. The notion of technological paradigms and technological regimes present in the evolutionary literature (Dosi, 1982; Malerba and Orsenigo, 2000) and, from a different perspective, the notion of bounds by Sutton (1998) are useful ways to represent these limits. In this framework, the specificities of technological paradigms and regimes and the knowledge base of an industry provide powerful limits to the patterns of learning, competencies, and behavior within firms, as well as to the organization of innovative and productive activities. More in general, a given knowledge base, technological environment, or demand defines the nature of the problems firms must solve in their innovative and production activities and the types of incentives and constraints to particular types of behavior and organization. Within these constraints, however, extensive and persistent heterogeneity in the ways that firms behave and organize their innovative and productive activities is possible.

The boundaries of knowledge for firms and industries that we have discussed so far may be accompanied by a more or less extensive division of innovative and productive labor among different actors. Knowledge differs very much in terms of tacitness and codification and, consequently, also in terms of transmission and transferability (Winter, 1987; Arora et al., 2001; Foray, 2004). If knowledge is codified and modular and interfaces can be created in the production of new artifacts, a division of innovative and production labor among different firms is possible even when complex product systems are involved.

Division of innovative labor does not necessarily mean a lack of centralized governance of knowledge integration. Often, knowledge stemming from different sources and having different content has to be integrated into products and systems. This often requires interaction, coordination, information flows, absorptive capabilities, and control of technological and organizational interfaces. Although the knowledge boundaries of firms may be extensive and articulated and encompass a range of different organizations and individuals that provide sources of knowledge, ideas, and feedback, the governance of that knowledge often remains in the hands of a few groups within firms. These groups are able to control and coordinate the direction of change in innovation, production and commercialization processes. The works by Prencipe (1997), Brusoni et al. (2001), and Brusoni and Pavitt (2003) clearly underscore the key role that a few actors – the system integrators – may play in the process of generation of new products and processes. Similarly, in a sectoral system perspective, the governance of knowledge does not imply an equal and symmetric involvement of all the organizations engaged in knowledge generation, use, and exchange. Usually, a much smaller number of companies govern these processes. For example, in several sectors such as ICT, pharmaceuticals and biotechnology, aerospace, and chemicals, a limited number of companies coordinate the spectrum of both production and innovation processes. In ICTs, the control of key interfaces or the setting of standards that govern how innovation and production take place is often in the hands of few large companies, which set the direction of technological change and have a major structuring effect on new product development. Similarly, in pharmaceuticals and biotechnology, some large pharmaceutical firms coordinate the innovation process of a variety of other actors such as university laboratories, new biotech companies, or medical schools for the introduction and delivery of new drugs on the market. In the aircraft industry, some large assemblers control the division of labor and coordinate the activity of a large number of component suppliers, engine producers, and software deliverers. Finally, in machine tools, some key players develop new machines, integrating their system competencies with the specific knowledge and inputs that come from users and new advanced component producers.

In the following sections, this discussion on the nature, characteristics, and dimensions of knowledge and of its relevance for the boundaries of firms and industries will be placed in a long-term perspective. In the third section we discuss the supply-side dynamics that have pushed and pulled the knowledge boundaries of firms and industries, and in the fourth section we turn to the demand side. As mentioned in the introduction, our discussion is broad. It is our intention to highlight major trends and long-term changes rather than analyze in depth any specific period or dimension.

KNOWLEDGE BOUNDARIES AND PRODUCTION BOUNDARIES: THE SUPPLY SIDE

The interplay among knowledge sources, the division of labor, and the integration of knowledge provide useful lenses through which to observe the long-term evolution of industrialized economies. As Brusoni and Pavitt (2003) attempt to demonstrate, the recent emphasis on vertical disintegration and network dynamics is but the last stage of a long process of reciprocal adaptation between the dynamics of firms' legal boundaries, the activities firms carry out to design and deliver products and services, and the capabilities they need to perform them.

Table 3.1 ambitiously summarizes what we think has been happening in the past 200 years. This section focuses on the interplay between productive knowledge and production (i.e., the "supply side" of innovation, for our present purposes). The next section looks at parallel developments on the demand side. Briefly put, Table 3.1 shows two related trends. First, certain major advances in technology have been key factors of change in organizational specialization, sometimes leading to disintegration and sometimes leading to integration. Second, the degree of disintegration in the production of artifacts has always been greater or equal than that in the production of technological knowledge.

As many times highlighted by Keith Pavitt, Adam Smith's pin factory is mainly a story about innovation in production processes. The conditions for the mechanization of repetitive manual operations emerged from the specialization of tasks within the factory. As anticipated by Smith, the design and building of these machines would become " . . . the business of a peculiar trade." The supply of product components and machine parts became specialized businesses as they became standardized and interchangeable. Looking at the U.S. and British economies in the second half of the nineteenth century, Lamoreaux and Sokoloff (1999) and, earlier, Saul (1967, 1970) discussed, respectively, the rise of patent agents, that is, intermediaries in the trade of mechanical inventions, and the rise of consultant engineers, that is, professionals engaged in design activities on a fee-based system with limited, or no, involvement in the actual implementation of their designs. Saul (1970) discusses at length which factors led to the emergence of such knowledge professionals, highlighting how the emergence of a large demand for homogeneous consumer goods played a pivotal role in explaining first the quick catch-up of the U.S. economy and subsequently the rapid diffusion of the U.S. way of designing and manufacturing of engineering goods toward the UK.

At the same time, as documented by Chandler (1977, 1990), Mowery and Rosenberg (1991), Freeman and Louca (2001), and scholars from the middle of the nineteenth century, we observe a rapid process of reintegration of productive and innovative labor. On the one side, the emergence of modern management techniques, as well as reduced transport costs and the rise of new, reliable, and flexible power sources (e.g., first coal and then, crucially, electricity and oil) made it possible to exploit economies of scale and scope to an extent unthinkable before. In the late nineteenth century and even more rapidly after the beginning of the twentieth, increasing size led to increasing functional specialization within – not between – firms, and the need for coordinated planning among material purchase, production, and marketing. Langlois (2003) related the rise of the Chandlerian visible hand of management to the increasing urgency of buffering activities made necessary by increasingly complex production technologies. This type of organization of production and related knowledge became the dominant form in the twentieth century.

However, in the last twenty years, new forces that begin to modify this pattern have surfaced. Products are becoming increasingly complex, embodying both an increasing number of subsystems and components and a widening range of fields of specialized knowledge. This increasing product (or system) complexity is itself a consequence of increased specialization in knowledge production, which has resulted in a better understanding of cause–effect relations, as well as better and cheaper methods of experimentation. This has, in turn, reduced the costs of technological search and thereby enabled greater complexity in terms of the number of components, parts, or molecules that can be successfully embodied in a new product or service. Increasing knowledge specialization and complexity challenges traditional ways of coordinating firms' activities. Specialization in knowledge production has increased the range of fields of knowledge that contribute to the design of each product. The recent evolution of a seemingly simple product such as a tire is quite telling. Far from being the archetypal ring of rubber, tire production requires nowadays extensive knowledge of a variety of chemistry subfields to increase safety while reducing rolling resistance (thus saving on fuel). At the same time, new process technologies imported from other sectors (e.g., plastic) are increasingly used to turn the traditional batch product process of rubber-based raw materials into a continuous process. Robotics is extensively used in tire production. Electronic sensors are embedded into the tire itself to foster online control technologies. The increasing diversity found in tire firms' patent portfolios is quite revealing of this increasing breadth of their knowledge boundaries.

The growing number of specialized fields that are embodied in increasingly complex products also leads to an increasing number of specialized

Table 3.1. The Evolution of Production and Demand in Terms of Knowledge

Time Line	Changes in Technology	Implications for Firm Management	Organizational Integration/Disintegration of		Characteristics of Consumer Demand	Implications for Knowledge Interface with Demand
			Production	Knowledge		
1850s	Improvements in metal cutting and shaping	Interchangeable parts	Vertical disintegration	Vertical disintegration	Consumption focused on fulfilling basic needs; homogeneous demand	Stimulation
	Energy (coal) Materials (iron and steel)	Mass production of standard commodities	Specialization & integration of purchasing, production, marketing Vertical disintegration in capital goods	In-house development of specialized skills In-house knowledge of design, & operation of capital goods		Producers transfer knowledge to create and stimulate the growth of demand
	Organic chemistry, Physics	Synthetic products Electrical & electronic products	Integration of product design, manufacture, & marketing	Growth of in-house R&D as dominant source of innovation		

Various (e.g., metal cutting, chemistry, computing, ITC)	Technological convergence in segments of production	Partial vertical disintegration in production segments (e.g., machine tools, continuous processes & instrumentation, CAD, robots, applications software)	In-house knowledge of design, & operation of producers' goods	Consumerism focused on the accumulation of goods, moderated by group pressures	Consultation: Producers consult consumers to gain knowledge about their needs and wants; producers use this knowledge to deliver value satisfaction
Increasing product complexity (more components, subsystems, and bodies of knowledge) + ICTs	Modular product designs, Mass customization	Vertical disintegration in design & production of product components and subsystems	In-house knowledge of design, & operation of subsystems & components		
2000s ICTs	Platform competition	Vertical disintegration in production	Knowledge integration capabilities, which require In-house competence in systems design	Informed and connected consumers seek self-expression, involvement, and experience with products	Engagement: Producers involve consumers directly in all phases of product cycle; knowledge is shared between producers and consumers as well as among consumers

professions and communities whose activities need to be monitored and coordinated to be competitive. Firms designing these increasingly complex products have found it more difficult to master advances in all of the fields embodied in them. Hence, the growing importance of differentiated knowledge sources and of modular designs, in which component interfaces are standardized and interdependencies among components are decoupled. This, in principle, enables the outsourcing of the design and production of components and subsystems within the constraints of an overall product (or system) architecture. Also, much research is nowadays focused on the role played by advanced ICTs in fostering distributed learning processes (see, e.g., Zammutto et al., 2007, for a review). Similarly, many researchers are looking at the exchange of physical or digital artifacts – so-called boundary objects (e.g., D'Adderio, 2001; Cacciatori, 2008) – and how they enable collaboration and control across interacting communities of specialists who rely on different bodies of knowledge and practice and often collaborate in geographically distributed settings.

Opportunities have also emerged for further vertical disintegration between product design and manufacture, based on technological convergence (i.e., convergence based on technical change in specific production operations across firms, products, or industries) and the development of a global market for intermediate goods. The size of the market for such operations often became large enough to sustain the growth of small specialized firms focused on delivering what Stigler (1951) called "general specialties." For example, Arora and Gambardella (1994) discussed the factors driving the emergence of specialized engineering firms (SEFs), engineering and design firms that delivered design and construction services to the global chemical industry. Similar trends have been observed in the automotive industry and telecommunication industry, from whom large manufacturing customers could therefore buy machines and even entire plants that incorporated the latest improvements fed back from many users and that were therefore superior to what they could make by themselves. In contemporary terms, large manufacturing firms no longer had a distinct competitive advantage in designing and making hardware and machines.

Another factor now modifying patterns of specialization is the impact of advances in ICT, reflected in reductions in the cost and increases in capacity, by several orders of magnitude, for storing, manipulating, and transmitting information. These changes open up options for more complex systems (through digitalization), reduce the costs of experimentation (through simulation techniques), and allow greater disintegration (through lower costs of transmitting information) (Arora and Gambardella, 1994; D'Adderio, 2001; Pavitt and Steinmueller, 2001).

At first sight, these changes appear to point to a neatly specialized system in the sources of knowledge and in the production of innovations, with product and systems designers, their subcontractors for components and subsystems, and their manufacturers working together through arm's-length market relations. Many have argued in favor of the so-called modular production networks (e.g., Sturgeon, 2002) within which "distinct breaks in the value chain tend to form at points where information regarding product specifications can be highly formal," thus enabling greater division of labor and coordination through established physical and organizational interfaces. In other words, as pointed out by Sanchez and Mahoney (1996) and Radner (1992), because components' interfaces are not permitted to change within a specified period of time, a modular architecture would create an "information structure" that smoothly coordinates decentralized design teams. In this way, the information structure would also act as a "compensation mechanism" that holds the systems together without the need to exert explicit managerial authority.

This line of analysis, which emphasizes a clear overlap between production and knowledge boundaries, has been extensively criticized, starting with the seminal paper by Prencipe (1997), who observed a distinctively different pattern of division of labor when comparing outsourcing at the manufacturing level versus outsourcing at the design level. More recently, Ernst (2005) used the example of chip design to argue that the competitive dynamics and cognitive complexity set limits to the extent of organizational and technological modularization. Ernst actually argues that the increasing reliance on interfirm networks is creating the need for more, not less, coordination through corporate management. As argued elsewhere, it is one thing to coordinate the development and production of artifacts and another thing altogether to coordinate the evolution of the underlying knowledge bases (Brusoni and Prencipe, 2001). Detailed sectoral studies confirm that (some) firms within networks of vertically related companies maintain science and technology (S&T) capabilities over a set of fields wider than that justified by their in-house activities (Davies, 1997; Prencipe, 1997; Chesbrough and Kusunoki, 2000; Orsenigo et al., 2001; Takeishi, 2001; Brusoni, 2005; Ernst, 2005).

The gap between firms' production and knowledge boundaries has led to the emergence of so-called loosely coupled networks (Brusoni et al., 2001). Such networks are generated by the increasing reliance of manufacturing firms on external suppliers. This is consistent with what is predicted by the advocates of modularity as a technological and organizational strategy. However, a distinctive feature of loose coupling is the presence of systems integrators: firms that lead and coordinate the variety of the sources of knowledge and the work of suppliers involved in the network from both a technological and an organizational viewpoint.

Loosely coupled organizations are led by "systems integrators" (Prencipe, 1997; Prencipe et al., 2003). Systems integrators are more than the assemblers that operate within core networks. Systems integration includes the technological and organizational capabilities to integrate changes and improvements in internally and externally designed and produced inputs within existing product architecture. Recent research on "platforms" is providing new insights into the role played by systems integrating firms, and into the reasons why, despite ICTs and modularity, the governance of knowledge still appears to rely on the presence of focal organizations. Platforms are defined as broad architectures of product families within which customers can tailor products to their specific needs, embodying both physical technologies and service technologies. Gawer (2009) argues that the emergence of platforms is changing the patterns of competition across firms in a variety of sectors. To put it simply, the idea is that firms do not compete over specific products anymore. Rather, they compete on their differential abilities to develop a broad range of options open to their customers. Such options are embodied in physical and software objects open to customers to fill and, so to speak, complete them on the basis of their specific needs. Examples of such platforms include traditional industries such as the automotive industry, in which firms compete now by defining broad architectures that cut across traditional product families. Semiconductors' system-on-chips architectures have enabled some producers to introduce very versatile architectures that they have been to redeploy across different market niches. Software's open source development models have enabled distributed communities of programmers to develop software that has challenged the leadership position of giants such as Microsoft.

The interplay of modularity and ICTs explains the openness of platforms to their customers. ICTs may now play a much more proactive role in design solutions that fit the customers' needs. Yet, at the same time, their degrees of freedom are limited by what the platforms enable them to do. Customers of semiconductors can codesign the products they need through online interfaces. Yet, which products are open to such codesign projects and the limits within which such products can actually be customized are the key strategic decisions left to "platform leaders" (Gawer and Cusumano, 2002).

To conclude this section and introduce the next one, we argued that we are observing the last stage of a process of increasing disconnectedness among the dynamics of production (what firms do), the dynamics of the types and sources of knowledge (what kinds of knowledge are needed for innovation), and the dynamics of the governance of that knowledge (what firms know and govern). Knowledge integration activities have become the core competence of the large, postindustrialist firms, and such competencies appear to require less and less direct involvement in actual manufacturing and in all sources of knowledge generation. Yet, the ability to govern and influence the evolution of a complex set of interrelated bodies of specialized knowledge is crucial to being able to govern and lead the evolution of product platforms. This section largely focused on the supply-side dynamics that has led, through a long process of specialization and integration, to the emergence of specific forms of governance of knowledge (i.e., loosely coupled networks) and of markets (i.e., platforms) needed to develop complex products within wide and distributed networks of specialized suppliers. We emphasized the growing presence of a variety of knowledge sources on the production side, an extensive division of labor in production together with the centralization of the monitoring, and the coordination of a variety of scientific and technological disciplines. Yet, as the next section argues, firms will have also to deal with customers in their design and development processes.

THE KNOWLEDGE BOUNDARIES OF FIRMS: THE DEMAND SIDE

This analysis of the evolution of knowledge boundaries on the demand side focuses on final end users or consumers rather than on intermediate or industrial users who buy goods in order to make other products. This focus was chosen because the evolution of the knowledge boundaries between industrial users and their suppliers has already been covered in the previous section. Our objective here is to expand this analysis to include the demand side as defined by individual users or consumers and their interactions with developments on the supply side. Over the past two centuries, we contend that there has been a progressive redefinition of the knowledge boundaries between firms and consumers from an identifiable separation focused on sales transactions to an increasingly open interaction in all phases of the product cycle. In this section, we attempt to map this evolution and the implications of such developments for the role of demand in sectoral systems.

We divided the evolution of knowledge boundaries between producers and consumers over the past 200 years in the economies of Europe and the United States into three broad periods that we call demand stimulation, demand consultation, and demand engagement. These periods have been characterized by different trends in consumer behavior as well as by different patterns of interaction between firms and consumers.

The first period dates roughly from the beginning of the first industrial revolution up to the end of the First World War. It has been described as an era of homogeneous demand. As populations migrated from rural to urban areas, there was a subsequent transition from traditional societies with norms based on self-sufficiency and modest consumption levels to the development of new mass markets with few guiding precedents (Fraser, 1981; Hounshell, 1984; Fullerton, 1988). Consumers had only limited experience with the many new products that were introduced into the market, and technical knowledge was not widespread (Benson, 1994). As a result, consumers were dependent on producers not only for the provision of their basic necessities but also for new solutions and advice about new products.

Producers, on the other hand, were benefiting from significant breakthroughs in knowledge that they were able to apply to overcome constraints in supply. Large-scale production, in fact, came increasingly to be seen as the key to success. Yet, authors such as Shaw (1916), Gilboy (1932), and McKendrick et al. (1982) argue that, in their quest for production efficiency, producers could not completely ignore the demand side. Mass production required the creation of mass demand. Marketing therefore had to work alongside production to educate consumers about new products, help develop consumer tastes and preferences, and generate sales (Cochran, 1977). Large producers such as Unilever (Britain), Singer (United States), and Henkel (Germany), for example, developed strong marketing programs to generate awareness and desire for their products and to make them readily available to buyers (Fullerton, 1988). In this process, producers were aided by the advent of the advertising industry (Fox, 1984; Fullerton and Nevett, 1986) as well as the development of the distribution trade (Converse, 1930). It was during this period, in fact, that retailing was transformed from roaming, outdoor markets to fixed shops where loyal clients could get trusted advice about new products (Brewer and Porter, 1993; Blondé, 2005).

Knowledge flows during this period were mostly unidirectional from producers to consumers and were aimed at educating the market in order to stimulate demand for new products. Only rarely, in fact, did producers begin to seek out the ideas and opinions of consumers in the development of new products. In some high-end categories such as textiles, fashion, and tableware, for example, companies such as Wedgewood and Boulton studied the tastes of their elite clients and then turned them into more inexpensive product lines for the wider mass market (McKendrick et al., 1982). Notwithstanding these limited attempts to learn from the market, however, the locus of knowledge for product innovation and manufacturing during this first period of industrialization was clearly located within producer firms. Consumer demand played a relatively passive role in the product development process in most sectoral systems across the economy.

During the second period, which runs roughly from the 1940s to the 1970s, the role of consumers changed significantly. This evolution occurred for a number of reasons. First, experience with consumer products became more widely dispersed throughout the general population. Industrialization produced affluence and a burgeoning middle class with more discretionary income to spend and more leisure time to fill (Fox and Lears, 1983). In addition, greater consumption was touted in these countries, especially in the United States, as a way to help their economies transition out of wartime conditions (Galbraith, 1958; Katona, 1964; Cohen, 2003). As a result, the sheer number of consumers with first-hand experience with new products increased dramatically during this period. At the same time, the character of consumer demand became more heterogeneous. New lifestyles emerged, and new participants, including women and teenagers, entered the market arena with highly differentiated needs in categories such as food, white goods, beauty products, clothing, and entertainment (Benson, 1994; Baudrillard, 1998). Finally, as Bowlby (1997) notes, the growth of both supermarkets and department stores changed the shopping experience, leaving shoppers with little assistance from store personnel to navigate through a vast assortment of products. Consumers became increasingly active and empowered actors who were responsible for their own choices.

As knowledge became more dispersed and segmented and as consumer decision processes became more complex and mediated through a vast distribution system, producers became farther distanced from their markets. As a result, they began to seek ways to reconnect with buyers and to tap into often unfamiliar and diverse knowledge bases to uncover new trends emerging in markets. A new approach to market research was developed with "consumer engineers" who were able to use sophisticated tools to research consumer needs (Levitt, 1960; Heskett, 1980). This was followed by the development of mass survey techniques and consumer behavior research from fields such as psychology, sociology, and anthropology. The objective of this research was to break through the complexity of behavior patterns in order to segment the market into manageable groups and allocate resources efficiently (Martineau, 1958). Companies such as Procter & Gamble led the way in thinking that "sound marketing objectives depend on knowledge of how segments which produce the most customers for a company's brand differ in requirements and susceptibilities from the segments which produce the largest number of customers for competitive brands" (Yankelovich, 1964, p. 2).

Throughout these processes, companies reached out to learn from consumers and, in doing so, redefined the knowledge boundaries between producers and consumers. Producers recognized the need to consult the wider mass of consumers to find untapped needs and preferences in saturated markets. Yet, the locus of innovation and responsibility for the design of solutions in terms of product and process elements remained firmly in hands of the producers. The knowledge gained from the market was brought back into the confines of the firm where solutions were designed and produced. The process of value creation, epitomized by the model of the value chain proposed by Michael Porter (1980), remained clearly within the confines of the firm.

In more recent decades, this company-centric view of product development is increasingly being replaced by new models based on the direct engagement of consumers in the innovation process. This evolution reflects a recognition that consumers have accumulated in-depth knowledge and experience with a wide variety of product categories over the past decades (Saviotti, 1996; Bianchi, 1998; Witt, 2001) and that this stock of knowledge and experience has important consequences for consumption (Stigler and Becker, 1977). Witt (2001), for example, postulates that demand for more differentiated products is a consequence of how consumers learn and specialize in certain consumption activities. Consumers not only learn about products, but they learn how to satisfy their wants. Consumers therefore have developed both specialized contextual knowledge as well as highly evolved sets of wants.

But the move to engage consumers more directly in product development processes also mirrors broader changes in the nature of consumer behavior (Gronow and Warde, 2001). Over the past thirty years, purchasing patterns have moved away from Veblen's conspicuous consumption toward a more individualistic approach. According to marketing scholars, the new consumers tend more and more to purchase goods to impress themselves rather than the community. Satisfaction is achieved by being different rather than by conforming to group norms. As a result, the influence of reference groups on purchase decisions has given way to tendencies to "do your own thing." In Maslow's hierarchy of consumer needs, it is the need for "self-actualization" that motivates these consumers.

Such trends in consumer behavior have also been noted by research within the postmodernist school (Brown, 1995; Firat et al., 1995). According to these authors, postmodernity represents a transition phase in the history of western societies. It is an era in which a plurality of styles and trends have come to coexist without the constraints of a dominant or defining ideology or utopia (Cova and Badot, 1995). The postmodern consumer "takes elements of market offerings and crafts a customized consumption experience out of them . . . (They) lack commitment to grand projects and universal images and seek different and local experiences. They want to become part of processes and experience immersion in thematic settings rather than merely encounter finished products and images. The essence of postmodern experience is participation; without participation, the consumer is merely entertained and does not experience" (Cova, 1996, p. 17).

These changes in behavior have gone hand in hand with the development of a new ethos and new capabilities based on connectivity. Consumers who have grown up with the Internet are natives to relationships based on collaboration, participation, dispersion, and distributed knowledge (Lankshear and Knobel, 2006). Technology has also enabled them to access nodes of information that were previously inaccessible and has enhanced consumer-to-consumer horizontal communication (Iacobucci, 1998). The growth of both online connectivity and social web services has facilitated the development of networks and communities within which consumers can exchange information with large numbers of individuals who share specialized interests. The popularity of such services is demonstrated by the rapid growth of social networks such as MySpace or Facebook and media sites such as YouTube and Flickr (Universal McCann, 2008). In sum, consumers are now more informed, capable, connected, and empowered (Prahalad and Ramaswamy, 2004).

From the supply side, the difficulties of managing product development in a "consultation" mode have also become more apparent. Hamel and Prahalad (1994), for example, note that consumers are notoriously lacking in foresight and are unable to imagine products that do not yet exist. Other studies have shown that as the knowledge base of consumers grows and becomes more specialized and "sticky" through the use of products in specific contexts, gathering, transferring, and using this knowledge also becomes more costly (Von Hippel, 1994). Finally, by listening to the needs of their current customers and focusing on standards that satisfy the average consumer, companies often ignore outliers who offer better insight for product innovation (Cristensen and Bower, 1996).

As a result, the old division of labor in which producers make and sell and consumers buy and use is being dismantled. Consumers, who were once thought of as passive targets, are becoming active participants in the product development process. Problem solving is moving from a product-driven focus on the articulated needs of consumers to learning environments in which consumers discover their needs through interactive processes focused on innovation. Companies are developing new solutions to engage consumers in the design, testing, and improvement of products.

These solutions have taken many forms. A first and limited version lies in the extension of existing models of mass customization (Pine, 1993; Piller, 2003). Producers attempt to meet both consumers' needs for personalized solutions and their requirements for efficiency and scale economies: in other words, perfect relevance at minimum cost. Customers are integrated into the value creation process by defining or modifying their individualized solutions from a list of options and predefined components, parts, or features (Wind and Rangaswamy, 2001). This may be done offline or online: IKEA offers standard products and components in their stores that customers may mix and match according to individual tastes, whereas Dell (computers), NikeID (sportswear), and Expedia and Orbitz (travel websites), for example, all provide single customers with a user-friendly web interface to personalize their selection from a host of standardized product parts, services, and processes. In other cases (Von Hippel, 2001, 2005), companies provide platforms or toolkits that allow selected customers to access company information and develop solutions through experimentation and iterative processes. These platforms not only provide active consumers with customized solutions, they also increase customer satisfaction through experience with the codesign process (Prahalad and Ramaswamy, 2004;

Novak et al., 2000). Companies may also use platforms to solicit ideas and solutions directly from consumers. Threadless.com, for example, collects the t-shirt proposals of hobby designers on its website. The designs are then rated by the community and Threadless.com decides which of the top-rated designs will pass into production and sale.

But platforms and toolkits are not only used for interaction between consumers and producers. They may also get consumers and users to interact directly with each other. There is a small but growing body of research, in fact, that explores how consumer communities may contribute to the process of innovation both from within and from outside of firms (Sawhney and Prandelli, 2001; Wind and Rangaswamy, 2001; Franke and Shah, 2003; Jeppesen and Molin, 2003; Piller, 2003; Füller et al., 2006). The models proposed differ somewhat in terms of the openness of the system (any member of the community may get involved (Adidas and Lego) or only lead users (video games) and of the nature of user involvement focused on the use, improvement or customization of existing products (e.g., Wii) or on the development and design phases of new products) (Piller et al., 2005; Aoyama and Izushi, 2006). But in all of these models, platforms are used to form communities of practice in which interactive learning takes place consumer-to-consumer and leads to innovation.

Consumer engagement in innovative processes therefore has become increasingly prevalent over the past decades in many sectors. It is not relevant in all sectors, however (Pavitt, 1984). We are still far, in fact, from the world of "creative consumers" envisioned by Toffler in 1980. For many goods, consumers do not recognize the advantage of investing resources in development and are satisfied enough with the mass-produced alternatives that provide basic value for money. In other cases, consumers will decide that the cost of using the platforms and participating in the processes (in terms of time, effort, and knowledge) outweighs the advantages of the experience in designing their own products.

In conclusion, the boundaries of knowledge between firms and demand have changed over the past two centuries in several ways. They have changed in terms of the direction, intensity, and nature of knowledge flows. Companies have gone from searching for preferences in their markets, to seeking in-depth contextual knowledge, to sharing knowledge bases with their customers. There has also been a change in terms of the numbers of customers involved in these processes of knowledge exchange and generation. Firms have gone from interacting with a selected group of customers in order to serve a homogeneous mass market, to focusing on large but differentiated market segments,

112   PAMELA ADAMS, STEFANO BRUSONI, AND FRANCO MALERBA

to aiming to serve each customer on an individualized basis. Finally, the boundaries have changed in terms of activities and functions involved. Initially, information was gathered as an input for the commercialization process and in order to assist the adoption process by consumers and users. Firms then began to involve their customers in their production processes to test solutions and eventually to personalize limited aspects of products according to specific preferences. More recently, producers are bringing users directly into the innovation process, giving them access to the firm's own knowledge bases to find their own solutions or the solutions already developed by lead users in the market.

Yet, although the boundaries of knowledge have clearly evolved, the governance of knowledge has changed much less. Although consumers are becoming more involved in an increasing number of activities and functions that were once the domain of the research and development department of firms, producers still dominate the flows of knowledge concerning product and process innovation in most categories. They do so in several ways: by framing the choices that customers have in terms of customization, by providing relevant libraries of knowledge and methods to educate users, by structuring the production processes at the base of these interfaces and interactions, and by making involvement more or less user-friendly and economical. They also continue to dominate the production and commercialization processes that resulted from consumer-led innovation strategies. In industries such as computer games (Jeppesen and Molin, 2003) and in companies such as Threadless.com, in fact, producers benefit from outsourcing part of the value chain to the intelligence and manpower of a mass of free volunteers. In sporting goods such as rodeo kayaks, on the other hand, user innovations are often turned over to large, established manufacturers once the design space had been mined out, and high-volume production and distribution become the key to success. Although knowledge is being shared between producers and consumers more than ever before, firms still determine most of how and when this knowledge will be used.

CONCLUSIONS

In this chapter, we advanced several points. First, we proposed that an understanding of the long-run changes in the knowledge boundaries of firms and industries requires a historical and dynamic analysis of both supply and demand and consequently of the various activities in which firms and industries are involved – innovation, production, and commercialization. Second, we claimed that an analysis of the changing knowledge boundaries entails a detailed examination of three related levels: knowledge in terms of content and sources, division of labor among the various actors involved, and governance of knowledge. Third, we pointed to the rather symmetrical processes taking place on the supply side and on the demand side. Taking a historical perspective, for the supply side we argued that we are witnessing a last stage of a process of increasing disconnectedness among the dynamics of production (what firms do), the dynamics of the types and sources of knowledge (what kinds of knowledge are needed), and the dynamics of the governance of that knowledge (what firms know and govern). Knowledge integration capabilities have become the core competence of the large, postindustrialist firms and require less and less direct involvement in actual manufacturing and in all sources of knowledge generation. On the demand side, we illustrated that companies have gone from processes of transferring knowledge to consumers to stimulate demand, to ones of consulting consumers to learn about their specific preferences and satisfy demand, to ones of engaging consumers directly in value creation at all stages of the product cycle. And we claimed that on both the supply and the demand side these processes have been gradual, incremental, and evolutionary.

We also proposed that the changing knowledge boundaries of firms do not necessarily correspond to the legal boundaries and that the division of labor and governance of knowledge do not necessarily overlap. Although division of labor and the knowledge boundaries of firms have greatly expanded beyond the legal boundaries of firms to reach different scientific and technological realms and various contextual and application loci, the governance of knowledge is often quite concentrated because of the need to coordinate, integrate, and control dispersed relevant knowledge. Therefore, one can understand why today in the presence of an increasing dispersion of the significant knowledge and of a major emphasis on social networks, the governance of that knowledge becomes more complex and challenging.

The focus of this chapter has been intentionally broad in order to identify major long-term trends, to highlight interdependencies and links, and to propose a system view in the analysis of the changing knowledge boundaries of firms. As a consequence, in this chapter we have drawn from existing research, interpretation, and evidence. At the same time, however, in this chapter we also hope to provide a call for new and original research on the knowledge boundaries of firms.

REFERENCES

Arora, A., & Gambardella, A. (1994). The changing technology of technical change: General and abstract knowledge and the division of innovative labor. *Research Policy, 23*, 523-32.

Arora, A., Fosfuri, A., & Gambardella, A. (2001). *Markets for technology: Economics of innovation and corporate strategy*. Cambridge, MA: MIT Press.

Arora, A., Gambardella, A., & Rullani, A. (1998). Division of labour and the locus of inventive activity. *Journal of Management and Governance, 1*(1), 123-40.

Baudrillard, J. (1998). *The consumer society*. London: Sage.

Benson, J. (1994). *The rise of consumer society in Britain 1880-1980*. London: Longman.

Bianchi, M. (1998). Taste for novelty and novel tastes. In M. Bianchi (Ed.), *The active consumer: Novelty and surprise in consumer choice*. London: Routledge.

Blondé, B., Briot, E., Coquery, N., & Van Aert, L. (2005). *Retailers and consumer changes in early modern Europe: England, France, Italy and the Low Countries*. Tours, France: Presses Universitaires François-Rabelais.

Bonaccorsi, A., & Giuri, P. (2001). The long term evolution of vertically related industries. *International Journal of Industrial Organization, 19*, 1053-83.

Bowlby, R. (1997). Supermarket futures. In P. Falk & C. Campbell (Eds.), *The shopping experience*. London: Sage.

Brewer, J., & Porter, R. (Eds.). (1993). *Consumption and the world of goods*. London: Routledge.

Brown, S. (1995). *Postmodern marketing*. London: Routledge.

Brusoni, S. (2005). Limits to specialization: Problem solving and coordination in modular networks. *Organization Studies, 26*, 1885-1907.

Brusoni, S., & Fontana, R. (2010). Incumbents' strategies for platform competition: Shaping the boundaries of creative destruction. In R. Leoncini & N. De Liso (Eds.), *Internationalization, technological change and the theory of the firm*. New York: Routledge.

Brusoni, S., & Pavitt, K. (2003). Problem solving and the co-ordination of innovative activities (SPRU Electronic Working Paper Series No. 93).

Brusoni, S., & Prencipe, A. (2001). Technologies, product, organisations: Opening the black box of modularity. *Industrial and Corporate Change, 10*(1), 179-205.

Brusoni, S., Prencipe, A., & Pavitt, K. (2001). Knowledge specialization, organizational coupling, and the boundaries of the firm: Why do firms know more than they make? *Administrative Science Quarterly, 46*, 597-621.

Cacciatori, E. (2008). Memory objects in project environments: Storing, retrieving and adapting learning in project-based firms. *Research Policy, 37*, 1591-601.

Chandler, A. D. (1977). *The visible hand: The managerial revolution in American business*. Cambridge, MA: Belknap.

Chandler, A. D. (1990). *Scale and scope: The dynamics of industrial capitalism*. Cambridge, MA: Harvard University Press.

Chesbrough, H., & Kusunoki, K. (2000). The modularity trap: Innovation, technology phase- shifts, and the resulting limits of virtual organisations. In K. Nonaka & D. Teece (Eds.), *Knowledge and the firm*. Oxford, UK: Oxford University Press.

Christensen, C. M. & Bower, J. L. (1996). Customer Power, Strategic Investment, and the Failure of Leading Firms, *Strategic Management Journal*, *17*, 3, 197-218.

Cochran, T. C. (1977). *200 years of American business*. New York: Basic Books.

Cohen, L. (2003). *A consumer's republic: The politics of mass consumption in postwar America*. New York: Knopf.

Converse, P. D. (1930). *The elements of marketing*. New York: Prentice-Hall.

Cova, B. (1996). The postmodern explained to managers: Implications for marketing. *Business Horizons*, *39*(6), 15-23.

Cova, B., & Badot, O. (1995). Marketing theory and practice in a postmodern era. In M. J. Baker (Ed.), *Marketing theory and practice*. Basingstoke, UK: Macmillan.

D'Adderio, L. (2001). Crafting the virtual prototype: How firms integrate knowledge and capabilities across organisational boundaries. *Research Policy*, *30*, 1409-24.

Davies, A. (1997). The life cycle of a complex product system. *International Journal of Innovation Management*, *1*, 229-56.

Dosi, G. Technological Paradigms and Technological Trajectories, *Research Policy*, *11*, 3, 147-62.

Dosi, G., Nelson, R., & Winter, S. (2002). *The nature and dynamics of organizational capabilities*. Oxford, UK: Oxford University Press.

Ernst, D. (2005). Limits to modularity: Reflections on recent developments in chip design. *Industry and Innovation*, *12*, 303-35.

Firat, A. F., Dholakia, N., & Vendatesh, A. (1995). Marketing in a postmodern world. *European Journal of Marketing*, *29*(1), 40-56.

Foray, D. (2004). *The economics of knowledge*. Boston, MA: MIT Press.

Fox, S. (1984). *The mirror makers: A history of American advertising and its creators*. New York: William Morrow.

Fox, R. W., & Lears, T. J. J. (1983). *The culture of consumption*. New York: Pantheon.

Franke, N., & Shah, S. (2003). How communities support innovative activities: An exploration of assistance and sharing among end-users. *Research Policy*, *32*(1), 157-78.

Fraser, W. H. (1981). *The coming of the mass market 1850-1914*. Hamden, CT: Archon Books.

Freeman, C., & Louca, F. (2001). *As time goes by*. Oxford, UK: Oxford University Press.

Füller, J., Barti, M., Ernst, H., & Mühlbacher, H. (2006). Community based innovation: How to integrate members of virtual communities into new product development. *Electronic Commerce Research*, *6*, 57-73.

Fullerton, R. A. (1988). How modern is modern marketing? Marketing's evolution and the myth of the production era. *Journal of Marketing*, *52*(1), 108-25.

Fullerton, R. A., & Nevett, T. R. (1986). Advertising and society: A comparative analysis of the roots of distrust in Germany and Great Britain. *International Journal of Advertising*, *5*(4), 225-41.

Galbraith, J. K. (1958). *The affluent society*. Boston: Houghton Mifflin.

Gawer, A. (Ed.). (2009). *Platforms, markets and innovation*. Cheltenham, UK/Northampton, MA: Elgar.

Gawer, A., & Cusumano, M. A. (2002). *Platform leadership: How Intel, Microsoft, and Cisco drive industry innovation.* Boston, MA: Harvard Business School Press.

Gilboy, E. W. (1932). Demand as a factor in the Industrial Revolution. In *Facts and factors in economic history.* Cambridge, MA: Harvard University Press.

Gronow, J., & Warde, A. (Eds.). (2001). *Ordinary consumption.* London: Routledge.

Hamel, G., & Prahalad, C. K. (1994). *Competing for the future.* Boston, MA: Harvard University Press.

Heskett, J. (1980). *Industrial design.* New York: Oxford University Press.

Hounshell, D. A. (1984). *From the American system to mass production 1800–1932.* Baltimore: Johns Hopkins University Press.

Iacobucci, D. (1998). Interactive marketing and the meganet: Networks of networks. *Journal of Interactive Marketing, 12*(1), 5–16.

Izushi, H. & Aoyama, Y. (2006). Industry Evolution and Cross-Sectoral Skill Transfers, Environment and Planning *38*, 10, 1843–61.

Jeppesen, L., & Molin, M. (2003). Consumers as co-developers: Learning and innovation outside the firm. *Technology Analysis and Strategic Management, 15*(3), 363–83.

Katona, G. (1964). *The mass consumption society.* New York: McGraw-Hill.

Lamoreaux, N., & Sokoloff, K. (1999). Inventors, firms and the market for technology: US manufacturing in the late nineteenth and early twentieth centuries. In N. Lamoreaux, J. Raff, & R. Temins (Eds.), *Learning by firms, organizations and countries* (National Bureau of Economic Research Conference Report). Chicago, IL: Chicago University Press.

Langlois, R. (2003). The vanishing hand: The changing dynamics of industrial capitalism. *Industrial and Corporate Change, 12*, 351–85.

Lankshear, C., & Knobel, M. (2006). *New literacies: Everyday practices and classroom learning.* Berkshire, UK: McGraw-Hill.

Levitt, T. (1960). *Marketing myopia. Harvard Business Review,* July-August, *38*, 45–56.

Malerba, F. (1992). Learning by firms and incremental technical change. *Economic Journal, 102*, 845–59.

Malerba, F. (2002). Sectoral systems of innovation and production. *Research Policy, 31*, 247–64.

Malerba, F. (Ed.). (2004). *Sectoral systems of innovation.* Cambridge: Cambridge University Press.

Malerba, F. (2005). Sectoral systems: How and why innovation differs across sectors. In J. Fagerberg, D. Mowery, & R. Nelson (Eds.), *The Oxford handbook of innovation.* Oxford, UK: Oxford University Press.

Malerba, F., & Orsenigo, L. (2000). Knowledge, innovative activities and industry evolution. *Industrial and Corporate Change, 9*(2), 289–315.

Martineau, J. (1958). Social classes and spending behavior. *Journal of Marketing, 23*(10), 121–30.

McKendrick, N., Brewer, J., & Plumb, J. H. (1982). *The birth of a consumer society: The commercialization of eighteenth-century England.* London: Europa Publications.

Mowery, D., & Rosenberg, N. (1991). *Technology and the pursuit of economic growth*. Cambridge: Cambridge University Press.

Nelson, R. (1991). Why do firms differ, and how does it matter? *Strategic Management Journal, 12*(S2), 61-74.

Nelson, R. (1994). The co-evolution of technology, industrial structure and supporting institutions. *Industrial and Corporate Change, 3*, 47-63.

Nelson, R., & Winter, S. (1982). *An evolutionary theory of economic change*. Cambridge, MA: Belknap.

Novak, T., Hoffmann, D., & Yung, Y. (2000). Measuring the customer experience in online environments: A structural modeling approach. *Marketing Science, 19*(1), 22-42.

Orsenigo, L., Pammolli, F., & Riccaboni, M. (2001). Technological change and network dynamics: lessons from the pharmaceutical industry. *Research Policy, 30*, 485-508.

Pavitt, K. (1984). Sectoral patterns of technical change: Towards a taxonomy and a theory. *Research Policy, 13*, 343-74.

Pavitt, K., & Steinmueller, W. (2001). Technology in corporate strategy: Change, continuity, and the information revolution. In T. Pettigrew & R. Whittington (Eds.), *Handbook of strategy and management*. London: Sage.

Piller, F. (2003). *Mass customization*. Wiesbaden, Germany: Gabler.

Piller, F., Schubert, P., Koch, M., & Moslein, K. (2005). Overcoming mass confusion: Collaborative customer co-design in online communities. *Journal of Computer-Mediated Communication, 10*(4), 1-25.

Pine, J. (1993). *Mass customization*. Boston, MA: Harvard Business School Press.

Porter, M. (1980). *Competitive strategy: Techniques for analyzing industries and competitors*. New York: Free Press.

Prahalad, C. K., & Ramaswamy, V. (2004). *The future of competition: Co-creating unique value with customers*. Boston, MA: Harvard Business School Press.

Prencipe, A. (1997). Technological competencies and product evolutionary dynamics: A case study from the aero engine industry. Research Policy, 25, 1261-76.

Prencipe, A., Davies, A., & Hobday, M. (2003). *The business of systems integration*. Oxford, UK: Oxford University Press.

Radner R. (1992). Hierarchy: The economics of managing, *Journal of Economic Literature, 30*, 1382-415.

Sanchez, R. & Mahoney, J. T. (1996). "Modularity, Flexibility, and Knowledge Management in Product and Organization Design, Strategic Management Journal, 17, 63-76.

Saul, S. B. (1967). The market and the development of the mechanical engineering industries in Britain, 1860-1914. *Economic History Review, 20*(1), 111-30.

Saul, S. B. (Ed.). (1970). *Technological change: The United States and Britain in the nineteenth century*. London: Methuen.

Saviotti, P. (1996). *Technological evolution, variety and the economy*. Cheltenham, UK: Elgar.

Sawhney, M., & Prandelli, E. (2001). Communities of creation: Managing distributed innovation in turbulent markets. *California Management Review, 42*(4), 24-54.

Shaw, G. (1992). The European scene: Britain and Germany. In J. Benson & G. Shaw (Eds.), *The evolution of retail systems*. Leicester, UK: Leicester University Press.

Shaw, I. (1916). *An approach to business problems*. Cambridge, MA: Harvard University Press.

Stigler, G. J. (1951). The division of labor is limited by the extent of the market. *Journal of Political Economy, 59*(3), 185–93.

Stigler, G., & Becker, G. (1977). "De gustibus non est disputandum." *American Economic Review, 67*(2), 76–90.

Sturgeon, T. (2002). Modular production networks: A new model of industrial organization. *Industrial and Corporate Change, 11*, 451–96.

Sutton, J. (1998). Technology and Market Structure, Cambridge: MIT Press.

Takeishi, A. (2001). Bridging inter- and intra-firm boundaries: management of supplier involvement in automobile product development. *Strategic Management Journal, 22*, 403–33.

Tee, R., & Gawer, A. (2009) Industry architecture as a determinant of successful platform strategies: a case study of the i-mode mobile Internet service. *European Management Review, 6*, 217–32.

Toffler, A. (1980). *The third wave*. New York: Bantam Books.

Universal McCann, *Wave.3: Power to the People Social Media Tracker*, March 2008 available at http://www.universalmccann.com/Assets/wave_3_20080403093750.pdf.

Von Hippel, E. (1994). "Sticky information" and the locus of problem solving: Implications for innovation. *Management Science, 40*, 429–39.

Von Hippel, E. (2001). Innovation by user communities: Learning from open source software. *MIT Sloan Management Review, 42*(4), 82–6.

Von Hippel, E. (2005). *Democratizing innovation*. Cambridge, MA: MIT Press.

Wind, R., & Rangaswamy, V. (2001). Customerization: The next revolution in mass customization. *Journal of Interactive Marketing, 15*(1), 13–32.

Winter, S. (1987). Knowledge and competencies as strategic assets. In D. Teece (Ed.), *The competitive challenge*. Cambridge: Cambridge University Press.

Witt, U. (2001). Learning by consumers: A theory of wants and the growth of demand. *Journal of Evolutionary Economics, 1*, 23–36.

Yankelovich, D. (1964). New criteria for market segmentation. *Harvard Business Review*, March/April. Available at http://www.danyankelovich.com/new-criteria.pdf.

Zammutto, R., Griffith, T., Majchrzak, A., Doughtery, D., & Faraj, S. (2007). Information technology and changing fabric of organizations. *Organization Science, 18*, 749–66.

4

Organizing the Electronic Century

RICHARD N. LANGLOIS

INTRODUCTION

Talk of a third industrial revolution presupposes that there has been a second.[1] Alfred Chandler (2006, pp. 1-2) tells us that the second industrial revolution began in the 1880s, when the development of the railroad, steamships, electricity, and the telegraph and telephone called forth economies of scale and set in motion genuinely multinational enterprises (Chandler, 1977, 1990). The revolutionary barricades were manned by a large number of integrated multidivisional firms wielding a multiplicity of technologies. By 1930, that revolution was over, leaving behind the infrastructure of the industrial century – the twentieth century. As Chandler (2006, p. 48) reminds us, with what one suspects is a great deal of satisfaction, 98 of the 100 largest industrial enterprises in the United States in 1993 had been founded by the early 1930s.

The third industrial revolution, which Chandler tends to call the electronic or information revolution, began just as its predecessor was ending. It would eventually generate the infrastructure for the electronic

---

[1] Disclaimer: I am not actually interested in what industrial revolutions are, whether they exist, or whether these particular ones are correctly specified. I use the terminology only as a convenient container for my narrative.

century now upon us. Unlike the second industrial revolution, the information revolution bubbled up from a narrow set of technologies – the vacuum tube, the transistor, the integrated circuit, and the microprocessor – and thus involved a smaller set of players (Chandler, 2001, p. 12). But the organizational outcome was identical, because it would be the same kind of large multidivisional firms that would commercialize the scientific and technological ideas of the new century. As first movers, and occasionally fast followers, these firms developed an *integrated knowledge base* from which they could launch innovative products. Although a "supporting nexus" of smaller, more-specialized firms was crucial to the success of the overall industrial enterprise, it was the multidivisional firms, not the web of specialists, who did the heavy lifting. So long as the pioneering firms employed the *virtuous strategy* of related diversification and remained on the straight-and-narrow *paths of learning* the first movers had mapped out, those firms were able to enjoy economies of scale and scope and to become the perpetrators rather than the victims of creative destruction. But when the pioneers strayed from the path, and especially when they succumbed to the temptation of unrelated diversification, they stumbled and fell (Chandler, 2001, 2006).

This is clearly a coherent framework for understanding the organization of technological change, and one with a good deal of appeal. Unlike many accounts of organization, especially those emanating from economics departments, Chandler's framework stresses the knowledge and economic *capabilities* (Langlois and Foss, 1999) that underlie production and the ways in which organization is both shaped by and shapes such capabilities. Nonetheless, one might legitimately wonder whether an explanation honed in the fires of the second industrial revolution retains a sharp edge for the third. To many observers, the most recent manifestations of the electronic revolution, those involving personal computers and the Internet, are notable precisely for the ways in which they have diminished the role of the large multidivisional firm as a generator of innovation and a repository of economic capabilities. There are still large firms with integrated knowledge bases and economies of scale and scope, but those firms – Intel, Microsoft, Dell, Cisco – are far more vertically specialized than firms of old. And it is far from clear nowadays whether it is these large firms or the "supporting nexus" that tends the industry's overall path of learning. This alternative view implies a discontinuity not merely between the second industrial revolution and the third, but perhaps even between the two dimensions of the industrial century itself, consumer electronics and computers. Viewed in this way, we can see the path of learning in consumer electronics through the classic Chandlerian lens as a dance of large multidivisional firms like RCA, Philips, Matsushita, and Sony. However, understanding the path of learning in the computer industry, especially in its more recent phases, requires an entirely different optic.

My approach is to steer between – or rather to recombine elements from – these competing accounts of the electronic revolution. In accord with the "new economy" view, I am sensitive to the ways in which changing technology and other factors have affected the nature, role, and scope of both the multidivisional firm and the supporting nexus. Indeed, I concur in the view that the forces of the modern age have led to a widespread "deverticalization" of production in this and other industries, although, as in previous work (Langlois, 2003, 2004, 2007), I locate the source of that phenomenon less in the specific demands of digital technology and the Internet than in the larger Smithian forces of specialization attendant on a growing economy, increasing globalization, and an expanding base of technological knowledge. At the same time, however, I do not consign the multidivisional firm to the dustbin of history. I attempt to tell a tale of the electronics industry that is fundamentally Chandlerian in character, as it focuses on the development of technological and economic capabilities and on the paths of learning in the industry. Like Chandler, I see the dynamics operating in consumer electronics and computers as essentially similar rather than as dramatically different. The result may or may not have pleased Chandler himself;[2] but it is my attempt to walk a path of learning that he, as "first mover," has marked out.

CAPABILITIES AND ARCHITECTURE

As Chandler noted, the consumer electronics and computer industries of the twentieth century emerged from a handful of related technologies, namely, the vacuum tube, the transistor, the integrated circuit, and the microprocessor. These technologies arguably qualify as general-purpose technologies (GPTs), and their general-purpose character accounts for the rapid pace of economic growth both in and because of the

---

[2] Chandler (2005, p. 595, note 1) vented his annoyance at a related attempt by Lamoreaux et al. (2003) to create a new synthesis of business history in light of present-day organizational trends. He accused them, perhaps a bit unfairly, of imagining a world dominated by small specialized firms and of neglecting the importance and visibility of global capitalism.

electronics sector (Helpman, 1998; Langlois, 2002a). At the same time, however, these technologies became useful only when embedded in larger systems like radios, televisions, and computers. In this respect, the products of the electronics industry have always been what Merges and Nelson (1994) call cumulative systems technologies. A technology is a (complex) system when it is composed of many parts, each of which may draw on its own potentially distinctive knowledge base; and a technology is cumulative when "today's advances lay the basis for tomorrow's, which in turn lay the basis for a next round, and so on, with the sequence often progressing very far from the original invention starting place" (Merges and Nelson, 1994, p. 7). In industries based on cumulative systems technologies, advances do indeed follow a path of learning.

How many of the capabilities necessary to produce a complex system will reside within the boundaries of a (large multidivisional) firm and how many will be left to other (perhaps more-specialized) firms? And – what is not the same question – which pieces of the system will a (large multidivisional) firm produce itself and which will it buy from other (perhaps more-specialized) firms? That specialization has its benefits is, of course, an idea that predates Adam Smith. George Richardson (1972) recast the issue in terms of economic capabilities: The greater the extent to which the complementary capabilities needed to produce a (complex systems) product emerge from distinct bases of knowledge, the more expensive it will be to manage those capabilities effectively within a single organization. This suggests, with Chandler, that successful integrated knowledge bases will consist in capabilities that are related to one another. But how related? And how integrated?

In making their case against a broad patent scope, Merges and Nelson (1990, 1994) point out the value of a process of innovation in which many different agents can participate, as competition in ideas can lead to rapid trial-and-error learning (Nelson and Winter, 1977.) In the case of a complex systems product, patents on crucial components can make it costly to assemble a state-of-the art system; but broad patents covering large parts of the overall system can be especially damaging, as they allow the patent holders to block or retard the innovative activity of others. The same logic suggests that, even in the absence of explicit patent protection, broad and tightly integrated capabilities within a few first movers can have a similar effect. Baldwin and Clark (2000, 2006) make the argument more formally when they suggest that a given set of innovative activities – of economic experiments – are more valuable in a market than in a (large multidivisional) firm: The value of a portfolio of options is always greater than the value of an option on a portfolio.

A complex systems product is underlain by an *architecture*: a set of parts and a way of fitting those parts together. An *integral* architecture is one in which the parts depend on one another in complex and often unpredictable ways: the system is a tangle of spaghetti. By contrast, a *modular* architecture is one that regularizes the dependencies among the parts, forcing them to interact only in relatively formalized and predictable ways (Langlois, 2002b). Such modularity reduces the costs of specialization and permits actors to participate with only a limited repertoire of capabilities. In the case of a complex systems product, a certain degree of modularity is inevitable to the extent that the parts of the system call on a wide set of dissimilar technological and economic capabilities.

Although the degree of modularity of an architecture is an important determinant of organizational structure, there is no one-to-one mapping between the architecture of a complex systems product and the industrial structure under which that product is actually produced. For example, a large multidivisional firm can choose to produce internally most of the components of a more-or-less-modular systems product in order to appropriate rents or to maintain the kinds of first-mover advantages Chandler describes. In such a case, the full *option value* of the architecture may lay untapped (Baldwin and Clark, 2006). Alternatively, the causality may run in reverse: Vertical integration may persist precisely because the firm or firms controlling the architecture are relatively insulated from competition by intellectual property protection or industrial structure (Langlois, 2003). It is competition that unleashes the option value of a (potentially) modular architecture. Moreover, architecture is itself a decision variable that may be under the control of a Chandlerian first mover, and such a firm may choose a more-integral system design as part of a strategy of rent appropriation or because the conditions of competition do not require it to do otherwise.

On one side of the ledger, then, is the benefit to modularity and vertical disintegration of *modular innovation* (Langlois and Robertson, 1992), the rapid trial-and-error learning that comes from tapping into the larger universe of external capabilities that lie outside the boundaries of the firm. On the other side of the ledger, however, is the potential benefit to integration and integrality of *architectural innovation* (Henderson and Clark, 1990), improvements that come from reorganizing the list of parts and the way the parts fit together. It is the importance of integrative capabilities that resonates in Chandler's discussion of paths of learning. In the second industrial revolution, first movers emerged and grew into large multidivisional firms because of their ability to create and manage the architecture of a new product (or, more typically, process) the parts for which were not initially available cheaply through arm's-length transactions (Langlois, 1992b, 2003; Langlois and Robertson, 1995). Many writers continue to insist on the importance of integrative capabilities even in today's world of greater modularity and vertical disintegration. Now as then, there remains a need for a systems integration capability (Pavitt, 2003). This is why, in general, successful firms "know more than they do" (Granstrand et al., 1997; Brusoni et al., 2001). That is, firms retain internal capabilities not only in systems integration, but also in fabricating many of the parts of the system, even though they may actually source those parts from others.

What can we learn from all this? The present-day theory of capabilities has much to say about paths of learning; but it does not prescribe that those paths be trodden by large multidivisional firms alone or, for that matter, by small, highly specialized ones. Rather, it provides a toolkit I use in creating an account of how the infrastructure of the electronic century came to be organized.

CONSUMER ELECTRONICS

At the turn of the twentieth century, the strands of technology that would lead to what we now think of as consumer electronics were not yet electronic: They were electromechanical (radio) or strictly mechanical (sound and video reproduction). With John Fleming's invention of the vacuum-tube diode in 1904, followed quickly by Lee de Forest's invention of the triode "audion" in 1906 (Hong, 2001, pp. 119-20), a genuinely electronic paradigm began to emerge. What would spur the development of that paradigm, however, was not the prospect of consumer demand but rather telecommunications, notably military telecommunications.[3]

The Radio

At the end of the nineteenth century, Guglielmo Marconi had demonstrated the possibility of wireless telegraphy using a spark-gap transmitter. By the turn of the twentieth century, he had incorporated in

---

[3] Unless otherwise noted, the next few paragraphs draw generally on Maclaurin (1949), Aitken (1985), Graham (1986), and Chandler (2000).

Britain what would become Marconi's Wireless Telegraph Company, along with a series of similar companies around the world, including one in the United States. Although there were other players, Marconi was a formidable competitor who generally refused interconnection with other networks; American Marconi held a virtual monopoly on wireless telegraphy in the United States. A major use for wireless was communication with ships at sea, something that became more significant as the First World War broke out; the war also thrust wireless into the land-to-land business as the warring factions cut each other's undersea telegraph cables. Understandably, wireless technology did not escape the notice of the U.S. Navy, which effectively nationalized American Marconi for the duration.

The spark-gap transmitter was a relatively crude device that spewed electromagnetic radiation indiscriminately over the spectrum. Marconi continued to depend on this technology, however, as he concentrated on the geographical expansion of his empire at the expense of technological development. By the First World War, American companies, along with some in Europe, had developed electromechanical approaches to the transmission of cleaner waveforms. But these companies, including GE, were in the equipment business, not the radio-transmission business. At war's end, the Navy, fearing dominance of a crucial military technology by what was ultimately a British company, wanted badly to nationalize wireless telegraphy.[4] When it became clear that Congress would not accede, the Navy changed tack and pushed for the "Americanization" of American Marconi through an organizational alliance with GE (Maclaurin, 1949, p. 103; Howeth, 1963, Chapter 27). GE would become the major shareholder in a new entity, the Radio Corporation of America (RCA), that would absorb most of the assets of American Marconi, including personnel and patents. The new company would then provide radio services using American (GE) equipment.

RCA received its Delaware charter in 1919. Within the next two years, a number of significant players joined in with capital and technology: AT&T, United Fruit, and Westinghouse. In part, RCA attracted these partners because of the systemic nature of the service. In the case of AT&T, for example, RCA needed access to AT&T's lines as feeders for its service.

---

[4] The case in favor of nationalization was pressed at a 1919 Congressional hearing by the assistant secretary of the Navy, one Franklin Delano Roosevelt (Aitken,1985, p. 386, note 42). A year earlier, the case against had been eloquently argued at another hearing by a rising star in the American Marconi organization, David Sarnoff. Navy ownership, Sarnoff argued, would have a chilling effect on innovation (Graham, 1986, p. 36).

The more compelling motive, however, was intellectual property. RCA was a way to pool the many patents that would be needed to produce the complex systems products of radio transmission and reception.[5] Seeing vacuum tubes as important for amplifiers in its wire-based transmission system, AT&T had purchased the de Forest triode patent. Marconi had acquired the Fleming diode patent. Prior to the U. S. entry into World War I, development of vacuum-tube technology had been at a standstill as the two firms dueled in court in a classic case of blocking patents[6] (Merges and Nelson, 1990, pp. 892–3; Aitken, 1985, pp. 248–9). By 1920, RCA controlled both patents. United Fruit, which had developed wireless technology for use with its extensive fleet of ships, contributed patents and facilities, thereby ridding itself of concerns far from its core competences. The last piece of the puzzle was Westinghouse, America's other electrical-equipment giant, which contributed, among other things, the rights to the crucial heterodyne principle.[7] As a result of this agglomeration, as well as numerous international cross-licensing agreements, "RCA obtained rights to over 2,000 issued patents, including practically all the patents of importance in the radio science of the day" (Maclaurin, 1949, p. 107). It remains an open question as to why all this took the form of an equity joint venture rather than a contractual patent pool alone, though most commentators point to the role of the government in pushing for the development of what they saw as a national champion in radio technology (Maclaurin,1949, pp. 100ff.). In the words of founding chairman Owen D. Young, RCA for its part "was anxious to create an industry in which competition would be 'orderly and stabilized'" (Maclaurin, 1949, p. 105).

RCA's original business model was wireless telegraphy. Everyone recognized that vacuum tubes would eventually be important in this enterprise, even if they were not initially capable of providing the power

---

[5] A 1919 Navy memorandum had "found that there was not a single company among those making radio sets for the Navy which possessed basic patents sufficient to enable them to supply, without infringement, . . . a complete transmitter or receiver" (quoted in Maclaurin, 1949, p. 105). Maclaurin (1949, p. 97) also reports that there were twenty major issues of patent infringement between AT&T and GE between 1912 and 1926.

[6] During World War I, the U. S. Government effectively inactivated all radio-related patents for the duration and assumed financial responsibility for any resulting infringements (Reich, 1977, p. 214).

[7] The heterodyne technique involves adding two waveforms in order to produce two new signals at different wavelengths. The superheterodyne receiver became the eventual dominant design in radio.

levels of the electromechanical alternator. Vacuum tubes could produce a cleaner waveform, something of great use if one were to modulate the signal to transmit and receive sound and voice, not just dots and dashes. But few at the time saw any potential in sound broadcasting. There was, however, one crucial exception, and even he underestimated its potential. David Sarnoff was a Russian immigrant who rose through the ranks from office boy and key operator to a management position at American Marconi, where he had conceptualized what he called a "Radio Music Box" (Graham, 1986, p. 32). The business model was to make money from selling receivers to a mass market while providing broadcasting content free of charge as a kind of advertising. American Marconi had no interest in the idea, but, when Sarnoff moved over to RCA, he eventually found a warmer reception.

We are accustomed nowadays to the rapid penetration of new technologies - the DVD, the cell phone, the Internet - and may be accustomed to thinking of such rapid penetration as unique to our age. But the speed with which the American home adopted the radio was on a par with anything our age has to offer; the penetration of the personal computer proceeded at a snail's pace by comparison.[8] Sarnoff apparently thought that the total cumulative demand for radios would be about a million sets at $75 each. In the event, the industry sold $60 million worth in the first year (1922) alone; $136 million in 1923; and $358 million in 1924. RCA's own sales were $11 million in 1922; $22.5 million in 1923; and $50 million in 1924 (see Table 4.1). Over the next decade, 60 percent of American homes came to possess radio receivers (Scott, 2001). Sarnoff saw his sales staff burgeon from 14 people in 1921 to 200 offices nationwide the next year - and saw himself catapulted into the position of vice-president and general manager (Graham, 1986, pp. 38-9).

Because radio constitutes what economists now call a hardware-software network, what actually catalyzed the takeoff of radio was less RCA's entrance into receiver manufacturing than the impetus RCA's entry gave to the launching of broadcast stations. The broadcast of voice and music probably goes as far back as 1906, all in the context of amateur radio, which constituted a large "hobbyist" sector akin to what would later drive the early personal computer industry:

---

[8] In the first two years after introduction, IBM sold a total of 750,000 personal computers, and that represented 26 percent of the market for PCs (Langlois, 1992, p. 23).

Table 4.1. Sales of Home
Broadcast Radio Sets (in
Thousands)

Year	Number	Value
1922	100	$60,000
1923	550	136,000
1924	1,500	358,000
1925	2,000	430,000
1926	1,750	506,000
1927	1,350	425,600
1928	3,281	690,550
1929	4,428	842,548
1930	3,827	496,432
1931	3,420	300,000
1932	3,000	200,000
1933	3,806	300,099
1934	4,084	350,000
1935	6,027	370,000
1936	8,248	500,000
1937	8,065	537,000
1938	6,000	350,000
1939	10,500	375,000
1940	11,800	584,000
1941	13,000	610,000

Source: Maclaurin (1949, p. 139).

By the 1920s wireless had become the hobby of thousands of young Americans. No other modern industry has been supported by so many ardent participants. It is hard today [i.e., in 1949] to recapture the spirit of this period: amateur clubs were started in every state, comprising all types and classes – schoolboys, professors, electricians, and ex-servicemen who had operated radios during the war. Radio was a new toy, not only technically interesting, but the means by which people could reach out into unknown regions and communicate with new-found friends. (Maclaurin, 1949, p. 112)

In 1920, Westinghouse set up a radio station (under the call sign KDKA) at its East Pittsburgh plant to cater to this ham radio market and earn some cheap goodwill. The effect was to alert other commercial enterprises, including AT&T and RCA, to the potential that already existed because of amateur radio (Aitken, 1985, pp. 469ff.). The number of broadcast stations on the air leapt from 5 in 1921 to 556 in 1923, leveling off at 765 by 1940 (Sterling and Kittross, 1978, cited in Scott, 2001). Most early stations did indeed broadcast for free to earn goodwill (and maybe sell receivers); but by 1927, the tide had turned in favor of the advertising-revenue model.

Most of the first commercial producers of radio receivers were hobbyists and garage-shop operations. Between 1923 and 1926, by one estimate, an average of 187 new firms entered the business every year, most of which failed quickly (Maclaurin, 1949, p. 134). Despite its formidable capabilities, RCA was not in a good position to compete on price with the garage shops, as it had costly and often unwieldy supply relations with GE and Westinghouse for parts. As the architecture of the radio receiver matured, RCA and its owners–suppliers struggled with the problem of standardization for parts like vacuum tubes (Graham, 1986, pp. 39–40). Like personal computers decades later, radios were in fact relatively inexpensive to assemble; and increased standardization and the emergence of a dominant design quickly eroded the rents one could earn from selling assembled receivers. RCA initially tried to extract rents at the level of the vacuum tube, because this was indeed the high-tech core of the radio, but they did this by insisting on full-line forcing and exclusive dealing in their arrangements with distributors, practices of dubious value that were in any event struck down by the Federal Trade Commission (Graham, 1986, p. 40; Chandler, 2001, p. 19). In the late 1920s, RCA's market share had slipped to between 18 and 20 percent (Chandler, 2001, p. 21).

By 1927, however, courts had affirmed the validity of RCA's dominant patent portfolio, which opened the door to what would be the company's strategy for the next three decades: package licensing. Chandler (2001, p. 18) takes pains to point out that by the end of the roaring 'twenties, garage-shop radio manufacturers had faded away in favor of significant firms founded before 1920 in related technologies like batteries, automotive equipment, telephone equipment, or electrical equipment.[9] The superior capabilities of incumbents may indeed have won out in the end; but in this case the demise of the newcomer was mostly the result of RCA's patent policy: only twenty-five large assemblers would initially have the rights to RCA's patents, in exchange for a sizable royalty of 7.5 percent plus back damages for infringement.[10] The licensing was a package in the sense that an assembler had to pay royalties on RCA

---

[9] The two exceptions were start-ups Zenith and Raytheon.

[10] RCA had initially wanted to limit licenses to customers whose royalties would amount to at least $100,000, though this minimum was never enforced (Maclaurin, 1949, p. 135).

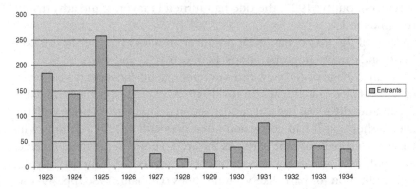

Figure 4.1. Effect of RCA patent licensing on entry into radio. (*Source:* Maclaurin, 1949, p. 134).

patents for all relevant parts of the radio even if the assembler did not use all those parts (Figure 4.1).

Although RCA did later extend the deal to others and reduce royalty demands somewhat, it was nonetheless RCA's control of the patent portfolio that gave shape to the radio industry. In part, this meant more rapid consolidation. More important, as Graham noted,

> the most enduring consequence of the [package-licensing] policy was that it made it uneconomic for most other companies to do radio-related research, because they could not recoup the investment. This left control of the rate and direction of technological change in the radio industry largely in the hands of RCA. For RCA, the effect was to make licensing fees the major payoff of its research activity. RCA was effectively in the business of selling research.[11] (Graham, 1986, p. 41)

Thus, in radio, it was not the case that an integrated path of learning within a large firm gave rise to innovation; it was, rather, that innovation, channeled within a particular structure of property rights, contained the path of learning within a single large firm. One might indeed wonder whether, far from representing the *optimum optimorum* of capability building, RCA's integrated structure failed ultimately to tap the option value of what was potentially a powerful modular architecture.

Sarnoff understood that, because the firm was not a cost leader and had essentially no source of rents in the receiver value chain other than its patents, RCA needed to look elsewhere for future sources of rents.

---

[11] On this point, see also Reich (1977).

This meant pouring money into research. It also meant a move away from hardware to "software": broadcasting and content. Taking over the broadcasting assets of AT&T, RCA famously created the National Broadcasting Company (NBC) in 1926, from which the American Broadcasting Company (ABC) would eventually spin off in 1942.

Sound Recording

In addition, Sarnoff began to see the relevant architecture broadly as one of "consumer electronics" rather than of radio as an appliance.[12] The core of all consumer electronics in the era was the vacuum-tube amplifier, which could be linked to electromagnetic speakers to reproduce sound. The amplifier could receive its input from a radio tuner. But it could receive other inputs as well. At the system level, then, consumer electronics in the age of sound was potentially highly modular, and at the high end explicitly so. The principal source of input to an amplifier other than radio was prerecorded sound. In 1930, Sarnoff purchased the Victor Talking Machines Company, a prominent maker of phonographs based on the techniques of Edison.[13] Initially, the phonograph was entirely mechanical: A needle picked up vibrations in the tracks of a recording, and a horn then amplified the sound acoustically. But as technology advanced, it became possible to capture the vibrations electronically and transmit them to a vacuum-tube amplifier. The research department at Western Electric (later to become Bell Labs) developed electric sound recording in the early 1920s, but Victor initially refused to adopt the technology.[14] A company called Brunswick was first to market with an electronic phonograph it called the Panatrope. Sarnoff clearly understood the potential of such technological convergence, and RCA began to offer not only electronic Victrolas but also a device called the Duo Jr., a $9.95 record player that plugged into an existing radio. Smaller producers of audiophile equipment pursued an even more forceful modular strategy, offering (and often specializing in) separate amplifiers, preamplifiers, tuners, phonographs, and speakers. A principal element of the standardized interface within this modular system is still called an RCA plug.

---

[12] This paragraph and the next draw on Robertson and Langlois (1992).

[13] At the same time, Sarnoff also engineered the sale of both GE's and Westinghouse's stakes in RCA, thus bolstering the company as an independent entity (Chandler, 2001, p. 22).

[14] Supposedly on the grounds that consumers were accustomed to the tinny sound of the Victrola and would find the new sound unpleasant (Robertson and Langlois, 1992, p. 330).

Because of the integrated structure of RCA, however, meaningful competition by specialists was decidedly limited. But there did emerge one relatively integrated rival, and the ensuing competition did much to spur technological change in the industry. Columbia began its life in the late nineteenth century as a distributor of Edison's phonographs and cylinders in the Washington, DC, area (hence the name) and by the 1920s was Victor's principal rival in phonographs. Columbia also owned a small network of radio stations that had formed as an outlet for talent snubbed by Sarnoff's NBC. In 1927, a young Philadelphia cigar maker named William Paley bought the whole operation on the strength of his enthusiasm for radio advertising. The Columbia Broadcast System (CBS) competed with RCA's networks and was also integrated into phonograph records.[15] An excellent example of the benefits of Columbia's competition with RCA is the famous battle of the speeds. Adapted to the acoustic phonograph, standard records of the time were made of shellac and spun at 78 rpm. The new electronic technology suggested slower speeds and a new material, vinyl. RCA experimented with 33-rpm recordings, but was unable to increase playing time significantly and abandoned the project at the onset of the Depression. Columbia took up the idea under the direction of Peter Goldmark and Edward Wallerstein, the latter the erstwhile general manager of RCA's Victor Division. As a result, Columbia stole a march on RCA, whose attempt to retake the standard with the large-spindle 45-rpm disk fell short. After World War II, phonographs adopted a gateway technology that enabled a user to play records at all three speeds.

Television

Advancements in radio and phonograph technology proceeded largely in modular fashion through improvements in components. As many of these, notably vacuum tubes, were general-purpose technologies, their manufacturers benefited from scale and learning economies from demand – including military demand – outside of the consumer sector. But the next big advance in consumer electronics required innovation that was much more systemic in character.

---

[15] In fact, the Columbia record label had spun off from CBS after Paley purchased the Columbia networks. Columbia merged with the British firm Gramophone (controlled by RCA) in 1931 to form EMI, but, because of antitrust concerns, the American assets of Columbia were not part of the deal. CBS eventually reacquired the Columbia label in 1938.

Dating back to the nineteenth century, there had been numerous attempts to transmit pictures. All of these required some kind of electromechanical apparatus, and the results were never satisfactory. By the mid-1920s, Vladimir Zworykin was making progress on a fully electronic method of scanning and transmitting images. His work attracted Sarnoff's attention, and RCA began funding the work, first at Westinghouse and then at RCA's own facilities. Whereas radio did not strictly depend on vacuum tubes and could benefit from the independent development of tubes and other components, television depended on the simultaneous development of a design architecture (for both transmitter and receiver) and many new and specialized components, including highly complex electron tubes. Moreover, television raised many more issues of technical standardization than had radio. Zworykin evidently believed that television could in fact develop in an incremental, modular and decentralized way (Graham, 1986, p. 53), but he grossly underestimated the resources that development would require. And, as the rapid development of technology made early standard setting problematic, it is likely that Sarnoff was right to regard the technology as an ideal fit with the model of the well-funded industrial research laboratory.

Although entrepreneurial start-ups – like those created by Philo Farnsworth and Alan B. Du Mont, who had invented technology parallel to Zworykin's – did attempt to develop television, it was more substantial enterprises like CBS, Philco, and Zenith who provided a challenge to Sarnoff, even if these competitors were obliged to license much of the technology from RCA. Far more than up-front costs, it was, however, the systemic nature of the innovation in its early (or "preparadigmatic") stages that created what Chandler (2001, p. 25) refers to as barriers to entry. The initial dearth of programming reduced television's attractiveness to early adopters, as Sarnoff discovered after the first RCA TVs rolled out at the 1939 World's Fair. But RCA's integration into a broadcast network placed it in a more favorable position than competitors, who had banded together to push a standard different from RCA's. At the behest of the Federal Communications Commission (FCC), the radio manufacturers trade association formed the National Television Standards Committee (NTSC) that, in 1941, promulgated standards largely identical to those RCA favored.

TV broadcasting began in earnest later that year – just in time for the American entry into World War II and the consequent ban on the manufacture of commercial television equipment. Nonetheless, the war proved immensely beneficial for the development of the television. The

military demanded technology closely related to that used for television, notably the cathode-ray tubes crucial to radar. As a result, the end
of the war presented commercial industry with numerous advances in
both product and process technology, including techniques for mass
producing cathode-ray tubes that halved the postwar price of TVs (Graham, 1986, p. 59). Component makers, working with glass-making firms,
continued the trajectory of improvement in product and process after
the war (Graham, 2000, p. 144). A year after the war ended, RCA was
selling mass-market TV sets bundled with a contract for installation and
service[16] (Graham, 1986, p. 60).

RCA encouraged competition in the production of sets, even to the
extent of holding technical seminars for competitors.[17] This ought not
to be surprising, as RCA was in a position to benefit from its portfolio
of television patents, its position as key producer of a crucial bottleneck component (picture tubes), and its sale of complementary software through the NBC network. Indeed, in the early 1950s, NBC turned
handsomely profitable (Graham, 1986, p. 60). In the period 1952-6, RCA
received some $96 million in TV patent revenues – some 77 percent of
all industry revenues (Levy, 1981, p. 124) – which Levy (1981, p. 162)
estimates to have raised the price of televisions by 2.26 percent. As it had
in the case of radio, RCA licensed its TV patents (as well as its patents
in other technological areas) as a package – until a 1958 antitrust consent decree mandated a patent pool among American (but not foreign)
producers.

The American public adopted the TV with an enthusiasm that rivaled
its earlier infatuation with radio. Production ramped up to 3 million units
by 1949, peaking at 7.79 million in 1955, and then declining slightly
as the market for black-and-white sets reached saturation (Levy, 1981,
p. 99). In 1950, five years after the war, 9 percent of American homes
could boast a television set; after ten years, 64.5 percent could; and
by 1960, the figure was 87 percent (Levy, 1981, p. 116). Klepper and

---

[16] This was arguably the cheapest way to provide what consumers really wanted – reliable
television services – when technology was both unreliable and unfamiliar to consumers.
Because reliability was the central issue, and because knowledge of television technology
was not widely diffused to independent dealers, it was cheaper to provide such contracts
through vertical integration (as RCA did) than through contracts with independents.

[17] "In 1947, Frank Folsom, then president of RCA Victor, invited representatives of all other
television makers to visit the RCA plant in Camden, New Jersey. He then proceeded to
give them a tour of RCA's production facilities and presented each one of them with a
copy of the blueprints for RCA's most popular television model" (Levy, 1981, p. 129,
citing Fortune, September, 1948, p. 81).

Simons (1997) document the resulting flurry of entry of new firms into the market for black-and-white TVs. American manufacturers peaked at 92 in 1951, after which a shakeout reduced the number to 38 in 1958.[18] Of these, RCA and Zenith accounted for about a third of sales in the 1950s, and the top four firms held more than half the market (Levy, 1981, p. 86).

The move to color television required systemic innovations that were more expensive and arguably more complex than those of monochrome TV, and the attendant standardization issues were equally daunting. Here again, RCA took the lead (Levy, 1981; Graham, 1986; Chandler, 2001). Systemic innovation of this sort was well suited to RCA's corporate research apparatus, which had grown in capability through war-related research as well as commercial TV research. Once again, RCA's owner-ship of NBC reduced the coordination costs of launching a product with substantial network effects. But, as happened in the battle of the speeds, CBS quickly emerged as formidable competitor, having since added tube manufacture to its portfolio of broadcasting, records, set assembly and corporate research (Graham, 1986, p. 61). In 1947, Goldmark petitioned the FCC to approve a partially mechanical system that CBS had been tin-kering with since before the war. RCA was at work on a fully electronic system compatible with the existing black-and-white standard, but the company could not work out the bugs fast enough to forestall FCC approval of the CBS system in 1951. Unfortunately for CBS, however, the Korean War put a hold on production of color (but not black-and-white) technology. By war's end, growth in black-and-white sales had made compatibility a bigger issue; moreover, the likes of Zenith, Philco, and Philips much preferred an all-electronic system.

RCA earned the imprimatur of the NTSC, and CBS slunk off to concen-trate on broadcasting and records. But the technology remained expen-sive and finicky. RCA was forced to absorb high overheads in research and production, and at NBC, overheads on which competitors chose to free ride until color reached its tipping point. Unsurprisingly, the rate of penetration of color TV was much slower than that of black-and-white: Five years after introduction, only half a percent of American homes had a color set; ten years after, only 2.9 percent did (Levy, 1981, p. 115). Nonetheless, RCA was eventually able to capture rents from color TV through the production of sets, the sale of picture tubes (of which it was

---

[18] Klepper and Simons (2000) also show that almost all the producers who survived the shakeout tended to be those with prior experience in radio.

initially the sole producer), and the broadcasting of color programs by NBC.[19]

So far, we have seen evidence to support Chandler's insistence on the importance of integrated capability building in large research-equipped multidivisional firms. Both the monochrome and the color TV – if not, however, the radio – were systemic innovations well suited to early development through strong corporate research; and all three technologies partook of network externalities that could be partly internalized in an integrated structure. But we have also seen evidence of the importance to technical advance of vibrant competition and of innovation at the level of suppliers.

The Demise of American Consumer Electronics

The major integrated firms, notably RCA and Zenith, continued to provide most of the product innovations in television through the 1970s (Klepper and Simons, 1997, p. 421), though much process innovation came from suppliers and from advances elsewhere in electronics, like the wave-soldering techniques developed in connection with military applications (Levy, 1981, pp. 64ff; Klepper and Simons, 1997, p. 428). As the technology of television, including color television, began to mature in the 1960s and 1970s, RCA's rents from production of color picture tubes began to decline as other firms entered tube production, and NBC's early lead in color programming dissipated as all three networks began broadcasting almost entirely in color. Advantage began to shift to those who could produce receivers cheaply. And that increasingly meant foreign, especially Japanese, firms. (See Figure 4.2.)

With the exception of Sony, which pursued a strategy of product innovation akin to that of American firms like RCA and Zenith, most Japanese firms entered the American market as low-cost producers dependent on American technology, notably that of RCA (Levy, 1981, p. 97). They concentrated on black-and-white sets, portable sets, and private-label production for retailers like Sears, eventually moving up to higher-end branded products. Figure 4.2 understates the penetration of foreign firms into the American market, as many "American" producers – indeed half of all American producers in 1979 (Levy, 1981, p. 82) – were actually

---

[19] The 1958 antitrust consent decree limited RCA's ability to collect rents from color TV patents, as these became subject to a patent pool in which all comers could dip for free so long as they tossed in some of their own patents (Levy, 1981, p. 159).

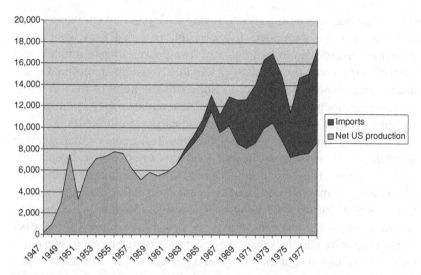

Figure 4.2. Net U.S. production and imports of television receivers, 1947-78 (thousands of units.) *Note:* U.S. production includes units manufactured in the U.S. by foreign-owned firms. (*Source:* Levy, 1981, p. 99).

subsidiaries of foreign (mostly Japanese) firms.[20] By 1971, Sony had set up an assembly plant in California, with a picture-tube plant to follow in 1974. In the same decade, Sharp and Hitachi also set up *de novo* American facilities. Meanwhile, many existing American producers were gobbled up by foreigners. In 1974, Matsushita bought Motorola's television business. In the same year, Philips acquired Magnavox and by 1981 had picked up the remnants of Philco and Sylvania. In 1976, Sanyo formalized its growing hold on Sears's Original Equipment Manufacturer (OEM) business by buying out Warwick, which had been Sears's American assembler. In 1986, the mighty RCA sold its television operations (including NBC) to its quondam parent GE, which promptly swapped the electronics part for the medical-technology business of France's Thomson. Zenith, the last domino, fell in the early 1990s (Perry, 1988).

Why? Chandler (2001) lays great stress on the strategic mistakes. RCA (and other integrated American firms) strayed from the virtuous strategy of technological development and related diversification that would have maintained paths of learning on which they had originally embarked. Instead, they succumbed to the temptation of conglomerate

---

[20] The remainder of this paragraph draws on Levy (1981, pp. 109-10) and Chandler (2001, pp. 44-7).

diversification, thus ultimately destroying the integrated knowledge base on which success depended. It is certainly true that RCA went in for unrelated diversification in a big way. The process began under David Sarnoff in 1966 with the purchase of Random House and continued apace after the accession of David's son Robert to the helm of RCA in 1968. Acquisitions included golf equipment, car rental, paper manufacture, frozen food, real estate development, and carpet manufacture.

Economists tend to be less inclined than historians or management scholars to see strategy as an independent causative force, especially when all firms in the environment seem to be adopting the same one. The strategy of massive unrelated diversification in this reading is merely the proximate rather than the ultimate cause. As Michael Jensen (1986) taught us, unrelated diversification is one possible symptom of "free cash flow," corporate windfalls that allow managers to pursue their own interests and visions without the short-run discipline of product markets and financial markets. Although it is not often remarked on, the heyday of the large American multidivisional firm coincided with a period of relative economic isolation. The Depression, tariffs, and wars of the first half of the twentieth century constitute what economic historians now see as a massive collapse of nineteenth-century globalization (James, 2001; Bordo et al., 2003). And with the destruction of the German, Japanese, and other economies in World War II, that isolation continued for the better part of two decades. In a general sense, then, the postwar golden age of the large multidivisional American firm was one in which competition was relatively relaxed by later globalized standards – and in which managers found themselves with sources of free cash flow. The resulting (relatively) slack environment not only encouraged diversification (as Chandler insists), but also reinforced the multidivisional form itself, a form of which unrelated diversification is the logical if extreme extension, and isolated that form from economic realities to which it was increasingly ill-adapted (Langlois, 2003, pp. 370–1).

In the case of RCA, as we saw, free cash flow came importantly from patent licensing. In addition, government, especially military, contracts propped up RCA's research laboratories, thus increasingly insulating them from contact with the market. Both the postwar federal research climate and RCA's own addiction to patent royalties moved the labs in the direction of more basic research (Graham, 1986, pp. 68–71). Sarnoff believed that profit lay in continuing RCA's founding strategy of staying abreast of – or ahead of – all knowledge in electronics. Thus came RCA's ultimately disastrous foray into digital computers.

As Adam Smith might have predicted, however, this strategy would become increasingly problematic as both the extent of such knowledge and the extent of the market expanded after World War II. As technological leaders in electronics, American firms found themselves with a broad menu of product and process options. And, because of the ultimate limit of capabilities within even a large organization, those firms became the prey of competitors who could pick off and specialize in pieces of technology or market. However valuable the integration-cum-research structure had been in the generation of systemic innovations like television, it became a liability in a globalizing world that could take advantage of outsourcing, low-cost production abroad and withal the option value of increasingly mature and thus relatively modular technology. Moreover, for Japan in particular, specialization in production led to the creation of technological, organizational, and institutional approaches (notably in miniaturized electronic and electromechanical devices) that constituted a kind of general-purpose technology that could be applied to newly emerging devices like video-tape and optical-disk storage peripherals. Importantly, as we will see again presently, the diffuse focus of American systems houses like RCA, GE, and Philco made it difficult for them to compete with specialized American firms in the fabrication of semiconductor devices and with Japanese firms in the incorporation of such devices into electronic systems (Klepper and Simons, 1997, p. 421).

DIGITAL TECHNOLOGY

Even though semiconductors and computers were born in the years immediately following the Second World War, their institutional origins were quite different. The invention of the computer involved both universities and direct government research funding. By contrast, the transistor, the basic building block of the semiconductor industry, emerged from private research at AT&T's Bell Labs. Because of its success and its secure status as the nation's telephone monopoly, AT&T was able to pursue a policy of research that, although arguably more focused toward commercial ends than basic research at universities, was nonetheless willing to indulge basic science and to envisage a research agenda quite far from commercial fruition.[21]

---

[21] For a classic account of how the research environment at Bell Labs led to the transistor, see Nelson (1962).

140   RICHARD N. LANGLOIS

The Transistor

More imminently, the Bell System was facing the long-run problem that had motivated the acquisition of the de Forest vacuum-tube patent: the difficulty of expanding a switching system based on electromechanical relays. By the 1930s, Mervin Kelly, the research director at Bell Labs, was voicing the opinion that electromechanical relays would eventually have to be replaced by an electronic alternative in order to handle the growing volume of traffic. William Shockley, one of the three Bell scientists to receive the Nobel Prize for the transistor, was impressed by this observation, and believed that the objective would be best realized with solid-state technology.

Bell Labs announced the invention of the transistor in December, 1947.[22] Almost immediately, transistor technology began spilling out to other firms. This was not, however, a process in which slippery knowledge leaked unintended to others, but rather a deliberate and systematic attempt by AT&T to disseminate know-how through inexpensive licenses, technical symposia, and site visits (Tilton, 1971, pp. 75–6; Braun and Macdonald, 1982, pp. 54–5). The main driver of this policy was the consent decree AT&T had just signed with the Antitrust Division of the U.S. Justice Department, which specified how the company was to treat technology outside the scope of the company's primary mission.[23] But there is also reason to think that AT&T pursued a strategy of dissemination because, like RCA in the case of color television, the company saw profit in the widespread adoption of the technology. AT&T was still primarily concerned with the usefulness of transistors to its own line of business, telephone switching. The company believed that if it allowed access to the transistor, telephony would reap the benefits of spillovers from the development of the capabilities of others in the electronics industry to an extent that would outweigh the foregone revenues of proprietary development[24] (McHugh, 1949; Bello, 1953; Braun and Macdonald, 1982, p. 54; Levin, 1982, pp. 76–7).

[22] For detailed histories of the invention of the transistor, see Braun and Macdonald (1982), Morris (1990), and Nelson (1962).

[23] AT&T's strategy of dissemination may also have been motivated in part by a desire to preempt any thought the military might have had of classifying the technology (Levin, 1982, p. 58).

[24] An AT&T vice president put it this way: "We realized that if this thing [the transistor] was as big as we thought, we couldn't keep it to ourselves and we couldn't make all the technical contributions. It was to our interest to spread it around. If you cast your bread on the water, sometimes it comes back angel food cake." Quotation attributed to Jack Morton, in "The Improbable Years," *Electronics, 41, 81* (February 19, 1968), quoted in Tilton (1971, pp. 75–6).

Unlike the triode vacuum tube, which had been entangled in patent litigation and then formed part of RCA's onerous package licensing, the transistor became easily available at relatively low royalties. The result was a large cohort of entrants (Mowery and Steinmueller, 1994). Existing producers of vacuum tubes, as well as Bell Labs itself, continued to be major sources of transistor innovations through the 1950s, especially in the realm of process and materials. The work of this period ultimately led to a pivotal innovation that allowed for rapid experience-based improvements and cost reductions: the *planar process*, a development responsible for the increasing-returns trajectory on which the semiconductor industry now finds itself. Notably, the planar process was not developed by Bell Labs or by any of the established vacuum-tube firms. Instead, in what would become a pattern characteristic of the American semiconductor industry, the new approach was developed by a small start-up organization.

Among the many Bell Labs researchers who had struck out on their own in the 1950s was Shockley, who returned home to the San Francisco peninsula to found Shockley Semiconductor Laboratories. Apparently prompted by dissatisfaction with the company's orientation toward product breakthroughs at the neglect of the commercially richer area of process technology (Braun and Macdonald, 1982, p. 84; Holbrook, 1999), eight of Shockley's team defected in 1957, and, with the backing of Long Island entrepreneur Sherman Fairchild, founded the semiconductor division of Fairchild Camera and Instrument Corporation. The Fairchild group mounted an ambitious plan to produce silicon mesa transistors using technology developed at Bell Labs (Malone, 1985, p. 88; Lydon and Bambrick, 1987, p. 6). In attempting to overcome some of the limitations of this transistor design, one of the eight defectors, Jean Hoerni, found a way to create a device by building up layers on a flat surface – a "planar" device (Dummer, 1978, p. 143; Braun and Macdonald 1982, p. 85; Morris, 1990, p. 38). The planar structure made it easy for Fairchild to devise a way to replace the mesa's clumsy wires with metal contacts deposited on the surface.

By 1961, two Americans, Robert Noyce of Fairchild and Jack Kilby of Texas Instruments (TI), had created prototypical integrated circuits (ICs).[25] Unlike Kilby, who had started with the monolithic idea and then sought to solve the problem of fabrication and interconnection, Noyce began with a process for fabrication and metallic interconnection – the

---

[25] The idea of the integrated circuit was probably first propounded in 1952 by G. W. A. Dummer of the British Royal Radar Establishment (Braun and Macdonald, 1982, p. 108).

planar process – and moved easily from that to the idea of the integrated circuit. Under pressure from the industry, TI and Fairchild forged a cross-licensing agreement in 1966 under which each company agreed to grant licenses to all comers in the range of 2–4 percent of IC profits (Reid, 1984, pp. 94–5). This practice served to reproduce and extend the technology-licensing policies of AT&T, again broadly diffusing the core technological innovation to all entrants and thereby reasserting the principle that innovative rents should flow to those who could commercialize and improve on the key innovation.

As important as the innovation of the IC was, the planar process is the more important technological breakthrough, not merely because it underlay the IC but because it provided the paradigm or technological trajectory the industry was to follow.[26] By either etching away minute areas or building up regions using other materials, semiconductor fabrication alters the chemical properties of a "wafer," a crystal of silicon. Each wafer produces many ICs, and each IC contains many transistors. The most dramatic economic feature of IC production is the increase in the number of transistors that can be fabricated in a single IC. Transistor counts per IC increased from 10 to 4,000 in the first decade of the industry's history; from 4,000 to over 500,000 in the second decade; and from 500,000 to 100 million in the third decade. The ten-million-fold increase in the number of transistors per IC has been accompanied by only modest increases in the cost of processing of a wafer and almost no change in the average costs of processing the individual IC. This factor alone has been responsible for the enormous cost reduction in electronic circuitry since the birth of the IC. Electronic systems comparable in complexity to vacuum-tube or transistor systems costing millions of dollars can be constructed for a few hundred dollars, a magnitude of cost reduction that it is virtually unprecedented in the history of manufacturing. The cheapness of electronic functions has reduced the costs of electronic systems relative to mechanical ones and lowered the relative price of electronic goods in general – developments that have had a major effect on the industrial structure of the electronics and IC industries.

Langlois and Steinmueller (1999) have pointed to the critical role of end-use demand in shaping industrial structure and competitive advantage in the worldwide semiconductor industry throughout its history. In the early years, demand in the United States came first from military sources and then, importantly, from the computer industry. Government

---

[26] Canonical sources here are Abernathy and Utterback (1978) and Utterback (1979).

procurement demand proved valuable to the development of the industry not only because of its extent, but also because of the military's relative price insensitivity and insistence on reliability (Dosi, 1984). Commercial demand eventually grew more rapidly than military, however, and, by the mid-1970s, government consumption had declined to less than 10 percent of the market (Kraus, 1971, p. 91).

The American government also pushed the development of the transistor and the IC through support of R&D and related projects. Scholarship on the subject is essentially unanimous that this activity was far less important for, and less salutary to, the industry than was the government's procurement role. All the major breakthroughs in transistors were developed privately with the military market (among others) in mind. And, although the government tended to favor R&D contracts with established suppliers, notably old-line systems houses like RCA, it *bought* far more from newer specialized semiconductor producers (Tilton, 1971, p. 91). The pragmatic policy of awarding work to those firms that could meet supply requirements was particularly important for encouraging new entry.

A significant feature of the transition to the IC was the virtual disappearance of those vertically integrated American electronics companies that had led in the production of vacuum tubes. Although these firms had been able to stay in the race during the era of discrete transistors, their market shares began to plummet in the era of the integrated circuit. Why? Wilson et al. (1980) point out that the new leaders were either specialized startups or multidivisional firms (like TI, Fairchild, and Motorola) in which the semiconductor division dominated overall corporate strategy and in which semiconductor operations absorbed a significant portion of the attention of central management. By contrast, the semiconductor divisions of the integrated system firms were a small part of corporate sales and of corporate strategy, thereby attracting a smaller portion of managerial attention and receiving less autonomy.

The Digital Computer

The history of the digital computer has much in common with that of semiconductor technology, even if there are a number of important differences. Like the transistor, the digital computer was developed with a specific bottleneck in mind. But, unlike the transistor, the digital computer was developed not privately but at universities, with explicit government subsidy from the start.

During World War II, the U.S. Army contracted with J. Presper Eckert and John W. Mauchly of the Moore School at the University of Pennsylvania for a device "designed expressly for the solution of ballistics problems and for the printing of range tables"[27] (Stern, 1981, p. 15). By November 1945, they had produced the Electronic Numerical Integrator and Computer (ENIAC), the first fully operational all-electronic digital computer – a behemoth occupying 1,800 square feet, boasting 18,000 tubes, and consuming 174 kilowatts of electricity. Universities continued to play an important role throughout the early life of the technology, helping to create the wholly new discipline of computer science. Indeed, Rosenberg and Nelson go so far as to call the computer "the most remarkable contribution of American universities to the last half of the twentieth century" (1994, p. 331).

Government, especially military, support for the computer remained significant throughout the 1950s, and government funding helped spur important technical developments like ferrite-core memory, which emerged from the military-funded Whirlwind project at MIT (Redmond and Smith, 1980; Pugh, 1984). But, as Bresnahan and Malerba (1999, pp. 89–90) argue, government research support had little to do with the success of the *commercial* computer industry. Moreover, much of government policy, notably in the areas of R&D funding and antitrust, was actually aimed at *forestalling* the emergence of IBM as a dominant "national champion" in computers. As in semiconductors, however, the military's pragmatic approach to procurement favored those firms who could deliver the goods, and in computers that meant IBM (Usselman, 1993; Bresnahan and Malerba, 1999, p. 90).

By the mid-1960s, however, IBM found itself riding herd on a multiplicity of physically incompatible systems – the various 700-series and the 1400-series computers, among others – each aimed at a different use. Relatedly, and more significantly, software was becoming a serious bottleneck. By one estimate, the contribution of software to the value of a computer system had grown from 8 percent in the early days to something like 40 percent by the 1960s (Ferguson and Morris, 1993, p. 7). Writing software for so many incompatible systems greatly compounded the problem. In what *Fortune* magazine called "the most crucial and portentous – as well as perhaps the riskiest – business judgment of recent times," IBM decided to "bet the company" on a new line of computers

---

[27] The end of the war reduced the urgency of this goal, and the first major task given the ENIAC was actually to perform calculations for the development of the hydrogen bomb (Stern, 1981, p. 62).

called the 360 series. The name meant to refer all the points of the compass, for the strategy behind the 360 was to replace the diverse and incompatible systems with a single modular family of computers (Flamm, 1988, pp. 96–9). Instead of having one computer aimed at scientific applications, a second aimed at accounting applications, and so forth, the company would make one machine for all uses. This was not to be a homogeneous or undifferentiated product; but it was to provide a framework in which product differentiation could take place while retaining compatibility.

As Timothy Bresnahan suggests, the 360 was the first major computer *platform*, by which he means "a shared, stable set of hardware, software, and networking technologies on which users build and run computer applications" (Bresnahan, 1999, p. 159). To put it another way, the 360 was a *modular system*, albeit one that remained mostly closed and proprietary despite the efforts of the "plug compatible" industry to pick away at its parts. Carliss Baldwin (2006a, 2006b) argues that IBM never understood the tremendous option value implied in the 360 architecture. Had the company opened the architecture up to the market while retaining control of key bottlenecks in the system, they could have created considerably more value.

As the market for computers picked up speed, the symbiosis between computers and semiconductors became stronger: Competition among computer makers drove the demand for ICs, which lowered IC prices by moving suppliers faster down their learning curves, which in turn fed back on the price of computers, and so forth. The result was a self-reinforcing process of growth for both industries. Indeed, the falling prices of semiconductor logic fueled a second computer revolution, that of the minicomputer. Minicomputers were smaller than mainframes and geared toward specialized scientific and engineering uses. Digital Equipment Corporation (DEC), founded in 1957, was the pioneer in the field. Among the other firms to enter the minicomputer market were Scientific Data Systems, Data General (founded in 1968 by defectors from DEC), Prime Computer, Hewlett-Packard, Wang, and Tandem (Flamm, 1988, p. 131).

Japanese Challenge and American Resurgence

Japan had responded to the American competitive advantage with high tariffs, and in addition imposed quotas and registration requirements[28]

---

[28] This is in contrast to European policy, which featured high tariffs but no prohibition on foreign direct investment. As a result, much of the European demand for semiconductors

(Tyson and Yoffie, 1993, p. 37). The Japanese government essentially forbade foreign direct investment, which forced American firms to tap the Japanese market only through licensing and technology sales to Japanese firms rather than through direct investment.

In Japan, the principal producers of transistors in the 1950s and 1960s were diversified systems houses, including firms that had previously produced vacuum tubes, rather than companies that principally specialized in semiconductors. Moreover, the main end use for transistors in Japan was consumer products rather than the military. The Japanese vacuum-tube firms were much smaller than their American or European counterparts at the beginning of the transistor era. As Tilton (1971, p. 154) notes, the small size and rapid growth of the Japanese firms "also helped create a receptive attitude toward change on the part of the [Japanese] receiving tube producers by reducing the risks associated with new products and new technologies and by increasing costs, in terms of declining market shares, to firms content simply to maintain the status quo." In many ways, then, Japanese systems firms faced many of the same constraints, and adopted many of the same approaches, as the aggressive American merchant firms rather than those of the American systems houses. The Japanese also sought licenses primarily from the American merchants rather than from the American systems firms.

Despite their early success in transistors, Japanese firms found themselves in a weak position by the 1970s. These firms were slow to make the transition to batch-produced silicon devices in the early 1960s, and, when they turned later in the decade to the production of bipolar ICs, they could not compete with the likes of Texas Instruments and National Semiconductor; some Japanese firms accused the Americans of "dumping" (Okimoto et al., 1984, pp. 14–15). After 1967, indeed, the purchase of American ICs created a Japanese trade deficit in semiconductors (Malerba, 1985, p. 136).

How did Japanese industry move from this weak position in the 1970s to its dominant position by the mid-1980s? Until recently, the tacit assumption of most commentators had been that Japanese success was the result of some combination of (1) Japanese industrial structure,

---

was satisfied by European subsidiaries of American companies. Japanese companies have typically supplied some 90 percent of the Japanese semiconductor market, whereas American firms – through imports or foreign direct investment – have supplied between 50 and 70 percent of the European market (Tyson and Yoffie, 1993, p. 34).

Table 4.2. Demand for Integrated Circuits by End-use Market, United States, Japan, and Western Europe, 1982 and 1985, in Percent

	United States		Japan		Western Europe	
End-use	1982	1985	1982	1985	1982	1985
Computer	40	45	22	36	25	20
Telecommunications	21	10	10	13	20	29
Industrial	11	10	17	6	25	19
Military and Aerospace	17	18	0	0	5	7
Consumer	11	16	51	45	25	25

Note: Includes captive consumption.
Source: OECD (1985).

understood as superior to American industrial structure in a very general or even absolute sense; and (2) Japanese industrial policy, understood as a highly intentional – and even prescient – system of government-industry planning and control. Langlois and Steinmueller (1999) suggest a somewhat different picture. Although both industrial structure and government policy played important roles in the rise of the Japanese semiconductor industry, the benefits of that industrial structure were far less timeless than commentators supposed, and the effects of government policy were far less intentional, and perhaps somewhat less significant, than the dominant accounts suggested.

As in the earlier rise of the American semiconductor industry, the pattern of end-use demand was crucial in shaping the bundle of capabilities that Japanese industry possessed, as well as in narrowing and limiting the choices the Japanese firms had open to them. In this case, that end-use demand came largely from consumer electronics and, to a somewhat lesser extent, from telecommunications, especially purchases by NTT, Japan's national telephone monopoly. (See Table 4.2.) Consumer demand helped place the Japanese on a product trajectory – namely MOS and especially CMOS ICs – that turned out eventually to have much wider applicability.[29] Moreover, Japanese firms adopted a strategy of specialization in high-volume production of one particular kind of chip. The DRAM, or dynamic random-access memory chip, is a technology that benefited from increasing returns to scale not only because of the volume effects of mass production but also because it is arguably a

[29] MOS stands for metal-oxide semiconductor and CMOS for complementary MOS.

Table 4.3. Maximum Market Share in
DRAMs by American and Japanese
Companies, by Device

Device	Maximum Market Share (%)	
	United States	Japan
1K	95	5
4K	83	17
16K	59	41
64K	29	71
256K	8	92
1M	4	96
4M	2	98

Source: Dataquest, cited in Methé (1991, p. 69).

general-purpose technology of considerable importance – a device that can store digital information for a wide variety of purposes.[30]

Established American firms, accustomed to providing customized devices, were slow to recognize the cost-reduction advantages of a standardized memory chip (Wilson et al., 1980, p. 87). Two new firms – National and Intel – quickly gained advantage over their established competitors in the merchant market by moving more quickly into the production of high-volume standardized devices. Both firms were spin-offs from Fairchild – two of the first of what came to be called the "Fairchildren". In pushing standardized DRAM chips, however, these firms precipitated a "memory race" in which Japanese firms were eventually to prove dominant. American firms led in the early 1K and 4K DRAM markets. But an industry recession delayed the American "ramp-up" to the 16K DRAM, which appeared in 1976. Aided by unforeseen production problems among the three leaders, Japanese firms were able to gain a significant share of the 16K market. By mid-1979, sixteen companies were producing DRAMs, and Japanese producers accounted for 42 percent of the market (Wilson et al., 1980, pp. 93–4). (See Table 4.3.) The opportunity opened for Japanese producers in the 16K DRAM

[30] DRAMs are "dynamic" in the sense that the electric charges containing the remembered information decay over time and need periodically to be "refreshed." This stands in contrast to the static RAM (or SRAM), which does not require refreshing, but which therefore has disadvantages in size, cost, and power consumption because it requires more transistors per memory cell.

market had proven sufficient for them to advance to a position of leadership in the 64K DRAM. Japanese dominance accelerated in the 256K (1982) and 1-Mbit (1985) generations. Intense price competition, combined with the general recession in the U.S. industry in 1985, caused all but two American merchant IC companies to withdraw from DRAM production.[31] In 1990, American market share had fallen to only 2 percent of the new generation 4-Mbit DRAMs.[32] (See Table 4.3.)

Why did the Japanese succeed? In broad terms, circumstances had staked out for the Japanese industry a strategic path that fit well the existing competences of the firms - namely those in mass production and quality control - and supported the thrust of their final products, which, despite government efforts to create a computer industry, were still in consumer electronics and telecommunications.

Rather than feeling that they were on the verge of overtaking American companies, the Japanese saw their computer industry as relatively weak against IBM and perceived that a key feature of IBM's advantage was technology, specifically its position in ICs. From the viewpoint of Japanese firms, the American IC industry was enormously innovative but did not share much of the manufacturing culture that had developed in the larger Japanese electronics companies, where quality, systematic capacity expansion, and long-term market position were regarded as key variables to control. The fact that Japanese IC producers were large companies in comparison with their American counterparts gave them one particular advantage: They were able to mobilize internal capital resources to make investments in the IC industry in a way that U.S. companies could not.

James March (1991) has pointed out that there is a necessary trade-off between exploration and exploitation - a trade-off between searching for new ideas and running with the old ones. As the technology leaders, the American firms found themselves with a full plate of alternatives to pursue, in both product and process technology. Sitting somewhat behind the frontier, Japanese firms could pick one item off the plate and run with it. Their morsel was the mass production of DRAMs.

These events certainly did not go unnoticed by American industry and policy makers, and alarms went up as early as the 64K generation. More worrisome than the loss of the memory market was the possibility that

---

[31] The exceptions were Texas Instruments, which produced in Japan, and Micron Technology, which produced in Idaho.

[32] These figures do not take into account the sizable captive production at IBM and AT&T.

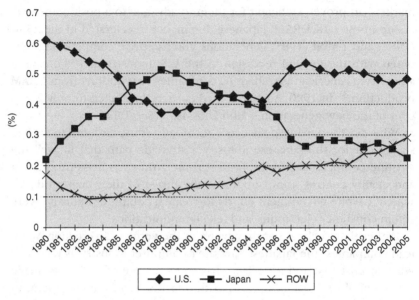

Figure 4.3. Worldwide semiconductor market shares (in percent), 1980–2005. (*Source:* Semiconductor Industry Association.)

Japanese dominance in DRAMs would be translated into equal success in other kinds of chips. Although memory chips constituted at most 30 percent of the IC market, many believed them to be "technology drivers" essential for continued progress in increasing the number of transistors on an IC. If American firms could not use DRAM production to develop and gain experience in the next generation of technology, then Japanese producers would soon be able to climb up the design-complexity ladder and challenge U.S. positions in logic markets (Ferguson, 1985; Forester, 1993).

In 1986, Japan's overall market share in semiconductors moved ahead of that of the American merchants. Thus in 1988 the U.S. industry appeared to stand on the brink of oblivion, with no haven in product or process that could be counted on to ensure its survival into the 1990s. But the predicted extinction never occurred. (See Figure 4.3.) Instead, American firms surged back during the 1990s, and it now seems that it is the Japanese who are embattled.

Langlois and Steinmueller (1999) argue that the American resurgence is not the result of imitating Japanese market structure and policy, but rather of taking good advantage of the distinctly American market structure and capabilities developed in the heyday of U.S. dominance.

Just as the innovation of, and the growing market for, the standardized DRAM had favored the Japanese, another semiconductor innovation and the burgeoning market it created came to favor the Americans. That innovation was the microprocessor, an integrated circuit
designed not to store information (like the DRAM) but rather to provide on a single chip the information-processing capability of a digital
computer.

In 1969, a Japanese manufacturer asked Intel to design the logic chips
for a new electronic calculator. Marcian E. ("Ted") Hoff, Jr., the engineer
in charge of the project, thought the Japanese design too complicated to
produce. The then-current approach to the design of calculators involved
the use of many specialized hardwired circuits to perform the various
calculator functions. Influenced by the von Neumann architecture of
minicomputers, Hoff reasoned that he could simplify the design enormously by creating a single, programmable IC rather than the set of
dedicated logic chips the Japanese had sought (Noyce and Hoff, 1981).
By using relatively simple general-purpose logic circuitry that relied
on programming information stored elsewhere, Hoff effectively substi-
tuted cheap memory (then Intel's major product) for relatively expensive special-purpose logic circuitry (Gilder, 1989, p. 103). The result
was the Intel 4004, the first microprocessor. A sixth of an inch long
and an eighth of an inch wide, the 4004 was roughly equivalent in
computational power to early vacuum-tube computers that filled an
entire room. It also matched the power of a 1960 IBM computer
whose central processing unit was about the size of a desk (Bylinsky,
1980, p. 7).

Intel gained an early lead in microprocessors that it never relin-
quished. Early on, Intel did not push patent protection, and, in Hoff's
view, "did not take the attitude that the microprocessor was something
that you could file a patent claim on that covers everything" (quoted in
Malone, 1985, p. 144). Because the microprocessor is a general-purpose
computer, there are many different ways to implement the microprocessor idea without infringing on a particular implementation. And the
appropriation of rents in microprocessors has always depended on first-
mover advantage, rather than on patent protection for particular features
of the system design or on the ability to produce a microprocessor that
could not be emulated technically.

The microprocessor found uses in a wide variety of applications
involving computation and computer control. But it did not make
inroads into the established mainframe or minicomputer industries,

largely because it did not initially offer the level of computing power these larger machines could generate using multiple logic chips. Instead, the microprocessor opened up the possibility of a wholly new kind of computer - the microcomputer.

The Personal Computer

The first personal computer (or microcomputer) is generally acknowledged to have been something called the MITS/Altair, which graced the cover of *Popular Electronics* magazine in January, 1975.[33] Essentially a microprocessor in a box, the machine's only input–output devices were lights and toggle switches on the front panel, and it came with a mere 256 bytes of memory. But the Altair was, at least potentially, a genuine computer. Its potential came largely from a crucial design decision: The machine incorporated a number of open "slots" that allowed for additional memory and other devices to be added later. These slots were hooked into the microprocessor by a network of wires called a "bus." This extremely modular approach emerged partly in emulation of the design of minicomputers and partly because hobbyists and the small firms supplying them would have been incapable of producing a desirable (i.e., more-capable) nonmodular machine within any reasonable time. In effect, the hobbyist community captured the machine and made it a truly open modular system. The first clone of the Altair - the IMSAI 8080 - appeared within a matter of months, and soon the Altair's architecture became an industry standard, eventually known as the S-100 bus because of its 100-line structure.

The S-100 standard dominated the hobbyist world. But the machine that took the microcomputer into the business world adopted a distinctive architecture, built around a Motorola rather than an Intel microprocessor. Stephen Wozniak and Steven Jobs had started Apple Computer in 1976, quite literally in the garage of Jobs's parent's house. The hobbyist Wozniak, also influenced by the architecture of minicomputers, insisted that the Apple be an expandable system - with slots - and that technical details be freely available to users and third-party suppliers. With the development of word processors like WordStar, database managers like dBase II, and spreadsheets like VisiCalc, the machine became a tool of writers, professionals, and small businesses. Apple took in three-quarters

---

[33] For a much longer and better-documented history of the microcomputer, see Langlois (1992), on which this section draws.

of a million dollars by the end of fiscal 1977; $8 million in 1978; $48 million in 1979; $117 million in 1980 (when the firm went public); $335 million in 1981; $583 million in 1982; and $983 million in 1983.[34]

Existing computer companies were slow to develop competing microcomputers, largely because they saw the machines as a small fringe market. But as business uses increased and microcomputer sales rose, some computer makers saw the opportunity to get a foothold in a market that was complementary to, albeit much smaller than, their existing product lines.[35] By far the most significant entry was that of IBM. On August 12, 1981, IBM introduced the computer that would become the paradigm for most of the 1980s.

In a radical departure, IBM decided to produce the machine outside the control of company procurement policies and practices. Philip Donald Estridge, a director of the project, later put it this way. "We were allowed to develop like a startup company. IBM acted as a venture capitalist. It gave us management guidance, money, and allowed us to operate on our own" (*Business Week*, October 3, 1983, p. 86). Estridge knew that, to meet the deadline he had been given, IBM would have to make heavy use of outside vendors for parts and software. The owner of an Apple II, Estridge was also impressed by the importance of expandability and an open architecture. He insisted that his designers use a modular bus system that would allow expandability, and he resisted all suggestions that the IBM team design any of its own add-ons. Because the machine used the Intel 8088 instead of the 8080, IBM needed a new operating system. A tiny Seattle company called Microsoft agreed to produce such an operating system, which they bought from another small Seattle company and rechristened MS-DOS, for Microsoft Disk Operating System.

The IBM PC was an instant success, exceeding sales forecasts by some 500 percent. By 1983, the PC had captured 26 percent of the market, and an estimated 750,000 machines were installed by the end of that year. The IBM standard largely drove out competing alternatives during the decade of the 1980s. This happened in part because of the strength of the IBM name in generating network effects, principally

---

[34] Data from Apple Computer, cited in "John Sculley at Apple Computer (B)," Harvard Business School Case No. 9-486-002, revised May 1987, p. 26.

[35] Few people inside or outside IBM foresaw the sweeping changes the PC would make in computer markets. In April 1981, four months before the official announcement of the IBM PC, IBM gave presentations estimating it would sell 241,683 PCs over five years. In fact, IBM shipped 250,000 PCs in one month alone (Zimmerman and Dicarlo, 1999).

because it created the expectation among users that the key vendor would continue to provide services long into the future and that a wide array of complementary devices and software would rapidly become available. But in large measure, the "tipping" of the market to the IBM PC standard was a result of the openness of the IBM system, which could be easily copied by others, and the eagerness of Microsoft to license MS-DOS to all comers.

As it had with the 360/370 series, IBM had created a dominant computer platform. But in the case of the PC, the dominance of the platform would not translate into a dominant market share for IBM. Because of the strategy of outsourcing and the standards it necessitated, others could easily imitate the IBM hardware, in the sense that any would-be maker of computers could obtain industry-standard modular components and compete with IBM. A legion of clones appeared that offered IBM compatibility at, usually, a price lower than what IBM charged. By 1986, more than half of the IBM-compatible computers sold did not have IBM logos on them. By 1988, IBM's worldwide market share of IBM-compatible computers was only 24.5 percent. IBM's choice of an open modular system was a two-edged sword that gave the company a majority stake in a standard that had grown well beyond its control. For reasons that are debated in the literature, but that likely have to do both with strategic mistakes by IBM and with the inherently strong positions of key suppliers in controlling their proprietary "bottleneck" technologies – the microprocessor and the operating system – Intel and Microsoft gained control of the standard that IBM had originally sponsored (Ferguson and Morris, 1993). The PC architecture is now often referred to as the "Wintel" (Windows–Intel) platform.

Langlois (1992) has argued that the rapid quality-adjusted price decline in microcomputers resulted not only from the declining price of computing power attendant on successive generations of Intel processors, but also from the vibrant competition and innovation at the level of hardware components and applications software that resulted from the open modular design of the PC. A decentralized and fragmented system can have advantages in innovation to the extent that it involves the sampling of many alternative approaches simultaneously, leading to rapid trial-and-error learning. This kind of innovation is especially important when technology is changing rapidly and there is a high degree of both technological and market uncertainty (Nelson and Winter, 1977). Moreover, the microcomputer benefited from technological convergence, in that it turned out to be a technology capable of taking over tasks that had previously required numerous distinct – and more expensive – pieces of physical and human capital. By the early 1980s, a microcomputer costing $3,500 could do the work of a $10,000 stand-alone word processor, while at the same time keeping track of the books like a $100,000 minicomputer and amusing the kids with space aliens like a 25-cents-a-game arcade machine.

The personal computer grew rapidly in a niche that existing mainframes and minicomputers had never filled. Quickly, however, the microcomputer's niche began to expand to encroach on the territory of its larger rivals, driven by the rapidly increasing densities and decreasing prices of memory chips and microprocessors. In the early 1980s, a class of desktop machines called workstations arose to challenge the dominance of the minicomputer in scientific and technical applications. As in the case of personal computers, the workstation market was driven by open technical standards and competition within the framework of what was largely a modular system (Garud and Kumaraswamy, 1993; Baldwin and Clark, 1997). Initially, these workstations used microprocessors and operating systems different from those of personal computers.[36] By the early 1990s, however, the same process of increasing power and decreasing cost began pushing the Windows–Intel platform into what is today a dominance of the workstation space. At the same time, workstations hooked together (or hooked to personal computers) began to take over many of the functions of larger minicomputers and mainframes. By the 1990s, networks of fast, cheap, smaller machines were widespread, a development accelerated by the spectacular growth of the Internet.[37] This growth had a significant negative effect on the makers of larger computers, notably the Boston-area minicomputer makers. Many went bankrupt; and, in a telling development, the flagship maker of minicomputers – DEC – was acquired by Compaq, a maker of microcomputers. Bresnahan and Greenstein (1996, 1997) refer to this encroachment of smaller computers as the "competitive crash" of large-scale computing.

---

[36] So-called traditional workstations are built around Reduced-Instruction-Set-Computing (RISC) microprocessors and run variants of the UNIX operating system. Intel-platform workstations use high-end versions of the same microprocessors used in personal computers and typically run Microsoft's Windows NT or Windows 2000, which are compatible with Microsoft's operating systems for personal computers.

[37] In some respects, the demand for large websites created by the Internet has spurred demand for large central servers. Increasingly, however, even these servers are frequently networks of high-powered personal computers rather than traditional mainframes or minicomputers.

Former Intel CEO Andy Grove (1996) has famously described the evolution of the computer industry as a transition from a structure of vertical "silos" in the days of IBM and DEC to a horizontal structure today. Once, large multidivisional firms undertook virtually all stages of production internally and captured rents at the level of the system. Nowadays, computers – and electronics more generally – are the product of multiple independent suppliers competing at every stage of production. Such competition drives down costs and spurs modular innovation (Langlois and Robertson, 1992). But, because of the PC's relatively open modular structure, the assembly of computer systems themselves is not an obvious source of economic rent, and few assemblers prospered in a consistent way. Compaq, which had gobbled up the remains of DEC, was itself eaten by Hewlett-Packard. Gateway, an early mail-order success, has flirted with bankruptcy. And, in late 2004, the originator of the IBM PC sold the entirety of its PC operations to Lenovo of China (Williams and Kallender, 2004). The one spectacular success has been Dell Computer, which has been able to use the modular structure of the personal computer to its advantage by making good use of the "external" capabilities of a worldwide network of suppliers (Curry and Kenney, 1999; Kraemer and Dedrick, 2002; Field, 2004). More than any other major producer, Dell has abandoned the traditional model of the integrated electronics firm in favor of what Baldwin and Clark (2006) call a *small-footprint strategy*. Dell's source of rents lies in not in any physical assets it owns, but rather in the way it organizes the PC value chain, including through its own innovative logistics system.

Among suppliers, a principal beneficiary of the rise of the personal computer was the American semiconductor industry. The abandonment of the DRAM market by most American firms – including Intel – was a dark cloud with a bright silver lining. When Intel led the world industry in almost all categories, it and many of its American counterparts faced a full plate of product alternatives. With the elimination of mass memory as a viable market, these firms were impelled to specialize and narrow their focus to a smaller subset of choices. The areas in which American firms concentrated can generally be described as higher-margin, design-intensive chips. For such chips, production costs would not be the sole margin of competition; innovation and responsiveness would count for more. Innovation and responsiveness were arguably the strong suit of the "fragmented" American industry. As in the case of the personal computer industry, the decentralized structure of the American semiconductor industry permitted the sampling of a wider diversity of

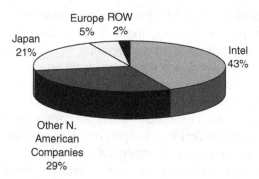

Figure 4.4. Production of MOS microprocessors and related devices in 1996 (percent). (*Source:* ICE, 1998).

approaches, leading to rapid trial-and-error learning (Nelson and Winter, 1977). And the independence of many firms from larger organizations permitted speedier realignment and recombination with suppliers and customers. Building on existing competences in design (especially of logic and specialty circuits) and close ties with the burgeoning American personal computer industry, American firms were able to prosper despite the Japanese edge in manufacturing technology (Ferguson and Morris, 1993).

The most important area of American specialization has been microprocessors and related devices.[38] Between 1988 and 1994, a period in which merchant IC revenues grew by 121 percent, revenues from the microprocessor segment grew much faster than did memory revenues (ICE, 1998). This evolution of the product mix in the industry has strongly favored American producers. In the microprocessor segment of the chip market, American companies accounted for 72 percent of world production in 1996 compared with a 21 percent share for Japanese companies. (See Figure 4.3.)

The importance of the microprocessor segment has meant that a single company, Intel, is responsible for much of the gain of American merchant IC producers. In 1996, Intel accounted for 43 percent of world output in the microprocessor segment. (See Figure 4.4.) Intel's strategy for recovery, begun in the 1980s, has proven remarkably successful (Afuah, 1999). In the late 1980s, the firm consolidated its intellectual-property

---

[38] This segment includes not only microprocessors but also microcontrollers (less-sophisticated microprocessors that are used in embedded applications) and related "support" chips, such as memory controllers, which are necessary for assembling a microprocessor system.

position in microprocessors by terminating cross-licensing agreements with other companies. More important, it also began extending its first-mover advantage over rivals by accelerating the rate of new product introduction. These developments pushed Intel into the position of the largest IC producer in the world, with 1998 revenues of $22.7 billion – more than those of the next three largest firms combined. Although Intel dominates the microprocessor market, it is not entirely without competitors; and it is significant that its principal competitors in microprocessors are also American companies, notably AMD and Motorola.

Another aspect of specialization that benefited the American industry was the increasing "decoupling" of design from production, a result in this case of growth in the extent of the market, which brought with it the development of computerized design tools (Hobday, 1991) and the standardization of manufacturing technology (Macher et al., 1998). On the one hand, this allowed American firms to specialize in design-intensive chips, taking advantage of a comparative advantage that arguably arises out of the decentralized and "fragmented" structure of American industry.[39] On the other hand, it also allowed many American firms to take advantage of growing production capabilities overseas. This "modularization" of the semiconductor industry is spurring the kind of decentralized innovation from which the personal computer industry has benefited.

Another area in which American suppliers have prospered is, of course, software, with Microsoft sitting prominently on at least one critical bottleneck. Effectively, the personal computer relies for its modular structure on three major technological standards. One involves the microprocessor, for which, as we saw, Intel (and now AMD) controls the standard. Another involves the architecture of the bus, along which the various pieces of the computer communicate with one another; this is in the public domain, shepherded by a committee of an industry trade group. And the third standard is the operating system, which regulates how the hardware communicates with the higher-level (or "applications") software that yields the services consumers ultimately demand. Here, Microsoft came to earn significant rents as first MS-DOS, and then the Windows operating system, over whose underlying code

---

[39] Perhaps surprisingly, the mid-1980s – that dark period for American fortunes – was actually, by a large margin, the most fertile period in history for the startup of new semiconductor firms. Most of these new firms were involved in design-intensive custom devices and ASICs (Angel, 1994, p. 38).

Microsoft owns copyright, became the dominant technical standard. American firms also remain strong in other key segments of the value chain, including disk drives (Kraemer and Dedrick, 2002). And, although PC production takes place in a global network of suppliers (Angel and Engstrom, 1995), American firms have in general retained those aspects of the production process requiring high skill levels and paying high wages (Dedrick and Kraemer, 2007, p. 22).

CONVERGENCE AND CONCLUSION

By the mid-1980s, by most accounts, America had "lost" consumer electronics and was in imminent danger of losing semiconductors and computers.[40] Contemporary analysis ran within Chandlerian channels. Innovation and production both necessarily emanate from large multidivisional firms. The leading American versions of these had either failed (RCA) or were embattled (IBM), while Japan's large multidivisional firms were on the ascendant. Ultimate reasons were sought in the realms of culture and government policy. If organization had a lesson, it was that American firms should become more like Japanese firms.

As it has a habit of doing, however, history failed to conform to predicted trends. The most striking development at the end of the electronic century was the convergence of consumer electronics into digital technology. As we saw, digital technology proceeded in important respects within an open modular framework in which specialized American players were often better positioned than large multidivisional firms to capture pieces of value. As digital technology developed, its various strands began to converge and to encompass what had been consumer electronics. Coupled to the Internet and cellular communications networks, the microprocessor has become the focal point for the generation and transmission not only of "data" (as we used to understand that term) but also of voice, music, text, and video. Sometimes, the microprocessor lies within a conventional personal computer; but increasingly it is the core of a device that combines the functions of a handheld computer, a phone, a camera, a music player, an arcade game, and even a video player.

The network that produces such devices, their components, and the attendant software (now increasingly broadly understood) is genuinely international, with significant players in Japan, Korea, Europe, and elsewhere, notably China. But whereas Japan was the hotbed of innovation

---

[40] And maybe even software (Cusumano, 1991).

in consumer electronics in the 1970s and 1980s – video-tape recorders and cameras, optical disks, and miniaturized devices like the Sony Walkman – by century's end, the United States had regained a significant measure of its stature in that field. At the turn of the millennium, Apple's iPod was arguably the signature device in converged digital consumer electronics.

What does all this imply? Paths of learning are not thoroughfares excavated by large multidivisional firms with entourage in train. They have always been, and are perhaps increasingly, trails beaten out by a variety of specialists working in cooperation and competition. The Chandlerian model works well for producing systemic innovations in their early stages (television was a prime example) and occasionally for generating fundamental new ideas (like the transistor). But many, if not most, important developments – from the vacuum tube to the planar process, from the radio to the personal computer – were the product of specialists within the network. (The digital computer was the product of a special kind of specialist, the university.) Moreover, by taking advantage of a range of capabilities far wider than the boundaries of what even the largest firm can encompass, a network of specialist suppliers and competitors is better able to exploit the value of a complex and potentially modular product architecture.

REFERENCES

Abernathy, W. J., & Utterback, J. (1978). Patterns of industrial innovation. *Technology Review*, June/July, *41*(80), 40-7.

Afuah, A. (1999). Strategies to turn adversity into profits. *Sloan Management Review, 40* (Winter), 99-109.

Aitken, H. G. J. (1985). *The continuous wave: Technology and American radio, 1900-32*. Princeton, NJ: Princeton University Press.

Angel, D. P. (1994). *Restructuring for innovation: The remaking of the U.S. semiconductor industry*. New York: Guilford Press.

Angel, D. P., & Engstrom, J. (1995). Manufacturing systems and technological change: The U.S. personal computer industry. *Economic Geography, 71*(1), 79-102.

Baldwin, C. Y. (2006a). *Architecture, modularity and unmanageable designs*. Paper presented at the Academy of Management Annual Meeting, Atlanta, GA.

Baldwin, C. Y. (2006b). *Unmanageable designs: What some designs need from the economy and how they get it*. Paper presented at the Academy of Management Annual Meeting, Atlanta, GA.

Baldwin, C. Y., & Clark, K. B. (1997). Sun wars – Competition within a modular cluster. In D. B. Yoffie (Ed.), *Competing in the age of digital convergence*. Boston: Harvard Business School Press.

Baldwin, C. Y., & Clark, K. B. (2000). *Design rules: The power of modularity* (Volume 1). Cambridge: MIT Press.

Baldwin, C. Y., & Clark, K. B. (2006). *Architectural innovation and dynamic competition: The smaller "footprint"* strategy (HBS Working Paper No. 07-014). Boston: Harvard Business School.

Bashe, C. J., Johnson, L. R., Palmer, J. H., & Pugh, E. W. (1986. *IBM's early computers*. Cambridge, MA: MIT Press.

Bello, F. (1953). The year of the transistor. *Fortune*, March, *50*, pp. 128-58.

Bordo, M. D., Taylor, A. M., & Williamson, J. G. (2003). *Globalization in historical perspective*. Chicago: University of Chicago Press.

Borrus, M., Millstein, J. E., & Zysman, J. (1983). Trade and development in the semi-conductor industry: Japanese challenge and American response. In J. Zysman & L. Tyson (Eds.), *American industry in international competition: Government policies and corporate strategies* (pp. 142-248). Ithaca, NY: Cornell University Press.

Bresnahan, T. F. (1999). New modes of competition: Implications for the future structure of the computer industry. In J. A. Eisenach & T. M. Lenard (Eds.), *Competition, innovation, and the Microsoft monopoly: Antitrust in the digital marketplace* (pp. 155-208). Boston: Kluwer Academic.

Bresnahan, T. F., & Gambardella, A. (1998). The division of inventive labor and the extent of the market. In E. Helpman (Ed.), *General purpose technologies and economic growth* (pp. 253-81). Cambridge, MA: MIT Press.

Bresnahan, T. F., & Greenstein, S. (1996). The competitive crash in large-scale commercial computing. In R. Landau et al. (Eds.), *The mosaic of economic growth* (pp. 357-97). Stanford, CA: Stanford University Press.

Bresnahan, T. F., & Greenstein, S. (1997). Technical progress and co-invention in computing and the use of computers. In M. N. Bailey et al. (Eds.), Ppin *Brookings papers on economic activity: Microeconomics, 1996* (pp. 1-77). Washington, DC: Brookings Institution.

Bresnahan, T. F., & Malerba, F. (1999). Industrial dynamics and the evolution of firms' and nations' competitive capabilities in the world computer industry. In D. C. Mowery & R. R. Nelson (Eds.), *The sources of industrial leadership* (pp. 79-132). New York: Cambridge University Press.

Bresnahan, T. F., & Trajtenberg, M. (1995). General purpose technologies: "Engines of growth"? *Journal of Econometrics, 65*, 83-108.

Braun, E., & Macdonald, S. (1982). *Revolution in miniature* (2nd ed.). Cambridge: Cambridge University Press.

Brusoni, S., Prencipe, A. & Pavitt, K. (2001). Knowledge specialization, organizational coupling and the boundaries of the firm: Why do firms know more than they make? *Administrative Science Quarterly, 46*, 597-621.

Bylinsky, G. (1980). Here comes the second computer revolution. In T. Forester, (Ed.), *The microelectronics revolution* (pp. 9-15). Oxford, UK: Blackwell.

Chandler, A. D., Jr. (1977). *The visible hand: The managerial revolution in American business*. Cambridge, MA: Belknap.

Chandler, A. D., Jr. (1990). *Scale and scope: The dynamics of industrial capitalism*. Cambridge, MA: Belknap.

Chandler, A. D., Jr. (2001). *Inventing the electronic century: The epic story of the consumer electronics and computer industries*. New York: Free Press.

Chandler, A. D., Jr. (2005). Commercializing high-technology industries. *Business History Review*, 79, 595-604.

Chandler, A. D., Jr. (2006). How high technology industries transformed work and life worldwide from the 1880s to the 1990s. *Capitalism and Society*, 1(2), Article 1. Available at http://www.bepress.com/cas/vol1/iss2/art1.

Cox, W. M. & Alm, R. (1998). *The right stuff: America's move to mass customization* (Annual Report). Dallas, TX: Federal Reserve Bank of Dallas.

Curry, J., & Kenney, M. (1999). Beating the clock: Corporate responses to rapid change in the PC industry. *California Management Review*, 42(1), 8-36.

Cusumano, M. A. (1991). *Japan's software factories: A challenge to US management*. New York: Oxford University Press.

David, P. A. (1990). The dynamo and the computer: An historical perspective on the modern productivity paradox. *American Economic Review*, 80, 355-61.

David, P. A., & Greenstein, S. (1990). The economics of compatibility standards: An introduction to recent research. *Economics of Innovation and New Technology*, 1, 3.

Dedrick, J., & Kraemer, K. L. (2007). *Globalization of innovation: The personal computing industry*. Irvine, CA: Personal Computing Industry Center, The Paul Merage School of Business, University of California.

Dosi, G. (1981). *Technical change and survival: Europe's semiconductor industry*. Sussex, UK: Sussex European Research Center.

Dosi, G. (1984). *Technical change and industrial transformation*. New York: St. Martin's Press.

Douglas, G. H. (1987). *The early years of radio broadcasting*. Jefferson, NC: McFarland.

Dummer, G. W. A. (1978). *Electronic inventions and discoveries*. New York: Pergamon.

Economides, N. (1996). The economics of networks. *International Journal of Industrial Organization*, 17, 673.

Ferguson, C. H. (1985). American microelectronics in decline: Evidence, analysis, and alternatives (VLSI Memo No. 85-284). Cambridge, MA: Microsystems Research Center, Massachusetts Institute of Technology.

Ferguson, C. H., & Morris, C. R. (1993). *Computer wars: How the west can win in a post-IBM world*. New York: Times Books.

Fields, G. (2004). *Territories of profit: Communications, capitalist development, and the innovative enterprises of G. F. Swift and Dell Computer*. Stanford, CA: Stanford University Press.

Fisher, F. M., McKie, J. W., & Mancke, R. B. (1983). *IBM and the U. S. data processing industry*. New York: Praeger.

Flamm, K. (1988). *Creating the computer*. Washington, DC: Brookings Institution.

Forester, T. (1993). Japan's move up the technology "food chain." *Prometheus*, 11(June), 73-94.

Fransman, M. (1990). *The market and beyond: Information technology in Japan*. Cambridge: Cambridge University Press.

Garud, R., & Kumaraswamy A. (1993). Changing competitive dynamics in network industries: An exploration of Sun Microsystems' open systems strategy. *Strategic Management Journal, 14*, 351-69.

Gilder, G. (1989). *Microcosm: The quantum revolution in economics and technology.* New York: Simon & Schuster.

Graham, M. B. W. (1986). *RCA and the videodisk: The business of research.* New York: Cambridge University Press.

Graham, M. B. W. (2000). The threshold of the information age: Radio, television, and motion pictures mobilize the nation. In A. D. Chandler, Jr., and J. W. Cortada (Eds.), *A nation transformed by information: How information had shaped the United States from colonial times to the present* (pp. 137-75). New York: Oxford University Press.

Granstrand, O., Patel, P., & Pavitt, K. (1997). Multi-technology corporations: Why they have "distributed" rather than "distinctive core" competencies. *California Management Review, 39*(4), 8-25.

Grove, A. (1996). *Only the paranoid survive.* New York: Bantam.

Henderson, R. M., & Clark, K. B. (1990). Architectural innovation: The reconfiguration of existing product technologies and the failure of established firms. *Administrative Science Quarterly, 35*(1), 9-30.

Hobday, M. (1991). Semiconductor technology and the newly industrializing countries: The diffusion of ASICs (application specific integrated circuits). *World Development, 19*, 375-97.

Holbrook, D. (1999). Technical diversity and technological change in the American semiconductor industry, 1952-65. Unpublished doctoral dissertation, Carnegie Mellon University, Pittsburgh, PA.

Hong, S. (2001. *Wireless: From Marconi's black-box to the Audion.* Cambridge, MA: MIT Press.

Helpman, E. (Ed.) (1998). *General purpose technologies and economic growth.* Cambridge, MA: MIT Press.

Howeth, L. S. (1963). *History of communications - Electronics in the United States Navy.* Washington, DC: Bureau of Ships and Office of Naval History. Available at http://earlyradiohistory.us/1963hw.htm.

Integrated Circuit Engineering Corporation (ICE). (Various years). *Status of the integrated circuit industry.* Scottsdale, AZ: Author.

James, H. (2001). *The end of globalization: Lessons from the Great Depression.* Cambridge, MA: Harvard University Press.

Jensen, M. C. (1986). Agency costs of free cash flow, corporate finance, and takeovers. *American Economic Review, 76*, 323-9.

Katz, B., & Phillips, A. (1982). The computer industry. In R. R. Nelson (Ed.), *Government and technical progress: A cross-industry analysis* (pp. 162-232). New York: Pergamon.

Klepper, S., & Simons, K. L. (1997). Technological extinctions of industrial firms: An inquiry into their nature and causes. *Industrial and Corporate Change, 6*, 379-460.

Kraemer, K. L., & Dedrick, J. (2002). *Dell Computer: Organization of a global production network.* Irvine, CA: Center for Research on Information Technology and Organizations (CRITO), University of California, Irvine.

Kraus, J. (1971). *An economic study of the U.S. semiconductor industry*. Unpublished doctoral dissertation, New School for Social Research, New York.

Lamoreaux, N. R., Raff, D. M. G., & Temin, P. (2003). Beyond markets and hierarchies: Toward a new synthesis of American business history. *American Historical Review, 108*, 404-33.

Langlois, R. N. (1992a). External economies and economic progress: The case of the microcomputer industry. *Business History Review, 66*, 1-50.

Langlois, R. N. (1992b). Transaction-cost economics in real time. *Industrial and Corporate Change, 1*(1), 99-127.

Langlois, R. N. (2002a). Digital technology and economic growth: The history of semiconductors and computers. In Steil, B. et al., (Eds.), *Technological innovation and economic performance* (pp. 265-84). Princeton, NJ: Princeton University Press for the Council on Foreign Relations.

Langlois, R. N. (2002b). Modularity in technology and organization. *Journal of Economic Behavior and Organization, 49*, pp. 19-37.

Langlois, R. N. (2003). The vanishing hand: The changing dynamics of industrial capitalism. *Industrial and Corporate Change, 12*, 351-85.

Langlois, R. N. (2004). Chandler in a larger frame: Markets, transaction costs, and organizational form in history. *Enterprise and Society, 5*, 355-75.

Langlois, R. N. (2007). *The dynamics of industrial capitalism: Schumpeter, Chandler, and the new economy*. London: Routledge.

Langlois, R. N., & Foss, N. J. (1999). Capabilities and governance: The rebirth of production in the theory of economic organisation. *Kyklos, 52*, 201-18.

Langlois, R. N., Pugel, T. A., Haklisch, C. S., Nelson, R. R., & Egelhoff, W. G. (1988). *Microelectronics: An industry in transition*. London: Unwin Hyman.

Langlois, R. N., & Robertson, P. L. (1992). Networks and innovation in a modular system: Lessons from the microcomputer and stereo component industries. *Research Policy, 21*(4), 297-313.

Langlois, R. N., & Robertson, P. L. (1995). *Firms, markets, and economic change: A dynamic theory of business institutions*. London: Routledge.

Langlois, R. N., & Steinmueller, W. E. (1999). The evolution of competitive advantage in the worldwide semiconductor industry, 1947-96. In Mowery, D. C., & Nelson, R. R. (Eds.), *The sources of industrial leadership* (pp. 19-78). New York: Cambridge University Press.

Levin, R. C. (1982). The semiconductor industry. In Nelson, R. R., *Government and technical progress: A cross-industry analysis* (pp. 9-100). New York: Pergamon.

Levy, J. D. (1981). *Diffusion of technology and patterns of international trade: The case of television receivers*. Unpublished doctoral dissertation, Yale University, New Haven, CT.

Lydon, J., & Bambrick, R. (1987). Fairchild semiconductor, the lily of the valley, 1957-87. *Electronic News, 33*.

Macher, J., Mowery, D. C., & Hodges, D. (1998). Performance and innovation in the U.S. semiconductor industry, 1980-1996. In Landau, R., & Mowery, D. C. (Eds.), *Explaining America's industrial resurgence*. Washington, DC: National Academy Press.

Maclaurin, W. R. (1949). *Invention and innovation in the radio industry.* New York: Macmillan.

Malerba, F. (1985). *The semiconductor business: The economics of rapid growth and decline.* Madison, WI: University of Wisconsin Press.

Malone, M. S. (1985). *The big score.* New York: Doubleday.

March, J. G. (1991). Exploration and exploitation in organizational learning. *Organizational Science, 2*, 71–87.

McHugh, K. S. (1949). Bell System patents and patent licensing. *Bell Telephone Magazine,* January, 28, 1–4.

Merges, R., & Nelson, R. R. (1990). The complex economics of patent scope. *Columbia Law Review, 90*, 839–916.

Merges, R., & Nelson, R. R. (1994). On limiting or encouraging rivalry in technological progress: The effect of patent-scope decisions. *Journal of Economic Behavior and Organization, 25*, 1–24.

Methé, D. T. (1991). *Technological competition in global industries: Marketing and planning strategies for American industry.* Westport, CT: Quorum Books.

Mokyr, J. (1990). Punctuated equilibria and technological progress. *American Economic Review, 80*, 350–4.

Moore, G. (1965). Cramming more components onto integrated circuits." *Electronics, 38*, 114–17.

Moore, G. (1997). An update on Moore's law. Keynote address given to the Intel Developer Forum, September 30, San Francisco. Available at ⟨http://www.intel.com/pressroom/archive/speeches/GEM93097.HTM.⟩

Morris, P. R. (1990). *A history of the world semiconductor industry.* London: Peter Peregrinus on behalf of the Institution of Electrical Engineers.

Mowery, D. C., & Steinmueller, W. E. (1994). Prospects for entry by developing countries into the global integrated circuit industry: Lessons from the United States, Japan, and the NIEs, 1955–90. In Mowery, D. C. (Ed.), *Science and Technology Policy in Interdependent Economies.* Boston: Kluwer Academic.

Nelson, R. R. (1962). The link between science and invention: The case of the transistor. In Nelson, R. R. (Ed.), *The rate and direction of inventive activity* (pp. 549–83). Princeton, NJ: Princeton University Press.

Nelson, R. R., & Winter, S. G. (1977). In search of more useful theory of innovation. *Research Policy, 5*, 36–76.

Norberg, A. L. (1993). New engineering companies and the evolution of the United States computer industry. *Business and Economic History, 22*, 181–93.

Noyce, R. N., & Hoff, M. E., Jr. (1981). A history of microprocessor development at Intel. *IEEE Micro, 1*, 8–21.

Okimoto, D. I., Sugano, T., & Weinstein, F. B. (1984). *Competitive edge: The semiconductor industry in the U.S. and Japan.* Stanford, CA: Stanford University Press.

Pavitt, K. (2003). Specialization and systems integration: Where manufacture and services still meet. In Prencipe, A. et al. (Eds.), *The business of systems integration.* Oxford, UK: Oxford University Press.

Perry, T. S. (1988). The longest survivor loses its grip. *IEEE Spectrum, 25*(8), 16–20.

Pugh, E. W. (1984). *Memories that shaped an industry.* Cambridge, MA: MIT Press.

Pugh, E. W., Johnson, L. R., & Palmer, J. H. (1991). *IBM's 360 and early 370 systems.* Cambridge, MA: MIT Press.

Redmond, K. C., & Smith, T. M. (1980). *Project whirlwind: History of a Pioneer computer.* Bedford, MA: Digital Press.

Reich, L. S. (1977). Research, patents, and the struggle to control radio: A study of big business and the uses of industrial research. *The Business History Review, 51,* 208-35.

Reid, T. R. (1984). *The chip: How two Americans invented the microchip and launched a revolution.* New York: Simon & Schuster.

Rifkin, G., & Harrar, G. (1988). *The ultimate entrepreneur: The story of Ken Olsen and Digital Equipment Corporation.* Chicago: Contemporary Books

Richardson, G. B. (1972). The organization of industry. *Economic Journal, 82,* 883-96.

Robertson, P. L., & Langlois, R. N. (1992). Modularity, innovation, and the firm: The case of audio components. In Scherer, F. M., & Perlman, M. (Eds.), *Entrepreneurship, technological innovation, and economic growth: Studies in the Schumpeterian tradition* (pp. 321-42). Ann Arbor, MI: University of Michigan Press.

Rosenberg, N. (1963). Technological change in the machine tool industry, 1840-1910. *Journal of Economic History, 23,* 414-43.

Rosenberg, N. (1992). Scientific instrumentation and university research. *Research Policy, 21,* 381-90.

Rosenberg, N., & Nelson, R. R. (1994). American universities and technical advance in industry. *Research Policy, 23,* 323-48.

Scott, C. (2001). History of the radio industry in the United States to 1940. In Whaples, R. (Ed.), *EH.Net Encyclopedia.* Available at http://eh.net/encyclopedia/article/scott.radio.industry.history

Semiconductor Industry Association. (1999). *International technology roadmap for semiconductors: 1999 edition.* Austin, TX: International SEMATECH.

Siegmann, K. (1993, December 20). An American tale of semi-success: How American chip companies regained lead. *The San Francisco Chronicle,* 1-2.

Simons, K. L. (2000). Dominance by birthright: Entry of prior radio producers and competitive ramifications in the U.S. television receiver industry. *Strategic Management Journal, 21,* 997-1001.

Sparkes, J. J. (1973). The first decade of transistor development. *Radio and Electronic Engineering, 43,* 8-9.

Sterling, C. H., & Kittross, J. M. (1978). *Stay tuned.* Belmont, CA: Wadsworth.

Stern, N. (1981). *From ENIAC to Univac.* Bedford, MA: Digital Press.

Tilton, J. E. (1971). *International diffusion of technology: The case of semiconductors.* Washington, DC: Brookings Institution.

Tyson, L. D'A., & Yoffie, D. B. (1993). Semiconductors: From manipulated to managed trade. In Yoffie, D. B. (Ed.), *Beyond free trade: Firms, governments, and global competition.* Boston: Harvard Business School Press.

Usselman, S. W. (1993). IBM and its imitators: Organizational capabilities and the emergence of the international computer industry. *Business and Economic History, 22* (Winter), 1-35.

Utterback, J. M. (1979). The dynamics of product and process innovation in indus-
try. In Hill, C. T., & Utterback, J. M. (Eds.), *Technological innovation for a
dynamic economy* (pp. 40–65). New York: Pergamon.

Williams, M., & Kallender, P. (2004, December 7). China's Lenovo to buy IBM's
PC business. *InfoWorld, 1.*

Wilson, R. W., Ashton, P. K., & Egan, T. P. (1980). *Innovation, competition, and
government policy in the semiconductor industry.* Lexington, MA: Heath.

Zimmerman, M. R., & Dicarlo, L. (1999, December 23). Who would've known
where the PC would go? Nearly 20 years after the IBM PC was born, it still rules –
Thanks to its ability to evolve." *ZDNet News.*

5

Aircraft and the Third Industrial Revolution

ANDREA PRENCIPE

INTRODUCTION[1]

Widely regarded as a fast-paced, high-technology sector, the commercial aircraft industry is driven toward the continuous development of safer and faster aircraft in order to satisfy the travel demands of a globalized economy. No longer the province of the wealthy, air travel is a core infrastructure for the modern economy. The aircraft industry quickly assumed a pivotal position in society and the economy from its inception at the start of the twentieth century. The early stage of industry development was turbulent, as artisan firms competed with each other to push the design and reliability of new airships. Some of the giants of present-day aviation have histories going back to the early expansion of the industry, with the founding of Boeing in 1916 and Douglas in 1920 (Winship, 1998).

---

[1] This chapter builds on different types of data, namely interviews, technical literature, firms' annual reports and publications, and industry data. Technical literature and specialized journal articles (particularly *Flight International, Interavia*, and *World Aerospace Technology*) have provided the basis for the discussion of the technological drivers and developments of the aircraft engine. I have collected information through face-to-face and telephone interviews with aircraft manufacturers, suppliers (e.g., engines), airlines, industry experts, and regulatory bodies. This information has been used to describe the role of the main actors in the evolution of the industry.

Since the First World War, the aeronautics industry has served both commercial and military markets. Although we must acknowledge the dual nature of the industry and its important effects on technological learning, this study focuses on the commercial aircraft industry. The rationale for splitting the analysis is based on the very different nature of these two markets. Whereas the United States and Europe demonstrate different military investments, the market trends for commercial aircraft are very similar across the two regions, reflecting a global dimension for the industry. For both the European Union and the United States, peaks are apparent in 1989 and 1997, with a drop in 1994 that is due to the recession in the early 1990s (Bryant, 1996). The aircraft industry in the United States was worth more than $82 billion in 2000, or 0.8% of U.S. gross domestic product (GDP) and 1.9% of all manufacturing sales (AIA, 2001, pp. 15, 18). Of the $82 billion in aircraft sales in the United States, the commercial aircraft industry accounts for the largest share, $48.4 billion dollars in sales in the United States in 2000. In Europe, the commercial aircraft share is even higher, 72% in 2000 (AECMA, 2001), and growing.

Technological change has heavily affected improvements in aircraft performance. The introduction of jet engine technology (incorporated in the Douglas DC-8 and Boeing 707) in the 1950s, the introduction of the turbofan technology that extended aircraft range in the 1960s, and subsequently the emergence of wide-body aircraft affected various aircraft performance indicators. As Mowery and Rosenberg (1981, p. 348) put it, "Various measures of aircraft product performance [also] display impressive gains for the 1925–75 period. Direct operating costs per seat mile dropped by over 90% between the era of the Ford and Fokker trimotors in the 1920s and the wide-body transports, utilizing high-by-pass-ratio turbofan engines, in the 1970s. Passenger capacity and speed of aircraft have increased by a factor of 20 during this period."

The Aircraft Industry as CoPS Industry

Complex product systems (CoPSs) have been defined as "high cost, engineering-intensive products, sub-systems, or constructs [i.e., capital goods] supplied by a unit of production." Hobday has identified a number of dimensions to compare and contrast mass-produced products and CoPSs.[2] Accordingly, CoPSs differ from simpler, mass-produced

---

[2] For a comprehensive discussion of the main features of CoPS industries, see Hobday (1998). For a description of a CoPS product life cycle, see Davies (1997).

products in terms of product and production characteristics, dynamics of
the innovation process, competitive strategies, managerial constraints,
industrial coordination, and market characteristics.

Miller et al. (1995), relying on a study of the flight simulator industry, have shown that the industry life-cycle model is unable to explain
the determinants of the life cycle in CoPS industries. According to the
Abernathy and Utterback model, industries evolve through two phases
characterized by different rates of product and process innovations. In
the initial or *fluid phase*, the rate of product innovation is high, stimulated by a large number of small competing firms. Product innovations
are performance maximizing, and processes are uncoordinated and customized. The fluid phase is terminated by the selection by the market
of a particular product configuration, labeled *dominant design*. The
emergence of a dominant design has two main effects. First, it ushers
in an industrial shakeout as the industry becomes dominated by a small
number of large firms. Second, because of the standardization of product design, the rate of product innovation slows, whereas the pace of
process innovations increases to exploit economies of scales. By contrast, Miller et al. (1995) show that the flight simulator industry tends
to remain in the *fluid stage*. The emergence of a dominant design does
not pave the way for an industrial shakeout. Because of high barriers to
entry and despite radical technological shifts, the flight simulator industry is characterized by high stability of flight simulator suppliers (systems integrators) and high turbulence in the supply chain (component
suppliers).

The aircraft industry shares some of the characteristics of CoPS industries. An aircraft is a high-value capital good composed of many interacting and often customized elements that belong to different technological
fields. The number of components varies according to the size and therefore the thrust of the engine. Components and subsystems are also multitechnology, multicomponent artifacts. The avionics and engine systems
are cases in point. For instance, the engine powering such airplanes as
the Boeing 747 and the Airbus A340 may encompass up to 40,000 components. Further, although the same engine powers the two previously
mentioned airplanes, some engine parts need to be customized to each
application. The software governing the engine control unit is a case
in point because it has to be fine-tuned with the avionics system of the
airplane.

Aircraft are batch produced. The design, development, and production of a new aircraft involve several firms, and the degree of user

involvement is very high. Airlines, regulatory bodies, specialized suppliers, and aircraft manufacturers closely collaborate during new engine development programs. The development costs of a new aircraft program are so extremely high that a failure of the program may have a bad impact on the financial situation of manufacturers and/or push them to the brink of receivership. Again, this holds true for suppliers of large subsystems: During the development of the RB211 engine in the 1970s, Rolls-Royce went bankrupt and was saved through its nationalization. This huge financial effort has paved the way to collaborative financial agreements between engine makers and suppliers for the development of new engines.

Regarding the dynamics of the innovation process in the aircraft industry, the Abernathy and Utterback life-cycle model does not seem to capture its salient characteristics. Although current configuration can be regarded as the industry's dominant design, its emergence does not seem to have slowed down the rate of product innovation. In the aircraft engine industry, product and process innovations are tightly intertwined and product innovations are always performance maximizing.

Miller et al. (1995) argued that the appropriate unit of analysis for studying the process of innovation in CoPS industries is the network of actors involved in the process as well as the single-supplier firms. They suggest that the innovation parameters of CoPS industries can be described in terms of a mesosystem composed of three main groups, notably the innovation superstructure, the systems integrators (in this case, the aircraft manufacturers), and the innovation infrastructure.

The aircraft manufacturers make up the core of the mesosystem. They coordinate the functioning of the innovation process by organizing the roles of the different actors involved. Suppliers are part of the innovation infrastructure. They provide materials, components, subsystems, machine tools, and software to engine makers. Suppliers are increasingly involved in new engine programs, both financially as risk- and revenue-sharing partners (RRSPs) and technologically as they take on larger chunks of engine design and manufacturing tasks. Government-funded laboratories and universities are also part of the innovation infrastructure. They provide research infrastructure as well as technologies and training. Aircraft manufacturers and the innovation infrastructure are the supply side of the industry. They can be regarded as the sources of technological change.

The innovation superstructure represents the "market" for engines. Airlines, certification agencies, and professional organizations heavily influence the pace and direction of technical change. The airlines are the buyers of the aircraft. Certification agencies and professional bodies form the remaining part of the innovation superstructure. The former determine engine certification requirements, whereas the latter act as the context of information exchange among the different parties involved in the process. The high level of regulations imposed by national governments and international organizations also plays a substantial role in directing technological change.

Nature of the Markets

The commercial aircraft industry comprises five markets: large commercial aircraft (planes of 100 or more seats); maintenance, repair, and overhaul (MRO); engines; business and regional aircraft (fewer than 100 seats); and avionics (including electrical systems such as power, entertainment, and cabin environment) (Acha et al., 2006). The market for large commercial aircraft is closely tied to the market for long-haul travel and transport, whereas the markets for business and regional aircraft are more diversified in scope. Frequent short-haul flights and regional links for transport require a greater number of aircraft in a variety of sizes and specifications. The Boeing 737 design family is the most ubiquitous aircraft flying (4,602 aircraft as compared with Airbus A320s 1,264 aircraft). More than half of all aircraft are operated in North and South America (10,100 aircraft) compared with Europe (5,140 aircraft), and this trend seems to be holding, as more than half of the large aircraft orders are held by airlines operating in the Americas. However, future growth is expected from the emerging economies in East Asia and the Middle East (Acha et al., 2006).

The MRO market is significant in this industry because these products have a long life cycle. For example, the first Boeing 747s were commissioned in 1968 and are still in operation. The customers for the MRO firms are the owners and operators of aircraft: the airlines, government agencies, and firms. The MRO market depends on the cumulative stock of aircraft in operation. Future MRO trends will be closely linked to the likely decommissioning of the oldest operating aircraft, as safety regulations and concerns lead to excessive refurbishment and maintenance costs. At some point, it is cheaper and less risky for airlines to buy a new airplane.

Although engines are supplied to the lead manufacturer for the appropriate airframe, the engine itself is specified or selected by the ultimate client – the airline, the government agency, or the firm. Until recently, the competition for engine sales was bound by two trends: first, the trend for airlines to pursue engine commonality across their fleet of aircraft to minimize MRO costs; and second, the selection provided by the prime manufacturers of several engine options. Recent events have indicated that airlines are now prepared to diversify engines across their fleets, following preferences for engine types. Also, prime manufacturers have begun to move toward exclusive engine–airframe agreements, generally in all U.S. or all European combinations (Storey, 2002). The engine market is somewhat countercyclical to the MRO market, rising directly with a growth trend for new aircraft purchases. Accordingly, engine manufacturers play a role in the MRO market, particularly with respect to power systems. In fact, some of the most important players in the MRO market are actually the airline firms, which seek returns on economies on a scale of their existing in-house MRO facilities and services. This is particularly true in Europe, where European airlines actively sell their MRO services to other airlines.

Industry Structure

National and supranational governments (i.e., the European Union) heavily influenced the vertical integration and disintegration process that characterized the industry's structure over time. In the late 1920s, the United States witnessed a wave of mergers that involved air transport and airframe and engine manufacture (Mowery and Rosenberg, 1981). "United Aircraft, founded in 1929, was comprised of Boeing Aircraft, Boeing Air Transport, Pratt and Whitney, Chance Vought Aircraft, the Hamilton Standard Propeller Corporation and Stearman Aircraft. North American Aviation, incorporated in 1928, included Curtiss Aeroplane, Wright Aeronautical, and had large minority stock-holdings in Transcontinental Air Transport and Western Air Express (subsequently combined to form TWA)" (Mowery and Rosenberg, 1981, pp. 104-5). Later, the Air Mail Act of 1934 mandated that air transportation and aircraft manufacture had to be separated. In the United States, during the postwar period (i.e., under the Civil Aeronautics Board [CAB] regime, 1938–78), military sales provided constant funding for "commercial gambles" (Mowery and Rosenberg, 1982, pp. 104-5). Airlines played aircraft manufacturers against each other to reap discounted price lists for innovative aircraft designs as they had impressive bargaining power in the bilateral oligopoly that emerged in the market. In addition, "the federal government was directly involved in determining the structure of the commercial aircraft industry" as it avoided bankruptcy of such companies as Douglas Aircraft Corporation (through an aid of US $75 million in 1966 that allowed the merger with McDonnell) and Lockheed in 1971 (with a federal loan guarantee of U.S. $250 million) (Mowery and Rosenberg, 1982, p. 113). In Europe, the Airbus consortium was born because of important funding guaranteed by the European state members of the firms involved (i.e., CASA, Spain; Aerospatiale, France; DASA, Germany; British Aerospace, Great Britain).

The aerospace industry as a whole has undergone considerable consolidation in the past decade, and the commercial aircraft sector has been equally affected. It is estimated that the mergers and acquisitions in the global aerospace and defense industries have exceeded $150 billion, with further deals (particularly among the smaller firms) lined up for the future (Velocci, 2001a). Beginning with the prime contractors, consolidation has now taken root at all levels of the value chain to bring added capital and market share weight to the bargaining table. Consolidation among the primes reflects the growing cost and complexity of aerospace development. "Those deals done so far, in Europe and the USA, have been inspired primarily by the need to attain mass due to the high capital expenditure involved in aerospace projects". Nevertheless, the industry is far less concentrated than expected: "The largest 20 manufacturers account for 75% of all sales in the Top 100, a figure that is relatively unchanged even though several big deals have been finalized. Ongoing and future mergers mean this will probably become an 85/15 split – although even the aerospace sector will fall well short of other industries in terms of its dominance by big players. In the pharmaceutical and auto sectors, says Roland Berger aerospace analyst Neil Hampson, the top 20 account for fully 95% of sales" (Flight International, 2000).

As a result of the consolidation process, in 2002, there were only two large commercial aircraft makers, Boeing and Airbus. Whereas Boeing has the cumulative strength in the industry, Airbus matches Boeing on the number of orders currently placed. Bombardier is the leading regional and business jet producer, holding 45 percent of regional order backlogs (Flight International, 2000). Other important regional aircraft producers are Gulfstream Air (owned by defense giant, General Dynamics), Textron (which owns the Cessna business), and Embraer (Brazil).

AIRCRAFT AND CARRIERS INDUSTRY: SOME STYLIZED FACTS

The Aircraft Industry as Technological Borrower

Aeronautics is growing in complexity as firms continue to look for solutions to provide greater product functionality and reduced costs in production and operation. The range of disciplines contributing to new developments in aeronautics includes mechanical engineering, mathematics, computer science, physics, chemistry, biology, electrical engineering, materials science, thermal dynamics, and digital communications and control systems (Acha et al., 2006).

The multitechnology, multicomponent nature and the high degree of systemic complexity that characterize the aircraft product led to an unusual extent to benefits from technological developments in a variety of other industries, such as metallurgy (new alloys and composites) and chemical and petroleum (new fuel compositions). According to Mowery and Rosenberg (1982), the commercial aircraft industry can be considered a *technological borrower*. Technological development of the commercial aircraft industry has relied heavily on developments in the military sector as well as in other industries. Regarding reliance on the military, Mowery and Rosenberg (1982, p. 102) noted that borrowing went "beyond applications to commercial design of components developed for military purposes," as aircraft and engine manufacturers managed to share development and production costs between military and commercial designs. For instance, Boeing benefited enormously from technological developments (such as the under-wing engine positions) that allowed the B-47 and B-52 military bombers to successfully enter the commercial market (where they had no reputation whatsoever as compared with the historical incumbent Douglas) with the Boeing 707 in the 1960s: "The 707 airframe design followed that of the KC-135 quite closely, so closely, in fact, that the first prototype 707 to be rolled out of the Seattle factory did not have windows in the fuselage" (Mowery and Rosenberg, 1982, p. 131).

Since 1940, the interindustry flow of innovations has increasingly coalesced around electronics (and information and communication technology), which has provided key innovations such as radar systems and navigational computers (Mowery and Rosenberg, 1982). The integration of aviation and electronics led to the emergence of avionics. The avionics industry continues to push for new breakthroughs in control and safety that are increasingly important to commercial aviation. Avionics firms have traditionally worked in radar or electro-optics–infrared sensor designs and tend to combine both areas because of the similarity in the physics of microwaves and electro-optics–infrared technology (Acha et al., 2006). Acha et al. (2006) analyzed both knowledge originating among the main participants of the commercial aircraft industry and knowledge originating from companies outside the commercial aircraft industry but applied in the production and development of aircraft, and they confirmed Mowery and Rosenberg's (1981) argument.

Modern aeronautics is arguably another area in which technology led to science, in which practical engineering fed into scientific discovery in an increasing variety of fields (Vincenti, 1986). Many advances in aircraft design and performance aircraft derive from what Vincenti (1986) calls *production-centered innovation*. Taking the example of the development of flush riveting, he explains "[s]ome knowledge did have to be generated for detail design, but the pivotal developments were in production, and it was there that the greater part of the innovative activity took place" (p. 542). Unlike patterns of diffusion from an initial creative source described with respect to other types of innovation, production-centered innovation appears to occur simultaneously and pervasively across the entire industry. Vincenti argues that this is possible only when fundamental ideas are already known or conceptually obvious and the relevant capabilities are widespread (1986, p. 570). In this type of innovative environment, technological breakthroughs are less amenable to closed in-house programs; rather, they diffuse and develop because of the distributed nature of production and of the contingent technological capabilities across a network of firms (Acha et al., 2006.)

Role of National Governments

Mowery and Rosenberg (1982) argued that government policy has influenced both demand and supply in the U.S. commercial aircraft industry. On the supply side, the industry has received government support via research on commercial application technologies undertaken at national laboratories such as the National Advisory Committee on Aeronautics (NACA, 1915–58) and the National Aeronautics and Space Administration (NASA, 1968–present); direct funding of firm internal research programs; and spillovers from the military side. The demand side has been influenced through ad hoc legislation (e.g., through the Civil Aeronautics

Board) and the imposition of heavy regulation for safety and subsequently environmental concerns.

As Mowery and Rosenberg (1982) put it, "consciously or not, the policies of the Post Office in the 1929–34 period, and those of the Civil Aeronautics Board during 1938–78, influence the structure and the conduct of the air transportation industry so as to provide substantial incentives for rapid adoption of innovation in commercial aircraft" (p. 140). After transferring responsibility for airmail transport from the U.S. Post Office to private contractors through the Kelly Air Mail Act of 1925, the increase in airmail volume that was due to a congressionally approved reduction of postal rates entailed an increase in contractors' profits (as payments remained stable at previous levels) (Mowery and Rosenberg, 1982). The McNary-Watres Act of 1930 "changed the method of computation of payments for mails from a pound-mile basis to a space-mile basis; that is, payment was made whether or not mail was carried in an aircraft. In addition, extra payments were made to carriers that used multi-engine aircraft, radio, and other navigational aids" (Mowery and Rosenberg, 1982, p. 141). The Air Mail Act of 1934 mandated a comeback in the per-ounce basis as a method of computation as well as divestiture by aircraft producers of subsidiary transport firms. Mowery and Rosenberg (1982, p. 141) concluded that although "it represented an inefficient mechanism for the support of air transport . . . this set of policies . . . coincided with rapid growth in passenger traffic and the introduction of the monocoque fuselage air transports, the B-247 and the DC-2, which were of great importance in the development of the commercial aircraft and air transportation industries." Subsequently, the U.S. Congress established the Civil Aeronautics Board (CAB) to overlook and control carriers' pricing policies and entry or exit from the air transportation sector through strict control of the award of routes. As a result of this heavy regulatory environment, competition became service based as major airlines were keen to rapidly adopt innovative aircraft designs. This relentless drive toward better and more innovative designs entailed, on the one hand, an impressive productivity growth, and on the other, heavy debts for airlines' balance sheets.

CAB regulation focused major research efforts on luxury aircraft for the transcontinental market, which had become the largest and most profitable industry segment (Mowery and Rosenberg, 1982). This bias in the direction of innovation had two major implications on the industry structure and on consumer welfare at large. As Caves (1962, p. 10) noted, "relatively forgotten were the airlines in need of large planes efficient on short hops, as well as the airlines needing low-cost equipment to serve low-density routes." As a consequence, "consumer welfare was impaired by the lack of variety in service quality and price" (Mowery and Rosenberg, 1982, p. 141). Caves (1962) argued that the turboprop engine was a missed opportunity as it could have been the appropriate engine for short-haul, economy flights because of its fuel efficiency that could compensate for its relatively low speed as compared with that of the jet engine. CAB regulation did not allow for price competition, however. Therefore, airlines did not have any incentive to differentiate their offering through prices.

Deregulation in the United States and, more recently, in Europe, led to a rediscovery of price as a differentiating lever. Price joined service quality to play a major role in airlines' strategic moves. Airlines vary and differentiate their offerings by using a variety of levers: for example, prices, service quality, advanced purchase, and business classes. Southwest Airlines in the United States and Ryan Air and Easy Jet in Europe have developed no-frill offerings that combine low price with low service and have stolen a march on national flag carriers. Besides technological innovation, strategy scholars introduced the concept of innovation in the business model.

The support of national governments for the development of new engine technologies through direct and indirect funding is still strong. Governments in both developed and developing countries fund research as well as development programs, the former to strengthen the technological leadership of their national champions, the latter to improve their technological capabilities in such a value-added industry. As confirmed by an industry expert,

"the reasons government [in developing countries] will do that [i.e., ask engine makers to involve national firms in the development of new engines] are very many, but essentially two. The first is the aero gas turbines are closely related to defense and therefore a country has to have the ambition in the medium or long term to have a defense capability equal to the best. The other issue is the view, totally correct view, that if you invest in very high value added technologies like the aero gas turbine, you get a spreading of the capabilities which are research, design and even management, because we are managing a very complex technology . . . So many developing countries will be opened to say why don't you invest in my organization to develop gas turbine technologies for this country, because there will be spin off effects for many other people in the country."

In Western countries, there are several differences between the organization of supports for technical progress between Europe and the United States.

Milestones in aviation technology emphasized the importance of experimentation in the development of design. In particular, wind tunnels have played an important role in airframe design. The contribution of the National Advisory Committee for Aeronautics (NACA), which provided the first significant wind tunnel facility, to early aviation design cannot be overstated. Testing fields provided by the Air Force and other national scientific infrastructures likewise have been important for the cumulative understanding of aircraft design, production and operation. Because of the number of variables at play in designing aircraft, simulation technologies have only recently advanced to a level whereby some of the expense of experimental trials can be foregone. Nevertheless, because of safety concerns, field testing remains an important stage of the learning cycle.

In the United States, the support of the federal government still continues by means of direct and indirect initiatives. The Glenn and the Langley Research Centers at NASA and the Wright Patterson Laboratory of the U.S. Air Force are considered the centers of excellence for commercial and military engine-related technologies, respectively. Cuts in the defense budget have reduced in part the role that military-related research programs used to have in the development of new technologies. The focus is now on the development of dual-use technologies. The latest major program, called Integrated High Performance Turbine Engine Technology (IHPTET), for instance, "addresses critical defense technology objectives," but also "develops dual-use technologies". IHPTET is a $4.5 billion program funded by the U.S. Government (65%) and industry (35%). It involves the U.S. Army, Navy, Air Force, Defense Advanced Research Project Agency (DARPA), NASA, as well as General Electric Aircraft Engines, Pratt & Whitney, Allison Engines, Allied Signal Engines, Williams International, and Teledyne Ryan Aeronautical. IHPTET is considered a major program because of its twenty-five-year time span, the areas it covers, and the magnitude of its goals. It covers the major jet engine component technologies, such as turbine and combustors, as well as the pervasive technologies such as materials and processes. The underlying objective is not to develop engines, but technologies that can be incorporated in demonstration and validation programs or full-scale development programs. The achievements (in terms of completion dates) of each objective per engine technology have been scheduled in three stages, notably in 1991, 1997, and 2003.

European governmental support for the technological developments in the aircraft engine industry is less visible than in the United States. Europe does not have organizations that can match the sheer size of the NASA Research Centers and the Wright Patterson Laboratory. Nonetheless, it is well known that European governments support national engine firms through direct funding of research programs and new engine development programs. Likewise, the European Union has funded and continues to fund important research programs where industry and universities collaborate within the framework programs. Special initiatives cover the specific subprogram on the aircraft industry labeled "Aeronautics" within the Brite-Euram Program, the work of the "Aeronautics Task Force" to coordinate the various aeronautics research programs, and the broad and heavily funded subprogram on "Aeronautics" within the recently launched 5th Framework Program.

Coordinating Changing Division of Labor and Division of Knowledge

Mowery and Rosenberg (1981, p. 348) emphasized the complexity of the knowledge bases underlying the aircraft industry:

Central to an understanding of the innovation process in the commercial aircraft industry is the high degree of systemic complexity embodied in the final product. The finished commercial aircraft comprises a wide range of components for propulsion, navigation, and so on, that are individually extremely complex. The interaction of these individually complex systems is crucial to the performance of an aircraft design, yet extremely difficult to predict from design and engineering data, even with presently available computer-aided design (CAD) techniques ... This pervasive technological uncertainty has been and remains an important influence upon producer structure and conduct in the industry. Such uncertainty also introduces an additional dimension to the innovation process "learning by using."

From an early stage, there was a division of labor between airframe manufacturers and suppliers. Aircraft manufacturers relied from the outset on suppliers of materials (such as wood, fabric, and aluminum) and components (such as tires and mechanical parts). Such a division of production has evolved alongside the growth in the market for aircraft and the complexity of design. Suppliers to the aircraft industry comprise the broad range of materials, components, support services and consumables necessary for air travel.

Mowery and Rosenberg (1981, p. 347) argued that "Fierce price competition coexists with very high levels of producer concentration and significant product differentiation. The industry also exhibits relatively low levels of vertical integration–contractual relationships predominate in the pursuit of extremely complex and highly uncertain goals in price and performance."

The multitechnology nature of aircraft production has implications for the management of technology and the industry's structure. The number of technologies involved in the design, development, and manufacturing of multitechnology products is too large to be managed entirely within a single-firm organization; external sources of technology must be integrated in one way or another. Consequently, firms compete in terms of their ability to manage the external relationships they need to develop and foster and be involved in the development of new, specialized bodies of knowledge. Literature on multitechnology settings focused on understanding which technologies and components are developed and kept in-house and which are those that are contracted out, as well as the characteristics of interfirm relationships and the nature of the coordinating mechanisms that enable firms to compete successfully (Brusoni et al., 2001).

The aircraft industry is characterized by an increasing number of vertical and horizontal contractual relationships because of the multitechnology nature of the product (and its components) and the related increasing development costs. The increasing development costs of aircraft, which are due mainly to the introduction of jet engine technology and avionics, forced manufacturers to exploit the largest production runs to reap economies of scale. Learning economies (as derived by the process of learning by doing) played an important role in the production of airframes (Mowery and Rosenberg, 1981). In addition, high development costs led manufacturers to conceive and design aircraft in terms of family. According to the family concept, an original aircraft design engendered a succession of versions through the stretching of the fuselage. For instance, the Boeing 737 aircraft family comprises the 737-100, 737-200, 737-200 Advanced, 737-300, 737-400, 737-400 HGW, 737-500, 737-500 HGW, 737-600, 737-700, and 737-800.

The manner in which labor is divided and coordinated is related to how knowledge is divided and coordinated, but this matching occurs in complex and untidy ways that often require the effort of large, general-knowledge firms called systems integrators (Miller et al., 1995). Previous literature has illustrated that in a number of engineering-intensive, intermediate industries, the division of labor and the division of knowledge are not necessarily isomorphic so that the production boundaries of the firm seem to differ from their knowledge boundaries (Brusoni and Prencipe, 2001). Brusoni et al. (2001) argued that systems integrators know more than they do and that processes of knowledge specialization lie at the core of the emergence of "loosely coupled" net-works of integrators, assemblers, and suppliers of physical equipment as well as specialized expertise. Paoli and Prencipe (1999) further argued that product systems, such as aircraft, that are intrinsically systemic in character can be adequately represented only through complex interpretative models of understanding and that the complexity of these models in terms of specificity and contingencies relies on a firm's tacit process of knowledge development.

Systems integrators' knowledge bases rely on capabilities developed across multiple knowledge bases. Eliasson (1996, p. 130) has further emphasized the hierarchical role of the integrator in the design and development process: "It is not difficult to understand that when the design, construction, prototyping and production problems are seen as a whole, there are thousands of different ways of organizing this solution, and that only some of them are economical. The *ability*, then, *to conceptualize the whole at an early stage becomes the important, dominant competence.*" Systems integrators in commercial aircraft – the prime contractors – must maintain integrative capabilities across the range of technologies and scientific disciplines that impact aircraft design and development, and this is revealed in a broad portfolio of patenting behavior. Eliasson's emphasis on the integrator's ability to conceptualize the whole at an early stage is reflective of the design concept in aircraft, which is still the preserve of Boeing and Airbus. Amesse et al. (2001) identified distinctive subcontracting arrangements based on economy, specialization, and supply, in which arrangements based on economy tended to dominate in number, but subcontracting on specialization and supply was apparent where the relationship between the two companies was very close (pp. 566–7). Nevertheless, the arguments from the literature discussed place the central governance of learning and the diffusion of technological knowledge in the commercial aircraft industry in the hands of the systems integrator.

As discussed in Prencipe (2001), systems integrators develop four different types of capabilities: *absorptive capabilities* – capabilities to monitor, identify, and evaluate new opportunities emerging from general advances in science and technology; *integrative capabilities* - capabilities to set the requirements, specify source equipment, materials, and components designed and produced internally or externally, and integrate them into the architectures of existing products; *coordinative capabilities* - capabilities to coordinate the development of new and emerging bodies of technological knowledge; and *generative capabilities* - capabilities to innovate both at the component and architectural level.

Component Integration: The Airframe–Engine Interface

Airframe–engine integration is of paramount importance for efficient and safe air transport. Radical changes concerning the engine design configuration involving new airframe–engine installation solutions require the joint and close effort of both airframers and engine makers. Radically new airframes involving a step change in the airframe–engine integration configurations require the joint effort of expertise in airframe- and propulsion-related technologies. A case in point is a three-year NASA technology development program whose aim is to assess the technical and commercial viability of an advanced, unconventional aircraft configuration, namely the blended-wing body (BWB). This airframe configuration is a flying wing with embedded engines. It is a very large subsonic transport with a design payload of 800 passengers, a 7,000-mile range, and a cruise Mach number of 0.85. As reported by NASA in 1999,

Because the BWB configuration is such an extremely integrated design, a multidisciplinary optimization process will be utilized extensively to address technical issues in configuration design, aerodynamics, structures, propulsion, and flight mechanics. An initial evaluation of this configuration indicates significant cost and performance benefits over conventional configurations: a 56-percent increase in lift-drag ratio, a 20-percent decrease in fuel burn, and a 10-percent decrease in the operating-empty weight. The research team consists of McDonnell Douglas Aerospace, Stanford University, the University of Southern California, the University of Florida, Clark-Atlanta University, NASA Glenn Research Centre, and NASA Langley Research Center the Technology Study funded by NASA is to assess.

During the development of new engine programs, airframers' involvement is highly interactive. The discussion between airframers and engine manufacturers starts when a potential business opportunity arises (new or derivative engine for a new aircraft or a stretched version of an existing aircraft). If the discussion is fruitful and the business opportunity seems promising, a technical and/or business agreement is signed by both parties. This agreement is called a memorandum of understanding (MoU). It contains detailed engine specifications such as thrust, fuel consumption, noise, weight, stability, and vibration. Relying on its internal technical capability, the aircraft manufacturer performs a detailed technical audit to assess engine technological characteristics (thermodynamic cycle, component efficiency, and installation losses). The technical audit also covers the engine's overall structural–mechanical design in terms of installation (accessibility and maintainability), materials used, and component durability. The aircraft builder also evaluates the engine test program. The technical audit is the beginning of the ongoing dialogue between the airframer and the engine manufacturer. The actual involvement of the airframer goes through engine development, flight tests, and certification of the airframe–engine combination.

Airframers have acquired a substantial in-house expertise of engine technology to cope with its increasing complexity (Mowery and Rosenberg, 1981). As mentioned, functional and aerodynamic relationships between aircraft and engine render their integration a critical task. Boeing has strengthened its in-house engine technology expertise following the severe difficulties encountered during the installation of the all-new high-bypass engines in the all-new wide-body 747 aircraft in the early 1970s. Similarly, the shift from sole sourcing to dual or even triple sourcing has required aircraft manufacturers to become competent transactionists.

It is worth noting that the use of information and communication technology-based tools has enormously improved the management of such complex interface.Three-dimensional computer-aided design (CAD) design systems, such as CATIA, allow airframers, engine makers, and suppliers to electronically define their products and make changes to the design on the screen. This has reduced the need for costly physical mock-ups. Computer modeling also helps to design maintainability, a critical factor for airline operation.

The aircraft–engine interface is a major area of concern for airframers and engine makers. There are around 300 mechanical interfaces between engine and airframe that are critical for the operation of the aircraft. These interfaces encompass air, hydraulics, electrics, fuel, electronic and mechanical controls, health monitoring, fire sensing, and protection. The airframe–engine integration necessitates close collaboration throughout the design, development, and assembly of the aircraft–engine combination. At the airframer level, it is coordinated by the propulsion department. A number of specialist departments of the airframer are involved in specific issues of the engineering integration of the engine. These are structures, aerodynamics, nacelle design, performance, noise, and systems (e.g., avionics, electronics, and hydraulics). For a large aircraft builder, the aircraft–engine integration can involve up to 300 people.

The aerodynamic integration of the aircraft-propulsion system combination is another important activity in which airframer and engine-maker roles are closely coordinated. The engine has to be integrated with the nacelle and the nacelle with the aircraft. The location of the propulsion system combination is of paramount importance for aerodynamic reasons. In long-range aircraft, the engine under-wing configuration has become the dominant location. Studies carried out at the National Advisory Committee on Aeronautics (NACA) supported the under-wing engine location: "By a comprehensive survey of net efficiencies of various engine nacelle locations, the optimum position in the wing was found. This NACA engine location principle, together with other refinements, had a revolutionary effect on military and commercial aviation the world over" (Hunsaker, 1941, as quoted in Mowery and Rosenberg, 1981, p. 129). As Cumpsty (1997, p. 7) notes, "Because engines are heavy there are good aerodynamic and structural reasons for mounting engines under the wing...Most of the lift is generated by the wings so hanging the comparatively massive engines where they can most easily be carried makes good structural sense by reducing the wing root bending moment." However, the trend toward higher bypass ratios and the ensuing larger fan diameters may render the under-wing configuration unsuitable because of its negative effects on the landing gear length. In short-range aircraft, the alternative mounting from the rear fuselage is preferred.

SPECIALIZED SUPPLIERS

The industry is characterized by an ever-increasing number of international collaborative agreements for the design, development, and manufacturing of new aircraft. This practice has been borrowed from the military side of the industry from which collaborations have been launched since the early 1970s among firms belonging to different countries. The reasons why the development of new aircraft is split among different firms lie in the increasing development costs and related risk of failure of the program. Competition is, in fact, cutthroat and price based. Industry trade journals report that aircraft list prices are heavily conceded by engine makers in order to secure a foothold in the spares market business, considered to be the "gold mine" of the industry.

The production of a commercial aircraft is a cascade of hierarchical contracting relationships, often led by the two remaining large aircraft manufacturers, Boeing and Airbus. Boeing and Airbus are the leading prime contractors or "primes," which then contract with Tier 1 (the largest engine and supplier firms) and smaller (and often more niche) Tier 2 suppliers for the design and construction of an aircraft for delivery to the customer (airline, business, or government). For example, the Airbus A380 aircraft includes suppliers for fifty-nine subsystems provided by thirty-nine firms (Airbus A380 Suppliers, 2002). These include elements of the structure (e.g., vertical stabilizers, stringers, and stiffeners provided by Jamco), components (e.g., fuel pumps provided by FR HiTemp), and engines (GP7000 engine by Pratt and Whitney). The ultimate role of systems integration of these contributions falls to the aircraft manufacturer or prime, in this case EADS and BAe Systems, which provide fully specified aircraft tailored to the needs of the airline firms and other key customers.

The engine market is dominated by the big three: General Electric, Pratt and Whitney and Rolls-Royce. Fourth in the ranking is Snecma, but its market dominance is growing due to its alliance with GE on the CFMI engines joint venture. The maintenance, repair, and overhaul (MRO) market is heavily dominated in Europe by the European airlines, whereas the largest U.S. airlines maintain their own MRO services in-house. In fact, suppliers of MRO are often suppliers of major subsystems or indeed the airframe (notably Boeing).

Engine manufacturers design, develop, and manufacture engines according to requirements set by the airlines, the airframers, and the regulators. They coordinate the activities of a large number of specialized suppliers, integrate components, and add value through their systems capabilities. The large turbofan market (over 35,000 lb) is dominated by the so-called Big Three or primes, notably General Electric Aircraft Engines, Pratt and Whitney, and Rolls-Royce. In the medium- and small-sized engines market (below 35,000 lb), the main actors are AlliedSignal Engines, Rolls-Royce Allison, General Electric Aircraft Engines, Pratt and Whitney Canada, Williams International and two international joint-ventures, CFM International and International Aero Engines. CFM International has been set up by General Electric and Snecma, whereas

International Aero Engine (IAE) is composed of Pratt and Whitney, Rolls-Royce, Motoren und Turbinen Union, Fiat Avio, and Japanese Aero Engine (a consortium of Japanese aerospace firms). In the turboshaft-turboprop market, in addition to the previously noted engine makers, it is worth mentioning the French firm, Turbomeca. In the aircraft engine industry, East Asian firms play a relatively minor role. They are, in fact, suppliers, or at the most, joint venture partners, such as Mitsubishi Heavy Industries and Kawasaki Heavy Industries from Japan and Samsung Aerospace from Korea.

In the last ten years, a number of mergers and acquisitions (M&A) have further concentrated the industry. AlliedSignal Engines has acquired Textron Lycoming and Garret Engines, whereas Allison Engines has been acquired by Rolls-Royce. M&A have also taken place at the supplier level within the larger M&A movement of the entire aerospace sector.

New engines are developed using a new form of contractual relationship, labeled RRSP. Accordingly, suppliers, typically first-tier ones, are invited to join the engine program early on and to buy a stake in it (usually one or more components or an entire subsystem) in order to share the risks and future revenues (if any) of the program. The shares held by suppliers have been increasing over time. On the one hand, engine makers want to "split" risks and revenues across several suppliers to reduce their own stakes and to gain customers (i.e., airlines) by means of the involvement of suppliers of the same nationality as that of the customers. According to some industry experts, airlines (usually state funded) are more likely to place engine orders when national component suppliers have been involved in the engine program. On the other hand, component suppliers, especially from developing countries, push to get bigger engine program shares in order to learn about more engine parts.

The industry is therefore characterized by a three-tier structure made up of engine makers, RRSPs, and suppliers. The world's largest RRSPs are MTU, Snecma, and Fiat Avio. It is worth noting that the boundary between the RRSP and supplier categories is fuzzy and not explicitly defined. A supplier can be invited to buy a stake in an engine program and become an RRSP and at the same time, be a mere supplier in another program. According to the component suppliers interviewed, RRSP is a risky business as it links the revenues of the supplier to the success of the program. The fierce competition between engine makers has drastically reduced the prices of the engines. In this way, RRSPs end up relying on spare part sales. In a mere supplier situation in contrast, suppliers' revenues are linked to the extent of the supply regardless of the success of the engine program.

The boundary between engine makers and RRSPs is more defined. On the one hand, engine makers may decide to be mere RRSPs in a specific engine program where they are in charge of the design and development of one or more engine part. On the other hand, RRSPs do not and cannot take on integration responsibilities at will. They lack the required systems integration capability. These capabilities are built over a long period of time and require large investments in multiple technical fields and across several knowledge domains, such as concept and detailed design and development. The boundary between systems integrators and RRSPs is therefore one-way permeable.

The Role of Universities

Universities are also part of the innovation infrastructure. Their role is not confined to being a mere provider of abstract and general knowledge. Rather, universities are heavily involved in research projects and with a large scope. In fact, the scope of academic research projects ranges from the design of components, verification of firm's design, and development and verification of design codes, through population of experimental database and exploration of component physical behavior, to training of researchers and technical process improvements. Firms fund scholarships on specific topics and hire in-house professors for trouble-shooting and problem-solving activities as well as for longer-term research guidelines. The importance of the role covered by academic units is evidenced by the fact that the firms interviewed here consider the technological areas researched by their academic units as highly confidential. It is worth noting that academic collaboration is a phenomenon that interests engine makers as well as first- and second-tier suppliers.

The Regulatory Network

The effects of regulation on aircraft demand are both *direct* and *indirect*. Direct effects concern the issue of rules that regulate certification of new aircraft. These effects are analyzed in the following subsections through a discussion of the role of certification bodies and the International Commercial Aviation Organization (ICAO). Indirect effects are subsequently discussed.

The indirect effects concern the heavy regulatory network imposed by national governments and international bilateral and multilateral agreements to control the exploitation of the air space over each national state by air carriers. These rules influence air carriers' competition in terms of price and routes structuring. According to such rules, air carriers are granted licenses to exploit the air space.[3] The International Air Transport Association (IATA) is the regulatory body that oversees fares. Bilateral air carriers' agreements (for instance, code sharing) are overlapped in this heavy regulatory network.

This dense regulatory structure has started shrinking dramatically in the last twenty years. In the United States, the tight control of the Civil Aeronautics Board (CAB) that since 1938 has controlled pricing policies and entry and exit from air transportation, came to an end in 1978 (Mowery and Rosenberg, 1981). The deregulation has had profound impact on the U.S. air carriers' route structures. Air carriers have in fact adopted a *hub-and-spoke* strategy. Accordingly, airlines choose an airport as the hub where they concentrate passengers coming from other airports (spokes) to redirect them to others (spokes).

In Europe, the European Union's Third Package of aviation liberalization became effective in April 1997, giving airlines the right to cabotage in another country. However, according to industry sources, this last stage in the European liberalization has been a symbolic move by European governments, since national carriers still enjoy big cost advantages in their respective domestic market (Boeing, 1999; Rolls-Royce, 1997). At the end of 1998, a new Japan–United States bilateral agreement was signed. This represents a significant step toward the liberalization of the trans-Pacific market (Boeing, 1999).

The Certification Agencies and the Professional Bodies

Aircraft have to comply with the rules defined by regulatory agencies, such as the Federal Aviation Administration (FAA) in the United States and the Joint Aviation Authorities (JAA) in Europe. There is a close,

---

[3] The Chicago Convention of 1944 has regulated most of the issues related to air traffic control. The so-called "freedoms of air" have been instead left to international agreements. As reported by Rolls-Royce (1997), there are eight "freedoms of air": "1. Overfly foreign territory, for example en-route from one country to another. 2. Make a non-traffic stop in another country, for example to refuel. 3. Carry passengers from the home country to another country. 4. Carry passengers to the home country from another country. 5. Carry passengers between two countries by an airline of a third country, with the route beginning or ending in the home country. 6. Carry passenger between two foreign countries by stopping or connecting in the home country. 7. Carry passengers between two foreign countries, without extending the route to the home country. 8. The right to carry traffic wholly within a foreign country [cabotage]."

dialectic, and ongoing dialogue between engine makers and regulatory agencies during the design and the development of new engines. Safety requirements play an important and constraining role for the application of new technologies. The introduction of new technologies is, in fact, always extensively discussed between manufacturers and regulators. New technologies often attract specific new regulation and stringent testing procedures. In this way, the severe testing procedures imposed by means of new rules act as *targeting devices* for innovation (Miller et al., 1995). The dialogue between manufacturers and regulators ends with the formal certification of the aircraft after long and arduous testing activity carried out by the engine maker and overseen by the regulator. According to Miller et al. (1995), this *focusing role* played by the regulator for the introduction of the innovation is a salient characteristic of many CoPS industries as compared with mass productions in which innovation is instead predominantly mediated by the market.

The fact that the introduction of new aircraft parts based on innovative technologies is discussed between engine manufacturers and certification authority does not lessen, however, the importance of feedback as mediated by the market. Information related to engine behavior gathered by airlines and maintenance engineers is considered extremely valuable by the manufacturers during the innovation process. Recent acquisitions of maintenance firms carried out by some aircraft engine manufacturers has had as a by-product the acquisition of important sources of information about customer requirements. It is worth noting, however, that the main reason why engine manufacturers entered the maintenance business can be found in the increasing profit margins characterizing this business as opposed to the nearly negative cash flow deriving from the sale of engines. By strengthening their posture in the maintenance business, engine manufacturers claim to be able to provide a total engine service, from physical product to engine life maintenance. The acquisition of information related to the engine behavior is now facilitated by digital engine control technologies that have replaced the hydromechanical control system. Digital engine control units, also labeled FADEC (i.e., full authority engine control unit) are able in fact to monitor and store engine performance data throughout the engine life.

Two other points on certification are worth mentioning. The first is related to its scope. Certification procedures cover design, operations, maintenance, and licensing standards. The second is related to the recent move toward the global harmonization of certification procedures. The lack of common certification requirements throughout the world requires engine makers and airframers to certify and validate their products according to the different standards defined by the major national regulatory bodies. Meeting these different standards inevitably results in additional costs for the engine manufacturers. In Europe, a body representing the commercial aviation authorities of twenty-nine European countries was created in 1970 (Ashford, 1994). This body is called the Joint Aviation Authorities (JAA), and ensures common high levels of safety standards within the member countries. The JAA has also set up a Certification Group that is used for certification of new aircraft and engines. After the completion of a JAA certification program, Type Certificates can be issued by all member countries. The JAA and the FAA are currently working to harmonize the aircraft and engine certification procedures.

It is worth noting that the discussion of amendments to current rules occurs with study groups and committees belonging to national or international industry associations such as the Society of the British Aerospace Firms (SBAC), the European Association of Aerospace Firms (AECMA), and the Aerospace Industries of America (AIA).

Aircraft Carriers

Customers for large aircraft are primarily the airlines, whereas regional and business jets are sold to airlines, government (in particular, the military), and firms. The importance of military customers for commercial aircraft development was critical until the mid-1950s. At that point, the mismatch in demand interests between the military and commercial aircraft operators became more apparent. This resulted in less direct extension from military product designs to what was desirable to the airline industry. Since the introduction of the Stratocruiser line, Boeing had suffered failures in the commercial aircraft market in trying to extend their military product aircraft design families to commercial aircraft products. The strategy at Boeing changed significantly in 1955 with the decision to disengage the development of the Boeing 707 from planned Air Force contracts (Happenheimer, 1995). Nevertheless, Boeing remains one of the largest suppliers to the U.S. Department of Defense, as well as a leader in the commercial aircraft market. Therefore, we must not underestimate the valuable spillovers of technologies from military development programs to the commercial market; the difficulty is in actually defining these spillovers effectively. As Almeida

(2002, p. 270) pointed out, "The economic and technological impacts of military-commercial 'spin-off' are not undisputed. Indeed for every scholar who touts the benefits of spin-off there is another whose attempts to quantify the impact have demonstrated that the costs associated with maintaining large military-industrial complexes far outweigh any measurable benefit."

In general, the focus for airlines in selecting new aircraft is the cost-per-seat-mile, reflecting both original investment and maintenance. The Boeing 747 has been a leading market design precisely because of its superior economics in this sense. Tennekes (1997, pp. 112–13) estimated the cost of the 747, taking into account depreciation, interest, and income from freight (worth one-third of the total revenue earned) and passengers, at 2.5 cents per seat-mile. This cost ratio compares favorably with estimates for cars (ten cents per passenger-mile) and ocean liners (twenty-five cents per passenger-mile). Travel by train is nominally cheaper, but Tennekes argues that this is underestimating the real cost per passenger-mile because of required state subsidies for the infrastructure. Of course, other design features (in particular, safety features) have added importance to the nature of demand for aircraft; nevertheless, these are superfluous if the aircraft has not met the acceptable basic economics of operation and maintenance.

As final customers of the engine, airlines are in a position of considerable power to affect the performance characteristics of an engine. Airlines demand reliable aircraft and engines at low operating costs for a variety of reasons, but ultimately to boost their profit margins. Engines' fuel consumption and reliability influence around 60 percent of the total airline direct operating cost (DOC). The remaining 40 percent concerns airframe-related costs. In addition, airlines demand quieter and less polluting engines to comply with rules set by airports and regulatory agencies.

Airlines' strategy heavily influences the rate and direction of technical change in the aircraft engine industry. The demands placed on size and range of aircraft depend on airlines' route structures. Route structure in turn depends on firms' individual strategies, but it is also influenced by the rules imposed by national governments. As mentioned earlier regarding the deregulation in the United States, airlines have adopted a hub-and-spoke strategy that requires a change in the composition of airlines' fleet in terms of long- and medium-range aircraft. Long-range or medium- and short-range aircraft and twin or quad designs require the optimization of different engine design parameters such as specific fuel consumption and noise.

Airlines' preference for particular aircraft and engine brands is due to historical and regional factors. Historically, in the aircraft engine market, U.S. air carriers have preferred U.S. engines, whereas British Airways has been a loyal Rolls-Royce customer. However, complicated financial deals, privatization of national flag carriers, and offsetting practices have caused profound changes in the relationships between airlines and engine makers. Airlines who remain loyal to a particular manufacturer still exist mainly because of the heavy investments in support infrastructure, but also because of consolidated pricing policies. In the last five years, major airlines have teamed up to extend their market coverage by means of global alliances. The world's thirty largest airlines have formed four major alliances, notably *Oneworld* (American Airlines, British Airways, Canadian, Cathay Pacific, and Qantas), *Star Alliance* (Air Canada, SAS, Lufthansa, United, Varig, and Thai), *KLM* and *Northwest* (including also Alitalia and Continental), and *Atlantic Excellence* (Swissair, Delta, Austrian, and Sabena). These four major groupings accounted for around 60 percent of the world's passenger traffic in 1997. By forming these alliances, airlines have combined their marketing efforts in order to provide passenger capacity more efficiently. According to industry sources, however, the impact of these alliances on the structure of the competitive environment and on aircraft and engines purchases has been negligible so far.

Regarding airline involvement during new aircraft development programs, it is worth noting that in the last decade the airlines have been involved far more heavily. For instance, during the development of the Boeing 777 and the GE90, engine teams involving airframers, engine makers, and airlines were set up. These teams were labeled "Working Together Teams" (WTT). Boeing also has set up WTT with the other engine suppliers and subsequently applied the same principles to other aircraft programs.

The Demand for Aircraft

Aircraft and engine manufacturers develop specific econometric models to forecast such demand. The long time scale of the industries (both aircraft and engine) requires manufacturers to develop forecasts that cover twenty years. The determinants of demand and the direction of their impact are well known. However, the relatively large number of these determinants and their complex causal intermingling make aircraft demand highly unpredictable. As a consequence, forecasting techniques may prove to be unreliable. As noted in the *Market Outlook* published by Rolls-Royce (1997, p. 3.4), "In sympathy with many other forecasters we believe the forecasting of such cycles is fraught with danger. In particular, the timing and depth of the cycles and the regional traffic sensitivity to such perturbations are very unclear. Therefore, as a baseline case, and considering a long term view with possible upturns and downturns canceling each other out, a smooth growth in traffic is assumed."

Two main forecasting approaches are used by aircraft manufacturers, top-down and bottom-up. In the top-down approach, the main inputs include macroeconomic variables, such as institutional factors, route structures, airlines' substitution policies and changes in fleet capacity, and aircraft manufacturers' production plans. The main output is an estimate of the impact of such factors on aircraft aggregate demand and segmented by regions. For instance, Rolls-Royce uses a regionally segmented top-down approach. The bottom-up approach takes into account instead the fleet plans of individual airlines to analyze the characteristics of specific market niches. Airbus Industries, for example, relies on an internal database covering 359 airlines and cargo carriers worldwide segmented into 81 submarkets.

Factors Influencing Future Demand

The primary factors influencing demand are growth in air transportation, airlines' strategy and their financial situation, regulation, and airport congestion. By analyzing these factors, engine makers derive a demand forecast for aircraft broken down according to seat bands. The demand forecast is converted to an aircraft supply forecast and then to an engine supply forecast. It is worth noting that as in the case of other capital goods, aircraft demand, and therefore demand, is composed of two main components: one related to the replacement of existing equipment, the other related to the growth of fleets' capacity. The variables influencing these two components are similar, but the peculiar characteristics of airlines' substitution policies render demand forecast more unpredictable. Moreover, engine substitution and aircraft substitution policies may follow different dynamics that makes aircraft and aircraft engine demand somehow disjointed.

Relying on and integrating engine and aircraft manufacturers' publications on demand forecast and information gathered through interviews, I illustrate the main factors influencing aircraft and aircraft engine demands. The discussion here focuses on passengers' aircraft. Although some of the determinants of the passengers' market apply to the cargo market, the latter follows different dynamics. Demand forecast in cargo market is, in fact, treated separately by both engine and aircraft manufacturers. The growth in air transportation fluctuates according to macroeconomic and political issues. In particular, traffic growth is influenced by growth in world gross national product and cost reduction in airfares. The two main components constituting passengers' traffic, notably business travel and tourism, are characterized by different demand elasticity in relation to the preceding factors. Business travel's elasticity is in fact lower than tourism's. Traffic growth is measured in *revenue passenger miles*[4] (RPMs). This indicator has grown steadily since the end of World War II, but registered a slowdown at the beginning of the 1990s that was due to the world recessions and the Gulf War (1991). The more recent Asian economic crisis has had a more marginal impact on the growth trend in air transportation. Air traffic grows unevenly across regions. Rolls-Royce has forecasted a world traffic growth rate of 4.9 percent per annum in the period 1996–2014. Intraregion traffic in China has been forecasted to grow at 10.9 percent per annum, but at 3.3 percent per annum in North America. Intercontinental traffic also shows different growth rates. According to Rolls-Royce's forecast, the "North America to Asia/Pacific market" will become the largest of the intercontinental regions, showing a growth rate of 6.6 percent per annum, followed by the "Europe to Asia/Pacific market" with 6.2 percent.

Air traffic growth does not directly affect airlines' fleets' capacity growth[5] (i.e., aircraft demand). Increase in traffic growth is, in fact, met not only by increases in airlines' fleet capacity (i.e., new aircraft demand,) but also by airlines' productivity improvements. Airlines try to bring their existing fleet capacity to full strength by increasing load factor (through yield management policies and code-sharing alliances), increasing the number of flights per aircraft, and expanding routes' length. Annual world load factor has risen steadily for the last fifty years. World load factor averaged 50 percent in the 1950s, 60 percent in the 1970s, and

---

[4] Revenue passenger-mile is given by the product of revenue passenger and miles.
[5] A fleet's capacity is measured in available seat miles (ASMs).

65 percent in the 1980s. Engine and aircraft manufacturers assume it will continue to grow and reach a value of 72.5 percent at the end of 2015.

Airlines' strategies also influence aircraft demand. Aircraft demand is made up of two main components, one related to the increase of airlines' fleet capacity, the other to the replacement of existing aircraft. Fleet substitution policies are influenced by institutional, economic, and technical factors. Regarding institutional factors, regulation requires aircraft to meet stringent noise requirements so that old aircraft need to be replaced or equipped with proper hush-kits to comply. Technical and economic factors also affect substitution policies. Aircraft planned retirement age is around twenty years. The planned retirement age of narrow-body and wide-body aircraft should differ because they are exposed to different operating conditions. Narrow-body aircraft cover short and medium hauls and therefore are used for a higher number of cycles (takeoffs and landings). This makes narrow-bodies' retirement age lower than wide-bodies'. However, as explained previously, retirement ages depend also on the availability of a secondhand market. According to Rolls-Royce, there is evidence that wide-bodies leave passenger service earlier than narrow-bodies because of the limited secondary passenger market. In aircraft demand forecast, aircraft retirement age is assumed to be between twenty-four and twenty-six years (Rolls-Royce). However, airlines may find it economically convenient to upgrade aircraft to further extend their life, rather than to buy new ones. In particular, with the use of special maintenance procedures (also called *retrofitting*), aircraft life is extended well beyond that planned by the manufacturers.[6] Retrofitting can involve different parts of an aircraft. Sometimes, airlines may decide to re-engine part of their fleet. In other words, airlines ask engine makers to provide new engines or upgrade existing ones to take advantage of more fuel-efficient engine technology.[7] With the use of re-engine practice, engine demand does not follow aircraft demand.

Further, airlines adopt a phased retirement policy. Old aircraft are first used for less frequent routes, then stored (or parked) to be used in case of need (sudden increase in demand) or converted for cargo uses. The availability of a secondhand market for old aircraft is also important for airlines' decisions to park aircraft. These factors constitute elements that

---

[6] Some aircraft properly hush-kitted are retired at the age of thirty-five years (Rolls-Royce, 1997).

[7] An example may illustrate this case. The Rolls-Royce RB211–524 engine has been retrofitted with the core of the Trent 700, making a big improvement in specific fuel consumption (Howse, 1998).

render the demand for new aircraft even more unpredictable. Airlines' substitution policies and fleet upgrades are also influenced by the launch of new aircraft programs. Airlines, in fact, can delay their decisions to launch new aircraft to take advantage of newer technological solutions that entail lower operating costs. This causal loop between supply and demand makes forecasting new aircraft demand even more difficult.

CONCLUSIONS

Using the illustration of the key milestones of the recent evolution of aircraft and carrier industries, I explored whether and how some of these milestones may be regarded as (weak) signals of a third industrial revolution. Although technology, arguably the basis of the previous two industrial revolutions, has played and still plays a large role in affecting industry performance indicators – for example, electronic-based innovations such as avionic systems in the aircraft industry and ICT-based reservation systems in the airline industry – other sources of change may have had a more relevant impact. Innovation scholars have put forward the concept of a business model as "a heuristic logic that connects technical potential with the realization of economic value" (Chesbrough and Rosenbloom, 2002, p. 529). Logic underlying a business model unlocks latent values from a technology, but it may well constrain new technologies. Henceforth, changes in the business model will matter in realizing economic values of innovation (also technology based). It may be worth thinking of the recent impressive success of no-frill, low-cost airlines, such as Ryan Air (in Europe) and Southwest (in the United States) in terms of business model innovation, and question whether changes in the logic underlying it may (or may already) have had a strong impact on industry's performance indicators. Ryan Air, which started off as a national carrier (in Ireland), now commands the European carriers industry in terms of load factor, profits, and growth rate. When all carriers were stuck in their hub-and-spoke strategy, relying on major airports, mainly using travel agents for reservations, Ryan Air introduced the point-to-point strategy, relied on and revived minor airports, and wiped out reliance on travel agents (by using the Internet.) Apparently, its business model (although it relies on a new technology) exploits the benefits of organizational innovations. Using Chesbrough and Rosenbloom's (2002) terminology, the articulation of value proposition, the definition of its market niche, the definition of its value chain and value network, and the estimation of its cost structure and profit potential led it to formulate a competitive strategy that is outplaying its rivals.

REFERENCES

Acha, V., Brusoni, S., & Prencipe, A. (2006). Exploring the miracle. *International Journal of Technology and Innovation Management* (under review).

Aerospace Industries Association of America (Economic Data Service) (2001). *Aerospace facts and figures*. Washington, DC: Author.

Airbus A380 Suppliers (2002, July 12). http://www.speednews.com/stw/A380-Suppliers.pdf in *SpeedNews This Week* (Speednews).

Almeida, B. A. (2002). Aerospace industry. In Lazonick, W. (Ed.), *The IEBM handbook of economics* (pp. 269–77). UK, US: International Thomson Business Press.

Amesse, F., Dragoste, L., Nollet, J., & Ponce, S. (2001). Issues on partnering evidences from subcontracting in aeronautics. *Technovation*, 21, 559–69.

Brandenburger, A. M., & Nalebuff, B. J. (1966). *Co-option*. New York: Doubleday.

Brusoni, S., & Prencipe, A. (2001). Technologies, products, organisations: Opening the black box of modularity. *Industrial and Corporate Change*, 10(1).

Brusoni, S., Prencipe, A., & Pavitt, K. (2001). Knowledge specialization, organizational coupling and the boundaries of the firm: Why do firms know more than they do? *Administrative Science Quarterly*, 46, 597–621.

Bryant, A. (1996, October 20). U.S. airlines finally reach cruising speed. *The New York Times*, 179–205.

Caves, R. E. (1962). Air Transport and Its Regulators, Cambridge: Harvard University Press.

Chesbrough, H., & Rosenbloom, R. (2002). The role of business model in capturing value from innovation: Evidence from Xerox Corporation's technology spin-off companies. *Industrial and Corporate Change*, 11, 529–55.

Cumpsty, N. A. (1997). Compressor Aerodynamnics, Englewood Cliffs, NJ: Prentice Hall.

Done, K., & Nicoll, A. (2002, July 22). Industry turns to attack as its best defence (Aerospace Survey). *Financial Times* (London), I.

Eliasson, G. (1996). Spillovers, integrated production and the theory of the firm. *Journal of Evolutionary Economics*, 6, 125–40.

European Association of Aerospace Industries (AECMA) (Policy Research) (2001). *The European aerospace industry: Facts & figures 2000* (p. 40). In *RP134*. Brussels: Author.

Frenken, K. (2000). A complexity approach to innovation networks. The case of the aircraft industry (1909–97), *Research Policy*, 29, 257–72.

Fritchman, B. (Boeing Mathematics and Computing Technology) (2000). *Integrating Boeing's systems design environment*.

Hatchuel, A., Saidi-Kabeche, D., & Sardas, J. C. (1997). Towards a new planning and scheduling approach for multistage production systems. *International Journal of Production Research*, 35, 867–86.

Happenheimer, T. A. (1995). *Turbulent skies: The history of commercial aviation*. New York: Wiley.

Miller, R., Hobday, M., Leroux-Demers, T., & Olleros, X. (1995). "Innovation in Complex Systems Industries: the Case of Flight Simulation," *Industrial and Corporate Change*, 4(2), 363-400.

Mowery, D. C., & Rosenberg, N. (1981). Technical change in the commercial aircraft industry, 1925-75. *Technological Forecasting and Social Change*, 20, 347-58.

Mowery, D., & Rosenberg, N. (1982). The commercial aircraft industry. In R.R. Nelson (Ed.). *Government and technical progress: A cross-industry analysis* (pp. 101-61). New York: Pergamon.

Odell, M. (2002, July 22). Design focus on the value of speed (Aerospace Survey). *Financial Times* (London), IV.

Ott, J. (2001, March 19). A380 landing gear work started early at Goodrich. *Aviation Week and Space Technology* (Article No. 20010319.htm.0). Available at http://www.awstonline.com/. Accessed December 6, 2002.

Paoli, M., & Prencipe, A. (1999). The role of knowledge bases in complex product systems: Some empirical evidence from the aero engine industry. *Journal of Management and Governance*, 3, 137-60.

Prencipe, A. (2001). Exploiting and nurturing in-house technological capabilities: Lessons from the aerospace industry. *International Journal of Innovation Management*, 5(3), 299-321.

Slack, B. (1996). *La nouvelle geographie de l'industrie aeronautique Europeene* [The story of geography in the European aeronautical industry]. Paris: Editions L'Harmattan.

Slack, B. (1997). Book reviews: La nouvelle geographie de l'industrie aeronautique Europeene (P. Beckouche, Trans.). *Economic Geography*, 73, 356-7.

Storey, J. W. C. (2002, January 14). Engine makers vie for bigger market shares. *Aviation Week and Space Technology* (Article No. 20020114.aw115.htm.0). Available at http://www.awstonline.com/. Accessed December 6, 2002.

Tennekes, H. (1997). *The simple science of flight*. Cambridge, MA: MIT Press.

Velocci, J. A. L. (1997, July 21). Merger wave to hit suppliers unevenly. *Aviation Week and Space Technology* (Article No.199811230111547.aw55-48.html). Available at http://www.awstonline.com/. Accessed December 2, 2002.

Velocci, J. A. L. (2001a, December 3). Consolidation juggernaut yet to run its course. *Aviation Week and Space Technology* (Article No. 200111203.aw48.htm.0). Available at http://www.awstonline.com/. Accessed December 6, 2002.

Velocci, J. A. L. (2001b, December 3). U.S.-Europe strategic alliances will outpace company mergers. *Aviation Week and Space Technology* (Article No. 200111203.aw56.htm.0). Available at http://www.awstonline.com/, Accessed December 6, 2002.

Vincenti, W. G. (1986). The innovation of flush riveting in American airplanes. *Technology and Culture*, 16(37), 540-76.

Winship, W. (1998). Boeing & Douglas: A history of customer service. *Aero, Boeing Magazine*, 1. Available at www.boeing.com/commercial/aeromagazine/aero_01/ps/ps01/index.html. Accessed July 9, 2002.

6

Aluminum and the Third Industrial Revolution

MARGARET GRAHAM

INTRODUCTION AND FRAMEWORK[1]

Aluminum is a child of the second industrial revolution. Without electricity it would never have been more than an expensive curiosity.[2] There's a special symmetry, therefore, in studying how this industry is faring in the third industrial revolution. I take as the framework for my argument the following issues paralleling those of Manuel Castells in his The Rise of the Network Society (2000a): the restructuring of the industry from the 1960s on; the aluminum industry's use of information and information technology and the degree to which that has enabled other changes; the rate and direction of change in other aluminum-related technologies; the differential effects of certain economic shocks on different parts of the industry; the internationalization of production capacity; the changing face of government regulation, especially antitrust, in Europe and North America; the outlook for sustainability and the

[1] Thank you to Ivan Grinberg, Institute of Aluminum History, and Russell Seidle, McGill University.
[2] As a metal more precious than gold, aluminum was used for cutlery by Napoleon and for the cap to the Washington Monument.

comparative effect of all these things on human morale, identification, and motivation.[3]

If we take note of pronouncements by senior aluminum company executives in North America who have long controlled most of the production capacity in the developed world and a significant piece of the capacity in the developing world as well, the established aluminum industry has had a rude awakening since the turn of the millennium. Despite the surge in demand for aluminum as for other commodities since 2000, the industry has belatedly acknowledged a revised, more sober view of both the promises and the threats of the third industrial revolution.

Three very serious economic shocks in the space of one managerial generation have contributed to this changing sensibility (Rolfes, 2005; Evans, 2001; Brooks, 2005). As a consequence, aluminum has transformed itself into a global industry. But has there been an industrial revolution for aluminum? As most of the aluminum-related shocks have revolved around energy, the question they raise is whether a change in energy source remains essential to the completion of any industrial revolution worthy of the name. If a third industrial revolution has been taking place, can it be said to be complete without a radical change in the source of energy? Manuel Castells maintains that the reliance on energy is characteristic of the industrial mode of development. The case of aluminum is a reminder that much of the world is only now industrializing and that information alone will not power the transformation processes that are swiftly being transferred from industrialized to industrializing economies, although it may have a profound effect on how these processes are deployed (Edgerton, 2007).

THE MATERIAL

Aluminum has a special nature and unique history: it is not and never has been a representative metal, certainly not a base metal (Smith, 1986; Graham and Pruitt, 1990; Cailluet, 2003).[4] Aluminum in its metallic form does not exist in nature. It is made from alumina, which is a refined version of bauxite. The refining process used throughout the twentieth

---

[3] See also Castells's "Information Technology and Global Capitalism" in Hutton and Giddens (2000) for a summary article focusing on the phenomenon of disconnection by countries suffering the effects of the Asian monetary crisis.

[4] See also the IAH website for books and articles about all the various national companies. Eric Rosenberg portrays aluminum as the iconic modern metal, trapped in its symbolism.

century was invented by Bayer. The smelting process by which aluminum became a mass-produced metal was invented simultaneously by Frenchman Paul Heroult and American Charles Martin Hall; hence, the Hall–Heroult process, from which sprang two companies – Pechiney and the Aluminum Company of America (Alcoa). The process of smelting alumina is so energy-intensive (second only to paper and pulp making) that the metal is often referred to by people in the industry as an "energy bank" (Evans, 2001).

CONTINUITIES

The question of industrial revolution, *oui ou non*, requires an assessment of the power of continuities and discontinuities. A constant for aluminum is the international location of sources of inputs. Aluminum producers were international from the beginning. The holders of the fundamental processing patents controlled the central processes until shortly before World War I, but they needed to move swiftly to secure reliable sources of raw material. Deposits of bauxite are found everywhere, with the most concentrated lying between twenty degrees on either side of the equator.[5] An early twentieth-century memoir by Edwin Fickes, chief engineer of Alcoa,[6] records long ocean voyages in search of bauxite deposits to secure for his company. On one such voyage, Fickes reached Moscow in 1917 just at the time that the Bolsheviks were seizing power and found there a veritable conference of aluminum pioneers, all of whom had recognized the potential of Russia's bauxite resources. Early aluminum pioneers got around, and their work was not for the faint of heart.

France, Switzerland, England, and the United States all had well-established aluminum producers before 1909, founded to exploit the Heroult and the Hall patents, and they produced over 60 percent of the world's aluminum before additional aluminum producers were found in England, France, Norway, and Italy. Because the capital requirements of smelting aluminum were so great and the threats from overcapacity so problematic, the European companies soon formed a cartel.[7] The Aluminum Company of America was the odd man out and was very much

---

[5] France and Greece had the bauxite in Europe – enough to last until after World War II.

[6] Fickes was prevailed on to write his memoirs in the 1930s as an important document in Alcoa's anticipated defense against monopoly charges, so this is no ordinary memoir.

[7] For interesting work on cartels, see Jeffrey Fear, *Oxford Handbook on Business History*.

affected by competing European products before World War I, especially AIAG's Swiss–German ingot, which compared favorably in quality with Alcoa's ingot and threatened to enter its markets. Alcoa joined the European aluminum cartel, but when strong anticartel policies and sentiments in the United States forced it to withdraw, the owners participated through their Canadian subsidiary, the Northern Aluminum Company, formed in 1901. Alcoa was further and more definitively barred from participating directly in the cartel by the provisions of a consent decree in 1912.

In 1928, Alcoa formally severed its ties with its Canadian subsidiary and divested virtually all of its foreign holdings, which included major production facilities in Canada, to Aluminium, Ltd, later known as Alcan. From then on, Alcan participated in and benefited from the European cartel, while Alcoa officially did not.[8] Until as late as 1970, Alcan operated as a holding company, with highly decentralized assets organized mainly around markets (Lanthier, 2003). From Alcoa, Alcan inherited mining, refining, and smelting operations scattered all over the world, including holdings in India, Burma, and South America. The original Aluminum Company investors continued to have the controlling interest in both companies until 1951.[9] In short, the early aluminum industry was no stranger to the search for resources on a worldwide basis or to global business networks (in this case, in the form of cartels) and the problems of being excluded from them, a situation that Castells presents as one of the defining characteristics of a network society (Fear, 2006).

In aluminum, the advantages of scale and integration were great. Early primary aluminum companies found it necessary to integrate backward to control their sources of raw material and forward into downstream production of worked materials, and even finished products.[10] Concentrated supplies of high-quality bauxite were neither ubiquitous nor plentiful until the late 1940s when huge deposits were discovered first in Central America, equatorial Guinea, and later, in Northeast Australia.

[8] In fact, A.V. Davis, who was actually chairman of both companies, was routinely present each winter in Switzerland where the members of the aluminum cartel had their meetings.

[9] Arthur Vining Davis, whose younger brother Edward K. Davis ran Alcan, handled the international affairs of both companies out of Geneva. He set up a company school to train Alcan managers in international, especially European, management. This company school eventually accepted non-Alcan people, and in the 1990s merged with Imede to become the modern-day IMD in Lausanne.

[10] Here, the aluminum company was following the model of Carnegie and the other powerful iron and steel companies that secured their sources of ore in order to ensure steady throughput.

Table 6.1. "Big Six" Capacity in
1971 (thousands of tons)

Company	Capacity	% Total
Alcoa	1,717	15
Alcan	1,582	13.8
Reynolds	1,276	11.1
Kaiser	1,021	8.9
Peychiney	886	7.8
Alusuisse	476	4.2

The most economical power source was hydropower, and countries like Canada (Quebec) and Norway that had plentiful waterpower sources combined with stable governments and low populations were ideal sites for smelters.[11] After World War II, there was the prospect of using nuclear energy as the next major power source. In North America, this did not develop as anticipated, but it was a major advantage for the aluminum industry in France because power supplies there were publicly owned and allocated.

By the 1960s, it was estimated that the capital costs of investing in a fully integrated aluminum operation were of the order of $800 million for a competitive scale facility, roughly three to seven times the cost of integrated steel works with similar capacity (Leurquin, 1986, p. 368; Pezet, 2000). Even aluminum rolling, which was the first aluminum process to be automated, enjoyed such economies of scale by the 1960s that it was mainly controlled by the large integrated producers. Such barriers to entry ensured that aluminum production in the non-Communist world was dominated by "the Big Six," four North American majors, Alcoa, Alcan, Reynolds, and Kaiser, and two Europeans, Pechiney and Alusuisse (see Table 6.1). The fragmented state of the remaining European industry meant that smaller European companies tended to specialize more in downstream production, sourcing their primary aluminum from Canada, the United States, and the one European company that was both partially government owned and a net exporter, Norsk Hydro. For a short period of time, Japan became the second largest national producer, although

[11] In fact, Norsk Hydro, one of today's largest aluminum producers, was until the 1980s primarily an energy company, with major activities in fertilizers, magnesium, and, only later, in aluminum oxide. Norsk Hydro is the result of a merger between several European companies, including the German VAW, and the acquisition of certain Alcan assets in Eastern Europe.

its importance was greatest in semifinished products like aerospace materials and cans. Little was known in the West about the industry in the Communist world during the Cold War, although some scientific publications were available and it was known that the USSR was doing advanced work in alloy research.[12]

Although the industry fell into the habit of assigning importance on the basis of volume and size, smaller companies were contributing more to the industry than the output tables would indicate. After World War II, when military funding supported research and development (R&D), a number of smaller high-tech firms were founded to develop some of the more exotic military-funded metal products. European firms, recognizing the advantage that access to both the funding and the technical knowledge sharing these firms represented, became involved with a number of them, for example, Howmet and Pechiney (see Table 6.2).

FROM PRECIOUS METAL TO STRATEGIC METAL

From the time of World War I, most aluminum companies, with the exception of Norsk Hydro, which was established as a net exporter, were nationally oriented. They remained closely identified with their respective countries and the localities in which they operated for most of the rest of the century. In Germany, France, Switzerland, Canada, and the United States, the industry became closely identified with the material aspirations of the communities in which plants were located. In places like Shawinigan, Quebec, Addy, Washington, Alcoa, Tennessee, and Saint-Jean, France, often the location of remote power sources, the aluminum plants were the only employers for miles around, providing good jobs for whole families through several generations. In general, the industry was symbolic of advanced technical capabilities and a source of many thousands of jobs that were considered such high priority that aluminum workers were generally excused from wartime military service.

Because of its light weight, the metal was particularly useful for military outfitting, and early on it came to be used on military aircraft – first, for lightweight Liberty engines, dirigibles, and trainers, and thereafter as a key structural element for airplane fuselages.[13] Because the

---

[12] Francis Frary, the founder and director of Alcoa's corporate research center for many years, devoted his retirement years to learning Russian and translating Russian technical documents.

[13] Eric Schatzberg maintains that it is doubtful that aluminum was technically superior to wood for this purpose, but it was believed to be, and every belligerent country went to

Table 6.2. Worldwide Aluminum Production, 1973–2005

				Reported Primary Aluminum Production (Thousands of Metric Tons)						
Period	Area 1: Africa	Area 2: North America	Area 3: Latin America	Area 4: East Asia	Area 5: South Asia	Area 6A: West Europe	Area 6B: East/Central Europe	Area 7: Oceania	Total	Daily Average
1973	249	5,039	229	1,149	290		2,757	324	10,037	27.5
1974	278	5,454	256	1,167	296		3,150	330	10,931	29.9
1975	272	4,400	275	1,061	329		3,062	323	9,722	26.6
1976	337	4,485	316	963	402		3,150	372	10,025	27.4
1977	367	5,093	358	1,235	379		3,292	393	11,117	30.5
1978	336	5,409	413	1,126	385		3,345	414	11,428	31.3
1979	401	5,421	668	1,084	376		3,425	425	11,800	32.3
1980	437	5,726	821	1,168	399		3,595	460	12,606	34.4
1981	483	5,603	793	817	513		3,551	536	12,296	33.7
1982	501	4,343	795	376	627		3,306	548	10,496	28.8
1983	436	4,448	942	270	717		3,322	700	10,835	29.7
1984	413	5,327	1,035	304	878		3,502	998	12,457	34
1985	472	4,781	1,160	245	918		3,327	1,091	11,994	32.9
1986	556	4,402	1,397	158	916		3,399	1,119	11,947	32.7
1987	572	4,889	1,486	927			3,462	1,273	12,609	34.5
1988	597	5,475	1,553	981			3,488	1,407	13,501	36.9
1989	603	5,587	1,698	1,093			3,580	1,501	14,062	38.5

Year										
1990	602	5,617	1,790	1,118		3,561		1,498	14,186	38.9
1991	612	5,947	1,996	1,223		3,505		1,495	14,778	40.5
1992	617	6,016	1,949	1,379		3,319		1,483	14,763	40.3
1993	616	6,000	1,949	1,530		3,236		1,653	14,984	41.1
1994	576	5,554	1,976	1,585		3,961		1,583	15,235	41.7
1995	631	5,546	2,058	1,656		5,885		1,566	17,342	47.5
1996	1,015	5,860	2,107	1,624	3,192		3,185	1,656	18,639	50.9
1997	1,106	5,930	2,116	1,910	3,297		3,316	1,804	19,479	53.4
1998	1,043	6,086	2,075	1,843	3,549		3,419	1,934	19,949	54.7
1999	1,095	6,169	2,093	1,966	3,720		3,584	2,028	20,655	56.6
2000	1,178	6,041	2,167	2,221	3,801		3,689	2,094	21,191	57.9
2001	1,369	5,222	1,991	2,234	3,885		3,728	2,122	20,551	56.3
2002	1,372	5,413	2,230	2,261	3,928		3,825	2,170	21,199	58.1
2003	1,428	5,495	2,275	2,475	4,068		3,996	2,198	21,935	60.1
2004	1,711	5,110	2,356	2,735	4,295		4,139	2,246	22,592	61.7
2005	1,753	5,382	2,391	3,139	4,352		4,194	2,252	23,463	64.3

Source: **The International Aluminum Institute** http://www.world-aluminium.org/iai/stats/historical.asp?currentYear=2006&material= 1&formType=1&dataType=1&period=4&fromYear=1973&fromMonth=1&toYear=&toMonth=1&area=&submitSearch=Find+Stats

Germans perfected the alloy, Duralumin, they were the first to use aluminum structurally, not only in zeppelins, but in Junkers and Breganets. One of the clearest signs of German intentions in the 1930s was Germany's tenfold increase in capacity to produce aluminum, from 19,000 tons to nearly 200,000 tons per annum.[14] One part of its longer-term plans that did not come to fruition until after Germany's defeat was the development of the major Norwegian hydropower center Ardal, which was completed with funding from the U.S. Marshall Plan.

In the United States, there was a perennial government concern that Alcoa's investors, fearing overexpansion, would not add sufficient capacity to meet estimated wartime needs in World War II. To ensure adequate supply and to forestall war profiteering, the U.S. government created two new aluminum companies, Kaiser and Reynolds.[15] The Roosevelt administration's concern about Alcoa's stranglehold on national capacity also manifested itself in a Justice Department antitrust action against Alcoa. The suit, initiated in 1937, but settled only after the war, found Alcoa to be a monopoly simply by virtue of its market share. Judge Learned Hand, in a precedent-setting judgment that based a complete reinterpretation of antitrust law on the Alcoa case, ruled that it was not necessary for a company to misuse its market power to be a monopoly. For decades afterward, a U.S. company could be found to be a monopoly simply by controlling a dominant share of its market regardless of how it deployed its market power (Graham and Pruitt, 1990).[16]

The U.S. government's attempts to ensure ready access to aluminum did not abate after World War II. Fears of a recurring arms race, this time with the Soviet Union, increased aluminum's importance as a strategic metal. After World War II, while the government sold to Reynolds and Kaiser at a few cents on the dollar the plants that Alcoa had built using its latest technology, Alcoa was required to license its new competitors with its latest technology. This ensured vigorous competition, but inhibited knowledge sharing between the majors. It also resulted in seriously

---

great lengths to secure its own supplies when possible (Schatzberg, 2003). The Germans were also planning to use aluminum for the new Volkswagen or Peoples' Car designed by Porsche (Tolliday and Zeitlin, 1987).

[14] Norsk Hydro got its start in aluminum when the Germans built, but did not complete, large aluminum smelting facilities at the Ardal site in Norway, using forced labor from France, Ukraine, and Russia. - www.hydro.com.

[15] Mr. Kaiser

[16] "Dissolution," wrote Judge Hand, "is not a penalty, but a remedy." It's not hard to see why Alcoa, having suffered the distribution to its competitors of nineteen out of twenty plants built using its latest technology, would consider it otherwise.

adversarial relations for several decades between the government and the technology leader of the U.S. aluminum industry. Meanwhile, the U.S. government accumulated a strategic aluminum reserve, to which Norwegians contributed much of their aluminum output as debt repayment in lieu of currency payments.

In Europe and Canada, by contrast, there was a more collaborative relationship between the various aluminum companies and between the governments and the companies, even though or possibly because they were domiciled in different countries. Some were nationalized for a period. Many had long-term contracts with their respective governments, as Alcan did for many years with the British government, making aluminum companies more like public sector companies even though they were privately owned. Pechiney, for instance, was nationalized for a period in the 1980s and 1990s.

Despite widespread investor concern that demand for aluminum would not be great enough to use the huge production capacities built during World War II, the postwar picture for aluminum was brilliant. Owing to the twin requirements of rebuilding in Europe and providing the armaments for the Korean War and the Cold War, after a period of insufficient demand in Europe (and barely a pause in the United States), the industry grew at twice the rate of the rest of the economy right through the 1960s.

For much of the twentieth century, aluminum was the coming metal for civilian uses as well as military ones in all industrialized countries, poised to oust steel from automobiles, cans, and other high-volume markets. It also achieved an important position in building construction, the electrical industry, aeronautics, transportation and communication equipment, consumer goods, containers, and, especially in the United States, packaging. In Japan, aluminum was a major area of activity for industrial entrepreneurs, generating so much investment and activity that Japan became for a brief time the second largest aluminum-producing country in the world (Odajiri and Goto, 1993).

WESTERN OLIGOPOLIES AND COMPETITION

During the second half of the century, aluminum enjoyed two remarkable periods of sustained growth, known in the industry as "golden ages" (Knauer, 2003). The first of these lasted from 1950 to 1973, and the second, particularly for aluminum can stock in North America, was from 1983 until 1990. Until the 1970s, the Big Six aluminum companies, which controlled more than 60 percent of the non-Communist world capacity of 11.5 million tons, managed to keep prices stable worldwide through a web of joint ventures and alliances. Part of the ability to control prices was the advantage of long-term supply contracts with governments and part was the industry leaders' policy of maintaining moderate and predictable pricing that would encourage higher-volume aluminum use.

Beyond traditional efforts to secure sources of bauxite and power, Alusuisse, Alcan, Pechiney, and, in the 1950s, Alcoa and Reynolds, invested in operations throughout the developing world as a way of reaching markets that were at first protected by tariffs, and when tariffs came down in the 1960s, were still guarded by nontariff controls. The European majors also found ways to sell into the fast-growing and lucrative North American market, often by investing directly in or buying outright smaller aluminum producers.

Although the industry was concentrated in regional oligopolies, and although the larger companies, aided by governments, were able to maintain very stable prices until 1970, from the industry's point of view there was never a traditional monopoly or oligopoly. Aluminum was always in competition with other materials. It began by competing with copper and zinc for volume production of electrical wire and transmission cable. It made huge efforts to displace steel in automobiles, efforts that mainly stalled before World War I (with French and German exceptions), but resumed in the 1960s. But even as it reached the industry goal of truly high-volume production by replacing steel and glass as the drinks container material of choice, other "younger" metals like titanium and magnesium were nipping at its heels. From the late 1960s on, aluminum had to defend itself against the twin assaults of a resurgent steel industry, awakened from its torpor by a wave of minimills, and by the petrochemical industry, which introduced plastics that competed aggressively for almost all the markets that aluminum had fought so hard to establish only a few years earlier. The second Golden Age – mainly a North American phenomenon – reflected the displacement of steel from cans and packaging and came to an end when plastics succeeded in muscling aluminum aside for beer and soft-drink containers.

TECHNOLOGY, INFORMATION, AND INFORMATION TECHNOLOGY

In the early years of the industry, aluminum grew and coevolved with the nascent electricity industry that made it possible to produce aluminum in sufficient quantities. If electricity made it possible to smelt aluminum, aluminum in its turn enabled the long-distance transmission of large amounts of electricity through hybrid cables made of aluminum and steel. Aluminum was also important to trams and streetcars, making the Westinghouse Company, for instance, one of the largest sources of knowledge about how aluminum worked in applied settings. In other words, aluminum momentum, as historian Thomas Hughes would have termed it, was heavily dependent on the electrical industry.

Although not strictly a "high-tech" industry as that term came to be used in the 1960s, aluminum invested more in R&D than did conventional metals companies. Before World War II, this was a German and North American phenomenon, but in the 1960s, France, Japan, and the USSR all stepped up research in light metals. Nor do R&D figures tell the whole story because many of the efforts to increase productivity in aluminum took place in smelters and on plant floors where they were counted as part of regular operational activities. Much R&D was lavished on the twin problems of replacing the bauxite-refining process, which was energy-intensive and left large residues of what was called "red mud," and replacing the smelting process, which was even more energy-intensive, emitted fluoride fumes, and released huge amounts of carbon into the air as the carbon anodes broke down (Gagne and Nappi, 2000).[17] Despite serious technical campaigns on the part of more than one leading company to find replacement processes for these two original sins of the industry, the process at the end of the twentieth century was only a much-improved version of the process used at the beginning of the century. The Hall–Heroult process consumes 13,000–16,000 kilowatt-hours per ton, which sounds like a big number until you realize that it is half as much as was required in the 1930s. The size of smelters has increased dramatically, and the chemical control of the refining process has improved, but primary metal is still made much as it was. Because it is so energy-intensive and because the costs of power amount to 24-6 percent of the total costs, energy costs are the single most important factor in international differences in production costs. As of 1994, the full operating costs for producing aluminum in the 130 smelters worldwide ranged from $790 to $1,877 per ton.

---

[17] The Bayer Process used to refine bauxite into alumina uses 16-20 percent of the total energy consumed, whereas reducing alumina to aluminum requires 65 percent. The Soderberg Process, which feeds the carbon continuously, was used for decades to improve labor productivity, but the industry now regards prebaked anodes as state of the art because they allow for better control of off-gassing.

Information has been an essential asset to aluminum companies since
the beginning: The oligopoly shared detailed information about bauxite
supply, about public energy policies, about the status of demand, and
about supplies of "dumped metal coming into Europe" (Rinde, 2003).
Individual companies generated and collected information about the
physical qualities of countless alloys, and especially, data generated by
rigorous testing of the material under all sorts of conditions. From the
time of the early dirigible crashes starting in 1900, very public events
that were nearly fatal for the industry because the metal used for dirigible
structures was implicated, industry leaders recognized that generating
technical information about their product was key. It was Alcoa's ability
to supply verifiable data from rigorous testing programs set up by a
pioneering expert hired from the U.S. National Bureau of Standards that
convinced the Army Air Corps to adopt aluminum for trainers - the first
structural use of aluminum in aircraft beyond dirigibles (Graham, 1988).

Information was also a competitive weapon, and efforts were made
by all companies to jealously guard process information in particular.
After World War I, Alcoa gained much important process knowledge
from the British by stealing it, and from the Germans, by sequestering it
(Graham, 1988). When the company was safely protected by a technical
monopoly before World War II, it shared much alloy information with its
customers and with universities in the interests of gaining broader usage
for the material, but after the technical monopoly period ended, secrecy
was the norm for decades. Indeed, during the Cold War when labor-
management strife was common in both North America and Europe,
technical knowledge was controlled even at the plant level because
of the fear of industrial spying (and also because some of the union
representatives in North America were members of the Steel Workers
Union and aluminum was competing with steel).

Between 1960 and 1985, partly in response to the urgent need
for better control of energy use, aluminum production was substantially automated. Here, Pechiney set the standard at the time with
its high capacity and highly automated potlines rated at 260,000 tons
that it installed in several joint venture facilities in the United States.[18]

[18] As the United States was by far the largest market, owing especially to military weaponry,
and as the Defense Department was funding nonferrous metal research, European firms -
especially Pechiney - purchased and allied with several North American enterprises
to operate in this regional market. Other North American metal firms like the Canadian
Noranda and the U.S. copper firm Revere followed a similar strategy to enter the aluminum
industry (Le Roux, 1998).

Computers were used to model, improve, and control rolling processes and to govern production scheduling at every stage of the production process (Graham and Pruitt, 1990). The era of technological self-sufficiency, of relying on in-house R&D as a competitive weapon, passed in the 1970s when companies began selling their technology and relying more heavily on outside consultants and sponsored research in universities. Techniques were adapted from steel minimills and advanced producers of other nonferrous materials that had developed technology based on government contracts.

Ever more sophisticated research tools - for example, the electron microscope and its successors - were adopted in aluminum laboratories as soon as they were available after World War II. By the 1980s, those tools made it possible to study and model the material and its behavior at the molecular level, to engineer materials, to recover nearly original chemical composition in recycling, and to design and test using sophisticated simulation techniques.

The discussion so far would suggest that for the aluminum industry the chief components of the Third Industrial Revolution - globalization of supplies and markets, the gathering of extensive data, and the application of information technology, are evolutionary matters, hardly the stuff of genuine revolution. Nevertheless, as I indicated earlier, the aluminum industry was visited by some profound economic shocks in the 1970s - the period that Manuel Castells identifies as the beginning of the Third Industrial Revolution. It is to this transition and its aftermath that I now turn.

THIRD INDUSTRIAL REVOLUTION CRISES AND RESPONSES

The aluminum industry experienced three major crises after the start of the Third Industrial Revolution: the two OPEC oil boycotts (1973-4 and 1977-8); the commodity listing crisis in 1978 following the second energy price hike; and the overproduction crisis in 1991-3. These shocks concatenated to form a formidable set of hurdles that only some companies managed to surmount.

After World War II, the worldwide aluminum industry, which was largely western, enjoyed a sustained period of high demand, growing at roughly 8 percent compounded yearly between 1950 and 1970. This incredible run came to a halt with the Middle East oil embargo of 1973-4, when one of the industries' two chief inputs tripled in price. In fact, there had already been signs in the 1960s that the days of

oligopolistic control were coming to a close as governments in less industrialized countries began to subsidize stand-alone smelters. During the
1960s, the percentage of world capacity that was government sponsored
grew from 16 to more than 20 percent (jumping even more sharply to
30 percent by 1985). The specter of excess world capacity, experienced by most companies in postwar periods, once again loomed large.
Substitute materials were also gaining in importance at this time. Plastics were popping up in markets as diverse as construction, transportation, machinery, and packaging, and steel was waking up to the challenge of countering the threat of aluminum in automobiles, packaging,
and aircraft. For the first time since the early decades of the industry,
hybrid materials like steel-reinforced aluminum for cans and car parts
and plastic-coated retort packaging seemed to be the wave of the future.

What might have been a gradual shift that required adaptation changed to a terrible cost spiral for the industry when first the petroleum-
producing countries represented by OPEC, and then the producers of
bauxite represented by a cartel of their own, caused ingot production
costs to rise by multiples of three or more for most aluminum producers.[19] There followed double-digit inflation, attempts at price controls
in the United States, and wage demands by both unions and salaried personnel in all industrialized countries. In October 1978, after the second
oil shock of the decade, the London Metals Exchange (LME) started listing aluminum for the first time, and it soon became evident that the days
of producer-controlled pricing were over. By 1980, there was serious
overcapacity of aluminum in world markets, and the ability of the old
regional oligopolies to maintain prices had disappeared. Companies that
had been in the business for a century in Western Europe, Japan (which
had the most expensive energy costs), and the United States were forced
to cut back their production at old uneconomic smelters and lower their
production rates, while Canada, New Zealand, and countries in Asia,
Africa, and Latin America increased their production significantly.

It was not long after the occurrence of the economic shocks of the
1970s – the twin oil price shocks and the LME listing – that the shape of
the aluminum industry altered irrevocably (Prokopov, 2005).[20] Because
many subsidized smelters in developing countries were stand-alones,

---

[19] See Smith (1986, p. 386) for a table on major cost elements at Alcoa between 1970 and
1986.
[20] The effect of the LME listing over time has been to stabilize prices through investment
holding – i.e., growth of unregistered aluminum stocks and their use as an investment
tool.

the large, formerly integrated producers had to compete on intermediate products. Essentially, although the larger established companies remained integrated, the industry disintermediated. Upstream operations aligned more with other mining and metals companies, and downstream operations became diversified. Established companies sought out new forms of energy supply, invested heavily in automation and downstream processing, shifted much of their new investment overseas, and considered their options for going forward.

Several majors had been trying independently to develop alternative smelting processes that would use less energy and overcome some of the worst environmental hazards of the old smelting process, including the need to change out carbon anodes on a regular basis. These research pioneers were so confident of ultimate success that several majors began selling off the most sophisticated of the old technology in the late 1960s. Pechiney made its technology available initially in the developing world, causing Alcoa to reverse its ironclad policy of never revealing process secrets to anyone and to begin an aggressive technology sales effort in 1972.

The split between upstream and downstream focused the integrated companies' attention more on downstream products and drove the companies to hitch their wagon to aluminum's superior sustainability relative to plastics, stressing the full life cycle of the product. More emphasis was placed on recycling techniques that would allow recovered aluminum to take the place of newly smelted metal for all but a few special products. Several companies did serious cumulative work on improving can sheet and can design, leading to an almost complete takeover by aluminum from steel of the aluminum beer and soda can business. This business took off in 1983 and grew rapidly until 1990 when it leveled off just as rapidly, yielding ground in turn to the successful efforts of Pepsi Co., Inc., to introduce plastic bottles for supersized drinks.

In the 1960s, in response to public demand, North American and European governments began implementing environmental pollution controls.[21] Companies that could not control energy costs or government mandates turned instead to cutting costs where they did have some control – reducing employment in their home countries and negotiating new energy pricing arrangements with energy suppliers. In a move that would continue steadily for the next several decades,

---

[21] Some of the earliest instances of this kind of public resistance occurred when Pechiney began installing its processes in the Netherlands in the 1960s.

established companies in high-cost industrialized countries moved even more aggressively abroad, not just to find cheaper labor, but even more to locate smelting and refining facilities where energy costs might be lower and more diversified.[22]

For a time in the mid-1980s, Alcoa, a technology leader on the product side of the industry, made an attempt to develop alternative strategic options through R&D, looking at product differentiation in addition to scale and overseas expansion. Seeing the drastic changes that had affected the industry, its then top management projected a new reality in which aluminum was no longer the metal of the future and in which the industry would have to find a different set of products to offer. In its famous Annual Report of 1982, Alcoa's outgoing CEO, Krome George, acknowledged that the world had changed for aluminum. Shortly thereafter, his successor, Charles Parry, predicted that Alcoa might be out of the aluminum business in ten years. In 1985, he shut down Alcoa's experimental smelting plant in Point Comfort, Texas, the fruit of a secretive attempt to develop the Alcoa Smelting Process (ASP) that the company had been pursuing for over a decade in an attempt to achieve a more efficient and environmentally friendly smelting process. If aluminum as such was going to be less important, Parry reasoned, then Alcoa would become a "specialty materials" company. In this case, secondary aluminum could supply a good deal of the necessary inputs and there was no point in pursuing expensive alternatives to the Hall–Heroult process. After making a significant investment in alternative technologies like composite materials based on alumina, and molded and machined computer disk drives, Alcoa nevertheless abandoned the path of significant technological diversification, and with it, the chance for the industry in the developed world to pursue meaningful options to primary aluminum.

Senior management at Alcoa other than the technical staff had never been comfortable with the phasing out of aluminum, and when the board began to share their discomfort, Charles Parry was fired and replaced by Paul O'Neill. O'Neill turned his attention to making Alcoa the largest and most productive company in the industry, stressing safety as the most important goal, flattening the organization, and forcing the company to adopt such progressive practices as the paperless office.[23] The search for

---

[22] Alcoa invested heavily in two countries, Australia and Brazil.

[23] Whether O'Neill's time in the paper industry between stints in government service prompted his insistence on ridding Alcoa of paper, it was one way of ensuring that

alternatives to aluminum was gradually curtailed. When Alcoa redirected its various R&D efforts, Alcan did much the same.

Instead of radical diversification, Alcoa followed the middle path of refocusing on higher value-added aluminum and invested heavily in a joint development program with Audi. Although there had been lower-volume aluminum cars like the Pierce Arrow and, later, the Dyna by Panhard in France, earlier efforts to pursue this kind of development with American carmakers had foundered. It was significant, therefore, that it was Audi, feeling greater pressures on the European car market to reduce fuel consumption, that was willing to partner with Alcoa. Some automobiles such as Land Rover, Jaguar, and Chevrolet (Corvette) had already used aluminum for selected parts of their cars. The first contemporary aluminum car was actually produced by Honda – a sports vehicle sold under the name Acura in the United States – and several high-cost sports vehicles had aluminum bodies, but the aim of the Audi–Alcoa collaboration program was to produce an aluminum-intensive vehicle (*Wall Street Journal*, 2006).[24]

More than ten years later, the cost penalty for an aluminum structure in an automobile had dropped considerably from the $500 it was estimated to be in 2001, but even Audi had backed off from introducing a completely aluminum body, adopting a hybrid instead. The Aluminum Intensive Vehicle could be more symbol than substance if large amounts of aluminum continued to be used, but steel fought back with new specialized steels and antirust treatments, making it possible that if aluminum prices rose, 2006 could be the high-water mark for aluminum in automobiles.

In hindsight, Alcoa's retreat from the pursuit of strategic diversification into advanced materials and much higher value-added products was a turning point for the industry as a whole, and certainly for the industry in the developed world. Alcoa, as traditional technology leader in the non-Communist world, had the chance to open a wider set of opportunities going forward for its industry. When the chance was foreclosed, the use of composite materials for aircraft, for instance, was significantly

---

his entire management was computer savvy and not technology averse, a problem that hampered many industrial companies and not a few IT companies in the 1980s and 1990s.

[24] Alcoa invested over $250 million dollars in the program with Audi. Sixteen years after Honda introduced the first car with an all-aluminum unibody, the Audi TT, which was originally supposed to switch to an all-aluminum structure in 2007, was announced as a hybrid framework containing one-third steel. Note that it was VW, related to Audi, that had been an early user of 60 percent of Norsk Hydro's magnesium output.

delayed. Instead, Alcoa threw its weight on the side of convincing customers like Boeing that aluminum was the material of the future – a line they were very willing to embrace – and the leadership in composites that aluminum companies might have had went to others with less of the potential capacity to make them into a conventional material any time soon.

CRISES OF GLOBALIZATION

Aside from pushing more value-added, downstream products in the 1990s, the majors strategically converged on a common path, choosing the uncertainties of international investment and the greater certainties of productivity seeking over the higher-risk, higher-return possibilities of technology-based innovation. Alcoa and Alcan absorbed other companies to gain scale, set up overseas alliances, and doubled and tripled their overseas production sites, moving from internally generated growth to acquisition wherever possible. They did this in the context of the first globalization crisis for the industry, when Russian aluminum flooded the market in the early 1990s following the disintegration of the USSR and the sudden privatization of its large companies.

Not surprisingly, the move by the North American companies to expand internationally excited nationalist feeling. Worldwide consolidation, which threatened the older and more inefficient plants in the home countries of the majors, would bring out even more. As early as the 1950s, this sort of reaction was experienced in the competition between Alcoa and Reynolds for British Aluminium (BA). Although BA was desperate for infusions of capital and not well managed, the British public, alarmed by critical newspaper articles, opposed the sale of these "national assets," even though the most valuable assets owned by the British company were actually located in Canada and Australia (Cailluet, 2003; Smith, 1986). At that time, the majors did not have coherent international strategies, but simply opportunistic ones of access to markets through acquiring assets. The majors later developed very clearly articulated international strategies, but they came too late to offer comfort to countries and regions that were trying to retain good jobs in manufacturing. By 2007, it became evident that aluminum companies, along with other commodity metals, were likely to be absorbed by cash-rich mining companies. This was due to the fact that mining companies lacked the overriding concern with energy sources that had kept aluminum companies in close touch with national and provincial governments that controlled power sources, especially hydropower and more exotic sources like Iceland's geothermal energy.

ANTITRUST RECONFIGURED

The renewed interest in consolidation and merger in the developed world in the last third of the twentieth century revealed a split between North America and Europe in antitrust policy similar to the one that had also tripped up several large U.S. firms – Coca-Cola, Microsoft, and General Electric. In the United States under the Reagan administration in the 1980s, there was a reversal of longstanding government policy against combinations that ultimately proved to be a turning point in U.S. antitrust policy (Galambos, 2006). Very little opposition arose to Alcoa absorbing Reynolds or Alumax, and by the late 1990s, the more pressing question was what the U.S. Energy Department and its laboratories might do to improve Alcoa's chances of making a success of its new inert anode approach to smelting (Aluminum Association, 1997).[25]

For the European Union, however, the matter of industry consolidation, especially under foreign control, was a more controversial issue. When Alcan first proposed to merge with Alusuisse and Pechiney in the late 1990s, the move was halted by the European Union monopoly authorities. Alcan and Alusuisse did merge, leaving Pechiney temporarily on the sidelines. Several years later, the outlines of a new world order became apparent in more than just aluminum, the European Union Monopolies Commission muted its objections. Alcan then also merged with Pechiney, thus moving control of a large segment of the entire industrialized world industry to North America. Acquiring Pechiney, whose process technology was still advanced but that had electricity contracts that were set to expire in the near future, with companies that might well be privatized, may not have been such a good deal for the acquirers. The remaining sizable European player, Hydro Aluminium (capacity approximately 1 million tons), announced in June 2006 that it would be closing a tenth of its European capacity – two German

---

[25] The 1997 report contains results of a joint technology planning initiative undertaken by the U.S. Department of Energy and the Aluminum Association to position the U.S. industry to compete effectively in world markets. Despite its free market rhetoric, the U.S. government has been giving considerable support to the U.S. aluminum companies' attempts to achieve success with the inert anode, which would not only improve efficiency, but also reduce carbon emissions. This project has been eagerly awaited by the U.S. investment community for some time, but currently seems no closer than it was five years ago.

operations – because it had been unable to secure favorable power contracts in Germany. Meanwhile, it was constructing a 570,000-ton smelting plant in Qatar.

GLOBAL INDUSTRY RESTRUCTURING

Once the North American aluminum industry largely absorbed the European industry, it became a worldwide industry that took on a form different from its twentieth-century model. In the twentieth century, the non-Communist aluminum industry had been split into regional oligopolies comprising large integrated companies with strong links through alliances to smelters and rolling plants in the developing world. In the twenty-first century, the industry appeared to be gradually splitting into developed countries' industry versus the developing countries' industry. Whereas the largest markets in the previous era were concentrated in the United States, China became the largest twenty-first-century buyer, accounting for 30 percent of total aluminum demand in 2006.

The developed world industry led by Alcan and Alcoa, as well as the Russian Rusal (speaking through organizations like the Aluminum Association – a North American association now making overtures to associations in China and Latin America) tried to convince the developing world that one global industry linked through associations and alliances and all adhering to the same standards would be in everyone's best interests. Seven strategic principles were articulated for the industry as a whole, charting both direction and priority: (1) Globalize the business, making the necessary geographic shifts that will minimize energy, raw material processing, and transportation costs; (2) use captive, self-generated power; (3) modernize smelting capacity to cut production costs and investments using Greenfield smelters; (4) increase ratios of value-added products; (5) maximize the use of secondary aluminum; (6) develop long-term production and technology alliances with the major customers; and (7) increase social responsibility of business and industry.

Through the linked channels of industry associations as well as through their current webs of alliances, Alcan and Alcoa started to share knowledge and link scientific efforts. In Manuel Castells's terms, these linked associations are networks for which the new information technologies are key, but in social terms they are basically only conduits. Whether the interpretation of mutual and balanced interest is accepted at both ends of the conduits is another matter. So far, the emerging powerhouse in the developing world is the Russian industry that, as of this writing, has just become one company through the merger of the two Russian companies, Rusal and Sual. The outcome may well determine the nature of the global industry going forward.

In autumn 2006, Rusal Ltd. acquired Sual, as well as some assets from the commodities trader USB-owned company Glencore, partly for its ore supplies and also for its power. The Russian company had made no secret of its goal of becoming the largest aluminum company in the world, and it unquestionably had access to plentiful cheap power as well as controlling large amounts of smelting capacity.

North American aluminum executives claimed to not take the latest expansions very seriously because many of the Russian company's smelters were old and very remotely located, but there was little doubt that the Russian enterprise had acquired the aggregate capacity to annually turn out more aluminum (5 million metric tons) than Alcoa (4 million metric tons). Meanwhile, new aluminum companies have started up in many areas that have access to cheap power in India, Africa, and the Middle East. In some cases, these countries also have good access to ore supplies. In the Middle East, countries continued to enjoy good capital positions owing to the radical rise in fuel prices and were anxious to diversify out of petroleum and natural gas (*Wall Street Journal*, 2006).

Sohar Aluminum Co. was building a large smelter in Oman, and Aluminium Bahrain B.S.C. (Alba) built the Alba smelter, one of the lowest-cost smelters in the world and the third largest anywhere, with 3,000 employees and capacity to make 840,000 tons of aluminum a year. Bahrain has plans to expand Alba to make as much as 1.3 million metric tons a year. Companies in these developing countries are diversifying their holdings so that they can not only supply the Chinese market, which has no sources either of ore or cheap energy, but can also be prepared to ride out the inevitable cyclicalities of the market.

In the face of such well-capitalized and partially subsidized developing world competition, and with the cash-rich mining companies nipping at their heels, former arch rivals Alcan and Alcoa were moved to share technology with each other in ways they would never have done before. They could point to both power plants they own outright in North America and to new smelters in locations as varied as Pakistan, Siberia, and Brunei, with power sources, in addition to hydropower, as varied as geothermal, natural gas, and coal. Moreover, in Iceland, Alcoa planned to bring online a 344,000-ton-a-year plant that it claimed would be the cleanest and most modern plant in the world, based on Alcan's AP30 technology for using geothermal energy (Bream, 2005; interview with Bernt Reitan of Alcoa).

Predictions are that the worldwide aluminum market by the year 2020 will double to 60 million tons per year from over 30 million tons in 2005. Asia is expected to consume about half of the world's aluminum by that time, with other emerging regions also experiencing a surge in demand. Even though modern highly automated facilities have more flexibility to changes in demand, and aluminum's commodity listing helps stabilize demand as well, episodes of past volatility create concern that the specter of overproduction could reappear and would hit the oldest facilities hardest.

The emergence of the newly combined Russian company as the largest aluminum company in the world, as well as the new companies in the Middle East, comes in the middle of yet another energy shock. This one, in 2005–6, in which oil prices soared from $32 per barrel to over $70 before dropping back again, caused at least one North American major to change some of its policies very quickly.

Aside from looming spreads in energy costs between different parts of the industry, environmental issues are another area in which the developed and developing industries may be differentially affected with major cost implications. The North American industry has adopted a vocal policy stressing corporate responsibility toward workers, toward communities, and toward the environment, stressing recycling as environmentally friendly and arguing that recovery and reuse of secondary metal makes up for the environmental problems of the primary stages of production. Responsible corporate policies have played a large part in the strategies of both Alcoa and Alcan for decades. Their argument for being the best metal for use on cars as well as in cans and packaging is the life-cycle argument that, despite its high initial energy usage and in spite of the continued carbon emissions emitted by standard smelter technology, aluminum's light weight and superior recyclability produces vehicles, cans, and packaging that lead to better fuel standards than steel and that aluminum's superior recycling capabilities make it better than plastics throughout the vehicle life cycle. In recent years, in fact, aluminum has topped a 50 percent recovery rate in North America and 40 percent in Europe.

The signing of the Kyoto Accord in Europe and Canada, however, has directed laserlike attention at the primary stages of aluminum production. Aluminum is charged with being one of the two largest polluters in Canada (along with oil sands production) at a time when carbon emissions are starting to be an issue between Quebec and the Canadian Federal government. In the United States, where Kyoto has been a more regional issue, the industry has a lower environmental profile.

The big question concerning the environment is whether all parts of the global industry will accept the same policy, which in the short term is certain to add cost, though in the longer run could yield significant, if uncertain, economies. Even if all regions were to embrace sustainability, older facilities will bear a higher penalty. If some parts of the industry were to choose not to embrace sustainability and seize competitive advantage instead, they could have a serious short-term cost advantage.

Moreover, it remains to be seen how well the idea of a global industry will play in the developing world, where most new smelters are partly owned by governments and where part of the appeal of participating in the industry is to exercise political power through control over resources and pricing. So far, China, the Middle East, and Africa have shown little inclination to accept environmental issues as necessary costs. Russia has committed to the seven priorities articulated by the North American industry and will presumably keep such commitments as long as it maintains its current joint venture agreements. These center on downstream processing, some of which it has outsourced to North American industry in order to gain the necessary technological expertise.

IMPLICATIONS FOR MORALE, MOTIVATION, AND RESISTANCE

One of the most striking reversals in the global restructuring story that is now unfolding is the way it is changing the nature of the playing field between developing and developed parts of the industry. The North American industry has enjoyed incomparable advantages for a century and still has better access to technological expertise and educated workforces than any other place on earth. Moreover, it is an industry that has globalized its management employees far more than other industries. Over half of its employees are from outside North America, as is half Alcoa's board of directors. Both companies predict that in ten years more than half their operations will be outside North America and Europe.

Even in anticipation of increasing demand and record revenues, the North American industry faces a number of daunting and as yet unresolved challenges arising out of the recent shifts in its strategy and the conditions it faces. In moves to reduce costs, it is closing down plants located in traditional aluminum communities both in Canada and the

United States. In keeping with their commitment to articulated principles of responsibility to communities and workforces, both Alcan and Alcoa have reinvested in modernizing some of their best plants in places like Davenport, Iowa, and Rockdale, Texas. But even in these exceptional "turnarounds," they are shedding workers. Alcoa alone announced 6,500 layoffs in 2006 and expects a 30 percent reduction in its U.S. workforce overall. Many older operations in Europe, too, which is considered a higher-cost place to operate because of its progressive labor and environmental regulations, will close if they have not already.

Despite its cost cutting, the developed world industry is vulnerable to the fluctuating favor of capital markets, which in the face of spikes in energy costs in 2005, downgraded the stock price by around 20 percent. This makes investment in new plant and plant modernizations more costly. Moreover, the economics remain uncertain owing to the privatization and deregulation of some energy sources and the failure to deliver on promised new technologies that have figured large in financial analysts' reports on the industry.

The set of challenges facing aluminum in the developed world makes it seem and act more like the mining industry or the steel industry, and less like the industry of the future that it was for most of the twentieth century. Indeed, in a real departure from the days when aluminum executives spent their entire careers in aluminum, the industry has been losing experienced high-level executives to these other industries. Most recently, Anglo-American Ltd. of South Africa has announced the hiring of Alcan's Cynthia Carroll to be its new CEO. Carroll is one of Alcan's several senior women executives, head of its Primary Metals business, key to implementing its merger with Pechiney, and one of the executives known to be directly in line for succession at Alcan. Her willingness to move outside the old industry is a sign of a new kind of mobility in which managers are identifying more broadly with a set of operations and activities they have experienced in many different settings around the world and less with the particular culture of a particular company.

The Russian aluminum industry offers a contrasting employment picture (Prokopov, 2005).[26] Through the difficult days of privatization following the fall of the Berlin Wall, it retained a loyal and skilled workforce, keeping motivation high by increasing productivity every year after privatization. Now, it is locating new plants in countries all over the old Soviet Union – smelters in Siberia, Ukraine, and Armenia. As

[26] Prokopov is president of the Association of Aluminum Producers of Russia.

mentioned, it is acquiring technological expertise through joint ventures with western companies, including several with Alcoa. It has also sold former Russian rolling mills to North American companies and sealed these deals with long-term contracts. In negotiations that appear highly innovative for Eastern Europe, it has worked out risk-sharing agreements with communities in which it is located. With a goal of being the largest in the world, a growing and loyal workforce, a sense of momentum, and a supply of capital that is not altogether constrained by western stock markets, Rusal, Ltd. and its affiliates resemble the North American industry in the takeoff period following World War II. Mastery of information technology and access to technological expertise through networks of associations certainly are helping it to achieve unprecedented scale in plant size, but the primary source of its momentum seems to be quite traditional – commitment to people and communities.

CONCLUSION

In theory then, both halves of the global industry – developed and developing – face the same demand conditions, but prospects for the industry in the developing world look considerably brighter. From a global perspective this is an encouraging picture, somewhat different from Castells's predictions, for it suggests a rebalancing between richer and poorer nations in which the global industry has an interest in sharing its technology in return for access to explosive markets and secure resources and energy supplies.

Revolutions are notoriously difficult to read from the middle. It is too soon to tell whether attempts at global industry governance through linked industry associations, reminiscent of efforts in the United States in the 1920s, will in fact help to stabilize the industry, or whether they are merely transitional mechanisms that will disappear or assume less importance when the revolution ends. It is also too early to tell whether new approaches to environmental policy through all-party negotiations, greater public transparency to NGOs and the public at large, will outweigh or at least help to balance the competitive pressures of a global marketplace. This is the approach now being tried by the European Union (Harribey, 2006). Will shared technology offer a sufficient payoff for developing countries to be willing to internalize the costs of environmental controls and good labor practices?

One thing this look at the aluminum industry suggests, however, is that for some industries at least, information sharing and networks repeatedly have been natural responses to turbulent times brought about by shifts in technology. Information technology has clearly been a combinatorial factor in this mix. It has also been a powerful enabler. It has enabled a spread of enterprises around the globe, a certain expansion of the span of control of any one enterprise, an increase in scale, an ability to automate processes and dramatically reduce direct employment, and possibly an increase in employee mobility, especially managerial employee mobility. But for the aluminum industry, the most important causal factor, perhaps the determining factor, in the discontinuity we see in the twenty-first century is energy. Until the economics of energy changes in some dramatic way, or until a renewable source of energy is found without the dangers and vagaries of nuclear power, aluminum will continue to go through highly volatile periods, causing major dislocations for its workforce, its customers, and the communities in which it is located. In this sense, the aluminum industry may well be the canary in the mine.

REFERENCES

Aluminum Association (1997). *Aluminum industry technology roadmap*. Brussels: Author.
Aluminium industry in Europe – Present and future profiled. (1998). *Metallurgia*, *65*(8), 264.
Amdam, R. P. (2003). Organizational changes in two Norwegian aluminium companies: The case of ASV and Alnor [Special issue on Europe]. *Cahiers d'Histoire de l'Aluminium*, No. 1.
Bream, R. (2005, November 2). Profitability depends on what you make of the opportunities that are out there. *Financial Times* (London).
Brooks, M. (2005). Insights on the global aluminum industry. Paper presented to the China Aluminum Association.
Cailluet, L. (2003). The British aluminium industry, 1945–80s: Chronicle of a death foretold? [Special issue on Europe]. *Cahiers d'Histoire de l'Aluminium*, No.1.
Cameron, K. (2006, October 22). Aluminum is striving for mass appeal, but with a lot less mass. *New York Times*.
Carbon fibre composites are posing a threat in the air (Special report on aluminium). FT.
Castells, M. (2000a). *The rise of the network society*. Malden, MA: Blackwell.
Castells, M. (2000b). Information technology and global capitalism. In Hutton, W., & Giddens, A. (Eds), *Global Capitalism* (pp. 52–74). New York: New Press.
Edgerton, D. (2007). *The shock of the old: Technology and global history since 1900*. New York: Oxford University Press.
Evans, R. (2001). 7 Deadly sins. Address to the International Aluminum Association, London.

Fear, J. R. (2006). *Cartels and competition: Neither markets nor hierarchies.* Boston: Harvard Business School.

Figuerol-Ferretti, I. (2005). Prices and production cost in aluminium smelting in the short and the long run. *Applied Economics, 37,* 917 (12).

Fonteyne, A. (2003). Semi-finished aluminium products in the Benelux: An open market and major exporters. [Special issue on Europe]. *Cahiers d'Histoire de l'Aluminium,* No. 1.

Fridenson, P. (2003). Conclusion. [Special issue on Europe]. *Cahiers d'Histoire de l'Aluminium,* No. 1, 123-4.

Gagne, R., & Nappi, C. (2000). The cost and technological structure of aluminium smelters worldwide. *Journal of Applied Economics, 15,* 4, 118-24.

Galambos, L. (2006, June). Globalization, antitrust, and the information age of Manuel Castells. Paper presented at the Business History Conference.

Global Aluminum (2006). *Industry Profile, DataMonitor.* New York: Author.

Graham, M. B. W. (1988). R&D and competition in England and the United States: The case of the aluminum industry. *Business History Review, 62*(2), 261-85.

Graham, M. B. W., & Pruitt, B. H. (1990). *R&D for industry: A century of technical change at Alcoa.* Edited by Louis Galambos. New York: Cambridge University Press.

Grinberg, I., Griset, P., & LeRoux, M. (Eds). (1997). *Cent ans d'Innovation dans l'industries de l'aluminium* [One-hundred years of innovation in the aluminium industries]. L'Harmattan, Paris.

Hachez-Leroy, F. (2003). The construction of Europe and its consequences on the French aluminium industry [Special issue on Europe]. *Cahiers d'Histoire de l'Aluminium,* No. 1.

Harribey, L. (2006). La theorie des parties prenantes dans le referentiel communautairee et son impact dans les politiques Europeennes de recherche et d'education. "Paper presented at the ADERSE Conference, Bordeaux, France.

Hunt, W. H., Jr. (2004). *The China factor: Aluminum industry impact.*

Hutton, W., & Gidden, A. (Eds). (2000). *Global capitalism.* New York: New Press.

Knauer, M. (2003). The "golden years": The European aluminium industry during the postwar economic boom [Special issue on Europe]. *Cahiers d'Histoire de l'Aluminium,* No. 1.

Lanthier, P. (2003). Alcan from 1945-75: The uncertain road to maturity. [Special issue on Europe]. *Cahiers d'Histoire de l'Aluminium,* Paris, No. 1.

Le Roux, M. (1998). *L'entreprise et la recherche: Un siècle de recherché industrielle a Pechiney.* Histoire Industrielle, Paris, éditions Rive Droite.

Lesclous, R. (2003). Nuclear power and the revival of primary aluminium production in Europe [Special issue on Europe]. *Cahiers d'Histoire de l'Aluminium,* No. 1.

Philippe Leurquin, *Marche Commun et Localizations* (Louvain, 1962) quoted in Smith From Monopoly to Competition.

Maier, H. (2003). From aircraft scrap to export boom: Production and consumption of the German aluminium industries from 1945-75 [Special issue on Europe]. *Cahiers d'Histoire de l'Aluminium,* No. 1.

New CEO for Angla-American. (October 25, 2006). *Financial Times.*

Odajiri, H., & Goto, A. (1993). The Japanese system of innovation: Past, present and future. In Nelson, R. R. (Ed), *National innovation systems : A comparative analysis*. New York: Oxford University Press.

Paquier, S. (2003). The Alusuisse Group, 1945–75: An analysis of a Swiss multinational company during the great growth period [Special issue on Europe]. *Cahiers d'Histoire de l'Aluminium*, No. 1.

Pezet, A. (2000). La décision d'investissement industriel: Le cas de l'aluminium. *Economica.*

Prokopov, I. (2005). The Russian aluminum industry: Trends and reflections of the global market. *Journal of Metals, 57*(2), 32.

Rinde, H. (2003). The powerhouse of Europe: The growth of the Norwegian aluminum industry: 1945–70 [Special issue on Europe]. *Cahiers d'Histoire de l'Aluminium*, No. 1.

Rolfes, R. (2005). Running ahead of discontinuity. In *Forward Online: Global Perspective from MSCI.*

Sanders, R. E., Jr. (2001). Technology innovation in aluminum products. *Journal of Metals, 53*(2), 21–5.

Schatzberg, E. (2003). Symbolic culture and technological change: The cultural history of aluminum as an industrial material. *Enterprise and Society, 4,* 226–71.

Smelting is migrating from the traditional industrial heartlands. (2005, November 2). *Financial Times*, Special Report on Aluminum.

Smith, G. D. (1986). *From monopoly to competition: The transformation of Alcoa, 1888–1986.* New York: Cambridge University Press.

Tolliday, S., & Zeitlin, J. (Eds). (1987). *The automobile industry and its workers: Between Fordism and flexibility.* New York: St. Martin's Press.

7

The Role of the State in the Third Industrial Revolution

Continuity and Change

ANDREA COLLI AND NICOLETTA CORROCHER

INTRODUCTION

Nearly 50 years ago, Alexander Gerschenkron published his seminal book, *Economic Backwardness in Historical Perspective* (Gerschenkron, 1963). The lessons that Gerschenkron derived from the economic history of the European nations trying to catch up with the leaders of the first industrial revolution proved to be useful for those who were interested in the forces behind economic growth. By examining the successful efforts of Germany, Russia, and Italy to escape the cage of economic stagnation, the Russian scholar illuminated an apparently easy way to jump on the fast train to industrialization. The presence of alternative factors fostering the industrialization process revealed a powerful model for closing that gap by exploiting relatively easy access to the most up-to-date technology through a virtuous mix of financial resources made available by skilled intermediaries (banks); human capital trained in technical school, universities, and polytechnics; and state policies directly and indirectly sustaining the industrialization process.

The notion of the state as an alternative variable that could accelerate the catch-up process since then has been a powerful concept. It has been applied to different historical and geographical contexts and still proves to be an attractive analytical tool for scholars trying to explain particularly successful stories of fast economic growth and development: for instance, in the case of late industrializing countries in the Far East and Latin America (Amsden, 2001; Amsden and Hikino, 1994). From a historical perspective, it proves to be extremely useful. The state has played an essential role not only during the catch-up process created by the first industrial revolution, but also during the second industrial revolution, and a strong continuity between the two industrial revolutions exists (Millward, 2005). Furthermore, the state was among the main forces behind the catch-up process between the two World Wars. In capital- and knowledge-intensive industries, it provided the necessary conditions for private initiative to take place. Even more, in some specific countries – for instance, Italy or Spain – direct intervention (the state entrepreneur) was the only way to fill the technological gap and to provide the financial, technical, and human resources necessary to cope with the challenges of the "new" industrial revolution.

A great deal of research on this issue is now available, examining both national cases and the articulated range of instruments employed by governments to implement economic and industrial policies in the capital-intensive sectors of the second industrial revolution (see, for example, Toninelli, 2000). Given all of this, a nonnegligible research question concerns the evolution of the state's intervention during the third industrial revolution, which here we define as a group of innovations that transformed some industries (e.g., chemicals and pharmaceuticals, telecommunication systems, electronics) or created *ab nihilo* new products and processes (e.g., biotechnology, new materials). The aim of this chapter is to provide some theoretical reflections and empirical evidence on the role of the state in stimulating knowledge-based entrepreneurship and growth during the third industrial revolution. We describe some of the essential features of this revolution, provide some empirical evidence on the role of the state in the third industrial revolution with particular reference to the case of information and communication technologies (ICTs) and biotechnology, and offer some theoretical reflections on the role of state intervention in different technological and organizational contexts by discussing continuity and change across the second and third industrial revolutions.

THE THIRD INDUSTRIAL REVOLUTION: GENERAL REMARKS

The process breakthroughs of the three industrial revolutions differ substantially not only in the specific technologies involved, but also in the resulting form of enterprise and in the nature and role of the actors involved. One crucial aspect of the third industrial revolution is the emergence of information processes linked to the automation of control following the introduction of radical innovations in information and communication technologies. Moreover, the peculiarity of this revolution lies not only in the central role of knowledge and information, but more prominently in the application of knowledge and information to different products and processes and the elaboration of knowledge itself, so that a virtual cycle of development and use of innovations unfolds (Von Tunzelmann, 1997, 2003).

The emergence of information technology contributed to the development of domains of innovation within which inventions and applications could be tested and learning by doing constituted a crucial component. Within these milieus, there was a concentration of actors interacting in a very proactive way: research centers, universities, high-tech small and large firms, venture capitalists, public institutions. This variety not only allowed the internal development of capital goods and human resources, but also attracted foreign knowledge in the form of technologies and people. As Castells (2002) suggests, this revolution took place within metropolitan areas that were able to create knowledge-based synergies that were subsequently transferred in industrial production and commercial applications. What is really crucial in the development of the information technology revolution is the interface between two forces: large research programs and public procurement on the one hand, and decentralized innovation driven by technological creativity by individual entrepreneurs on the other.

The new ICTs form the basis of a new technological paradigm that had a pervasive impact on the economy as a whole. Several new products and techniques were developed around these technologies, and this explains the rapid growth of ICT products over the past thirty years. The pervasive character of ICT is related to its impact on the more traditional industries in terms of methods of production and organizational structures of these industries, that is, management styles and interfirm relationships. The new sociotechnical paradigm emerging out of this interaction was centered on networks of technologies, organizations, and institutions. This paradigm possesses five distinctive features. First, information represents the core resource. Second, the technologies are general purpose, as they serve as the basis for different products, processes, and applications and have widespread effects on the economy as a whole. Third, networks become the dominant paradigm not only with reference to the intrinsic nature of the technologies, but also with regard to processes, organizations, and institutions. Fourth, the paradigm is highly flexible and, as a consequence, is able to reconfigure and restructure processes, organizations, and institutions without undermining their underlying structure. Finally, there is convergence, from a technological and organizational point of view, of knowledge base and research activities in different domains. This implies that sectoral boundaries diverge as a consequence of changes in the knowledge base and the actors involved in the production processes and institutions, paving the way for a coevolution among technical change, organizational forms of coordination, and regulatory framework.

With particular reference to "industrial demography," the third industrial revolution provides interesting examples of the advantages brought about by the presence of a "community of companies," that is, the existence of firms of different sizes and degrees of specialization within the same industry. In the initial phase of the third industrial revolution, small start-ups were the main actors in the exploitation of the new technologies, as demonstrated by the history of a number of different industries such as biotechnology and software. However, far from being simply driven by entrepreneurial private initiative, this process of creative destruction also took place through active government initiative. Moreover, as noted by Chandler and Hikino (1997), within contemporary advanced economies, the large firm has not ceased its role as knowledge and capabilities coordinator. Further, as stressed by Adams et al. in this book, the knowledge-intensive nature of the third industrial revolution has forced the firm to deal with different actors – including governments – in their learning processes, thus redefining its boundaries and organizational structures.

THE ROLE OF THE STATE IN THE EMERGENCE OF NEW TECHNOLOGIES

What has been the role of the state in the third industrial revolution? Given technological and organizational variety, the range of instruments employed by national governments in sustaining emerging sectors was quite complex. The scope and articulation of these instruments and policies make it almost impossible to give a complete account of all of them in a single overview (a synthesis is provided by Lundvall and Borrás, 2006). The situation is complicated also by the fact that policies are active at different levels (countries, industries, firms) and that firms are at different stages of their life cycle and are of different dimensions. When considering the set of policies undertaken by governments, one possible perspective is to look at public intervention in the emerging sectors related to ICT and biotechnologies. By "public intervention" we mean here a broad set of interventions ranging from regulatory policies to the creation of governmental bodies able to foster the generation and diffusion of new technologies, as well as the selection of standards.

The previously mentioned sectors are representative of the third industrial revolution both in terms of the *nature* of the technologies involved, which are largely general purpose, and in terms of the nature of the firms, which range from small entrepreneurial ventures to large integrated corporations. Moreover, differing institutional elements played a considerable role in both these industries. At first glance, it is reasonable to argue that science policy, technology policy, and intellectual property rights (IPR) policy have been crucial in pharmaceuticals and biotechnology, and standards, competition policy, and IPR policy have had major effects in telecommunications and software sectors.

PUBLIC POLICIES IN THE ICT SECTORS

The role of institutions has been crucial for development in the telecommunications sector. On the one hand, standards have played a major role in innovation and the success of European mobile telecommunications. On the other hand, deregulation has been an important factor in the diffusion of the Internet and mobile telecommunications. The relationship between firms and public institutions has been of fundamental importance in the functioning and the performance of these sectors. In particular, during the 1980s and 1990s these relations took the form of research funding, standard setting, and public technology procurement. Relations between different kinds of firms and other private research organizations are also important, as are relations between users and producers. In particular, public technology procurement was crucial for the early development of the Internet in the United States, and the formulation of standards was crucial for the very early development of mobile telecommunications in the Nordic countries in Europe (Edquist, 2003).

The U.S. government played an extremely important role in the very early stages of the development of fixed data communications. Government agencies financed research in this area and initiated the public procurement associated with the new technology. Furthermore, some public organizations receiving public economic support had to use specific data communications protocols in order to boost the diffusion of the new technologies. The development of the Internet drew on many of the same institutions and policies of the postwar American "national innovation system" that were influential in other postwar high-technology industries (Mowery and Simcoe, 2002). Examples are the prominent role of defense funding and procurement in the development of the Internet and the strength and breadth of intellectual property rights whose relative weakness in Internet-related technologies arguably supported the Internet's rapid development. The success of American firms in commercializing the Internet was strongly associated with the unique combination of institutions and policies characteristic of the U.S.'s national innovation system.

The state did not play a major role in the creation of standards for the Internet; rather, this was left to private firms. Nonetheless, the involvement and support of the government triggered the success of the U.S.'s Internet equipment producers, which are still very dominant globally precisely because they were the early movers in the new high-tech fields and were close to customers. It is in the very early stages in the development of a system of innovation that the uncertainty and risks are greatest, and private actors and markets therefore operate least efficiently and dynamically. Therefore, policy interventions in these very early stages often mean the difference between success and failure.

In the mobile communications sector, state-owned organizations were extremely important in creating the first successful standard in Europe. In particular, public telecommunications operators played a prominent role in defining the technical development of the standard and led the way for private equipment producers. They both placed orders to firms and used public technology procurement to create incentives for firms to develop equipment for the emerging standard. More than to a direct intervention of the government, the success of the mobile communications standards was due to the interaction between public operators and private equipment producers such as Nokia and Ericsson. In that contest, the European institutional setting differed remarkably from the U.S. one. The European Commission promoted one unique standard developed *ex ante* that diffused rapidly outside Europe as well. In contrast, the U.S. policy was against *ex ante* standardization and advocated an open-network architecture and competition among alternative standards. This proved to be a policy failure for the United States and led to a slower diffusion of mobile communications. The promotion of one single standard was of great importance for the European dominance in the production of equipment for the mobile telecommunications industry. This is notable especially if one considers the lack of European success and U.S. dominance in most ICT-related sectors.

In contrast to what happened in the telecommunications industry, the evolution of the software industry is closely related to the strategic interaction of private firms and users (consumers and businesses). Quite interestingly, the purposes that software innovations fulfill and the capabilities they require both for their development and for their commercialization have shifted substantially during the industry's evolution. This instability in the sector has had a fundamental impact on the strategies of the companies that derive their principal revenues from the sale of software products. This instability is also the main reason why it has been particularly difficult to develop an effective technology policy for the industry. Furthermore, it explains the centrality of intellectual property rights in the policy agenda of the dominant actors (Steinmueller, 2004).

PUBLIC POLICIES IN THE BIOTECH SECTOR

The evolution of the biotechnology industry in the United States and the changing nature of organizational boundaries of firms were determined by a strong interaction among academia, institutions governing property rights, and venture capital (Mowery and Rosenberg, 2000). Over time, there was an increase in the dealings between industry and university, as well as in the commercialization of the results of academic research through universities' patenting, licensing activities, and the creation of spin-offs. Although the role of the state was not as central in the early development of the sector, the establishment of a regime of intellectual property rights played an important part in encouraging the emergence of new firms in the United States. In particular, the Bayh-Dole Act in 1980 facilitated university patenting and licensing. At the same time, a series of judicial and congressional decisions strengthened the appropriability regime of the emerging sector (McKelvey et al., 2004). The regulatory revolution interacted with the scientific revolution in effecting change in the sector. In particular, during the 1980s, increasingly strict controls on product approval requirements emerged, especially in Europe. Even more significant was the development of cost containment policies. In general, these policies were very different across countries but were all characterized by vigorous publicity aimed at making patients and health providers more price conscious and more price sensitive. However, although there was no direct price control in the United States, indirect measures, such as the reduction of safety control procedures for generic drugs equivalent to branded products and the ability for pharmacists to sell equivalent generics instead of branded products, served a similar function. In Europe, in contrast, there were direct price controls (with the partial exception of Germany and Switzerland).

FURTHER EXAMPLES OF INSTITUTIONAL SPILL-OVERS: BIG SCIENCE, IPR, AND FINANCING

Institutional influence can involve a number of other specific instruments and policies, varying according to the activity or the final product. Frequently, the influence has been indirect, or beyond the intentions of the actors involved. Military demand for high-tech products provides one significant example. In examining the technological achievements of the postwar period, it is important to note the spill-overs from military research into civilian life: military demand in ballistics led to the development of the personal computer; the nuclear submarine program contributed to the development of the technology of nuclear reactors; and the space program drove the process of miniaturization that led to the introduction of the integrated circuit. More controversial has been the role of big science in developing mass consumption goods (Von Tunzelmann, 1995). On the one hand, this is related to the shift of research away from more socially acceptable products; on the other hand, it has to do with the typical "backward-looking" tendency of the military products and to their evaluation in terms of purely technological criteria more than by commercial standards.

At times, public policies have generated diversity by reducing the incompatibility among competing approaches and by offering a common base upon which different products may be developed (Cohendet and Llerena, 1997). This can be done through the diffusion of codified information about various competing technologies, so that firms can engage in the creation of gateway technologies. Important examples are the establishment of ETSI, the creation of standards within the ESPRIT program, and the role played by the National Institute of Standards and Technologies in the United States in the initial development of the semiconductor and computer industries.

The relatively high knowledge intensity typical of the third industrial revolution emphasizes the role of intellectual property rights and of institutional conditions fostering individual creativity. In the United

States, the protection of intellectual property played an important role in the postwar development of new firms in high-technology sectors. Patent policies have been particularly important in supporting the activities of small technology-based firms and university licensing – especially in biotechnology and chemicals. This has created the basis for a division of labor between technology suppliers and users and permitted the development of markets for technologies. As Coriat et al. (2004) suggest, the existence of an IPR regime protecting scientific discoveries though patents provides firms specializing in R&D with intangible assets. These assets are used in financial markets designed to finance risky, but potentially highly profitable, firms. At the same time, patent policies have been designed to enhance coordination through knowledge sharing and a variety of technologies. Complex technologies can also be seen to enhance governmental contribution. As the literature on national systems of innovation has widely illustrated (Lundvall, 1992; Nelson, 1993), although the role played by institutions in organizing markets is crucial, it does not necessarily imply direct intervention in the production of the private firms, but might involve the development of links among firms. Innovation policy should focus not only on the elements of the systems, but also on the relations among them. This includes the relations among various types of organizations and institutions. For example, the long-term innovation performance of firms in science-based industries is strongly dependent on the interactions of these firms with universities and research organizations. These links could be facilitated by means of policy, that is, by changing the laws and rules that govern the relationships between universities and firms. Incubators, technology parks, and public venture capital organizations may also be important in similar ways. In this phase, learning by interacting turns out to be a fundamental process behind entrepreneurship and competitiveness. Indeed, the general-purpose character of these technologies raises the question of possible direct governmental intervention. A convincing argument for state intervention in the promotion of high-tech industries is the dynamic benefit stemming from the choice of the right technological opportunity, which may translate into the ability to sustain increasing returns and maintain high value added over the long term (Von Tunzelmann, 1995).

Last but not least, the development of an adequate financial system, able to sustain investments in tech- and risk-intensive industries is another example of the indirect but key role played by the state. The example of the venture capital system, which acted as a catalyst for entrepreneurial activity especially in biotechnology and information technology, is telling. Between 1969 and 1977, the annual flow of venture capital within industrial investments is estimated to have been between 2.5 and 3 billion dollars. One slightly indirect but extremely relevant role played by the state was to support through adequate regulation the wide diversification of instruments for entrepreneurial finance. The history of the American venture capital industry (Reiner, 1991; Gompers, 1994) provides a vivid example of the direct influence of the regulation of financial markets on the availability of entrepreneurial finance during the technological wave of the third industrial revolution.

Policy makers across Europe and East Asia have fostered the emergence of Internet-based firms by developing a set of institutions needed to support entrepreneurial technological initiatives. Following Germany's first move in the mid-1990s, European countries as well as Japan and Korea generated public venture capital programs to promote the development of high-risk finance (Kogut, 2003). This arrangement somehow complemented the existence of high-risk stock markets as well as a series of fiscal and corporate governance reforms aimed at promoting equity-based financial schemes and employee remuneration (Soskice and Casper and Soskice, 2004). The creation of venture capital and other forms of financial incentives for start-up firms is not sufficient for these organizations to survive, as different sectors are characterized by very different organizational and technological risks, so multiple pathways exist for public intervention in the financial system. The arguments put forward here will be developed in further detail in the following section, examining the issue of continuity and discontinuity between the second and the third industrial revolution.

A TALE OF TWO REVOLUTIONS: CONTINUITY AND CHANGE

Changes in regulation regimes are recurrent features of the long trends (Perez, 1983, 1985). The rules of the game need to be changed from time to time in order to accommodate not only the new technologies, but also the changes in the balance of power in international relations, in the economic strengths of the various contending powers, and in the culture and ideology of the dominant social groups. The outcome of all this is a dynamism and articulation of policies. This dynamism has grown over time from the first to the third industrial revolutions and in more recent years has been characterized by a decline in the state's commitment to direct intervention.

In general, there are four main reasons behind the decline in state intervention, some of which were mentioned at the end of the last paragraph. First, the selection and coordination (among technologies, private and public organizations, and institutions) that existed in the past now takes different forms. Second, the creation and support of a variety of knowledge-based entrepreneurial processes has assumed a crucial role in the last few decades. Third, government involvement is still a critical bridging mechanism between microsystems and macrosystems. Finally, government policy acts at very different levels, and one of its most important roles is that of coordination. As Von Tunzelmann (1997) correctly points out, when countries have been performing very successfully, government intervention has declined slightly. However, empirical evidence suggests that state intervention is needed even at the *"height of Victorian laissez-faire"* in order to remedy specific shortcomings. The emergence of a new information paradigm requires a set of private and public arrangements (Amable and Boyer, 1995). The network among research, production, and other activities calls for mobility and communication both within and outside the firm in order to maximize productivity and competitiveness. In this context, learning becomes a crucial process and relies on education and continuous skill upgrading. In particular, new technologies require a richer cognitive content both within manufacturing and within human service resources.

When radical technical change takes place, the choice in the market lies between supporting existing systems – with their historically accumulated knowledge base – and sustaining the development of radically new products and processes. Indeed, large-scale changes in technological paradigms have often been accompanied by public intervention in Europe, the United States, and Japan. In such situations, an active role by public organizations in identifying, promoting, and creating the initial conditions for market success is called for. Specifically, governments can take the role of lead users of new technologies or simply support the use of new technologies by public organizations, as happened in the case of the Internet. However, as Edquist et al. (2004) have extensively documented, governmental ability to support the emergence of new technologies and new sectors differs substantially across countries. In any case, it is important that public intervention occur in the early stages of sectoral development in order to ensure that economies can harness the benefits of rapid technical change.

The government may increase economic variety by providing support for the entry and survival of new firms, which are typically characterized by different capabilities, resources, and cognitive frames as compared with those of the incumbents. This is important because growth, more than simple entry, is a fundamental process for the long-term survival of innovative firms that require continuous innovation as well as major managerial and organizational changes. For example, the U.S. computer industry has benefited from high entry rates of new actors in the sector characterized by different products and strategies and a high level of exploratory activities and variety. The maintenance of technological alternatives and variety has to take place in a very short period of time, usually at the beginning of a process of competition among technologies and standards. The government may help by using public technology procurement and R&D subsidies and by encouraging experimentation. However, one has to consider that the choice of which technology to support may cause problems for public institutions because of their lack of knowledge about the characteristics and potential success of technological alternatives, especially in the early stages of industry life cycle (David, 1987). In such a context, the government has two possible choices: It may focus its attention on organizations that explore or experiment with new technologies, such as universities, or it may sustain a specific technological alternative to the winning technology. In the U.S. semiconductor industry, public intervention was specifically directed at fostering the survival of alternative technologies through the support of different firms early in the history of the industry. This allowed the emergence of variety in the exploratory activity of firms and contributed to the selection of the winning technology (Bresnahan and Malerba, 1999).

THE STATE IN THE SECOND INDUSTRIAL REVOLUTION

The role of the state during the second industrial revolution has been widely investigated. In the leading country, the United States, the state's role in the process at the beginning of industrial evolution was largely indirect. As demonstrated in the early works of Alfred Chandler, antitrust policy was responsible for consolidation and growth of the *first movers* in the capital intensive industries, whereas policies directed toward the financial market empowered the stock exchange, which proved very efficient in providing the financial resources needed by firms in those sectors. In European countries that were trying to catch up with the United States, the role of the state was more decisive and intense. Beginning in the 1920s, in some countries the growth of capital-intensive industries was fostered, sustained, financed, planned, or even directly managed by the national government (Toninelli, 2000).

During the second industrial revolution, there was no explicit direct action in keeping variety or technological alternatives alive, which was largely left to the processes of competition across firms. The state, especially in European countries, stimulated selection mechanisms toward capital-intensive sectors, but apparently without explicit emphasis on knowledge generation and pervasive learning processes within firms. Some coordination was present. In the United States, this took the form of coordination between private and public research, even if it was limited first to the wartime effort, and again during the Cold War. In Europe, the rise of planning and nationalization during the decades of the Economic Miracle (1950-70) saw a further involvement of the state in the economy, mainly through direct intervention and economic policies aimed more at sustaining growth and employment than at coordinating research in science and new technologies.

In terms of intensity, direct intervention - through various instruments ranging from public procurement to rescues or protective tariffs - was clearly more relevant than other policies, such as the selection among different technologies and standards. The specificity of the technologies in use during the second industrial revolution, which required the employment of unskilled labor within large firms, was largely responsible for this. Even in Europe, training was either on the shop floor or provided at a very basic level by technical secondary schools as in Germany. In any case, as noted by Lazonick (1993), the innovation process characterizing the capital-intensive industries of the second industrial revolution was basically top-down and did not require large investments in the formation of a skilled labor force. Investments in human capital were confined to middle and top levels in the managerial hierarchy of the corporation (and in many European nations not even at those levels) or in the R&D laboratories. In this respect, the role of the state both in the United States and in Europe was not particularly significant in direct terms.

The Second World War marked a sharp difference. As much of the literature demonstrates (see Abbate, 2001, for an exhaustive review), military requirements and command of the war economy played a role in shaping many of the new technologies at the core of the industries of both the second and the third industrial revolutions. War efforts brought about two fundamental innovations. The first, which preceded the second industrial revolution, was the production of interchangeable parts

242   ANDREA COLLI AND NICOLETTA CORROCHER

generated by the needs of the U.S. Civil War. The second, which took place more or less 110 years later, was the Internet. These two innovations generated by war needs in two very different historical periods were developed with a prominent role played by the state, but with nonnegligible differences.

The origins of the Internet in the government-funded and sustained ARPANET project provide a significant example of the transformation in state policies for competitiveness between the second and the third industrial revolutions. In this case, the state not only played its "traditional" roles in terms of financing and procurement, but started to find itself in the position of selecting and shaping the emerging technology and defining standards while confronted with private enterprises. In this case, an important field of intervention was human capital formation. It appeared immediately clear that the new technologies would have a tremendous impact on the nature of the labor force, which was going to become a strategic element within various sectors. It was only during the second industrial revolution that the states realized the need to develop publicly funded institutes at the level of higher education and frontier scientific research, a call that has been intensified during the third industrial revolution. On the contrary, 100 years before, in the case of production of interchangeable parts, the direct effect on the labor force was a decrease in the skill level required of the individual worker and the consequent transformation of the nature of human capital. Human capital in high-tech industries was, in sum, not trained through basically learning-by-doing processes, which were typical of the first and, partially, of the second industrial revolutions: "The industries in which the United States forged ahead after World War II required organized R&D, in addition to experience and specialized training, for the effective advancement of technology . . . Employment in industrial research grew from around 40,000 just before World War II to approximately 300,000 in the early 1960s" (Ruttan, 2000, p. 438). In the United States, the consequence of this was that the state directed its policies and resources toward research, both through public funding of university research by a plethora of foundations, agencies, and departments, and by sustaining corporate research when related to national defense. In the mid-1960s, public money counted for half of private R&D.

Comparative studies stress the relevance of governmental policies in shaping the competitiveness of technology-intensive firms in the interwar period (e.g., Mowery, 1984). Because the roots of many of the industries typical of the third industrial revolution are to be found in the applied scientific research efforts during the Second World War (Ruttan, 2006), the involvement of the state in the process was quite pervasive (Owens, 1994). Both British and American governments understood the crucial role of physics and mathematics for nuclear weapons and for computer science (Freeman and Louçã, 2001). Since its beginning, the electronics industry has been at the heart of worldwide developments in communications technology (e.g., radio communications) that were even then the subject of intense government interest and regulation. One of the most significant examples, in this respect, is the support provided to the semiconductor industry through policies enhancing the circulation of information and knowledge among private firms (Holbrook, 1995). The particular climate created by the Cold War made compulsory a direct effort aimed at protecting new "strategic" products (such as semiconductors) while at the same time sustaining efforts in the pure research programs.

In other cases, the stimuli were more indirect in nature, through the influence of institutional changes that paved the way for a transformation in the industrial structure, competitive strategies, and technologies of production. The case of telecommunications illustrates this point well, as the breakup of the Bell system in the United States stimulated the privatization of the previously public monopoly services and paved the way for a new regulatory regime that would not only permit but also encourage new entrants into the world of telecommunications networks and services. This policy relied on the idea that a more competitive environment would act as a driver of growth of all kinds of new information services. The information revolution weakened the monopolistic power of the telecommunications utilities, especially those under state control. The old publicly owned state monopolies were replaced by private global multinational corporations. This specific case illustrates how the nature of the technology has influenced the character and configuration of the regulatory framework.

THE STATE DURING THE THIRD INDUSTRIAL REVOLUTION

A complete assessment of the role played by the state during the third industrial revolution proves to be quite complex. First, the very high number of breakthrough innovations characterizing the third industrial revolution called for a wave of liberalizations, which were accompanied by a massive retreat by the state from direct intervention in economic activity through an intense process of privatizations. In other words, at a first glance one might think that the present revolution is taking place in an environment characterized by the presence of "weak" and "light" states, an impression corroborated by the emergence of entrepreneurial models with small, innovative, and networked firms. However, as much of the literature clearly shows (Mowery and Rosenberg, 2000; Ruttan, 2000, 2006), the idea of an industrial revolution taking place *without* the support of the state is more than naïve. What is true is that the range and scope of the instruments employed by the state have enlarged during the last decades.

A second relevant element is that the constant growth of high-tech industries and the continuous generation of innovations occur in an increasingly complex environment from a technological, organizational and institutional perspective. Therefore, the relevance of public institutions is essential in establishing the framework in which the continuous generation of innovations and knowledge-based entrepreneurship can take place. The state not only plays an active role in the process of catching up, but it ensures also for first-tier countries the possibility of maintaining successful growth. Furthermore, although the ICT constellation had originally been characterized as a self-regulating network with relatively low central control, more recently it has witnessed the resurgence of some tendencies to new forms of control and regulation.

Third, the prominent role played by small firms in the process of commercialization of new technologies in electronics was a radically new phenomenon in the United States as compared with what had happened before. In both the information technology and the biotechnology sectors, a considerable number of innovations arose out of the effort of new firms. This somehow challenges (or, better, completes) the ideas put forward by Chandler and Hikino (1997) about the dominance of the large firms, which are increasingly to be seen as repositories of knowledge and capabilities of coordinating networks of minor producers and developers. These were responsible for the R&D activity in the emerging sectors, but very often had to rely on smaller firms in order to commercialize the results of the research. The wave of acquisition of small firms by large operators (e.g., AT&T) in the ICT sector can be partly explained by the need to exploit the marketing capabilities of small specialized actors.

As was the case in the earlier two industrial revolutions, the third one also has been characterized by an intense entrepreneurial wave. Similarly, entrepreneurial profiles have been conditioned by the form taken by the enterprise under the influence of the new technologies.

As Langlois (2003) recently suggested, referring to Adam Smith's idea of division of labor and specialization linked to the market extension, the growth of markets on a global scale typical of the third industrial revolution combined with the enhancement of new communication technologies has driven an increasing division of labor and specialization of firms. Galambos (2005) has also recently stressed that, even if the entrepreneurial models characterizing the second industrial revolution do not quickly disappear, the third industrial revolution will see a further increase in the strategic value of entrepreneurship as an asset for national competitiveness. Garage entrepreneurs and innovators, funded by an emerging and flexible entrepreneurial finance industry (venture capitalists, business angels, and later private equity firms) are the main characters in this world as is evident in the emergence of small and dynamic firms, often interacting within networks. The diffusion of vertical disintegration policies and downsizing strategies associated with the emergence of networks and other forms of cooperative behavior enforced by the diffusion of new complex technologies, seemed to strengthen the links among technology-intensive industries, individual entrepreneurial behavior, and industrial policies undertaken by governments and states to foster entrepreneurship. Quite often, the government, together with universities and private organizations, acted as an incubator for the development of innovations. High mobility of labor in microelectronics, biotechnology, and information technology served both to diffuse technological knowledge and to stimulate firms' agglomeration.

In some respects, the third industrial revolution has more in common with the first than with the second. There has been no linear move toward greater scale and scope, or higher product quality, or more intense labor saving. Even in cases in which cumulativeness could be strongly suspected on *a priori* grounds, as in the advance of S&T, the pattern has involved sharp breaks as well as forward momentum (Von Tunzelmann, 1997). A wide range of instruments and policies has been implemented during the last half of the twentieth century by national governments in advanced nations to sustain the competitiveness of high-tech industries involved in the technological shift driven by the new technologies. IPR legislation, public procurement, policies for local development (technological districts, clusters, scientific parks, consortia), education, R&D incentives, indirect stimuli through, for instance, the action over the financial system, up to direct involvement, are fully part of the industrial and economic policies of both industrialized and newcomer countries. Within this context, the state can adopt either *sectoral policies* aimed at sustaining the competitiveness of national players in specific industries, as in the case of the American semiconductor industries, or in that of telecoms (Fransman, 2002), or *national policies* that have an impact on all the sectors and aim at supporting the national economy as a whole.

The turnaround in government support of high-tech industries of the third industrial revolution was, in sum, directed toward the facilitation of private initiative and to the creation of an efficient framework for both private initiatives and collaboration between public and private research programs. The previously described spin-off effect would ideally be increasingly replaced by "spin-on," that is, the application of advanced technologies from the civilian to the military market (the most effective example is provided by semiconductors and later by microprocessors). The role of public institutions and governments is consequently shifting from direct intervention and involvement in research programs to the support of entrepreneurship in the private civil sector.

The story of technology policy in the United States during the second half of the twentieth century provides not only an interesting example of public involvement in science-intensive industries, but also of the necessity for first-tier countries to constantly fine-tune their policies in order to keep their position in the international competition among high-tech industries. Undoubtedly, the emphasis put on science and technology policies in the U.S. case was originated largely by the military effort first during World War II, and later during the Cold War period up to the end of the 1980s. On the one hand, research programs coordinated by the public agencies sustained the steady development of "big science," playing the role of sponsor, and selecting new technologies when the market was unable to direct sufficient resources in these fields. On the other hand, the selection bias toward defense programs in the years from World War II to the end of the Cold War has been heavily criticized. Nonetheless, in many cases the spin-off effect dominated: jet engines, electronics, satellites, and lasers are some examples of spin-offs in the civilian consumer markets.

The end of the Cold War brought an obvious reexamination of governmental policies regarding science and technology (Ruttan, 2006). The budget available to sustain research declined steadily up to the 1990s. At the same time, in many areas of commercial technology, the U.S. position in the international market seemed to increasingly weaken, bringing about pressure for a new science and technology policy not related mainly to defense industries. The U.S. case is interesting also for this reason. The Bush and then the Clinton Administrations issued two relevant reports (Ruttan, 2006). The first report (the Bromley Report) gave especially broad but effective recommendations for technology development and diffusion, addressing four relevant areas:

1. government incentives for the private sector, through fiscal and other incentives, aimed at providing an appropriate legal environment and better protection of intellectual property, and encouraging multilateral standardization efforts;
2. education and training, including federal coordination and cooperation in mathematics, science, engineering, and technology education;
3. federal R&D commitment, including joint venturing with the private sector in basic research; and
4. transfer of federally funded technology.

CONCLUSION

The third industrial revolution has been marked, as were the previous two, by a powerful shift in production technologies with strong consequences for the organizational structures of the corporations active in the industries involved. Also, as occurred previously, the revolution in technologies has brought with it another revolution in the ranking of the most advanced nations. Once again, technological leadership has to be correlated with the wealth of the nation. This has again demonstrated the need for a strong state intervention especially in those countries that for varying reasons were latecomers. However, public intervention has been relevant also among the nations leading the process of growth, through different policies, both direct and indirect. In contrast to the shift from the first to the second industrial revolutions that saw the decline of British leadership, the third industrial revolution has confirmed the leading role of the United States.

According to some research, this has largely, even if not completely, been connected to the ability of the large corporations of the second industrial revolution to jump into the new sectors and quickly apply the strategies and structures that made the difference more or less one century ago. However, we argue that although giant corporations have been undoubtedly among the main characters of the "electronic century," the characteristics of the new technologies have stressed much more than in the past the relevance of the "community of companies." The peculiarities of the technologies of the third industrial revolution, in other terms, allow the creative coexistence of large, medium, and small entrepreneurial firms, as well as the creation of networks and collaborations among different actors.

Although science and technology were the core of this process, human capital and knowledge became for the first time in history the main strategic asset for firms and countries. Furthermore, the union between science and technology called for a direct involvement of the state, given the fact that "big science" could not be left simply to the forces of the free market. The effect, which became apparent from the Second World War to the end of the Cold War, was that governments had the chance to intervene basically through defense and military procurement-related industries, as the case of the United States efficaciously demonstrates (Ruttan, 2006). In some sense, it can be said that the first approach by governments to the new sectors of the third industrial revolution was largely based on "old" policies among which procurement and research incentives provided by agencies, departments, and other public institutions played a primary role. With the end of the Cold War, however, a change in these policies became necessary, and governments had to find new ways to foster technology-intensive industries. In the most successful countries, direct involvement and procurement have been replaced by a bulk of policies aimed at sustaining entrepreneurial efforts – both in the large, but also in the small entrepreneurial firms – through the management of incentives, investments in human capital training, improvements in the flexibility of the financial system, and policies for local development.

From an evolutionary perspective, governments might be considered as having an important role in the selection of technological opportunities provided by individuals and creative entrepreneurs. During the third industrial revolution, the range of technologies, processes, and products has expanded much more than before, so that even the largest firms may be unable to be pioneers in the entire range of technological alternatives. Moreover, the increasing complexity of technologies and the multiple relationships among technologies, products, and processes calls for the development of a wide range of competencies. Learning by doing, by using, and by interacting become essential activities for firms in order to harness the potential of these pervasive technologies. Although firms may play the predominant part in these learning processes, governments can encourage such activities. However, governments may also act to build networks of firms and break down company insularity by stimulating interaction with users and other actors in the market.

In sum, state intervention has not ceased playing an essential role, even in the decades of the "weak" or "light" state. The point is that the nature and structure of government intervention (at least, in the most successful examples) have profoundly changed. Direct intervention has been replaced, even if not completely, by a more complex relationship with the private sector, which itself is populated by very different actors, from small to medium and large firms. To preserve this vitality, in terms of entrepreneurial effervescence above all, is probably the most important and delicate task of new public policies at the turn of the new millennium.

REFERENCES

Abbate, J. (2001). Government, business, and the making of the Internet. *Business History Review*, 75(1), 147-76.

Amable, B., & Boyer, R. (1995). Europe in the world technological competition. *Structural Change and Economic Dynamics*, 6, 167-83.

Amsden, A. (2001). *The rise of the rest. Challenges to the West from late-industrializing economies*. Oxford, UK: Oxford University Press.

Amsden, A., & Hikino, T. (1994). Staying behind, stumbling back, soaring ahead: Late industrialization in historical perspective. In Baumol, W. J. et al. (Eds.), *Convergence of productivity: Cross-national studies and historical evidence*. New York: Oxford University Press.

Bresnahan, T., & Malerba, F. (1999). Industrial dynamics and the evolution of firms' and nations' competitive capabilities in the world computer industry. In Mowery, D. C., & Nelson, R. R. (Eds.), *Sources of industrial leadership: Studies of seven industries*. Cambridge: Cambridge University Press.

Casper, S., & Soskice, D. (2004). Sectoral systems of innovation and varieties of capitalism: Explaining the development of high technology entrepreneurship in Europe. In Malerba, F. (Ed.), *Sectoral systems of innovation*. Cambridge: Cambridge University Press.

Castells, M. (2002). *The rise of network society*. Oxford, UK: Blackwell.

Chandler, A., & Hikino, T. (1997). The large industrial enterprise and the dynamics of modern economic growth. In Chandler, A. et al. (Eds.), *Big business and the wealth of nations*. Cambridge: Cambridge University Press.

Cohendet, P., & Llerena, P. (1997). Learning, technical change and public policy: How to create and exploit diversity. In Edquist, C. (Ed.), *Systems of innovation: Technologies, institutions and organizations*. London: Pinter.

Coriat, B. (2004). "The State of Organizational Reform in European Firms," Laboratory of Economics and Management, Working Papers Series 2004/04, Pisa, Italy.

David, P. (1987). Some new standards for the economics of standardisation in the information age. In Dasgupta, P., & Stoneman, P. (Eds.), *Economic policy and technological performance*. Cambridge: Cambridge University Press.

Edquist, C. (Ed.). (2003). *The Internet and mobile telecommunications system of innovation: Developments in equipment, access and content*. Cheltenham, UK/ Northhampton, MA: Elgar.

Edquist, C., Malerba, F., Metcalfe, S., Montobbio, F., & Steinmueller, W. E. (2004). Sectoral systems: Implications for European innovation policy. In Malerba, F. (Ed.), *Sectoral systems of innovation*. Cambridge: Cambridge University Press.

Ergas, H. (1987). The importance of technology policy. In Dasgupta, P., & Stoneman, P. (Eds.), *Economic policy and technological performance*. Cambridge: Cambridge University Press.

Fransman, M. (2002). *Telecoms in the Internet age*. Oxford, UK: Oxford University Press.

Freeman, C., & Louçã, F. (2001). *As time goes by*. Oxford, UK: Oxford University Press.

Galambos, L. (2005). Recasting the organizational synthesis: Structure and process in the twentieth and twenty-first centuries. *Business History Review*, 79(1), 1–38.

Gerschenkron, A. (1963). *Economic backwardness in historical perspective*. Cambridge, MA: Harvard University Press.

Gompers, P. A. (1994). The rise and fall of venture capital. *Business and Economic History*, XXIII (2), 1–24.

Holbrook, R. (1995). Government support of the semiconductor industry: Diverse approaches and information flows. *Business and Economic History*, XXIV(2), 134–65.

Kraakman, R. (2003). The durability of the corporate form. In DiMaggio, P. (Ed.), *The twenty-first-century firm: Changing economic organization in international perspective*. Princeton, NJ: Princeton University Press.

Kim, L. (1993). National system of innovation: Dynamics of capability building in Korea. In Nelson, R. R. (Ed.), *National innovation systems: A comparative analysis*. New York/Oxford, UK: Oxford University Press.

Kogut, B. (2003). *The global Internet economy*. Cambridge, MA: MIT Press.

Langlois, R. (2003). The vanishing hand: The changing dynamics of industrial capitalism. *Industrial and Corporate Change*, 12, 351–85.

Lazonick, W. (1993). *Business organization and the myth of the market economy*. Cambridge: Cambridge University Press.

Lundvall, B.A. (1992). *National systems of innovation: Towards a theory of innovation and interactive learning*. London: Pinter.

Lundvall, B. A., & Borrás, S. (2006). Science, technology and innovation policy. In Fagerberg, I. et al. (Eds.), *The Oxford handbook of innovation*. Oxford, UK: Oxford University Press.

McKelvey, M., Orsenigo, L., & Pammolli, F. (2004). Pharmaceuticals analysed through the lens of a sectoral innovation system. In Malerba, F. (Ed.), *Sectoral systems of innovation*. Cambridge: Cambridge University Press.

Millward, R. (2005). *Private and public enterprise in Europe. Energy, telecommunications and transport (1830–1990)*. Cambridge: Cambridge University Press.

Miyajima, H., Kikkawa, T., & Hikino, T. (1999). *Policies for competitiveness. Comparing business-government relationships in the golden age of capitalism.* Oxford, UK: Oxford University Press.

Mowery, D. C. (1984). Firm structure, government policy and the organization of industrial research: Great Britain and The United States, 1900–50. *Business History Review*, 58, 504–31.

Mowery, D. C., & Rosenberg, N. (2000). *Paths of innovation: Technological change in 20th-Century America.* Cambridge: Cambridge University Press.

Mowery, D. C., & Simcoe, T. (2002). Is the Internet a US invention? *Research Policy*, 31, 1369–87.

Nelson, R. R. (Ed.). (1993) *National innovation systems: A comparative analysis.* New York/Oxford, UK: Oxford University Press.

Nelson, R. R. (2005). *Technology, institutions and economic growth.* Cambridge, MA: Harvard University Press.

Owens, L. (1994). The counterproductive management of science in the Second World War: Vannevar Bush and the Office of Scientific Research and Development. *Business History Review*, 68, 515–76.

Perez, C. (1983). Structural change and the assimilation of new technologies in the economic and social system. *Futures*, 15, 357–75.

Perez, C. (1985). Micro-electronics, long waves and world structural change. *World Development*, 13, 441–63.

Reiner, M. (1991). Innovation and the creation of venture capital organizations. *Business and Economic History*, 20, 200–9.

Ruttan, V. W. (2000). *Technology, growth, and development: An induced innovation perspective.* Oxford, UK: Oxford University Press.

Ruttan, V. W. (2006). *Is war necessary for economic growth, military procurement and technology development?* Oxford, UK: Oxford University Press.

Steinmueller, W. E. (2004). The European software sectoral system of innovation. In Malerba, F. (Ed.), *Sectoral systems of innovation.* Cambridge: Cambridge University Press.

Toninelli, P. A. (2000). *The rise and fall of state owned enterprise in the western world.* Cambridge: Cambridge University Press.

Von Tunzelmann, G. N. (1995). Government policy and the long-run dynamics of competitiveness. *Structural Change and Economic Dynamics*, 6, 1–21.

Von Tunzelmann, G. N. (1997). Innovation and industrialization: A long-term comparison. *Technological Forecasting and Social Change*, 56, 1–23.

Von Tunzelmann, G. N. (2003). Historical coevolution of governance and technology in the industrial revolutions. *Structural Change and Economic Dynamics*, 14, 365–84.

8

Celebrating Youth

Historical Origins of the U.S. Stock Market's Appetite for Novelty

INTRODUCTION

In this chapter, I focus on the historical origins of one of the most distinctive contemporary features of the U.S. financial system: the capacity of its stock market to fund new industries and the young firms that enter them. The prominence of this capacity renders important the timing of, and conditions for, its historical emergence. However, an analysis of the existing evidence reveals considerable difficulty in pinpointing when and how it emerged.

Several candidates present themselves as potential milestones. The establishment of the NASDAQ market in 1971 is one plausible candidate. However, the postwar initial public offering (IPO) booms of the late 1950s and late 1960s, and even the boom in glamour stocks in the 1920s, suggest even earlier manifestations of the U.S. stock market's appetite for newness. In their ambitious study, Jovanovic and Rousseau (2001) even argue that the U.S. stock market began funding new industries and new firms as early as the 1880s and 1890s.[1]

---

[1] In this chapter, I focus on industrial stocks and ignore the emergence of public markets for the stocks of mining and other companies in resource-based industries like oil.

I begin with that claim and argue that problems with the evidence on which Jovanovic and Rousseau rely render it unpersuasive. Instead, I suggest that we must look to a later period for any significant involvement by the U.S. stock market in funding young firms in emergent industries. We begin to see signs of such activity in the midteens, but it was rather limited in scope, and it was not until after World War I, and especially in the 1920s, that we see significant numbers of securities of fledgling enterprises on the U.S. stock market. Important examples of such activity include the waves of securities issues to fund radio and aviation enterprises in the 1920s.

Such issues were facilitated by a number of changing characteristics of the U.S. stock market. First, the growing importance of New York's Curb market, the mid-Western and Western regional exchanges, as well as the over-the-counter market proved vital in creating trading markets for the securities of young firms. Second, the willingness of growing numbers of small, and often young, investment banks, to originate and distribute stock issues that were deemed risky by established firms played an important role. And, finally, there were important changes in the demand for stocks that made some investors more willing to buy stocks that they previously rejected because of their speculative character.

Notwithstanding the historical significance of the stock market's experiment with funding novelty in the 1920s, issuance activity by young firms in new industries represented a minority of overall stock issues on the U.S. stock market even by the late 1920s. Stock issues by established industries, especially to refund existing obligations and, even more so, to facilitate consolidation, dominated. As the example of the aviation industry suggests, the urge to consolidate sometimes became an important motivation for stock issues even in new industries.

The stock market's experience in funding new firms in new industries in the 1920s was not always a happy one. In the radio industry from the mid-1920s and in aviation in the late 1920s, investors in novel stocks were already licking their wounds. The stock market crash and the Great Depression, and then World War II, interrupted any further development of the stock market's relationship with new industries. However, beneath the stagnation of securities listing and trading that characterized these years, important regulatory developments were laying the groundwork for important changes to come. In some cases, these changes were intentional, but the most important changes were not.

After World War II, the stock market's involvement in the new markets and new technologies that had emerged by then, often as a direct consequence of the war effort, was initially rather tentative. This was true for the electronics sector, certainly one of the most exciting new domains of activity at the time. It was only in the late 1950s that substantial numbers of small electronics and other high-tech companies sold their stock to the public. The number of companies completing initial public offerings in the "hot issue" boom that lasted until the early 1960s was much larger than anything that had gone before and proved impressive even relative to subsequent developments.

In facilitating this development, we see once again the importance of the differentiation in the roles played by the various trading markets that constituted the U.S. stock market, but this time it was the Curb (renamed the American Stock Exchange in 1953), and especially the over-the-counter market, that were so crucial to the seasoning of the securities of new firms. Additionally, as was the case in the 1920s, hungry young investment banks and exuberant investors were important in securing funding for new firms in new industries in the late 1950s and early 1960s.

The scale of activity that characterized the post–World War II boom in new issues renders it a good candidate as a watershed in the evolution of the U.S. stock market's capacity to fund novelty. But it was also a watershed in another sense. The boom prompted widespread concerns about financial speculation, and then a major investigation by the Securities and Exchange Commission, and ultimately a variety of regulatory changes in the supervision of the U.S. stock market, especially the over-the-counter (OTC) market. Of particular importance were recommendations for the improvement of information about trading in, and issuing on, the OTC market, which ultimately gave rise to the establishment of the NASDAQ in 1971. And it was NASDAQ, more than any other institutional characteristic of the U.S. stock market, that served as the fulcrum for America's contemporary capacity for funding new firms and new industries.

TRACING THE ORIGINS OF THE U.S. STOCK MARKET'S APPETITE FOR NOVELTY

In contemporary discussions of varieties of financial systems in the advanced industrial economies, what is typically regarded as distinctive about the United States is the capacity of its financial system to cater to the funding needs of new industries and the young firms that enter them. For many commentators, the support that the U.S. financial system provides to new industries is crucial for fueling innovation and, in turn, for promoting the country's economic performance. Critics also attach importance to this feature of the American stock market for its role in fueling speculation and overinvestment in commercially unproven technologies.

Scholars have emphasized the importance of a constellation of institutions that interact with each other to support the nation's capacity to fund new industries. First, there is the NASDAQ stock market that, in providing a vibrant outlet for the stocks of promising new enterprises, directly funds these companies and indirectly induces other investments by allowing early stage investors to exit their investments through initial public offerings (IPOs). Second, there is the country's large venture capital industry, which specializes in making equity investments in the early stages of a company's development. Finally, U.S. institutional investors have proven willing and able to commit large amounts of financial resources to the stocks of newly public companies as well as to the funds that fuel venture capital activity.

Notwithstanding their contemporary prominence, these institutional arrangements are of relatively recent origin. The NASDAQ market was formed as recently as 1971, and it was not until the late 1970s and early 1980s that new companies began to list their stocks there in large numbers. Venture capital also emerged as a recognizable and self-conscious industry only in the early 1970s. Finally, the reinterpretation of Employee Retirement Income Security Act (ERISA) investment rules in 1979 marked the beginning of large allocations by institutional investors both to venture capital funds and investments in IPOs.

These developments certainly made a significant difference to the numbers and types of companies getting access to the U.S. stock market. Research by Eugene Fama and Kenneth French (2004) examined the characteristics of newly listed firms on the NYSE, Amex, and NASDAQ from 1973 to 2001. They found that the number of new firms listing on these markets increased dramatically from 156 per year from 1973 to 1979 to 549 per year from 1980 to 2001 and that there was a substantial increase among them in the incidence of firms with low profits and high growth. Unfortunately, given that their dataset begins only in 1973, it is hard to know how these developments compare with the situation prior to the early 1970s (Fama and French, 2004).

Earlier data on initial public offerings were compiled by Gompers and Lerner (2003) for the period from 1935 to 1971, and they show that IPO booms preceded the establishment of NASDAQ. The first IPO boom identified in their study took place just after World War II, but it was rather small. However, there were two subsequent IPO booms, one from the late 1950s to the early 1960s, and the other from the late 1960s to the early 1970s, which were much larger. Indeed, they rivaled those of the 1980s and 1990s in terms of the numbers of companies going public.

The data that Gompers and Lerner used began only in the mid-1930s. However, qualitative accounts of the development of the U.S. stock market suggest that the U.S. stock market's appetite for novelty may have emerged even earlier. Certainly, we know that companies competing in relatively new industries, including radio and aviation, featured prominently as "glamour stocks" in the 1920s. In fact, the most provocative and ambitious analysis of historical IPO activity, Boyan Jovanovic and Peter Rousseau (2001) pointed even farther back than the 1920s, to the late nineteenth and early twentieth centuries, in timing the emergence of the U.S. stock market's appetite for new industries and firms.

In "Why Wait? A Century of Life Before IPO," Jovanovic and Rousseau measured the age of companies at the time of their initial listing on the U.S. stock market for the entire period from 1885 to 1998. They showed that the companies that listed their stocks during the transition from the nineteenth to the twentieth centuries were just as young as the companies going public in the 1980s and 1990s. During the intervening decades, the age of companies going public rose to much higher levels, attaining a peak sometime during the 1950s and 1960s, depending on which measure of age one uses.[2] In other words, they claimed that an inverted U-shape curve can be observed from 1885 to 1998 in the age of firms listing on the U.S. stock market.

Jovanovic and Rousseau assumed that a new firm uses the period before its IPO to learn and develop its business plan and that it commits to a definite plan once it goes public. The better the idea, the higher is the opportunity cost of a delay in its implementation and, therefore, the earlier a firm will conduct an IPO (Jovanovic and Rousseau, 2001, p. 336). From this perspective, they attributed the concerted tendency for young firms to list to the emergence of general-purpose technologies (GPTs) and, specifically, to electrification for the earlier period and information technology for the most recent one: "the electricity-era and the information-technology-era firms came in younger because the

---

[2] Jovanovic and Rousseau measure age in three different ways: the period from founding to listing, from incorporation to listing, and from first product or process innovation to listing.

technologies that they brought in were too productive to be kept out very long." The ambition of the Jovanovic and Rousseau study, especially the long period of time it covers, makes it important to evaluate the provocative claims that its authors make. In fact, on close scrutiny there are a number of problems with their historical analysis of IPO activity.

The Illusion of Youth

The apparent youth of the majority of companies listing on the NYSE in the late 1880s, the 1890s, and the 1900s is the primary evidence that Jovanovic and Rousseau invoked to support their claim that large numbers of new companies listed on the U.S. stock market during the electricity era. However, on closer inspection, many of the "young" companies listing on the NYSE in the 1880s, the 1890s, and the 1900s were formed through consolidations of existing companies. Therefore, they came to the market with a history of business activities behind them and substantial assets already in place. In total, 152 companies joined the NYSE from 1891 to 1910. Of these, 44 industrial companies were products of the Great Merger Movement that led to the consolidation of U.S. industry during the period from 1897 to 1904. A further 35 of the new listings were railroad companies, which were newly incorporated shortly before they came to market and emerged in the process of consolidation underway in the railroad industry.

It is difficult to see how the process of electrification could account for the vast majority of these listings. Only General Electric seems like a plausible candidate for such an explanation even if it was hardly a new company; it was formed in 1892 from the merger of two of the leading companies in the electrical equipment industry. None of the other consolidations seem to have involved companies engaged in the development of product or process technologies related to electricity, the types of companies that Jovanovic and Rousseau seem to have in mind when they speak of new firms "bringing in" highly productive electricity-era technologies.

Once we remove these consolidations from the calculation, the average age of the remaining 73 companies at the time of their listing on the NYSE increases substantially. Only 42 of these companies were 10 years old or less and therefore could be classified as truly young companies, and they represented less than one-third of the total number of companies securing listings on the NYSE during this period. Even for this much smaller set of companies, it is not clear that the links that Jovanovic and Rousseau posit between technology and finance were operative. I was able to establish a direct link with electrification only for seven of these companies, which were all traction and lighting companies. The other companies were in established industries like metals and mining, and there does not seem to be any important or distinctive link between their activities and the process of electrification.

Conflating the U.S. Stock Market with the New York Stock Exchange

A second concern with the Jovanovic and Rousseau analysis stems from the proxies they used for IPOs for most of their period of observation, notably from 1885 to 1971. From 1885 to 1961, they rely on the dates of new listings on the New York Stock Exchange (NYSE).[3] From 1962 to 1971, they use the dates of new listings on the NYSE and the American Stock Exchange (AMEX) as proxies for IPOs. However, these proxies do not accurately reflect the way in which most U.S. companies developed public markets for their stocks during the period from 1885 to 1971.

The NYSE had already established itself as the premier trading market for corporate stocks in the U.S. by the late nineteenth century. It established and maintained this position by focusing on the highest-quality corporate securities available. Other trading markets for stocks – the New York Curb Market, the regional exchanges, and the over-the-counter market – survived in the United States by carving out niches that allowed them to avoid direct challenges to the NYSE's position.

The Curb grew rapidly at the beginning of the twentieth century, especially in the 1920s, as did a number of regional exchanges like Chicago. By 1929, the stocks of 1,246 companies were traded on the Curb, compared with 819 on the NYSE. By then, the Chicago Stock Exchange had grown to be the largest of the nation's regional stock exchanges, with the stocks of 383 companies traded there. The over-the-counter market, which was initially preoccupied with trading bonds, started trading stocks in growing numbers after World War I. It was on these trading markets, rather than on the NYSE, that companies with

---

[3] From 1885 to 1924, they use the year in which prices initially appeared in listings of NYSE stocks. For 1925 to 1998, they used the year in which firms entered the CRSP database as a proxy for IPOs. Until 1962, the CRSP database exclusively comprised NYSE firms, from 1962 firms on the American Stock Exchange were included in the database, and from 1972 NASDAQ firms were added.

limited track records and resources got their first exposure to the U.S. stock market.

From the 1930s, the U.S. stock market continued to be characterized by a hierarchy with the NYSE at its apex. The Big Board maintained its reputation for quality by establishing listing requirements that were the most stringent of all of the registered exchanges. These requirements tended to privilege scale and stability, so it is hardly surprising that almost none of the NYSE's new listings were IPOs.[4] Rather, they represented either transfers to the Big Board of companies already listed on other exchanges or companies whose shares were already traded in the OTC market. Robert Sobel described the normal trajectory for a public company at the time in the following terms: "[s]tocks in newly capitalized companies would be underwritten, sold to the public, then traded over-the-counter. After a while they might qualify for listing on the American Stock Exchange, which for years served as a sort of minor league, with the best issues going on to the big time. That, of course, was the N.Y.S.E." (Sobel, 1977, p. 67).

Given the institutional structure of the U.S. stock market, an analysis of new listings on the U.S. stock market during the period from the 1890s to 1933 ought to focus on the Curb Market and the regional stock exchanges. For the period from 1934 to 1970, the appropriate focus would be the over-the-counter market. In neither period are new listings on the NYSE a good proxy for initial public offerings. Unfortunately, the data on companies trading on the Curb Market prior to 1933 and on the over-the-counter market in the postwar period are patchy and their reliability and consistency over time is questionable. No doubt, it is for this very reason that Jovanovic and Rousseau relied on NYSE listings as a proxy for IPOs, but that does not change the fact that they are not up to the task. Relying on them is likely to lead to a systematic overstatement of the age of companies going public in the United States when other trading markets for stocks were important.

Learning About the Stock Market From the Histories of New Industries

The ambiguity about the historical emergence of the U.S. stock market's appetite for novelty reflects serious limitations of the existing data on initial public offerings in the United States. In principle, it is possible to

---

[4] Prior to 1983, in fact, only three IPOs took place on the NYSE.

draw on existing historical sources to compile a more systematic and comprehensive picture of the historical pattern of IPO activity in the United States. However, the practical demands of such a task are daunting. It is possible to identify stock issues by firm in the United States, at least from 1907, using data published in the *Journal of Commerce and Commercial Bulletin*. However, these data then need to be matched with information on the issuing companies to identify whether issues were IPOs or seasoned issues and to estimate the ages and other characteristics of the issuers. Precisely because many of these issuers were not listed on the NYSE, tracing that information poses considerable challenges.

An interim solution is to look to the historical emergence of prominent new industries in the United States and analyze the role that the stock market played in their early development. Although this approach does not eliminate data problems, it does make them more tractable. Moreover, focusing on a small number of new industries facilitates a more in-depth analysis of the relationship between the stock market and industrial dynamics than a more aggregated approach permits. For all of that, there are obvious problems with trying to learn about general historical trends from the particular experiences of a small number of industries. Such challenges can be alleviated only by accumulating more and more studies of new industries and the following analysis is offered here as only one step toward that end.

EARLY ENCOUNTERS WITH NEW INDUSTRIES IN THE TWENTIES

Prior to the development of a broad and deep national market for industrial securities in the United States, new industries were financed based on local networks. Some of the most important new industries of the Second Industrial Revolution, such as the steel industry, seem to have been funded in this way. By the time a national market for industrial securities emerged in the transition from the nineteenth to the twentieth centuries, these industries were ripe for consolidation, and it was this process, which culminated in the Great Merger Movement from 1897 to 1904, and to some extent the subsequent financing of the players that emerged from this consolidation, which the U.S. stock market facilitated when it became involved in their development (Navin and Sears, 1955; Doyle, 1991; O'Sullivan, 2011).

In contrast, a number of important industries experienced their initial takeoff following the establishment of a national market for industrial securities. If there were industries that would inaugurate the U.S. stock market's role in funding the emergence of new, innovative industries, these industries would seem to be good candidates for the job. The automobile industry is one example but, as I have argued elsewhere, the stock market was of limited significance as a source of funds for fledgling new entrants to this industry. When the stock market became involved in the early development of the industry, it tended to facilitate the consolidation of existing players through mergers and acquisitions or to fund investment by enterprises that were already significant competitors. This pattern started to change from 1915 to 1917, and again from 1919 to 1920, when the stock market funded some young, unproven companies but, by then, the industry was already large and its success understood, so that these entrants were behind, rather than ahead of, the curve.

In contrast, the stock market played a much more important role during the commercial takeoff of the radio and aviation industries. In both cases, the development of crucial technological breakthroughs for these industries occurred in the early twentieth century. Nevertheless, they found the markets they needed to sustain rapid growth only in the 1920s. As we shall see, the stock market was prominent in the development of both of these industries in the 1920s, although the nature of the role it played was somewhat different in each case.

Funding the Radio Industry

The origins of the radio industry are typically traced to the formation of the Marconi Company in Britain in 1897. The U.S. industry got off the ground when an American subsidiary was launched two years later. Besides Marconi, the other key players in the early development of the U.S. radio industry were companies established by two other prominent inventors, Reginald Fessenden and Lee de Forest. Financing did not prove to be a problem for any of these ventures. As Maclaurin (1971) put it, "The most difficult ingredient to supply proved to be effective management rather than capital. Marconi, De Forest and Fessenden – all succeeded in obtaining venture capital in substantial quantities to back their wireless enterprises."

However, the commercial success of the early radio companies was rather modest, and as late as 1920, the industry was of limited economic importance. That changed dramatically in the subsequent decade as the radio industry entered a period of rapid growth. The boon to the commercial potential of radio was the development of public broadcasting in

1920 (Maclaurin, 1971, p. 111). From its inauguration, radio broadcasting showed spectacular growth, and sales of broadcasting equipment and radio sets soared. By 1929, 69 million broadcast tubes and 4.4 million broadcast receiving sets were sold compared with 1 million and 100,000, respectively, in 1922. The total sales of equipment for broadcast reception rose from $60 million in 1922 to $843 million in 1929 (Maclaurin, 1971, p. 134).

By far the most important player in the radio industry at this time was the Radio Corporation of America (RCA). It was established in 1919 at the initiative of General Electric, with the approval of the U.S. government, to bring all of the important patents in the U.S. radio industry, primarily those of American Marconi, General Electric, American Telephone and Telegraph, and Westinghouse, under one roof. The dispersion of radio patents in the United States was increasingly seen as an obstacle to the country's ability to compete with other nations, especially Britain, in the development of international communications (Maclaurin, 1971, p. 103).

RCA was initially not intended to be a manufacturer of radio equipment. Instead, GE and Westinghouse would supply radio transmitters and receivers. Both companies started producing radio sets after World War I, but they were not able to keep up with the massive increase in demand that followed the launch of commercial broadcasting. As a result, the boom brought hundreds of entrants into the industry. As Maclaurin notes, "[l]ittle capital investment was required to assemble radio sets. And there were many companies which possessed the 'know-how' to manufacture the principal component parts" (Maclaurin, 1971, p. 260). He estimated that more than 700 firms entered the industry in the period of four years from 1923 to 1926.[5]

Many of the early entrants were engaged in the production of crystal radio sets in which patents could be worked around. However, it soon became clear that vacuum-tube sets were the wave of the future in radio and RCA exercised a dominant position in patents for all aspects of these sets from the circuit design through to the loudspeakers (Maclaurin, 1971, p. x). Some companies entered to do business on the basis of alternative patents for these technologies. Others competed by disregarding patent restrictions.

The wave of entry into the radio industry was accompanied by a boom in stock issues of radio companies. An expression commonly heard at

[5] One hundred eighty-five firms entered the industry in 1923, 144 in 1924, 258 in 1925, and 161 in 1926 (Maclaurin, 1971, p. 134).

the time was "a new radio stock a day," with pundits speculating that at least one share of stock was sold for every receiving set sold ("The Smash in Radio Shares," *Barron's*, May 3, 1926, p. 9). The most prominent new radio companies were listed on the New York Curb, and by 1925 there were eighteen of them represented there. A couple of them, such as De Forest Radio and Duplex Condenser and Radio, had been around for more than ten years, but most of them were new companies established in the early 1920s. Sometimes they boasted the involvement of men with long experience in radio technology, and a few of them came into existence to acquire a predecessor company with established operations. The Curb stocks may have been the most prominent of the radio stocks but that market was not the only outlet for the stocks of radio companies; the over-the-counter market, in particular, also played an important role in the distribution of radio stocks to a wider public ("The Smash in Radio Shares," *Barron's*, May 3, 1926, p. 9).

The stock market's enthusiasm for the radio industry dissipated in early 1925 largely because of the pressure on profitability that high entry had caused. The leading radio stocks lost 60 percent of their value from December 1924 to May 1926 ("The Smash in Radio Shares," *Barron's*, May 3, 1926, p. 9). If we exclude RCA's stocks from the calculation, the decline in the radio companies' market value was even more dramatic at 92 percent. And, as *Barron's* pointed out, "[t]his loss in market value in 18 different companies' stocks . . . is not the only loss suffered in radio stocks for other issues were floated in various sections of the country some of which were never actually listed on any market" ("The Smash in Radio Shares," *Barron's*, May 3, 1926, p. 9).

The crash was deemed by many commentators to be a response to the overcrowding of the industry. The *Wall Street Journal* claimed that "[w]ith a rush by all hands to scoop up some of the cream, the result was disastrous, inasmuch as it confused the public and actually stopped the boom in the sale of sets" ("Rapid Expansion Hurts Radio Trade," *Wall Street Journal*, May 26, 1925). One study observed that "all hands found the market tired and inventories at the peak. There was a rush to unload, and receiving sets were sold by the hundreds of thousands often at less than cost" ("Radio Stocks down $96,281,650 in Year," *New York Times*, May 2, 1926, p. E11).

Those with an interest in radio stocks were reportedly astonished by the sharp reversal of the industry's fortunes: "[o]verproduction, followed by cautious buying on the part of the public, astonished the promoters of the dozens of new companies" ("Rapid Expansion Hurts Radio Trade,"

Wall Street Journal, May 26, 1925). Investors in the stocks of many radio companies "found it impossible to get out without devastating losses. Four companies went into receivers' hands in the last year and application for receivership was announced for two others" ("Radio Stocks down $96,281,650 in Year," *New York Times*, May 2, 1926, p. E11).

Entry into the radio industry declined dramatically from its peak of 258 companies in 1925 to only 26 firms in 1927, 16 in 1928 and 26 in 1929 (Maclaurin, 1971, p. 134). In part the decline was a response to disappointed expectations, but the more important reason for the change was the success of RCA's attempts to enforce its patent rights. Concerned about the implications of hypercompetition for the profitability of the radio industry, RCA had been working through the courts to secure its future based on the control of key patents. By 1927, as Maclaurin put it, "the RCA group had . . . established a strong patent position in all the major branches of the radio industry, and an RCA license was considered essential for the manufacture of any up-to-date set or modern vacuum tube" (Maclaurin, 1971, p. 131). RCA was willing to license its technologies but only to a limited number of companies, which contributed to the reduction of the rate of entry to the business.

Following the crash of radio stocks in 1925, there was a lull in the public stock offerings of radio companies that lasted for almost three years, from July 1925 through February 1928. The only exception was an issue by Gold Seal Electrical in November 1928. Then, in March 1928, Grigsby-Grunow launched another burst of radio stock issues when it raised $500,000 in an issue of common stock. From March 1928 to September 1929, twenty-five public stock offerings were undertaken by radio companies to raise a total of $38.4 million.[6]

All of these issues were common stock offerings with the only exception being an issue of cumulative preferred stock by Stromberg-Carlson, which raised $1 million in July 1928. On average, these issues raised $1.6 million with a standard deviation of $1.6 million, and the median issue was $1.1 million. The issuing companies were on average 4.4 years old with a standard deviation of 6.3 years and a median age of 2.8 years.[7]

[6] These estimates are based on data compiled by the author from the volumes prepared by the National Statistical Service (Schwarzchild, various issues). They are the most comprehensive source of data on public stock issues in the United States for the period from 1925 to 1936.
[7] Data on the date of incorporation for issuing companies were obtained from Moody's. However, precise data were available only for 23 of the companies that issued stock.

However, on closer inspection, some of the very youngest issuers came into existence to acquire the assets of existing corporations. As a result, the radio companies completing public stock issues at this time tended to be older than earlier issuers of radio stock.

There was another bust in radio stock prices from 1929. Broader problems in the U.S. economy contributed to this downturn, of course, but industry observers also blamed another overexpansion of the industry. As Barron's pointed out, "[i]ncreased competition, narrower profit margins, and reduced sales forced some of the weaker concerns to the wall. Among them were Kolster Radio Corp, which went into receivership in January, 1930; Earl Radio Corp., which suffered a similar fate in November, 1929; and Freed-Eiseman Radio Corp., which experienced receivership in December, 1929" ("Radio Industry in the Doldrums," *Barron's*, June 8, 1931, p. 13).

Funding the Aviation Industry

The aviation industry was established only a few years after the automobile industry, with its origins usually traced to the first successful "powered" flight by the Wright brothers in December 1903. However, in contrast to that of the automotive industry, the development of aviation as a commercially viable industry took a longer time to achieve. In its early years, the industry was largely preoccupied with the manufacture of small numbers of planes for airplane enthusiasts. Investment in the industry was limited, output was low, and the number of competitors was small during the first decade of the industry's existence.

As far as financing was concerned, as Rae noted, "[t]he pioneering period of aircraft manufacturing in the United States shows a pattern characteristic of the growth of a new industry: that is, the emergence of a number of small companies financed from individual or local resources" (Rae, 1965, p. 99). There were a couple of exceptions to this pattern, with renowned inventors like the Wright brothers and Glenn Curtiss receiving the backing of nationally prominent financiers and industrialists (Rae, 1965, p. 100).

The outbreak of World War I stimulated the first major expansion in the industry's output with a dramatic increase in demand for airplanes from foreign governments and, eventually, the U.S. government. The anticipation of U.S. involvement in the war led to some important changes in the competitive structure of the industry. In particular, in 1916 the Wright-Martin Aircraft Corporation was formed through the merger of the Wright Aeronautical Company, the Martin Company, and the Simplex Automobile Company. In the same year, a merger took place between Curtiss and the Burgess Aeroplane Company to form the Curtiss Aeroplane and Motor Corporation (Rae, 1965).

The expectation and reality of higher military demand also brought new companies into the aviation industry (Dodd, 1933). For example, with a view to securing government contracts, the Dayton-Wright Company was formed in 1916 by Edward A. Deeds of National Cash Register and Charles Kettering of GM, among others, with Orville Wright as a consultant (Freudenthal, 1940). William Boeing also entered the aviation industry in 1916 after a highly successful career in the lumber business. He changed the name of his company, Pacific Aero Products, to Boeing Airplane Company in 1917 and made training planes for the navy during the war. At this stage, most new entrants to the industry continued to rely on their own funds or those invested by local financiers (Rae, 1965).

Estimates differ of the amount spent by the U.S. government on military aeronautics during World War I, but Rae puts the figure at somewhere over $400 million for the period from April 1917 to November 1918. This amount represented a huge influx of funds given the industry's small scale. The results, in terms of the delivery of suitable aircraft for the war effort, fell far short of expectations (Freudenthal, 1940; Rae, 1965). Nevertheless, when hostilities terminated, enough output had been generated to contribute to a major industry bust as a large number of surplus planes were dumped on the market (Dodd, 1933). Because commercial markets for airplanes were not sufficiently developed to compensate for the decline in military demand, the result was a collapse in industry output and investment.

In 1921, fewer than sixty companies were recorded in the Thomas Register of American Manufacturers as being active either in the production of airplanes or of airplane motors. Among the companies specializing in the aviation industry, only Wright Aeronautical, Curtiss Aeroplane and Motor Corporation, and Sturtevant Aeroplane were covered by Moody's, the best available source for information on listed or otherwise actively traded stocks in the United States. Of these three, only Wright and Curtiss were traded on an exchange: the NYSE for Wright and the Curb for Curtiss. As a measure of the stock market's limited involvement in the aviation industry, Dodd estimated that, until 1921, the total amount of publicly offered securities amounted to no more than $15 million (Dodd, 1933, p. 3).

Producers in the industry struggled to stay afloat in the early 1920s. Some companies went out of business (Dodd, 1933). Others sought to survive by merging with their competitors; for example, the Consolidated Aircraft Corporation was formed in 1923 through the merger of the struggling Gallaudet Aircraft Company with what remained of the Dayton-Wright Company. Other aviation companies diversified; Boeing, for example, produced furniture in the early 1920s to remain in business. By 1924, the total amount of capital invested in the airplane manufacturing industry had actually declined from where it had been in 1920 (U.S. Bureau of the Census, 1976).

However, in the second half of the 1920s, there was a dramatic turnaround in the industry's fortunes. By 1929, the total capital invested in aviation manufacturing reached $118 million in 1929 dollars compared with $19 million in 1919, and the number of wage earners employed reached 9,856 compared with only 1,395 in 1921 (Dodd, 1933, p. 181; U.S. Bureau of the Census, 1976, p. 685). By 1929, important investments had also been made in the development of the nascent airline business as well as in the construction of airports and the provision of services to the aviation industry. By the end of the boom in the late 1920s, aviation was still a relatively small industry in the United States. However, the decade from 1925 to 1935 proved to be a crucial one for the industry's development. It was a period of significant technological change that helped to lay the foundations for the development of major commercial markets for airplanes.

Several factors contributed to the expansion of the aviation industry in the second half of the 1920s. By then, postwar dumping had run its course and demand began to pick up again. There was some increase in airplane orders from the U.S. military but, much more important, a new source of business for the private sector emerged in the form of airmail service. Until 1925, the airmail service was operated by the government and, specifically, the Post Office Department. However, with the passage of the Kelly Bill or Air Mail Act of 1925, the postmaster general contracted with private companies to carry U.S. airmail, thus furnishing private companies with a flourishing and lucrative new business.

Appropriations by the post office to domestic airmail service increased from a mere $100,000 in 1918 to $2.75 million in 1925 and then to $12.4 million by 1929 (Dodd, 1933, p. 181). Initially, the post office paid for contracted services on the basis of the postage revenues that it received. However, it changed this arrangement in 1926 to pay its contractors based on the weight of what they carried. As a result, it provided a substantial direct subsidy to private contractors for the provision of airmail service (Freudenthal, 1940, pp. 75-6).[8] It also boosted demand for airplanes to service these airmail routes; U.S. aircraft production peaked in 1929 at 6,193 planes, of which 5,516 planes were for civil use (U.S. Bureau of the Census, 1976, p. 768).

The improvement in industry conditions led to an increase in the profitability of incumbent producers and also induced a new wave of entry to the industry. Although there had been some entry into the industry in the early 1920s, the number of producers of aircraft and parts was still relatively low in 1925 (Dodd, 1933, p. 181). There were few airline operators because commercial aviation was still in its infancy. By 1929, however, the number of producers had more than doubled (Dodd, 1933, p. 181) and there had been significant entry by operators competing for the emergent commercial airline business, by companies building and running airports, and by other suppliers to the aviation industry. By 1931, there were an estimated 459 companies operating in all branches of the aviation industry (Dodd, 1933, p. 2).

Some financiers understood the improved prospects for the aviation industry from an early stage. Clement M. Keys was a leading example. He was a Canadian who left Toronto for New York in the early 1900s to take a job as a journalist, and later as railroad editor, for the *Wall Street Journal*. Ten years later, he set up his own investment bank, C. M. Keys and Company (van der Linden, 2002, pp. 21-2).

In 1919, on a trip to Europe as a member of the American Aviation Commission, Keys became convinced of the potential of commercial aviation. When he returned to the United States, he bought Curtiss Aeroplane and Motor Company, which was in trouble, and borrowed money to keep it going until he turned it around. Then, in response to the passage of the Kelly Act, in May 1925 Keys established National Air Transport, the first U.S. company founded as an airline enterprise. He loaded the company's board with prominent industrialists and financiers and capitalized the company at $10 million, a very large sum for the aviation industry at the time. Initially, the company issued no stock to the public, but it was still able to raise so much money that it had surplus far beyond its investment needs (van der Linden, 2002, pp. 21-2).

[8] Freudenthal estimates that the U.S. Post Office provided a subsidy of 163 percent of the airmail revenues it received in 1929 (Freudenthal, 1940, p. 309).

Pratt and Whitney was also formed in 1925. Its founder was Frederick B. Rentschler who left Wright Aeronautical in 1924 and established a rival to that company with the approval of the Navy. Like Keys, he enjoyed the backing of powerful financial interests not least because of the help he received from his brother, Gordon, who was a director of the National City Bank. Later in the 1920s, Clement Keys and Frederick Rentschler would become rivals in a race to consolidate the aviation industry.

However, it took longer for most investment banks and the country's financial markets to get directly involved in the dramatic developments in the aviation industry's competitive structure. Practically no new securities were publicly issued from 1921 until the middle of 1927 (Dodd, 1933, p. 3).[9] Even the leading companies in the industry were relatively small, having shrunk dramatically from their wartime size; in 1926, Wright Aeronautical had sales of $3.2 million and total assets of $5.8m and Curtiss Aeronautical & Motor Company had sales of $3.7 million and total assets of 4.6 million in the same year. They were dwarfs compared with the giants of U.S. industry at the time, operating in an industry that as yet was greeted with skepticism by the investing public. As Freudenthal put it, "[f]lying was still generally considered a stunt, largely because of the postwar period of unrestricted flying which had resulted in many accidents. Serious flying seemed to be limited to the Army and Navy, which had captured a majority of the international air trophies" (Freudenthal, 1940, p. 89).

Charles Lindbergh's transatlantic flight in May 1927 changed all of that, contributing to great public excitement about the industry's prospects and massive speculation in aviation stocks. At the time, however, there were few such stocks from which investors could choose. Wright Aeronautical was the only aviation company with a listing on the NYSE. It made the engine that powered Lindbergh's plane, and its stock went from $25 per share in April 1927 to $94 ¾ by December 1927 (Freudenthal, 1940, p. 92). In October 1927, Curtiss Aeronautical and Motor Company moved from the Curb to join Wright Aeronautical on the NYSE, presumably to participate more centrally in the aviation boom, and its stock price also rose dramatically.[10]

---

[9] The only exception was the Aero Supply Manufacturing Company, which raised $375,000 in July 1925. Aero Supply was incorporated in Delaware in July 1925 as a successor to a company that had started business in 1920. Its stock was traded on the New York Curb.

[10] Dodd reports that an index based on ten aviation stocks moved from 104.9 in April 1927 to 1,147 in May 1929 compared with an increase from 110 to 192.6 over the same period for an index of 337 industrial companies (Dodd, 1933, p. 194).

In September 1927, Boeing Airplane Company completed the first public issue by an aviation company for more than two years, but of debt rather than equity, selling 6 percent notes to raise $600,000. The *Wall Street Journal* said the success of the issue was "another indication that investment demand has been stimulated" by Lindbergh's flight, noting that the entire issue was sold out in an hour or two with more demand left unfulfilled ("Broad Street Gossip," *Wall Street Journal*, September 2, 1927, p. 2). However, no further issues by aviation companies occurred for another six months.

In March 1928, Curtiss-Robertson Airplane Manufacturing Company sold shares to raise $500,000. Then, the floodgates opened. From March 1928 to June 1930, 124 public offerings of stock were conducted by aviation companies to raise more than $300 million.[11] Almost all of these issues were of common stock, a fact that reflected, as Freudenthal noted,

a tacit acknowledgement of the uncertainty the companies felt about their future. No bonds were issued because the underwriters and issuing houses were unwilling to obligate the companies to pay interest charges and retire their bonds on definite fixed dates. Common stocks, mostly of no par value, committed the management to no specific return on investment and, besides, made it possible to draw in capital far beyond what was warranted by the physical assets and current income (Freudenthal, 1940, p. 92).

The total amount of money raised by aviation companies through the sale of stock was enormous relative to the amount of invested capital in the industry at the time. It was also significant relative to overall levels of stock issuance that themselves were at all-time highs. In the first eight months of 1929, the aviation industry was reportedly the fourth most important industry in terms of stock issuance, generating proceeds of $158.7 million compared with a total of $4.2 billion for U.S. industry (Dodd, 1933, pp. 4–5). This ranking is remarkable given the small size of the emerging industry.

The issuers were involved in the whole range of activities in the aviation industry, including the manufacture of frames and engines, the operation of airlines, the production of aircraft parts, the provision of

[11] These estimates are based on data compiled by the author from volumes of stock issues publicly offered by banking and investment houses in the United States (Schwarzchild, various issues). In addition, twenty-seven stock issues by aviation companies, which were sold to the public without using the services of an underwriter, which were recorded in Dodd (1933), were also included.

aircraft services including runways, as well as the business of investing in aviation companies. The proceeds from these issues ranged in value from a low of $50,000 to a high of $40 million. The average issue was $2.6 million, with a standard deviation of $5.5 million, and the median issue was $1 million.

A couple of issues of stock were undertaken by established companies, like the Wright Aeronautical Company and the Glenn Martin Company, which had been around for more than 10 years and whose securities were listed on the NYSE. However, in general, the aviation firms undertaking these issues were very young. Their average age was only 1.6 years, with a standard deviation of 2.5 years, and their median age was only 0.4 years.[12] Many of these companies were small companies who were new entrants to the industry; a total of 46 issues raised proceeds of less than $1 million.

The wave of entry was a testament to how low the barriers to entry were in the aviation business at the time. However, some of the industry's most influential participants believed that this would soon change as more sophisticated technologies led to rising development costs. From their point of view, vertical integration was the appropriate strategy with which to confront this eventuality (van der Linden, 2002, p. 49). The post office created an added incentive for such integration by making the award of airmail contracts contingent on the reliability of the operator which, in those days, was closely linked to its manufacturing experience.

A dramatic process of consolidation got underway in the aviation industry in late 1928, less than a year after the start of the boom in aviation issues. It revolved around the creation of large holding companies that controlled both manufacturing and transportation companies. The stock market was heavily implicated in this process. Some of the very youngest aviation companies undertaking stock issues were, in fact, holding companies which were established to take active interests in existing companies. Moreover, the capacity of the most prominent holding groups to get access to resources from the stock market allowed them to extend their reach beyond all expectations.

These holding groups exercised an enormous influence on the competitive structure of the aviation industry. As Freudenthal put it, "[t]he flood of mergers engulfed all the old pioneers and aviation engineers who had managed to carry their own companies through the previous

---

[12] Data on the date of incorporation for issuing companies were obtained from Moody's. However, precise data were available only for 91 of the companies that issued stock.

Table 8.1. Distribution of Automobile, Radio and Aviation Stock Issues by
Trading Market

Industry/Period	No of Stock Issues Sold (% of total Stock Issues Sold)				
	NYSE	NY Curb	Regionals	OTC	Total
Automobiles: 1915–17	12	21	17		50
(50 issues)	(24%)	(42%)	(34%)		(100%)
Radio: 1925–29	1	14	10	11	34
(30 issues)	(3%)	(47%)	(33%)	(37%)	(120%)
Aviation: 1925–29	7	33	33	73	146
(126 issues)	(6%)	(26%)	(26%)	(58%)	(116%)

years of erratic development. They could not compete, they realized, with the large combinations backed by powerful interests that were now dominating the industry. So, they either sold out to the financiers, as Loening and Boeing did, or, like Douglas and Consolidated, admitted some financial interests" (Freudenthal, 1940, p. 99).

By the end of the 1920s, these holding groups dominated the aviation industry, soaking up the large majority of its revenues. United Aircraft and Transport accounted for 42 percent of all plane and engine sales over the period from 1927 to 1933 and Curtiss-Wright for a further 39 percent with independents such as Douglas, Glenn Martin, Great Lakes, Consolidated Aircraft and Grumman together accounting for the remaining 19 percent (Freudenthal, 1940, p. 120). Holding groups exercised an even more overwhelming dominance of the operating side of the aviation business: United received 57 percent of domestic airmail payments in 1929, the North American Group accounted for 23 percent, and the Aviation Corporation for a further 12 percent, bringing the total share of these three holding groups to an extraordinary 92 percent (Freudenthal, 1940, Table 8.1).

A GROWING, BUT LIMITED, APPETITE FOR NOVELTY

My analysis suggests that the U.S. stock market became actively involved in the development of new industries much later than Jovanovic and Rousseau suggested. In automobiles, the earliest possible timing would be from 1915 on, and, by then, the industry cannot really be thought of as "new" in the sense of being unproven, given the scale it had reached and the displayed success of some of its leading players. Based on aviation and radio, it would seem that the 1920s is a better candidate for a crucial turning point in the involvement of the stock market in the development of new industries in the United States.

Certain features of the U.S. stock market facilitated this development. As I suggested earlier, the variety of trading markets for stocks in the United States, and the differentiation in the roles they played, proved important in allowing new industries and new firms to raise funds through stock issues. The New York Curb Exchange, which started out some time before the Civil War, played a particularly important role in this regard.

Having witnessed the aggressive tactics that the NYSE used to eliminate its direct competitors, the Curb was careful to avoid looking like it was competing for the Big Board's business. It tended to list smaller, more speculative issues than those admitted to trading on the NYSE and served as a testing ground for some of these stocks that then graduated to the Big Board once they had proved themselves. As I previously noted, this pattern is very clear in the evolution of the U.S. automobile industry, with many of the leading companies in the industry starting out on the Curb (see also Leffler, 1957, p. 83). Once they made a transition to the Big Board, the Curb stopped trading these stocks.

The Curb flourished after World War I and especially in the 1920s after it moved indoors in 1921. Many of the stocks of radio and aviation companies initially traded on the Curb in the 1920s, and, in general, the decade proved to be a flourishing one for the exchange. By the early 1930s, more than 2,000 stock issues traded on the Curb Exchange, of which 400 were listed issues and about 1,700 were unlisted issues (Twentieth Century Fund, 1935, p. 256). In 1929, the volume of trading on the Curb was higher than that of the Big Board for the first time in its history. In the same year, to connote its elevated status, the New York Curb Market changed its name to the New York Curb Exchange (Bruchey, 1991, pp. 23-4).

In addition to the NYSE and the Curb, there were also more than thirty organized exchanges outside of New York City. The largest of them, in terms of the volume and value of securities traded, were in Chicago in the Midwest, Philadelphia and Boston on the East Coast, and San Francisco and Los Angeles on the West Coast (Twentieth Century Fund, 1935, p. 767). These exchanges had developed to provide markets for the securities of local corporations but, as the more successful of these companies graduated to the Big Board, they were increasingly concerned about generating new sources of business. Their problems were largely solved in the 1920s when they experienced a flood of new listings; for example, from 1926 to 1929, Chicago's listings more than doubled from 237 to 535 and Boston's listings increased from 300 in July 1925 to 437 in July 1930 (Securities and Exchange Commission, 1963, Chapter 8, p. 915). As Table 8.1 shows, the regional exchanges were the most important organized exchanges, besides the Curb, in facilitating the debuts of new industries on the U.S. stock market. The analysis in Table 8.1 confirms the dangers of using new listings on the NYSE as a proxy for initial public offerings. In all cases, especially for the radio and aviation industries, the NYSE was of limited importance as a market for the sale of newly issued stocks.

In addition to the organized exchanges, the U.S. had a growing over-the-counter (OTC) market, which also served as a seasoning ground for new securities. The OTC market was really a collection of dispersed markets in which broker-dealers conducted business with each other and with members of the public. When someone wanted to sell or buy a stock, a broker would seek to find a matching offer to buy or sell that stock and negotiate a price for the trade. Some dealers were described as market makers in particular securities to the extent that they carried inventories of these securities and stood ready to buy and sell them to other broker-dealers. The market was particularly useful for trading securities which had thin markets. As Table 8.1 shows, 37 percent of radio stocks and 58 percent of aviation stocks were sold in the OTC market in the 1920s.

Besides the characteristics of the trading markets for stocks, the changing character of competition in investment banking in the United States following World War I facilitated stock issues by new industries and new firms. In 1917 and 1918, the U.S. Treasury raised an unprecedented amount of $17 billion through the sale of Liberty bonds in the public markets and in 1919 it raised a further $4.5 billion with its Victory loan (Carosso, 1970, p. 224). In facilitating the government's efforts to sell Liberty and Victory loans, investment bankers developed their selling practices to reach as wide a public market as possible. There was a marked expansion in the size of selling syndicates that they used to distribute securities and the nationwide syndicate made its appearance at this time. In general, the investment banking industry experimented with more aggressive sales techniques and transferred these techniques to the sale of industrial securities in the 1920s (Carosso, 1970, pp. 253–4).

Some of the well-established investment banks participated in these developments but, as Carosso noted, "most long-established houses, while continuing to grow, maintained their conservative policies in the face of growing competition. They did not adopt aggressive sales tactics or openly solicit business. They sold few common stocks even though these were becoming the more popular securities" (Carosso, 1970, p. 255). For example, common stock accounted for just over three percent of the securities that the House of Morgan, which remained the leading investment bank in the U.S. in the 1920s, distributed to the public from 1919 to 1933 (Carosso, 1970, p. 256).

However, a growing population of new investment banks in the 1920s was willing to be much more aggressive. An analysis of the lead underwriters of aviation and radio stock issues in the 1920s reveals few of the investment banking firms that had featured prominently in the Pujo hearings. Instead, many of the underwriters were relatively small, and often young, players operating out of New York as well as regional players who had initially made their mark by underwriting local issues. Investment banking affiliates of commercial banks were also involved in originating and marketing these new, risky issues. The aggressive originating and selling tactics of these players were largely what facilitated and fueled the sale of stocks that previously had been considered too speculative for public consumption and remained so for the most prestigious U.S. investment banks.

These banks sold stocks to an increasingly receptive public. In the early twentieth century, the ownership of industrial stocks in the United States had been largely confined to the wealthiest households in the country. However, from the late teens through the 1920s, the dispersion of stockholding increased. Historians have emphasized the importance of the government's Liberty and Victory loan programs in bringing the savings of a new tier of American households into the securities markets. As the flood of government bonds dried up, especially in the 1920s, many of these investors were persuaded of the merits of holding industrial securities (Carosso, 1970, pp. 238–9). By the end of the bull market in 1929, the available estimates suggest that as many as 6.25 million Americans, that is, five percent of the U.S. population, owned stock (Goldsmith, 1969, p. 360).[13] It was not just households that plunged into the stock market during the 1920s; corporations and commercial banks also took their surplus funds and invested them there.

Even more important than the growth in the number of investors participating in the stock market was their increased willingness to take risks for the prospect of capital gains. Until the 1920s, preferred stocks

---

[13] Goldsmith drew his estimates from Cox, 1963.

were favored over common stocks for their promise of a steady income stream. The prevalence of preferred stocks is usually attributed to the efforts of corporations and their financiers to make stocks look as much as possible like the bonds that U.S. investors were more used to holding (Baskin and Miranti, 1997, p. 181). There was an important change in the composition of stock issues in the 1920s with a major increase in the importance of common stock. The trend accelerated in the late 1920s with common stock accounting for 60 percent of stock issues in 1928 and as much as 75 percent in 1929 (*Commercial and Financial Chronicle*, various issues).

This development seems to be explained by investors' growing interest in participating in the large capital gains that accrued to common stocks in the 1920s. An analysis of the real S&P index from 1890 to 1929 shows that the bull market of the 1920s was distinguished from earlier periods by its continuity and the rate of its acceleration. Common stocks gained ground in the 1920s, especially in the second half of the 1920s, as investors displayed increasing interest in the prospect of speculative gains, even if they came at the expense of steady dividends.

This change in attitude was crucial in allowing the aviation and radio companies to raise capital in the public markets in the 1920s. Almost all of them issued common stock to raise funds, and most of them took advantage of the discretion that this instrument accorded them to pay no dividends. In both industries, the stock market became actively involved in their development by riding on a wave of entry that had been set off by changes in the technological and/or market structures of these industries. However, the stock market's willingness to invest was set off by a public event – the start of commercial broadcasting in radio and Lindbergh's flight for aviation, which drew attention to their technological and/or market dynamics and stimulated huge run-ups in the stock prices of aviation and radio companies while the speculative momentum lasted.

The willingness of stockholders to bet their money on the future prospects of aviation and radio reflected their growing realization of the gains to be made from investment in industrial stocks. By the 1920s, the success of companies that dominated industries like electrical equipment and automobiles was very clear, as were the benefits that their stockholders had derived from that success. It generated great enthusiasm for getting in on the ground floor of new industries, even before their prospects were proven, and there was widespread discussion of the heuristics that might be used to select the stocks that would someday become the General Electric or General Motors of these industries.

However, it is important to recognize that the U.S. stock market's role in funding novelty in the 1920s was significant only in comparison with the limited extent of its involvement until then. It does not imply that the stock market's investments in the aviation and radio industries were representative of its general role in the U.S. economy at the time. To the contrary, based on his analysis of all of the security issues conducted in 1929, George Eddy concluded that "new productive enterprises were financed directly via public security issues in 1929 to the extent of no more than a few hundred million dollars at most" (Eddy, 1937, p. 86).

CRISIS AS INDUCEMENT TO STAGNATION AND CHANGE, 1930–45

The stock market crash and the economic crisis of the 1930s interrupted any further broadening of the stock market's relationship with new industries. Stock issues, whatever their provenance and motivation, fell to very low levels by the first half of the 1930s. Although there was an upsurge in stock issues in 1936, it quickly came to an end with the recession of 1937, and, not long afterward, the U.S. entry into World War II took a further toll on financial market activity. From what we currently know about the composition of stock issues at this time, few of the stock issues that took place from the mid-1930s through 1945 were initial public offerings.[14] Companies seeking funds from the stock market during this period were, for the most part, already publicly traded companies conducting seasoned issues often to refinance existing obligations.

These patterns are hardly surprising given that the stock market crash and the subsequent Depression had so resoundingly burst the bubble of investor enthusiasm not just for new stocks but for all stocks. Stock prices recovered from their low point in 1933 but the combination of recession, and then war, meant that in 1946 the Dow Jones Industrial Average was only slightly above its previous peak of a decade earlier. Even after World War II, there was limited enthusiasm for U.S. industrial stocks among individual investors or the mutual funds and other institutional investors that were becoming increasingly important in the U.S. stock market. The Dow Jones Industrial Average remained largely flat through the late 1940s.

---

[14] This statement is based on the data provided in Gompers and Lerner (2003) on the number of initial public offerings in the United States from 1935 to 1972.

Some observers attributed the decline of stock market activity in the 1930s and early 1940s to federal regulation of the securities markets and the banking industry, but this view has been hotly contested by other commentators. Wherever the truth lies, what is clear, and somewhat ironic, is that federal regulation shaped competition among trading markets for stocks and proved important in facilitating the U.S. stock market's involvement in funding new firms and new industries after World War II.

In influencing competition for new stock issues among trading markets, states had already led the way. In response to the speculation of the 1920s, most states enacted laws prohibiting unseasoned issues from trading on regional exchanges (Securities and Exchange Commission, 1963, Chapter 8, p. 916). In the postwar period, therefore, regional exchanges played a minimal role as markets for the seasoning of new issues. Instead, it was the OTC market that dominated this activity, an outcome that was encouraged by the important changes that federal regulation wrought in the relationship between America's organized exchanges and its over-the-counter market.

The Securities Act of 1933 required the registration of securities issues to the public and detailed public disclosure of material financial information about the issuers. It regulated the flotation of new securities and applied to all new stocks, wherever they were traded, so long as they could be deemed to be participating in interstate commerce. The only major exception to this act was for very small securities issues, known as Regulation A issues, and private placements. The Securities Exchange Act of 1934 extended these requirements to include the publication of periodic financial reports as well as the fulfillment of requirements with respect to proxy solicitation and insider trading. However, it mandated these disclosure requirements only for companies listed on a registered exchange. Companies whose securities traded in the OTC market did not have to comply with the periodic disclosure, proxy, and insider trading provisions of the 1934 Securities Exchange Act in contrast to companies listed on a registered exchange (O'Sullivan, in press).

The architects of federal securities regulation deemed the extension of the disclosure requirements of the 1934 Act to the over-the-counter market to be "vitally necessary to forestall widespread evasion of stock exchange regulation by the withdrawal of securities from listing on exchanges, and by transferring trading therein to 'over-the-counter' markets where manipulative evils could continue to flourish, unchecked by any regulatory authority" (S. Rep. No. 792, 73rd Cong., 2nd Sess. (1934)

quoted in Loss, 1951, p. 614). However, given how little was known then about the operation of the OTC market, they decided that further research was required to work out a framework for regulating these activities and the Exchange Act charged the SEC with the task.

The regulatory framework that was eventually established for the OTC market by the Maloney Act of 1938 required organizations of brokers and dealers to register with the SEC as national securities associations. In 1939, the SEC approved the registration of the National Association of Securities Dealers (NASD) that was, in fact, the only association registered under the Maloney Act. The NASD ultimately organized the vast majority of OTC brokers and dealers and took primary responsibility for the supervision of the OTC market (Seligman, 1995, pp. 183-9).

However, despite the earlier intention of federal security regulators, the SEC did not propose any regulatory scheme for issuers in the OTC market. As a result, OTC securities, in contrast to listed securities, remained beyond the purview of the ongoing disclosure, proxy, and insider trading requirements of the 1934 Act, even though, as Loss pointed out, "[i]n principle it seems self-evident that the disparity of regulation is without justification" (Loss, 1951, p. 615). The primary reason that the SEC offered in explanation for this omission was the practical difficulty in implementing such requirements in the absence of any sanction against the issuer, such as removal from an organized exchange, if it did not comply. As Seligman observed, there were also concerns at the time about the scope of appropriate federal regulation in this matter given recent interpretations of constitutional law (Seligman, 1995, p. 142).

Nevertheless, Congress enacted a provision in the 1936 amendment to the Exchange Act that made some effort to bring OTC securities within the Act's purview. It required companies with a share value of $2 million or more, making a new offering of securities any time after the effective date of the 1936 amendments, to provide periodic financial statements. Over time, it was hoped that more and more OTC securities would be covered by the Act at least to the extent that they made new issues (Seligman, 1995, p. 142). Nevertheless, important gaps persisted into the postwar period between the regulatory treatment of listed companies and those whose stocks traded on the OTC market; in particular, the latter were not subject to the periodic disclosure, proxy, and insider trading provisions of the 1934 Act. There were repeated attempts to close this gap in the late 1940s and the 1950s, but they all failed (O'Sullivan, in press). Instead, the regulatory gap persisted and contributed to the rapid expansion of the OTC market after the war.

Federal regulation also influenced the dynamics of investment banking in ways that influenced the origination and marketing of these issues. The stock market crash and the subsequent passage of the Glass-Steagall Act prompted an upheaval in the structure of the business by forcing banks to choose between their commercial and investment banking businesses. In particular, as commercial banks left the business, new investment houses were formed from the remnants of their underwriting and brokerage businesses and their relationships with issuers and clients were up for grabs. As Carosso put it, "[t]he disruption in issuer-banker relationships created by the Banking Act resulted in a general 'hustling for business,' in which old and new firms, small and large, sought to hold on to their clients and fought hard to win as many new ones as possible" (Carosso, 1970, p. 375).

Competition for issuance activity was heightened by a growing tendency for corporate issuers to privately place their bonds with institutional investors, notably life insurers, without help from an investment bank, as well as the growth in competitive bidding for utilities issues induced by the Public Utilities Act (Carosso, 1970; Smith and Sylla, 1993, p. 39). Underwriting commissions in the United States had been declining for some time and, by the late 1930s, commissions on bond issues reached levels of only 2 percent (Calomiris and Raff, 1996). In such highly competitive circumstances, as we shall see, investment bankers were just as hungry for new business as they had been in the 1920s and even more eager to consider issuing the stocks of fledgling enterprises.

FUNDING NOVELTY IN THE POSTWAR DECADES

Of the new markets and new technologies that emerged in the postwar period, the most exciting and dramatic developments were concentrated in a cluster of industries that made up the electronics sector. It was with respect to the new and untried enterprises that emerged to populate this sector that the U.S. stock market really developed a hearty appetite for novelty. However, this appetite took some time to stimulate, and pioneering electronics companies displayed considerable difficulties in finding the monies that they needed to fund their expansion.

THE DEVELOPMENT OF THE ELECTRONICS SECTOR

In 1939, factory sales of the electronics industry in the United States amounted to as much as $340 million but, until World War II, the industry was largely reducible to radios and related equipment. The war induced a major expansion of the industry; by 1946, factory sales of the U.S. electronics sector amounted to $1,750 million. Still the most dramatic expansion was yet to come in the 1950s and 1960s. By 1973, U.S. factory sales of electronics products amounted to nearly $32 billion, which represented a 94-fold increase over 1939 sales without any adjustment for inflation (Electronic Industries Association, 1974, p. 2).

This rapid expansion was driven by the development of new markets and technologies in the postwar period. Consumer products had dominated the industry prior to World War II, and they continued to play an important role in its aftermath especially with the growth of television. In 1939, they accounted for 55 percent of total factory output in electronics, and, by 1950, consumer products still amounted to 56 percent. During the decade of the 1950s, however, when the electronics sector really boomed, factory sales of consumer electronics were fairly flat (Electronic Industries Association, 1974). The dramatic growth of the electronics industry in this decade was driven primarily by the government market and, more precisely, by military applications of electronics.

The U.S. government's share of factory sales increased from 24 percent in 1950 to an extraordinary 64 percent by 1954, and it remained at about 60 percent through 1960. Industrial markets, in contrast, started out at very low levels of importance for the electronics sector, accounting for only 13 percent of factory sales in 1950. Their importance increased in the 1950s, and they surpassed consumer sales in importance for the first time in 1960, when they accounted for 19 percent of factory sales, but they still remained less important than military markets at that time.

One of the most important new electronics products of the postwar period for government, and then industrial customers, was the computer. Early computer technologies were pioneered during the war effort. Shortly after the cessation of hostilities, in 1946, the commercial computer industry came into existence when Eckert and Mauchly, who had developed the ENIAC computer at the University of Pennsylvania, established their own firm. However, technological change in the electronics sector can be understood only in part based on an analysis of new and improved final products. In the postwar period, some of the most dramatic technological innovations occurred in the components sectors of the industry, and it was these breakthroughs that created the possibilities for entirely new or greatly enhanced products.

Perhaps the most important development in the components segment of the industry was the rise of the semiconductor industry. Prior to 1945, the production of semiconductors was limited primarily to the crystal diodes used in radar equipment during the war. The real breakthrough came with the invention of the transistor in 1948 at Bell Labs. Commercial production began three years later, and an industry was launched. It grew in size from factory sales of $20 million in 1952 to $210 million, or ten times that amount, by 1958. Sales more than doubled again in the next two years to reach $560 million in 1960 and then grew from there to reach sales of close to $1 billion by the end of the 1960s.

In the rapid expansion of the electronics sector that characterized the postwar decades, entry rates were very high. However, both the rates of entry, and especially the success of entrants, differed dramatically by subsegment of the industry. In the early development of the computer industry, for example, new firms like Eckert-Mauchly Corporation, Electronic Research Associates, CDC, and SRS, entered the industry but, by the mid-1950s, the ranks of the country's leading mainframe manufacturers were dominated by large, established firms that had entered from other industries, notably the office equipment and consumer electronics industries (Flamm, 1988; Campbell-Kelly and Aspray, 1996; Mowery & Rosenberg, 1998, p. 139).

As far as the semiconductor industry is concerned, firms from a variety of backgrounds joined AT&T when its manufacturing affiliate, Western Electric, initiated commercial production in 1951. Large, established receiving tube firms including GE, RCA, and Sylvania entered the business. In addition, a large number of "new" companies started to produce semiconductors. Some of these players were large electronics companies, such as IBM, Hughes, and Motorola. Others were their smaller counterparts like Texas Instruments. Finally, a slew of companies were established to compete in the industry. By 1966, these new firms dominated the semiconductor industry, accounting for 65 percent of U.S. sales in 1966 (Tilton, 1971, p. 66).

FUNDING THE EMERGING ELECTRONICS SECTOR

As I noted earlier, Eckert and Mauchly inaugurated the commercial computer business in 1946 when they established their eponymous firm to develop general-purpose commercial computers. The Eckert–Mauchly enterprise survived its early years by obtaining capital advances or consulting fees from its customers, including Prudential, Nielson, and Northrop Aircraft. However, major cost overruns on the company's projects left it scrambling for resources until, in 1948, it seemed to have found a way to resolve its financial problems.

American Totalisator, a company that had developed a computing machine for betting in the 1920s, was persuaded by its leading inventor, Henry Strauss, to invest $500,000 in the Eckert-Mauchly Computer Corporation in return for 40 percent of its equity. The company also agreed to provide additional financing in the form of loans. Less than a year later, however, disaster struck when Strauss was killed in an airplane crash and American Totalisator withdrew its support for the computer company. In 1950, the Eckert-Mauchly Corporation, lacking the financial means to stay afloat, sold out to the Remington Rand Corporation (Campbell-Kelly and Aspray, 1996, pp. 110–11).

Much later, as late as 1957, the infamous story of the difficulties that the "traitorous eight" encountered in raising the funds to leave Shockley Semiconductor en masse suggests significant funding challenges for this entrant to the semiconductor industry.[15] With the help of Arthur Rock, then employed at Hayden, Stone, and subsequently one of Silicon Valley's best-known venture capitalists, they eventually raised the money they sought from Fairchild Camera and Instrument. The amount of investment capital that Fairchild invested to fund the spin-off from Shockley Laboratories is estimated at about $350,000 a year in both 1957 and 1958, the amount it spent before the venture began to make money (*Business Week*, March 26, 1960, p. 113).

Both of these cases suggest that there were limits to the supply of capital for start-up electronics companies in the postwar decades, which forced them to cede control to established industrial companies to get access to the funds they needed.[16] In fact, after the war, the alleged difficulties of small business financing – and, in particular, the "equity gap" that small, young firms faced – were much discussed in U.S. public policy circles. In explaining this "equity gap," the conservatism of U.S. financiers, many of whom were located in the money center in New York, was often invoked. In many accounts, it was the limits to the supply of risk finance from existing financial institutions, combined with strong demand for capital from the electronics sector, that set the stage for pioneering financial entrepreneurs to create the

---

[15] The eight men were Julius Blank, Victor Grinich, Jean Hoerni, Gene Kleiner, Jay Last, Gordon Moore, Robert Noyce, and Sheldon Roberts.

[16] Shockley Semiconductor was itself funded by Beckman Instrument.

institutions that ultimately supported the capacity of the U.S. financial system to fund the establishment and growth of new high-technology companies.

By the mid-1950s, and especially by the late 1950s, there were signs that funding was becoming more readily available from the U.S. capital markets for electronics ventures, even at a very early stage of their development. For example, General Transistor, an early entrant to the semiconductor industry, was established in 1954 with an investment of only $100,000. By 1956, the company was already generating sales of more than $1 million and a net profit of $183,784. During that year, less than two years after its establishment, the company raised money in a public offering in which it sold 100,000 shares. Three more share offerings – two public offerings and one private placement – followed later in the 1950s as well as an issue of convertible subordinate debt.

In the computer industry, the case of Control Data Corporation was a harbinger of things to come. Control Data was founded by a group headed by William C. Norris, formerly of Engineering Research Associates, in Minneapolis in 1957. It completed a stock offering in the same year, which was sold to friends and associates of Norris, and successfully raised $600,000. Only two years later, in 1959, it sold 99,591 shares of common stock to stockholders on the basis of one new share for each eight shares held and raised $1.2 million in the process (*Wall Street Journal*, August 24, 1959, p. 15). In 1960, it completed another public offering of shares, selling 125,000 shares at 39 $\frac{1}{2}$ each to raise $4.9 million. In 1961, it sold a further 300,000 shares at $33 per share to raise $9.9 million (*Wall Street Journal*, September 21, 1961, p. 16) and, in 1962, the company sold $15 million convertible debentures (*Wall Street Journal*, September 13, 1963). In total, during the first five years of this company's life, it raised $31.6 million and its stock traded in the over-the-counter market. It was listed for the first time in 1963 when it joined the New York Stock Exchange.

A more systematic analysis of the electronic stocks traded and issued on the U.S. stock market confirms that there was an important change in the funding of the electronics sector from the late 1950s. In its industrial classification of companies, Moody's *Industrial Manual*[17] identified

---

[17] In compiling this manual, Moody's endeavored to include most of the companies deemed to be of interest to U.S. investors. For practical purposes, this meant that the manual included all companies whose securities were traded on the country's organized exchanges as well as widely-held companies whose securities were bought and sold in

only five firms operating in the electronics industry[18] in 1950; the industry was not even included in the classification in 1945. By 1955, the number of electronics firms had risen to 40 firms but the really dramatic change occurred in the late 1950s and 1960s. By 1960, 140 electronics firms were included in the Moody's electronics classification. That number grew by another 34 percent in the first half of the 1960s to reach 187 by 1965 and then by a further 72 percent to 322 firms by 1970.

Consistent with this pattern in the trading of electronics stocks, I find that increasing numbers of electronics companies undertook stock issues from the early 1950s and, especially, from the late 1950s. In the period from 1950 to 1960 alone, 473 electronics companies completed more than 1,000 security issues. In the early 1950s, the number of issues per annum rose from 42 in 1950 to more than 60 in 1951 and 1952 before falling back to 44 in 1953. The number rose to 100 by 1956, dropped to 72 in 1958, but then boomed with issues by electronics companies numbering 187 in 1959, rising to 205 in 1960 and remaining at these very high levels through 1962.[19]

Even more striking than the increase in the number of electronics issues from the 1950s was a change in the characteristics of the issuing companies. In the early 1950s, the vast majority of issuers, accounting for between 64 and 82 percent of all security issues by electronics companies, were 20 years of age or more. As the decade unfolded, however, there was an unsteady but clear decline in the importance of older companies in total security issues by electronics companies. By the mid-1950s, younger companies of less than 20 years and older companies

---

the OTC market. Moody's industrial classification organized as many of these companies into their primary industries of operation although it was noted that "[a] few companies may be omitted because of their small size and relative unimportance or because they do not lend themselves clearly to a particular classification" (Moody, 1965).

[18] In principle, electronics firms could fall within at least three of the industries used by Moody's in its classification scheme: radio, TV, and phonographs; office equipment; and electronics. Radio, TV, and phonographs as well as office equipment were already of considerable importance by the end of World War II, but many of the firms listed as operating in these activities cannot be described as electronics firms. This fact makes it difficult to trace the rise of the electronics sector by focusing on the number of companies that Moody's lists as operating in these industries.

[19] In its Special Study of the Securities Markets, the SEC estimated that a total of 502 unseasoned issues of electronics firms were conducted during the period from 1959 to 1962. The importance of this number can be seen in comparison with IPO activity at a much later stage; for the entire decade of the 1980s, there were 578 IPOs of technology companies, including electronics, as well as 542 IPOs by companies that were originally financed by venture capitalists.

Table 8.2. Distribution of Electronics
Companies by Trading Market

Trading Market	1960	1965	1970
ASE	39	61	115
	(33%)	(33%)	(35%)
NYSE	56	69	125
	(37%)	(37%)	(38%)
OTC	45	57	89
	(30%)	(30%)	(27%)
Other	0	0	3
	(0%)	(0%)	(1%)
Total	140	187	332
	(100%)	(100%)	(100%)

Source: Author's analysis based on Moody's *Industrial Manual* and Standard & Poor's *Security Owner's Stock Guide.*

of more than 20 years were neck and neck in their share of security issues by electronics firms. From the late 1950s, the young ones took over and they accounted for more than 70 percent of all issues in 1959 and again in 1960 with a wave of "hot issues" by electronics companies that persisted until 1962.

THE FOUNDATIONS OF THE U.S. STOCK MARKET'S APPETITE FOR NOVELTY

As in the 1920s, the wave of hot issues was facilitated by the structure of, and competition among, the trading markets for stocks in the United States. To the extent that U.S. electronics firms sought listings on organized exchanges in the 1950s and 1960s, they looked to the New York exchanges. The NYSE experienced a marked growth in its listings in the postwar decades – in 1945, 912 companies were listed on the NYSE but by 1971 that number had grown to 1,426 (NYSE, 2003) – but it maintained its reputation for quality by establishing listing requirements that were the most stringent of all of the registered exchanges. The only electronic companies that could list there, as a result, were those that could meet the NYSE's requirements for size and stability.

In Table 8.2, I show the distribution of the electronics companies included in Moody's *Industrial Manual* by the primary trading markets in which their securities were bought and sold. The NYSE was clearly well represented, with just over 35 percent of electronics stocks listed

Table 8.3. Characteristics of Companies by Trading Market, 1965

Trading Market	Avg Sales	Min Sales	Max Sales	Avg Age	Min Age	Max Age
ASE	$16.0m	$2.3m	$102.3m	22.4	4	74
NYSE	$316.8m	$13.6m	$2,187.2m	32.6	4	93
OTC	$15.5m	$1.7m	$85.7m	20.9	<1	54

Source: Author's analysis.

there. As one might expect, and Table 8.3 confirms, the very largest and oldest electronics companies were listed on the NYSE. In terms of average sales, for example, NYSE electronics companies were more than twenty times as large as the other electronics companies traded on the U.S. stock market.

To a large extent, electronics companies whose stocks traded on the NYSE had transferred to the Big Board from other trading markets, and the American Exchange was particularly important as the provenance of these transfers. Coming out of World War II, the Curb Exchange, as it was then known, was the second largest organized exchange in the United States. However, after a brief recovery following World War II, it lost ground in terms of listings. From 1941 to 1950, 517 listed issues were removed from the Curb, mostly to graduate to the NYSE, and the Curb was unable to solicit enough new listings to replace them with only 214 new issues added during the decade.

These trends precipitated a crisis at the Curb and the need to attract new listings was recognized as urgent (*New York Times*, July 2, 1944, p. 85; Sobel, 1972, pp. 186–204). In 1951, former SEC Commissioner Edward T. McCormick was recruited as president of the Curb. His mandate was clear: to expand the exchange. As he put it on accepting the position: "We are fortunate at the moment in having no pressing administrative problems . . . Therefore, I shall be able to concentrate on the problem of bringing in new listings" (*New York Times*, April 3, 1951, p. 42).

McCormick proved energetic in his pursuit of growth in listings. The Curb began to invest heavily in public relations, making a film, starting a new magazine as well as a radio station, to draw attention to itself and its activities. In 1953, it was renamed the American Stock Exchange to impart it with a more respectable image. The number of issues approved for listing on the Amex grew steadily from 1951, with peaks in 1955 and 1956 when new listings reached nearly 70 per year, in 1960 and 1961 when the number was about 110 per year, and especially from 1967 to 1972 when the average reached nearly 160 per year.

In its aggressive pursuit of new listings, the American Stock Exchange sought out smaller, more speculative companies that would not be permitted to list on the NYSE just as its predecessor, the Curb, had done in an earlier era. The exchange flourished in the 1950s and 1960s largely because of its success in attracting new listings from young companies in the glamour industries of the day. Initially, in the early 1950s, uranium stocks proved attractive in this regard, and later Canadian stocks contributed to the expansion of the exchange. In the late 1950s, the Amex also began to pick up stocks from the electronics sector and soon ranked alongside the Big Board in terms of the numbers of electronics stock listed on its exchange (Sobel, 1972, p. 209). As Table 8.2 shows, by 1960, about a third of the electronics securities included in Moody's *Industrial Manual* were listed on the American Stock Exchange. It also suggests that the electronics companies that were listed on the Amex were, on average, much smaller and younger than those on the NYSE.

Most of the companies that listed on the Amex transferred there from the over-the-counter market. By 1939, the number of OTC stocks in the daily sheets was already 3,700 and by 1963 it had more than doubled to 8,200 (Hazard and Christie, 1964, p. 9). The value of trading on the OTC increased from approximately 25 percent of the combined total on the NYSE and the Amex in 1950 to 67 percent in the early 1960s.[20] Contributing to this expansion was the fact that the OTC market was by far the most important market for the seasoning of new issues at this time.

Certainly, the OTC market was crucial to the growing relationship between the stock market and the burgeoning electronics sector. As Table 8.2 shows, close to a third of the electronics companies included in Moody's industrial manual were traded in the country's over-the-counter market rather than in its organized exchanges. These companies were the smallest and youngest of the electronics companies even if the stocks of some older and larger electronics companies continued to trade in the OTC market.

The importance of the OTC market is even more striking if we focus only on electronics companies undertaking stock issues. The OTC market was already important in the early 1950s, with more than 40 percent of all securities issued being bought and sold there. Its share rose even

---

[20] These estimates are only indicative because the value of trading on the OTC market and the organized exchanges is not strictly speaking comparable because estimates of OTC market trading activity include the value of purchases and sales.

higher than that, notably in years in which the number of security issues by electronics companies was high. In 1955 and 1956, for example, between 55 and 60 percent of all issues were undertaken by companies whose stocks were traded on the OTC market and, in 1959 and 1960, the OTC's share was even higher at 69 and 65 percent, respectively. Many of these companies were small and young.

The dramatic postwar expansion of the OTC market, and its particular appeal to fledgling electronics and other companies, was facilitated by a variety of factors. Some companies preferred to trade in the OTC market rather than on an organized exchange. This was true of companies that were not sufficiently widely held for a liquid market in their stock to emerge. Still others preferred the system of trading in the OTC market with its multiple market makers rather than the dedicated specialists used by the exchanges. Companies, especially smaller companies, chose the OTC market because they did not want to pay the listing fees charged by the exchanges. However, as I previously discussed, the success of the OTC market was also substantially boosted by the lower standards of federal regulation that applied to the securities traded on it as compared with those traded on the exchanges.

Although, as I have noted, many companies moved up from the OTC market to the Amex as they matured, the division of labor between the two trading markets was not nearly as clear or as stable as that between the Amex and the NYSE. As Table 8.3 suggests, there was overlap in the characteristics of the companies that traded on the Amex and the OTC that gave rise to competition between them. In some cases, the Amex lost out as fast-growing electronics firms like Hewlett-Packard and Control Data Corporation went public on the OTC market and traded there until they were large enough to list directly on the NYSE without passing by way of a listing on the Amex.

Its competition with the OTC market was surely one reason for the laxity that came to prevail in the procedures for the admission of companies' stocks to listing on the Amex. As Sobel describes it:

New applications for listing were received by the Division of Securities, which checked to make certain that all the necessary papers had been filed, and then passed them on to the committee on securities. Once the new issues were approved there, they went to the board, which made final disposition of the application. In theory, the committee was to have screened the issues prior to sending them on, but in practice this rarely happened. As a result, firms not meeting the standards of economic viability were able to obtain listing. The quest for new listings was such that no member wanted the responsibility for having kept a security from a specialist who wanted it. (Sobel, 1972, p. 234)

The result was a profusion of low-quality issues; Sobel reports that 77 percent of the Canadian stocks listed on the Amex in 1960 generated losses the previous year and more than 50 percent of them recorded losses in the previous two years (Sobel, 1972, p. 234).

Concerns about the propriety of certain aspects of the Amex's activities eventually prompted the SEC to launch a major investigation of the exchange in 1960. The SEC discovered a wide range of problems in addition to lax listing standards, including price manipulation, rigged markets, and the sale of unregistered issues. As a result, in the early 1960s, the Amex was required to completely overhaul its activities.

In 1962, as part of this effort, the exchange explicitly defined minimum requirements for the initial listing of a stock for the first time in its history.[21] A comparison of these requirements with those for the NYSE shows that Amex explicitly positioned itself in a niche that was quite distinct from that targeted by the Big Board. The Amex also defined delisting standards, and these allowed the exchange to remove some of the more dubious issues that had listed on the exchange during McCormick's drive for expansion.

From 1960 to 1969, a total of 202 companies were delisted for failure to meet Amex's standards, which was higher than the total number of 194 companies that left the exchange in the normal course of business to list on the NYSE (Sobel, 1972, p. 324). Despite these losses, the exchange prospered, with the number of listed companies growing from 834 in 1962 to 1,315 in 1972. One of the benefits of its more stringent standards was that it allowed the Amex to argue that trading on its exchange was more respectable than anything the OTC market could offer. Prior to that, the exchange had trouble distinguishing itself from the OTC market and, in particular, justifying the listing fees it charged. The distinction proved compelling to some companies as the 1960s unfolded to the sound of growing criticisms of the lax standards that prevailed in the "under-the-counter" market.

A second important factor in facilitating the growing embrace by the U.S. stock market of the electronics sector was competition in investment banking after World War II. As I described, federal regulation and

---

[21] Prior to 1962, any stock that the committee on listing approved was admitted to the exchange.

increases in private placement and competitive bidding in the 1930s set the stage and, when the United States emerged from World War II, the country's investment bankers competed vigorously for underwriting business. Stock issues were particularly attractive because underwriting commissions on them tended to be higher than bonds. Many underwriters focused on competing for the issues of established utility and industrial companies, but some investment banks recognized that there was money to be made in underwriting issues by smaller companies.

The rates of commissions on smaller, more speculative issues were higher than on larger issues, and investment banks often sought and received noncash compensation, often in the form of stock or stock options, for participating in a deal (Securities and Exchange Commission, 1963, Part 1, Chapter 4, pp. 503–5). The fact that underwriting the stock of more speculative concerns was risky discouraged some of the older and more conservative investment banks like the Morgan firm. Nevertheless, an analysis of the underwriters involved in the smallest issues undertaken by electronics companies reveals the names of some of the leading underwriters in the United States at the time. In particular, some of the most aggressive of these players, notably Blyth & Company and Lehman Bros., were right at the top of the list.[22] These two players, together with Salomon Bros. and Kidder Peabody, were known at the time as the "fearsome foursome" for their efforts to challenge some of the longest-established investment banks for market share in the U.S. underwriting business. They were hungry for new business and therefore willing to compete in the sale of more speculative securities including electronics stocks.

Besides these very large underwriters, a second type of investment bank was also prominent among the underwriters of small, young electronics companies. These were smaller players in the investment banking business, often with operations based in, or focused on, regions other than New York City. Companies like Lee Higginson and Hayden, Stone, which were originally Boston-based firms as well as William R. Staats of Los Angeles and Schwabacher & Company of San Francisco are good examples.

---

[22] The leading U.S. investment bankers at the time, ranked in terms of their gross income in 1959, were as follows: First Boston, $1,042 million; Morgan Stanley, $965 million; Lehman Brothers, $880 million; Blyth & Co., $868 million; White, Weld, $833 million; Merrill, Lynch, Pierce, Fenner & Smith, $815 million; Kuhn, Loeb, $696 million; Halsey, Stuart, $650 million; Eastman, Dillon, $456 million; Stone & Webster, $388 million (Sobel, 1975, p. 335).

A third group of underwriting firms were specialists in OTC stocks. Some of these companies had been in business for several decades, but many of them were new entrants who flooded into the investment banking business in the 1950s. It was much easier to register as an OTC dealer than it was to become a member of an organized exchange, so it is not hard to understand why they entered this way. Large numbers of new firms were set up in the 1950s with limited capital and experience of the underwriting business.

Their role spawned perhaps the most striking pattern in the distribution of underwriters of small electronics stocks which is its diffusion. The top fifteen underwriters of these stocks together accounted for only 40 percent of all transactions. The remainder was distributed among brokers and dealers, many with only one or two issues to their credit, and some of whom were completely unknown. An analysis by the SEC of underwriters involved in unseasoned common stock issues offered in 1961 showed that the majority of them were younger than six years and more than 25 percent of them were one year old or less (Hazard and Christie, 1964, p. 19)!

As the market for new electronics stocks heated up, standards seem to have fallen across the board. Underwriters became very aggressive in the pursuit of new business. As the SEC put it in its *Special Study of the Securities Markets*:

In many instances the managements of companies going public had given little or no thought to it until they were solicited by underwriters or professional finders. Public enthusiasm as well as profitability to underwriters and their salesmen combined to channel much energy of the financial community into the origination of new issues. It was not unusual for persons connected with broker-dealer firms to attend meetings and exhibitions of the Institute of Radio Engineers and other organizations associated with the electronics, engineering, and aerospace industries in search of prospective new issuers. (Hazard and Christie, 1964, pp. 121–2)

As this description suggests, investment banks felt pressure not only to garner more underwriting commissions from the business of hot electronics issues; there was also pressure from salesmen within their own organizations to underwrite hot issues so that they could earn high sales commissions (Securities and Exchange Commission, 1963, Part 1, Chapter 4, p. 496). More generally, a huge increase in the number of brokers operating throughout the United States meant that the U.S. investment banking industry had access to more U.S. households so that there were more brokers canvassing for the business of selling securities than ever before.

As an indicator of this expansion, the membership of the National Association of Securities Dealers increased by more than 100 percent between 1945 and the early 1960s. The registered representatives employed by member firms grew from 25,000 to 95,000 and their branch offices expanded from 790 to 4,713 (Hazard & Christie, 1964, p. 9). As important as the increase in the scale of the business was a transformation in the way it worked. Brokers made door-to-door calls, like insurance salespeople, and employed sophisticated techniques, pioneered in the sale of consumer products, to sell securities to a mass market.[23]

The final factor that I want to emphasize in the growing enthusiasm by the stock market for the U.S. electronics sector was the increasing interest by the investing public in the stocks of new, unproven companies. However, this change can be traced only to the late 1950s. The Dow Jones Industrial Average increased from 1949 to 1952, but only at a modest rate, and then declined in 1953. Only in 1954, what Robert Sobel called the "tardy bull market" began, and, with occasional ups and downs, it took the country's stock market upward through the 1960s (Sobel, 1975). In its early stages, however, the bull market primarily benefited the stocks of established companies. Some of them were at the cutting edge of the new markets and technologies of the postwar period, like electronics, but they tended to be those that had already built up a track record. Although small companies had emerged to compete with the big players in electronics by this time, most investors were skeptical about their capacity to survive in competition with more established companies.

However, there was a major change in the valuation of electronics companies and, in particular, in the attitude of investors to fledgling electronics companies, in the late 1950s. Stock prices of the leading electronics companies began to rise in May 1958 and added 60 percent to their value by the end of the year. They continued to rise through 1959, 1960, and early 1961 and remained at high levels through early 1962. At their peak in May 1961, they were at three times their value in May 1958. During this period, investors became willing to invest large amounts of resources in the stocks not only of the leading companies in the electronics industry but also in unproven entrants to the industry. As

---

[23] For an account of Charles Merrill's important role in the postwar development of the U.S. brokerage industry, see Perkins (1999).

a result, stock prices of new issues of these entrants sustained spectacular rises in the aftermarket (Sobel, 1975, p. 362).

An important catalyst for change in investors' attitudes toward electronic stocks occurred in October 4, 1957, when the Soviets put the first Sputnik into orbit, an event that was greeted with shock and dismay in the United States for what it suggested about the country's relative technological and military prowess. Shortly afterward, the stocks of missile companies took off as investors realized that they would benefit from whatever response was forthcoming from the U.S. government.

The U.S. federal government was already allocating substantial resources to the development of technologies that could be employed in building its military capacity. Sputnik galvanized the U.S. political elite to make even greater financial commitments to the development of technology, and, in early 1958, Congress increased its appropriations to the development of its space program. It did not take much longer for U.S. investors to realize that the electronics sector would be a major beneficiary of increased expenditures on space technologies and weapons systems. Within two years, the term military–industrial complex would become commonplace and the stocks of the nation's electronics companies as well as its defense companies would be feted by U.S. investors.

At the time, institutional investors were becoming more important players in the U.S. stock market. They held less than 15 percent of U.S. corporate stock in the late 1950s, but their share in the trading of exchange-listed shares was much higher. However, in the over-the-counter market, in which the stocks of emergent electronics companies were bought and sold, individuals still accounted for the majority of transactions by public customers (Friend et al., 1958, p. 180ff). Not only did these investors become increasingly enthusiastic about speculative stocks in the late 1950s and early 1960s, but more and more of them plunged into the stock market as well.

The first systematic survey of share ownership in the United States, carried out by the NYSE and published in 1952, revealed that 6.5 million Americans or 4.2 percent of the population, held shares. These figures represented only small increases on earlier figures (Goldsmith, 1969, p. 360) but, from then on, household participation in the stock market increased rapidly. By 1959, 7.1 percent of the U.S. population, that is, 12.5 million people, held shares. Just three years later in 1962, those numbers had increased further to 9.2 percent and 17 million, respectively (Seligman, 1995, p. 658).

A TRUE WATERSHED

If one is looking for a watershed in the role of the U.S. stock market in funding new industries and new firms, then the late 1950s and early 1960s seems to me to be the most plausible candidate based on existing historical evidence. The numbers of stock issues undertaken by young firms in the electronics industry rivaled the experience of any other new industry that had gone to the stock market before it. The SEC estimated that a total of 502 unseasoned issues of electronics firms were conducted during the period from 1959 to 1962 alone. Certainly that makes the experience of the radio and aviation industries fade by comparison.

Furthermore, although the wave of hot issues that occurred during the period from 1959 to 1962 may have been dominated by the IPOs of electronics companies, it was not confined to them. Other glamour stocks were found in the fields of scientific instruments and research, photography, printing and publishing, sporting goods, and amusements. The SEC estimated that more than 85 percent of registered issues in these glamorous industries were companies with less than $5 million in assets (Securities and Exchange Commission, 1963, Chapter 4, p. 486). In 1959, 63 percent of all common stock issues were "unseasoned"; in 1960, 72 percent; and in 1961, 76 percent (Securities and Exchange Commission, 1963, Chapter 4).[24]

Based on existing evidence, it would seem that issues of the unseasoned stocks of new companies were much more important to overall stock issuance than in the 1940s, the 1930s, and even the 1920s (Securities and Exchange Commission, 1963, Chapter 4, p. 487). In fact, levels of activity in the hot issue boom from 1959 to 1962 even rivaled later years in their importance. The SEC estimated that a total of 502 unseasoned issues of electronics firms were conducted during the period from 1959 to 1962. For the entire decade of the 1980s, there were 578 IPOs of technology companies, including electronics, as well as 542 IPOs by companies that were originally financed by venture capitalists. Therefore, in timing the emergence of the U.S. stock market's affinity for new industries and new firms, the period from 1959 to 1962 presents itself as the most plausible candidate for a watershed.

---

[24] An issue was classified as "unseasoned" if the issuer had not registered stock previously under the Securities Act or Registration A and if its stock was not listed on a national securities exchange or known to be traded over the counter. On occasion, this classification resulted in the inclusion of large, well-established companies offering their stock to the public for the first time (Securities and Exchange Commision, 1963, p. 485).

The hot issue market of the late 1950s and early 1960s proved a watershed in a different sense because it set in motion a set of regulatory changes that led to the establishment of the NASDAQ market as we know it today. The speculative fervor that surrounded the hot issues focused critical attention on the operation of the OTC market, earning it the dubious moniker of the under-the-counter market. Concern about hot issues prompted the U.S. Congress to authorize the SEC to undertake a detailed study of the OTC market and recommend ways of improving its operation.

No sooner had the authorization been given in September 1961 than the hot issue market imploded in early 1962. Nevertheless, the SEC's Special Study of the Securities Markets went ahead and was a massive undertaking in terms of the resources devoted to it and the comprehensive nature of the analysis that it undertook. It highlighted a wide range of problems with the operation of the OTC market and provided a long list of recommendations for its improvement. Its greatest concerns were with the flow of information about trading in, and issuers on, the OTC market.

These concerns led the SEC to recommend the automation of OTC operations "to assemble all interdealer quotations and instantaneously determine and communicate best quotations for particular securities at any time" (Hazard and Christie, 1964, p. 263). As I have described elsewhere, the SEC's recommendations and its prodding of the NASD to deliver on them were the foundations for the establishment of NAS-DAQ in 1971 (O'Sullivan, in press). The electronics stocks that formed the backbone of NASDAQ's high-technology section at its establishment were those that had been distributed and traded in the OTC market in earlier periods and had survived to tell the tale.

CONCLUSION

In comparative perspective, the U.S. stock market's capacity to fund new firms in new industries strikes many commentators as one of the most distinctive characteristics of the American financial system. Notwithstanding its importance, there is a good deal of ambiguity about its historical origins. Based on the existing literature, there is some reason to think that it is of relatively recent origin, dating perhaps to as late as 1971 with the formation of NASDAQ, but there are also scholars who contend that the U.S. stock market displayed a substantial appetite for novelty as far back as the late nineteenth century.

The ambiguity turns on the limitations of the data that have been used to determine historical patterns in stock issues. Certainly, as I show, this is the case for claims that the U.S. stock market has been willing to fund novelty from the time of the emergence of a market for industrial stocks in the late nineteenth century. Although this chapter does little to improve on the general problem of data limitations, it uses a number of case studies of new industries to shed light on the timing of the emergence of America's capacity to fund the new firms that entered them.

From this analysis, I argue that the decade of the 1920s is the earliest possible period to which one could trace any substantial involvement by the U.S. stock market in new firms and new industries. During that decade, the structure of America's stock market, the dynamics of its investment banking industry, as well as the number and orientation of stock investors came together in ways that favored newer, more speculative stocks. Even so, issues by new firms represented only a small minority of overall stock issuance activity even in the late 1920s, raising questions about whether the period can be seen as a real watershed in the emergence of the stock market's appetite for novelty.

Instead, I point to a later period, from the late 1950s to the early 1960s, as the crucial transition. It was in funding enterprises that competed in the electronics sector, both the incumbent firms and, increasingly, the fledgling enterprises that entered it, that the U.S. stock market really cut its teeth with respect to funding new firms in new industries. By then, crisis and federal regulation had induced important changes in the structure of the U.S. stock market, which had an important impact on the market for new issues in the United States. In particular, these changes reinforced the role of the OTC market at the heart of the market for new issues in the United States. The investment banking industry had also changed by then, not least because of federal regulation, in a manner that created strong incentives for certain banks to seek out new issues even by speculative enterprises. Last, the public finally recovered sufficient enthusiasm from the Great Depression and war to take speculative risks in the stock market.

I have also underlined how the hot issue market of the late 1950s to early 1960s was a watershed in another sense. In response to an outcry about the extent of speculation that it entailed by brokers and dealers and bankers and investors, the SEC initiated the most comprehensive review of the nation's stock market since the early 1930s. Among the most important of the recommendations that emerged from its Special Study was its exhortation to the National Association of Securities Dealers

298   MARY A. O'SULLIVAN

to improve the information flow around issuers and purchases of stock in the OTC market. The solution that the SEC sketched out, and that the NASD eventually followed, was crucial in the establishment of NASDAQ in 1971.

REFERENCES

Baskin, J., & Miranti, P. (1997). *A history of corporate finance*. New York: Cambridge University Press.

Bruchey, S. (1991). *Modernization of the American Stock Exchange, 1971–1989*. New York: Garland.

Calomiris, C., & Raff, D. (1996). The evolution of market structure, information, and spreads in American investment banking. In Bordo, M. & Sylla, R. (Eds.), *Anglo-American finance systems: Institutions and markets in the 20th century*. New York: Irwin.

Campbell-Kelly, M., & Aspray, W. (1996). *Computer: A history of the information machine*. New York: Basic Books.

Carosso, V. (1970). *Investment banking in America: A history*. Cambridge, MA: Harvard University Press.

Dodd, P. (1933). *Financial policies in the aviation industry*. Philadelphia: University of Pennsylvania Press.

Doyle, W. (1991). *The evolution of financial practices and financial structures among American manufacturers, 1875–1905: Case studies of the sugar refining and meat packing industries*. Unpublished doctoral dissertation, University of California, Los Angeles.

Eddy, G. (1937). Security issues and real investment in 1929. *Review of Economics and Statistics*, 19, 79–91.

Electronic Industries Association (1974). *Electronic market trends*. Washington, DC: Author.

Fama, E., & French, K. (2004). New lists: Fundamentals and survival rates. *Working Paper, Dartmouth College*, Tuck School of Business, Hanover, NH, 73, 229–69.

Flamm, K. (1988). *Creating the computer : Government, industry, and high technology*. Washington, DC: Brookings Institution.

Freudenthal, E. (1940). *The aviation business: From Kitty Hawk to Wall Street*. New York: Vanguard Press.

Friend, I., Hoffman, G. W., & Winn, W. (1958). *The over-the-counter securities market*, New York: McGraw-Hill.

Goldsmith, R. (1969). *Financial structure and development*. New Haven, CT: Yale University Press.

Gompers, P., & Lerner, J. (2003). The really long-run performance of initial public offerings: The pre-Nasdaq evidence. *Journal of Finance*, 58(4), 1355–92.

Hazard, J., & Christie, M. (1964). *The investment business: A condensation of the SEC Report*. New York: Harper & Row.

Investment Dealers' Digest. (1960). Directory of corporate financing. New York: Author.

Jovanovic, B., & Rousseau, P. (2001). Why wait? A century of life before IPO. *American Economic Review, AEA Papers and Proceedings*, 91, 336–41.

Leffler, G. (1957). *The stock market* (2nd ed.). New York: Ronald Press Company.

Loss, L. (1951). *Securities regulation*. Boston: Little, Brown.

Maclaurin, W. R. (1971). *Invention and innovation in the radio industry*. New York: Arno Press.

Mowery, D., & Rosenberg, N. (1998). *Paths of innovation: Technological change in 20th-century America*. Cambridge/New York: Cambridge University Press.

Navin, T., & Sears, M. (1955). The rise of a market for industrial securities. *Business History Review*, 29(2), 105–38.

NYSE (Various). *Fact book, New York Stock Exchange*. New York: Author.

O'Sullivan, M. (2011). *Bonding and sharing industrial America: The US securities markets, industrial dynamics, and corporate development, 1885-1929*. Oxford, UK: Oxford University Press.

O'Sullivan, M. (in press). The deficiencies, excesses and control of competition: The development of the US Stock Market from the 1930s to 2001.

Perkins, E. (1999). *Wall Street to Main Street: Charles Merrill and middle-class investors*. Cambridge/New York: Cambridge University Press.

Rae, J. B. (1965). Financial problems of the American aircraft industry, 1906-40. *Business History Review*, 39(1), 99–114.

Schwarzchild, O. P. (Ed.): (Various issues from 1925/28-1936). *American underwriting houses and their issues*. New York: National Statistical Service.

Securities and Exchange Commission. (1963). *Special study of the securities markets*. Washington, DC: Author.

Seligman, J. (1995). *The transformation of Wall Street: A history of the Securities and Exchange Commission and modern corporate finance* (Rev. ed.). Boston: Northeastern University Press.

Smith, G., & Sylla, R. (1993). The transformation of financial capitalism: An essay on the history of American capital markets. *Financial Markets, Institutions and Instruments*, 2(2), 1209–14.

Sobel, R. (1972). Amex: A history of the American Stock Exchange, 1921-1971. New York: Weybright and Talley.

Sobel, R. (1975). *The Big Board: A history of the New York Stock Market*. Washington, DC: Beard Books.

Sobel, R. (1977). *Inside Wall Street: Continuity and change in the Financial District*. New York: Wall Street. Washington, DC: Beard Books.

Tilton, J. (1971). International diffusion of technology: The case of semiconductors. Washington, DC: Brookings Institution.

Twentieth Century Fund. (1935). *The security markets: Findings and recommendations of a Special Staff of the Twentieth Century Fund*. New York: Author.

U.S. Bureau of the Census (1976). *Historical statistics of the United States from the colonial times to the present*. Washington, DC: U.S. Government Printing Office.

Van der Linden, R. F. (2002). *Airlines and air mail: The post office and the birth of the commercial aviation industry*. Lexington, KY: University of Kentucky Press.

9

Labor in the Third Industrial Revolution

A Tentative Synthesis

STEFANO MUSSO

The most important change in the last three decades in developed countries regarding labor is the acceleration in the process of shifting the working population from the manufacturing to the service sector. The question arises as to how long it will take for the share of the working population in industry to be reduced in size to that occupied by agriculture workers at the end of the second industrial revolution. Thus, from the point of view of employment structure, the third industrial revolution should be called the services revolution. It is important to keep in mind that by the beginning of the twenty-first century, the largest simple group of big firms is found in retailing and financial services (see Howard Gospel and Martin Fiedler in this volume). The first industrial revolution was preceded and fostered by major innovations in agriculture (Jones, 1974). In the same way, currently, information and communication technologies foster nonmaterial production and give rise to vanishing boundaries between manufacturing and services. Here, we view the third industrial revolution as involving the advent of information-related technologies in production.

ICT AND CHANGING PRODUCTION METHODS

The third industrial revolution began to affect labor in industrialized countries by the late 1970s, when a combination of two forces caused a crisis in the Fordist system. On the one hand, in developed countries, increased income and living standards made customers more sophisticated and demanding, while the markets for durable consumer goods were saturated and demand grew very slowly. On the other hand, sharpening international competition made markets unstable and unpredictable because of both international free trade agreements and reduced transportation costs. Mass production of durable consumer goods had to be changed to a sort of neo-Sloanism (Sloan, 1964) by increasing the quality of products and, at the same time, diversifying them with multiple models, additional gadgets, greater choices of colors, etc.

To obtain economies of scale and flexible production to meet the changing demands of the markets, producers had to face these problems simultaneously. The introduction of information and communication technology (ICT) helped provide solutions through new flexible automation by means of computerized production systems that replaced old rigid automation that relied on single-purpose machinery and single-model dedicated assembly lines. At the same time, the need for cost reduction was met by adopting the "kan-ban" (or "just-in-time") system, first introduced in the Japanese automobile industry, especially by Toyota (Ohno, 1988), to realize mass production in small lots for a thin internal market. In particular, just-in-time was intended to eliminate the large buffers previously utilized when production was "pushed" by the producers in steadily growing markets. Buffers were also useful in diminishing the costs of strikes, in a period in which trade unions were strong and able to mobilize workers posing new demands in the process of collective bargaining. In the post-Fordist era, on the contrary, production has to be "pulled" by orders to reduce the costs of stored goods (and therefore of circulating capital).

Some observers have defined the new flexible automation as neo-Fordism because it pursued economies of scale while coping with the need to diversify products. Others scholars have called it flexible integration, a third approach between neo-Fordism and flexible specialization, because it has fostered flexibility at the general level of the company at which central coordination integrated the various plants or shops (or subcontracting firms), some of which had a flexible production method while others had a standardized one (Regini and Sabel, 1989).

According to the principles of "lean production" and "lean organization," the Western translation of the Japanese model, companies' production strategies progressively abandoned vertical integration for a new
tendency to concentrate on core activities or products for which the
company had special competencies, giving it competitive advantages.
This led to a sharp increase in outsourcing and partnerships, triggering
a decrease in the average size (in terms of number of employees) of
companies and plants.

From the point of view of labor force management, it was also considered a computer-aided neo-Taylorism, because workers' tasks and the
division of labor did not substantially change. On the contrary, some
scholars observed an increase in the level of skills required and predicted the advent of a neocraftsman system (Kern and Schumann, 1994).
Now, after twenty-five years, most scholars agree that ICT has increased
the skills required for some workers, especially those assigned to computerized machinery, whereas most tasks maintain a low skill content.
Nevertheless, new technologies make working tasks less exhausting and
improve the working environment, making it less dirty and less noisy
(Bonazzi, 1993).

What is more significant is that information technologies alone proved
unable to cope with the double challenge of flexibility and product quality. Difficulties and shortcomings experienced in highly automated and
yet traditionally managed production systems led companies to replace
the hierarchical–functional organization with the integration of functions at all levels, especially between staff and line. The adoption of
so-called high-performance work systems involves a reduction in organizational layers. In these systems, the hierarchical chain is shortened
in order to smooth the decision-making process and to solve problems
where they arise. Following the Japanese model again, self-managed
work teams and off-line problem solving groups (quality circles) have
been introduced. Workers are in a sense skilled, because in the work
team there are elements of job rotation.

With these new production methods, companies ask their employees for active cooperation in reducing costs and enhancing quality. In
particular, workers are asked to pay attention to the very first signals of
automated machinery malfunction so that quick intervention can avoid
damages. Shifting responsibilities from higher up to lower down can
motivate workers and increase satisfaction.

Thus, the adoption of ICT can lead to positive developments in the
quality of worker tasks when compared with the previous work system
in which decision making was in the hands of supervisors and workers

had poorly skilled tasks. In general, new technologies require higher levels of training and skills both for white- and blue-collar workers.

The adoption of ICT normally offers substantial efficiencies in production. Therefore, it implies a decrease in the amount of required manpower, thus functioning as a labor-savings investment. Restructuring, or as it is sometimes called, reengineering, normally caused reductions in the labor force. Increased use of information technology for manufacturing as well as for processing orders and managing supplier relations allows downsizing. According to some business schools' viewpoint, business success comes from these savings in the cost of the labor force, often triggering an increase in stock value. Yet, after an initial high level of dismissals, innovative ICT introduction together with the implementation of high-performance work systems is often associated with higher degrees of employee satisfaction, lower rates of voluntary quitting by workers, and higher training investment by companies (Osterman, 2000).

Here, the question arises as to the extent to which high-performance work systems have spread. Opinions on this matter are divided. Paul Osterman argues that the new forms of work organization, like quality circles and off-line problem-solving groups, job rotation, self-managed work teams, and total quality management, have been "one of the most important ways in which American firms responded in the 1980s and early 1990s to competitive challenges." In a comparison of 1992 and 1997, Osterman found a dramatic increase in the percentage of U.S. establishments with a high-performance work system involving at least half of core employees, from 26 percent to 70.7 percent for the establishments adopting two or more of these practices, and from 14.2 percent to 39.5 percent for the establishments adopting three or more. In his view, the diffusion of these practices is quite extensive, and this implies that firms will wish to maintain a commitment to those workers who are involved in them (Osterman, 2001). In contrast, in Piore and Safford's view (Piore and Safford, 2006), high-performance work systems have failed to diffuse because of organizational inertia and resistance by traditional middle and lower hierarchies (Voss and Sherman, 2000). The case of Saturn, created by General Motors in the 1980s as an attempt to meet the challenge of new competitive pressures coming from the Japanese automotive industry, is considered a prime example of the weak impetus of the new systems, because Saturn has not been copied by other car companies.

Yet Saturn, which is still operating and whose efficacy for business performance is proven (MacDuffie, 1991, 1995; Kochan et al., 1997), relies on a set of new labor–management relations that entails a high degree of collaboration and negotiation between management and union. This may be one of the major reasons for the Saturn model's inability to diffuse. In fact, it contrasts recent managerial trends toward unilateral initiative and efforts to block union organization. Nevertheless, the Saturn model cannot be taken as the only way to introduce high-performance work systems. Single practices can be implemented without union involvement, as with unilateral human resources policies intended to achieve individual commitment to the company. These practices are emphasized by human resources theories and appear to be quite widespread, as Osterman suggests.

Computerized automated machinery has made some typical consumer goods plants more similar to those of the process industries, such as basic chemicals or rolling mills in which the workers' tasks mainly involve looking after the functioning of machinery. Because workers are requested to pay attention to the very early signals of imminent malfunctioning to allow quick intervention, they cannot simply be ruled by coercive methods.

Whereas such developments seem to enhance new human resources policies in manufacturing, in several services and especially in new economy jobs such as call centers, e-commerce, online financial services and retailing, speeding up of the work pace and scientific management forms of controlling workers made even tighter by computer monitoring appear to be the rule (Joseph Rowntree Foundation, 1999; Marchington et al., 2005). Moreover, workers enjoy only very limited pay and benefit systems, even if they are requested to work under extremely flexible scheduling. In retailing, companies make intense use of young, female, and immigrant workers, the latter being decidedly anti-union, whose mixed identities hinder solidarity and opposition to management (Liechtenstein, 2006).

Overall, a growing diversity in work organization and managerial attitudes can be seen both between and within national systems (Katz and Darbishire, 2000). As Gospel puts it, different arrangements, "such as the provision of discretion for more skilled and higher level employees versus mass production type systems for many workers as well as elements of bureaucratic forms of management versus more differentiated and flexible systems" are to be found side by side, in so far as "some firms are pursuing so-called high-performance and high-involvement policies while many others have not developed sophisticated human resource strategies and provide little employee voice" (Gospel, 2007).

ICT, EMPLOYMENT, AND FLEXIBILITY: THE END OF LABOR?

Innovations in production processes connected with information technologies play a major role in increasing the speed of the shift of the active population from the industrial to the service sector. Increasing productivity and saturated markets for traditional consumer goods are the main forces underlying the changes in employment structure. Structural unemployment problems in the third industrial revolution are connected with difficulties in the accelerated process of the transfer of the labor force from industry to services.

The effects of increasing job insecurity on the welfare state are controversial. Growing demands for protection against risks caused an expansion of the welfare state, increasing public spending and debt. Beginning in the 1980s, a new wave of economic and social policies influenced by monetarism was promoted as a way to overcome the long-lasting fiscal crisis of the welfare state (O'Connor, 1973). But even if a series of reforms reduced some welfare benefits, the levels of public transfer payments and the expansion of social service provisions continued to increase, especially in the redistributive aspects of the welfare state, even if with growing differences between left- and right-oriented governments (Iversen and Cusack, 2000).

Rapid technical change and increasing competition in globalization force companies continuously to innovate and restructure production. To minimize labor costs and to enter new markets, enterprises delocalize production toward developing countries and, after the fall of the Berlin Wall in 1989, to the new transition economies. Restructuring, outsourcing, downsizing, and delocalization contribute to growing job instability, a topic frequently discussed by scholars and emphasized by public media. Feelings of insecurity are spreading into both the ranks of young people entering the labor market and the group of unskilled workers over the age of 40; people threatened with dismissal do not always have the skills required by the expanding sectors.

Uncertainty is fostered by the end of the so-called Fordist–Keynesian compromise that was able to guarantee economic growth, social inclusion, and improved standards of living in the golden age of Western countries. Under employers' pressure, a new wave of policies has reduced employment protection and labor legislation and curtailed trade unions' strength in order to facilitate appropriate labor adjustment by firms who have to face global competition. According to the new wave, flexible production on the bases of ICT has to be coupled with flexible labor.

In such a context, technological and organizational changes and new labor conditions have suggested a series of theoretical approaches as to how modern society is developing toward a postmodern one. According to the optimistic view, at an early stage the end of labor was foreseen, in that technological change was intended to reduce the amount of socially required work and would therefore liberate time for free social, political, or cultural activities (Gorz, 1980). In a more cautious approach, some scholars have proposed a distinction between labor and activity, the latter destined to substitute for the former (Dahrendorf et al., 1986; Offe et al., 1992). Labor was losing the major impact it had in shaping social identities, often on ideological bases such as the socialist and bourgeois labor ethics, which considered work as a moral and social duty. Because having a job was no longer a stable cornerstone of life and ideologies were declining in influence, new sources of personal identity were arising in consumer and leisure activities. The pessimistic view saw the advent of flexibility as a new and worse form of capitalistic exploitation of workers (Beck, 2000; Gallino, 2000, 2001). In a more general and encompassing view of the new, continuously changing society, sharp concerns have been expressed about anthropological changes in the personality of the flexible person (Sennet, 1998, 2006).

Notwithstanding these theories, labor seems to still play a major role both in social life and in the building of personal identity. Average working hours are not diminishing, quite the opposite in fact, and legal or contractual limitations to overtime are less rigid in the overall process of deregulating labor. Moreover, even if flexibility of labor is on the rise, especially for young people, there is no dramatic universal trend toward job instability (Accornero, 1997, 2006; Accornero et al., 2001; European Commission, 2001, 2006; Osterman, 2001; Semenza, 2004).

CHANGING EMPLOYMENT STRUCTURE IN DEVELOPING COUNTRIES: GLOBALIZATION AS AN EQUALIZING PROCESS?

As a consequence of delocalizing production, foreign direct investments from developed countries, and autonomous local investments, there has been a substantial increase over time in wage labor in developing countries. This has resulted in a move by workers from agriculture, for which unpaid family work is predominant, to manufacturing and services. Thus, at a global level, industrial workers are decreasing in number in developed countries, but increasing in number in the developing world. However, in developing countries, along with increasing wage labor, the sector that is growing fastest is not manufacturing but commerce, a sector in which family work still plays a significant role.

Asian countries seem to have seen the greatest changes in employment income in the last decade of the twentieth century. A general shift of employment out of agriculture was accompanied by declining numbers of the worst-off working poor (defined as workers whose income is under $1 a day) and rising numbers of working nonpoor (over $2 a day). Moreover, growth in Asia significantly increased "good" employment, as defined by a certain degree of stability, and reduced "bad" employment.

Changes in employment structure in African countries are not clearly observable. The working poor have increased, the working nonpoor have more or less stagnated, and there is no clear trend in either good or bad employment. In Latin America, the changes seem to be limited in extent and are marked by both rising informal and wage labor and a clear pattern of commercialization in agriculture. This change in employment structure is associated with stagnation in the numbers of working poor and increases in the numbers of working nonpoor. Overall, in developing countries, growth increases good employment, but reduces only very little the worst types of employment (Majid, 2005).

Market forces seem to shape wages and working conditions in most developing countries, in Asian industrializing countries (with a few exceptions), and Latin American left-oriented populist regimes, because trade unions as well as workers' rights are underdeveloped. In the relatively large establishments created by foreign investments or by joint ventures with local producers, work organization does not differ from the mother plants in developed countries. Economic growth in many developing areas offers new opportunities for skilled workers to start self-employment activities and small companies. Small companies have grown dramatically in countries like Mexico, India, and China. In both manufacturing and services, such companies make intense use of family work with no standard working rules at all.

Globalization, along with declining birth rates in developed countries (particularly Europe), works to a certain extent as an equalizing process in distributing both well-paid and poorly paid wage jobs. Skilled labor is required by advanced economies with strong service and tertiary sectors in which innovative enterprises are able steadily to acquire new technologies and appropriate human capital. Growing demand for skilled labor in developed countries attracts skilled workers from developing countries. These workers migrate to take up positions in the developed world, even if the pressure on migration is partially mitigated by foreign direct investment flows, which have an upward impact on the wages in developing countries. Therefore migrations are not limited to low-skilled workers moving from developing to developed countries to occupy the worst jobs abandoned by locally born workers. On the other hand, migrations and delocalization create a sort of globalized labor market in which low-wage jobs are no longer the exclusive preserve of the developing world, but are reallocated in developed countries to economic activities for which the capital and labor endowments are not being adequately retooled and reskilled. This seems to be the case with industries such as garments, furniture, packaging, and construction, and can be found regionally in cities in some developed countries, such as New York city in the 1990s (Sassen, 1997). In New York, the growth of casual employment was pervasive, with a high concentration of workers coming from specific communities, particularly immigrants who are endowed with specific craft skills. Such industries have to compete with cheaper goods from developing economies (Bhorat and Lundall, 2004). Finally, clandestine migrants find sources of income in the gray economy and "off-books" employment, so that informal employment and low-paid-wage jobs are on the increase in developed countries.

GLOBALIZATION AND JOB STABILITY IN EUROPE: EUROSCLEROSIS?

Poor-quality employment seems to have had a limited diffusion in the developed world, especially in Western Europe. A 2001 European Commission survey concluded that 75 percent of total employment in the European Community was of good or acceptable quality in terms of stability and wage level. Five years later, the situation seems to have undergone only very limited change (European Commission, 2001, 2006). The evolution of the share of dead-end jobs in total employment in fifteen European countries between 1992 and 2002 showed a slim increase, from 11 to 13 percent. Among the countries where shares of such jobs were the highest in 2002, Spain and Finland underwent a decrease in dead-end jobs (in Spain the share of dead-end jobs diminished from 34.2 percent in 1992 to 31.0 percent in 2002; in Finland from 18.1 percent to 16.0 percent). Only Portugal has shown a dramatic increase, from 12.5 to 21.7 percent (Semenza, 2004, p. 45). In 2002, the lowest shares were to be found in the United Kingdom and in Ireland (6.3 percent and 5.4 percent, respectively), because of the lack of regulations against dismissals. In 2002, under-average shares were found in Austria (7.1 percent), Belgium (8.1 percent), Denmark (9.1 percent), Italy

(9.9 percent), and Greece (11.2 percent) mainly because of norms limiting the recourse to fixed-term jobs.

Notwithstanding the limited levels of dead-end jobs, certain categories of workers, such as young people, women, ill-educated workers, and low-skilled aging workers, are more likely to suffer from job instability, short-term employment, and higher rates of unemployment. As a consequence, they risk social exclusion. Moreover, a general trend toward a growing number of nonstandard labor contracts is clearly observable. In Europe, the 2 percent increase in dead-end jobs, from 11 to 13 percent, represents a relative increase of almost 20 percent, and these contracts, according to Eurostat data, are increasingly associated with shorter job duration.

According to supporters of labor market deregulation, the limited presence in Europe of fixed-term labor contracts when compared with higher labor flexibility in the United States, is the cause of a sort of "Eurosclerosis." In 2003, the International Monetary Fund argued that if Europe were to reduce its labor protection legislation, adopting instead American-style flexibility, it could enhance output and productivity and reduce unemployment (International Monetary Fund, 2003).

Employment tenure, defined as the amount of time a worker has spent working for the same employer, can be considered as a proxy for job stability. Major differences emerge from comparisons between Europe and the United States. By 2002, the average job tenure in years was 10.6 in Europe (8.1 in the United Kingdom), 12.2 in Japan, and 6.6 in the United States. In Europe, workers with more than ten-year tenure represent 41.5 percent of total employees (32.1 percent in the United Kingdom). In the United States, the figure is only 26.2 percent. Workers whose tenure is less than one year are 14.8 percent of total employees in Europe (19.1 percent in the United Kingdom), and 26.6 percent in the United States (Auer et al., 2004).

Thus, employment stability remains a feature of European labor markets (Auer and Sandrine, 2003). The alleged negative effects of labor protection on employment and productivity have been questioned by scholars stressing the positive relationship between job tenure and productivity. According to Auer et al. (2004), regression analysis for several European sectors between 1992 and 2002 shows that employment tenure has a positive effect on productivity at the aggregate level, although there are some problems with excessively long tenure (productivity decreases for tenure over fifteen years). Therefore, European average tenure (ten years) does not appear to be detrimental to productivity.

The relationship between labor market regulation and unemployment rates is far less clear. According to Auer et al., a high percentage of short-tenure workers seems to be positively correlated with the employment-to-population rate. Thus, while it may still be true that more flexibility could be good for employment, it could be detrimental to productivity. Yet, according to other scholars, the positive effects of flexibility on employment rates have never been proven (Blanchard and Portugal, 1998; OECD, 1999). Protection against dismissals does not lessen employment rates, but does hinder exit flows from unemployment (Semenza, 2004). Starting with the oil shock in the 1970s, firms had to face a situation of volatility and uncertainty. In such a situation, firing costs, especially high in Europe, did not reduce the average level of employment because they induced firms to gradually diminish employment by attrition rather than by mass dismissals. At the same time, uncertainty reduced voluntary quitting, and the result was a fall in turnover that maintained the employment levels but increased the duration of unemployment, youth unemployment, and the number of jobs not covered by protection, for example, jobs in small firms and fixed-term atypical jobs as they were gradually legalized (Bentolila and Bertola, 1990). Therefore, long-term unemployment rates in total unemployment tend to be higher in countries with strong protection. For example, in 2005, unemployed workers with more than one year of unemployment represented 54.0 percent of total unemployed in Germany, 52.2 percent in Italy, 42.5 percent in France, and 40.1 percent in the Netherlands, as compared with 22.4 percent in the United Kingdom and 11.8 percent in the United States (see Table 9.1). Furthermore, protective regulations have positive effects on workers' bargaining power and tend to reinforce the positions of stable employees, thus enhancing the fragmentation of the labor market between insiders and outsiders (Snower and de la Teresa, 1997).

REGULATION, INDUSTRIAL RELATIONS, AND OTHER FACTORS AFFECTING EMPLOYMENT STABILITY

Job stability is not linked only to employment protection regulations. A variety of factors can affect the labor market. Aside from general market conditions linked to economic cycles and migrations, such factors can include collective bargaining agreements influenced by the respective power of employers and employees, as well as informal structures such as social values that encourage commitment on the part of both

Table 9.1. Unemployment Rates and Long-term
Unemployment (more than one year duration).
Selected Countries, 2005

Countries	Unemployment Rates (%)	More than One Year Duration (%)
Denmark[a]	4.9	25.9
France[a]	9.9	42.5
Germany[a]	11.3	54.0
Italy[a]	7.8	52.2
Japan[a]	4.6	33.3
Netherlands[a]	5.2	40.1
Sweden	7.8	18.9[c]
United Kingdom[b]	4.6	22.4
United States[b]	5.1	11.8

[a] Ages 15-64.
[b] Ages 16-64.
[c] 2004.
Source: OECD (2006), *Labor Force Statistics 1985-2005.*

employers and workers or unwritten customary norms that shape enter-prises' hiring and personnel practices in the so-called internal labor mar-ket (Doeringer and Piore, 1971). Such informal structures can have an inertia effect, undermining the implementation of new flexible regula-tions (Rodgers, 1994).

The quantity and quality of social spending can also influence job stability. An active commitment by the state to provide for laid-off work-ers may increase workers' feelings of job security, encouraging worker mobility, increasing voluntary quitting, and reducing job tenure. Further-more, high social protection for laid-off workers and the unemployed may reduce union interest and effort to obtain rigid dismissal regulations (Auer and Sandrine, 2003).

Both for the United States and Europe, there is clear evidence of the influence of unions on job stability. In the United States, for example, the proportion of workers with more than ten years of tenure in unionized companies is more than double that in nonunionized firms, and is very close to European levels (Auer et al., 2004).

In Europe, the length of job tenure is certainly positively influenced by employment protection legislation, but the different patterns of indus-trial relations in the various countries also play a major role. According to Visser (2001), four models can be identified. In the first two, Northern Corporatism (Sweden, Finland, Denmark, Norway) and Central Social

Partnership (Austria, Germany, Belgium, Netherlands), the state regulates and facilitates the relationship between unions and employers, the dominant wage bargaining level is sector, and conflict is highly organized and has low intensity. In the Latin Confrontational Model (France, Greece, Italy, Portugal, Spain), the state tends to intervene in the rivalry between unions and employers, the bargaining level alternates between sector and/or company, and the conflict is high and at times spasmodic. In the Anglo-Saxon Pluralism Model (United Kingdom and Ireland), the state abstains from direct involvement, the relationship between unions and employers is fragmented, the dominant bargaining level is that of the company, and conflict is medium and dispersed.

Differences among European countries lie not only in the degree of coordination versus confrontation, the role of the state and the bargaining structure, but also in social dialog and social spending. From this point of view, European labor market institutions differ among countries and do not constitute one rigid model, as opposed to an American flexible one, as has been suggested by the supporters of the Eurosclerosis model (Howell, 2002).

As far as union strength is concerned, the United States and the United Kingdom seem to have undergone quite different experiences when compared with continental Europe (with the probable exception of France). As in the field of work organization, in the field of industrial relations, diversity is on the increase within national systems. Nonetheless, in industrial relations, national traditions play an important role in differentiating the systems at the national level. A sort of path dependence seems to influence the different speed and depth in the shift from collective bargaining to market-oriented regulations. This shift has been greater in the United States and the United Kingdom than in Germany, the Scandinavian countries, or Italy, where trade union membership and the role of unions at the political level remain quite strong. In fact, in continental Europe, companies try to introduce more flexible employment systems with greater use of flexible pay and conditions and greater reliance on contingent workers. At the same time, in the building of new work arrangements, they tend to rely less on union bargaining and more on new forms of direct employee voice, for example, joint consultation and employee involvement through quality circles and team working (Feldenkirchen and Hilder, 2001). There has also been a shift in bargaining levels: The importance of national sector contracts is threatened by the growing weight of agreements at the level of the company that connects more strict wage levels to productivity increases.

Nevertheless, European firms did not succeed in proceeding as far as their U.S. and UK counterparts in developing a variegated and flexible employment system. Even if the strict employment protection regulations of the past have been gradually superseded by new labor laws, traditional arrangements still exercise their influence. In central and northern Europe, high job tenure reflects union constraints, whereas in Japan, the same effect is produced by customary and cultural influences (Gospel, 2007). Furthermore, Gospel recently pointed out a difference in company structure: German and Japanese firms have grown organically and are less diversified and divisionalized in comparison with their U.S. and UK (and partly French) counterparts (Gospel, 2006).

Alongside institutional and cultural traditions, a decisive structural difference between the United States and the United Kingdom on the one side, and Germany, Italy, and Japan on the other side, concerns the weight of manufacturing in the economy as a whole. In the United States and the United Kingdom, the share of industrial employment of the total active population has been reduced to a very slim level (13.1 percent and 14.4 percent, respectively, in 2004 – including mining and energy, but excluding the construction sector, whose figure is 7.7 percent in the United States and 7.6 percent in the United Kingdom). In contrast, in Germany, Italy, and Japan, industrial employment maintains a decidedly higher position (24.0 percent, 23.5 percent, 19.2 percent, respectively; construction being 6.8 percent, 8.25 percent, 9.2 percent, respectively) (ILO, 2005). As we know, the sharpest forms of flexibility and the lowest union presence are to be found in the service sector, alongside the newest forms of enterprises and technologies.

As a result, in the United States, new forms of enhanced flexibility are continuously introduced, especially in retailing, in the wave of the so-called "optimization" of working hours, with a firm such as Wal-Mart as the vanguard. In continental Europe, on the other hand, particularly under center-left coalition governments, some of the new regulations are intended to subject the new flexible arrangements to agreement with unions. For instance, the recourse to contingent workers in Italy is submitted to the control of the local Labor Office, is regulated by union agreements, and contingent workers must be paid according to sector national contracts (Musso, 2004). This seems not to be the case in the United Kingdom, which nowadays has "the most restrictive legislations in the western democracies" for the government and administration of trade unions. This legislation opens union funds to claims for damages in trade disputes and narrows unions' liberty to take industrial action (Smith, 2006). As a result, there has been "a dramatic shift from union to non-union representatives between 1980 and 1998" as well as an increase in nonunionized workplaces (Milward et al., 2000, p. 114).

In some cases, European Community recommendations and directives have compelled single-member states to make their labor legislation more flexible, as was the case with the abolition of the prohibition of private, lucrative, manpower supply agencies (a prohibition stated by the 1919 International Labor Organization convention in Washington). Until 1997, for instance, in Italy there existed a state monopoly for job placement that in the mid-1990s was condemned by the European Court in the case C-55/96 *Job Centre* (Ichino, 2000; Foglia, 2006). In the United Kingdom, in contrast, where legislation does not seem to comply with International Labor Office conventions, European Community directives imply an increase in worker rights, and various strategies have been used to transpose European Community directives on atypical workers and to reduce their impact (Kilpatrick, 2003).

Piore and Safford suggest that in the United States a shift has taken place in the axis of social mobilization, from economic identities associated with class and occupation to identities rooted outside the workplace: sex, race, ethnicity, age, disability, and sexual orientation. The new identity groups, as the authors put it, "seem to be motivated as much by the desire for social recognition as by economic gain, and the pressures they exert seem to be largely moral and symbolic rather than economic" (Piore and Safford, 2006). This shift is the consequence of the end of the model of social and economic organization that underlies the collective bargaining system, a model based on the separation between factory and family, between the realm of production with its rational and scientific standards and the realm of consumption ruled by affective and personal standards. In the case of the family, critical factors have been the rise in women's participation in the labor market and the increase in the divorce rate. As a result, the collective bargaining system has been replaced, not by a market regime, but by a regime of substantive employment rights intended to secure equal employment opportunities. This interpretation challenges the old conceptualization of industrial relations theory and its tendency to consider the epochal change of regime as a simple shift in the balance of power between employers and unions. Although Piore and Sanford's perspective is interesting, it might be argued that economic motivations remain quite important in a country in which the inequality in income distribution between upper and lower classes has increased dramatically in the last twenty years. In the American debate, ten years ago Richard Rorty condemned what in his view had been a "tacit collaboration between Right and Left in changing the subject from money to culture," stressing the opportunity to return to "class and money" issues (Rorty, 1998; Rorty et al., 1998). The recognition of economic strains and pressures as a potential source of collective mobilization does not represent a utopian dream of returning to a definitely surpassed era in the United States, a country in which, even if unemployment is at its historical low, the average dismissed worker finding a new job must take a 20 percent wage or salary cut. Under such growing income inequalities, the changing balance of power between companies and unions still plays a central role.

In any case, the epochal change sketched out by Piore and Sanford for the United States does not seem to suit the European institutional and social framework. In many European countries, in the industrial era the separation of the two realms of production and consumption was never as intense. Family and kinship ties have always and still play an important role in shaping supply and demand in the labor market as well as in the birth and operation of the numerous family-based small enterprises. An important feature in social and economic structures has been the multiactivity of individuals within their families, deriving from farming–artisan–temporarily industrial mixed activities in the early stages of industrial development. Such multiactivity lasted for a considerable time in several areas that maintained high levels of informal female productive occupations. European companies, even the biggest ones, have made and still make intense recourse to the internal extended labor market (Manwaring, 1984). Moreover, ethnic minority groups have not had a voice (with some exception in the United Kingdom and France for people coming from the old colonial empires), at least up until the very recent stabilization of groups of immigrants from outside the European Community. They had little voice because, in the recent past, immigrant workers were, and sometimes still are, considered not as citizens but as foreign guest workers (*Gastarbeiter* in Germany). Moreover, foreign immigrants themselves worked to save money to return to their villages of origin. Therefore, in Europe, the identities based on minority ethnic groups do not appear to have been an alternative source of mobilization to identities based on class or occupational groups. In sum, some of the factors of the epochal change delineated by Piore and Sanford do not appear to have been at play in continental Europe. Or, at least, they are not yet at play.

Historians have developed two different schools of thought regarding the history of strikes and union mobilization in Western countries (Boll, 1989, 1992). The first maintains the existence of an evolutionary trend toward regulated and limited conflicts thanks to growing social dialog between the parties and the state (Volkmann, 1978). The second viewpoint denies the existence of a secular development and stresses the emergence of irregular strike cycles, with new waves of labor unrest emerging whenever new working people's groups suffer from new sets of unsatisfied needs (Cronin, 1979). The first interpretation fits the Northern and Central Europe historical experience; the second, the Latin confrontational model. Referring to changes in the post-Fordist era, it can be said that an epochal shift is under way, and not merely a shift in the balance of power between unions and employers. Nonetheless, in Northern and Central Europe, the social dialog model will probably continue, whereas in confrontational countries a strengthening of the institutionalized experiences of social dialog may occur. New forms of labor mobilization may arise as well, as shown by the recent successful mobilization of workers and young people in Italy and France against the reduction in protection from dismissals and the introduction of new forms of flexible jobs.

In sum, work flexibility is not necessarily imposed by the new technologies, but depends more on management culture, organizational models, and company structure. Continental Europe's industrial relation models, rooted in their neocorporatist arrangements (Maier, 1975) that reached their highest point with the so-called "Rhineland Capitalism," seem to remain distant from their Anglo-American counterparts. The latter were fostered by a sharp, efficient, and successful discontinuity in work policies, which are not to be found in continental Europe. Here, attempts to foster flexibility are made by governments trying to introduce fixed-term workers in the public administration, thus modifying their historical role as a "model employer," showing private employers the way to guarantee worker rights, stability, and collective bargaining. The changing role of the state as employer has been especially relevant in the United Kingdom (Osborne and Gaebler, 1992; Massey and Pyper, 2005; Foster and Scott, 2006). Nevertheless, social dialog has never really been threatened. In many Europeans' eyes, a European social model, as opposed to the U.S. social model, is under construction and is characterized by "fundamental social rights, solidarity, involvement of the social partners and workers' participation, while individualism and profit-seeking dominate the American model" (Blanpain, 2003, p. 647). Such a view is schematic and oversimplified, and the European social model is part reality and part wish. Let us consider, for instance, the European Community (EC) directive on the employee right to information and consultation, adopted in March 2002 and connected to the directive on European works councils promulgated in 1994. These directives leave member states flexibility to adapt the general stated frameworks to their own industrial relations systems. The historical experience shows that worker councils within the company may represent a way for external unions to penetrate within the establishments or a way for employers to directly dialog with their employees to hold off the unions. As in the EC directives, workers' involvement retains the spirit of cooperation; in the implementation of the directive on the right to information and consultation a rift may arise between unionized and non-unionized companies. Therefore, even if recent EU statutes comply with International Labor Office conventions (Foglia, 2006), and in particular, with the principles on collective bargaining (Gernigon et al., 2000), the implementation of the mentioned directives may reinforce unions as well as employers' strategy of direct employee consultation. However, as far as it is debatable that a productive system can operate without formal or informal social regulations, Europe will not necessarily evolve along American lines. Formal work rules in continental Europe will probably continue to be shaped by union influence, at least in the medium run, and so far as industrial employment will continue to affect the labor market and working arrangements in important European member states.

CONCLUSION

Despite the sharp differences in employment stability between the United States and Europe, job tenure in the United States is remarkably high and long-term employment relationships remain quite common. Given the positive relationship between tenure and productivity, employment stability is important for enterprises, especially for those innovative industries for which job training is an essential component in the operation of the firm (e.g., through the use of work teams). As we have seen, according to Osterman (2001), the use of high-performance work systems increased in the American firms beginning in the 1980s, when the new sets of work practices were adopted in response to competitive challenges.

At the macro level, employment stability can help ensure constancy of aggregate demand. Thus, in terms of employment and productivity, employers and unions have more in common than is usually believed. Long-term employment relationships create economic stability, as steady and growing purchasing power over the life cycle of the working people becomes a positive source of consumption and thus, sustained aggregate demand growth. However, the positive relationship between extended tenure and consumer demand is based on the perception of job security. Such a perception can be undermined, even in a situation in which long-term employment relationships are widespread, if public discourse is dominated by the need for enhancing flexibility (Auer and Sandrine, 2003; OECD, 2004).

Anywhere in the developed world, even if to varying degrees, employers' needs for labor flexibility and pressure by employers' associations to reduce employment protection have been only partially successful. Union resistance to labor deregulation and the need of innovative businesses to preserve internal training and skilled personnel have strongly limited the amount of the so-called numerical flexibility (flexibility outside the firm). Nevertheless, atypical and short-term labor contracts are on the increase, especially for young people entering the labor market and old, fired workers. Deregulation on the one side and employment defense by unions on the other side seem to have enhanced fragmentation between insiders and outsiders in the labor market. Uncertainty is widespread in the labor world, probably more than may be justified by the current realities. Yet, flexibility drawbacks sharply impact some segments of the labor force, especially younger generations who face an uncertain future. Feelings of uncertainty are justified because most social security schemes are still founded on the assumption of stable employment work, based on the prevalent labor features of the time they were designed, that is, the 1950s and 1960s. Therefore, flexible workers enjoy very limited social protection, especially old age insurance. By the time the size and influence of the welfare state peaked, the dominant paradigmatic public discourse was centered on economic growth and social progress in terms of security as a human need; the state and collective efforts were supposed to play a central role in economic and social development. Now, the paradigm has shifted to one of change, risk, mobility, and individual adaptability.

Government policies generally have been intended to reduce labor market rigidity and to shift public intervention from curative measures (i.e., unemployment allowances) to labor market active policies such as training and retraining of laid-off workers. Union reactions to employers' pressure for flexibility have been centered on attempts to reduce numerical flexibility while enhancing functional flexibility within the firm. However, overall union strength is on the decrease, both because of diminishing membership that is due to the slimming of traditional industrial strongholds and to the lack of the general and encompassing unifying goals that were predominant in the Fordist era.

To understand what is at stake with flexibility, we can sketch out two different scenarios. In the first one, an optimistic view, flexibility provides a number of opportunities for individuals to experiment with different jobs and find their way in a much livelier and promising world of labor, where innovative businesses implement innovative technologies reducing fatigue, enhancing professional skills, emphasizing human capital, and fostering satisfying careers. In the second scenario, a pessimistic view, flexibility entails casual work, income uncertainty, lack of social security, the impossibility for individuals to plan their life; indeed, a sort of return to the early stages of capitalism when the world of labor was dominated by poverty and social exclusion.

Considering historical experiences, both scenarios seem unlikely. But, if future developments in the very rapid processes of social and economic change are left solely to market forces, perhaps weakly mitigated by regulations against discriminatory practices, the risk will be that the two scenarios will both become real, the first one for a minority of privileged workers, the second one for a vast majority of socially disadvantaged workers.

Indeed, history shows that in the field of technologies and organizational theories, as well as in the field of labor laws and policies, the real processes of implementation are characterized by complexity and unexpected results. Concerning work organization, there have always been large gaps between managerial theories and real practices, between ideal patterns and what really occurs. Let us consider for instance the adoption of high-performance work systems. Within the firms, a great deal of inertia and explicit resistance work against the new methods. Middle- and low-rank hierarchies are afraid of losing power and positions and reluctant to rid themselves of their habit of managing work simply by orders and discipline. Good education and high training levels are necessary to achieve a positive mix of human skills, cooperative teamwork, and advanced techniques in the new production methods. Yet, most workers and low-rank bosses in the traditional Fordist-style factory often lack such abilities. Any implementation of new methods is always an adaptation, differing from one to another company or plant. Thus, in the adaptation, some of the positive effects on job professional

content promised by the new models are often lost. From the viewpoint
of the workers, suspicious attitudes toward technological and organizational changes are widespread because of previous experiences with
the short-run unfavorable effects such changes have had on employment
and working conditions. Therefore, it is not easy for managers to obtain
workers' cooperation in explicating their tacit skills in order to enhance
the quality of product and smooth the production flow or to avoid damages and losses. The question arises as to whether managers can gain
workers' consent and collaboration solely through individual attraction
policies such as bonuses and benefits for a minority of core workers.
As far as teamwork is concerned, the kind of cooperation required of
workers is a collective one, and it necessitates a collective dialog that
implies the involvement of unions (Annibaldi, 1994), at least in countries
or companies where the presence of unions was, and still is, traditionally
strong.

Concerning flexibility and regulations, it can be noted that very rigid
protective rules were often simply bypassed or disregarded because they
contrasted too sharply with spontaneous social tendencies and market
forces, and were too difficult for public institutions to enforce. As the
Italian case shows, a rigid formal employment protection gave rise to
distortion in the active population structure. In 2002, the share of self-
employment in total active population was 25.4 percent, almost double
the average European number (14.6 percent). The rate of unemployment for young people (between the ages of fourteen and twenty-four)
was 27.2 percent, compared with the European average of 15.1 percent
(Semenza, 2004). Furthermore, in Italy, in an industrial structure characterized by the large predominance of very small firms, the amount of
irregular labor in the gray economy is especially high. The very rigid
regulation of the past still influences the Italian labor market, with a
sharp division between insiders and young outsiders. Many professionals and self-employed workers are, as a matter of fact, dependent workers
because they work for only one firm. The question arises, and not only
for the Italian case, of how a company's organization and functions
change (especially the personnel department and shop foreperson),
when required to deal with the growing use of formally autonomous
professionals and contingent workers, and what the related transaction
costs are.

As the Italian case shows, rigidity can have unexpected and undesir-
able effects. Nevertheless, a certain amount of labor market regulation

and social protection is necessary to avoid the risks of new waves of sharp labor conflicts like those of the past when the lack of social security recurrently flowed into social unrest. The fragmentation of the labor market may result from an excess of rigidity as well as from the lack of protection that divides privileged workers and socially excluded workers. A good balance between flexibility and protection is difficult to achieve.

Flexibility has always been a feature of many sectors of the labor market, and not only in the early stages of industrial development. Young and female workers in seasonal employment in agriculture, food industries, constructions, and small workshops in several manufacturing branches were the flexible components of the labor force. Their standard of living was guaranteed by a male breadwinner model that shaped labor and social protection, even if it was never fully achieved in many industrialized second-comer countries. The male breadwinner model is nowadays anachronistic, but it is not easy to adapt it to the increasing labor market flexibility that also hits adult male workers. In this process of adaptation, trade unions can play a role in organizing new flexible services and benefits for particular groups of workers, such as job placement or old age insurance funds. This will be a sort of return to the mutual benefit associations of the prewelfare state, to face the crisis of what the French call "État Providence." Social security, as we know it, was intended to solve the social problems that arose during labor's move from agriculture to industry. Now, it must be reshaped in order to face labor's shift from industry to the service sector.

Facing such difficulties, dialog between the social partners and the state seems the best way to tackle the labor problems within companies and in the broader labor market, as well as to overcome social problems linked to flexibility, and to build up a new "flexicurity" system (European Commission, 2006). Furthermore, social dialog is useful in facing local growth problems where the institutional framework plays a major role (Pyke et al., 1990; Pyke and Sengenberger, 1992). Overall, as Auer et al. put it, "if it holds true that the observed stability in the employment relationship accommodates productivity better than labor market flexibility, then the traditional positions of the social partners must be challenged. In such a case, employers should not only be interested in flexible employment relationships, but in stable ones as well [. . .] and unions should not fear more flexible labor markets if they are embedded in a framework of social security, while continuing also to ask for stable jobs [. . .] This is a good starting point for social dialogue on productive, decent employment" (Auer et al., 2004).

REFERENCES

Accornero, A. (1997). *Era il secolo del lavoro. Più interessanti ma meno tutelati i lavori del futuro?* Bologna: Il Mulino.

Accornero, A. (2006). *San Precario lavora per noi. Gli impieghi temporanei in Italia.* Milan: Rizzoli.

Accornero, A., Altieri, G., & Oteri, C. (2001). *Lavoro flessibile. Cosa pensano davvero imprenditori e manager.* Rome: Ediesse.

Annibaldi, C. (1994). *Impresa, partecipazione, conflitto. Considerazioni dall' esperienza Fiat. Dialogo con Giuseppe Berta.* Venice: Marsilio.

Auer, P. (Ed.). (2001). *Changing labor markets in Europe: The role of institutions and policies.* Geneva: ILO.

Auer, P., & Sandrine, C. (Eds.). (2003). *Employment stability in an age of flexibility. Evidence from industrialized countries.* Geneva: ILO.

Auer, P., Berg, J., & Coulibaly, I. (2004). *Is a stable workforce good for the economy? Insights into the tenure-productivity employment relationship* (Working Paper No. 15). Geneva: Employment Analysis and Research Unit- Employment Strategy Department, ILO.

Bauman, Z. (2000). *Liquid modernity.* Cambridge: Polity Press.

Beck, U. (2000). *The brave new world of work.* Cambridge: Polity Press.

Bentolila, S., & Bertola, G. (1990). Firing costs and labor demand: How bad is Eurosclerosis? *Review of Economic Studies*, 57, 381–402.

Bhorat, H., & Lundall, P. (2004). *Employment and labor market effects of globalization: Selected issues for policy management* (Employment Strategy Papers No. 3). Geneva: ILO.

Blanchard, O., & Portugal, P. (1998). *What hides behind the unemployment rate* (Working Paper No. 6636). Cambridge, MA: NBER.

Blanpain, R. (2003). *European labor law.* The Hague/ London/ New York: Kluwer Law International.

Boll, F. (1989). Changing forms of labor conflict: Secular development or strike waves? In Haimson, L., & Tilly, C. (Eds.), *Strikes, wars, revolutions in an international perspective: Strike waves in the late nineteenth and early twentieth centuries.* Cambridge: Cambridge University Press.

Boll, F. (1992). *Arbeitskämpfe und Gewerkschaften in Deutschland, England und Frankreich. Die Entwicklung von 19. Zum 20. Jahrhundert.* Bonn: Verlag Dietz.

Bonazzi, G. (1993). *Il tubo di cristallo.* Bologna: Il Mulino.

Cronin, J. (1979). *Industrial conflict in modern Britain.* London: Croom Helm.

Dahrendorf, R., Kohler, E., & Piotet, F. (Eds.). (1986). *New forms of work and activity.* Dublin: Europäische Stiftung zur Verbesserung der Lebens – und Arbeiterbedingungen.

Doeringer, P.B., & Piore, M. J. (1971). *Internal labor markets and manpower analysis.* Lexington, MA: Heath.

European Commission. (2001). *Employment in Europe*. Brussels: Author.
European Commission. (2006). *Employment in Europe*. Brussels: Author.
Feldenkirchen, W., & Hilder, S. 2001. *Menschen und Marken*. Duesseldorf, Germany: Henkel.
Foglia, R. (2006). *Il lavoro*. Torino: Giappichelli.
Foster, D., & Scott, P. (2006). *Deregulation of employment: The impact of the reorganisation of the UK state* (Mimeo). Paper presented to the working group for the project "State and Work Relations in the Twentieth-Century," Paris.
Gallino, L. (2000). *Globalizzazione e disuguaglianze*. Rome: Laterza.
Gallino, L. (2001). *Il costo umano della flessibilità*, Rome: Laterza.
Gernigon, B., Odero, A., & Guido, H. (2000). ILO principles concerning collective bargaining. *International Labor Review*, 139(1), 33–55.
Gorz, A. (1908). *Adieux au proletariat*. Paris: Galilèe.
Gospel, H. (2006). *The development of labor management in divisionalised companies* (Mimeo). London: King's College.
Gospel, H. (2007). Labor management in historical perspective. In Jones, G., & Zeitlin, J. (Eds.), *Handbook of business history*. Oxford, UK: Oxford University Press.
Haimson, L., & Tilly, C. (Eds.). (1989). *Strikes, wars, revolutions in an international perspective: Strike waves in the late nineteenth and early twentieth centuries*. Cambridge: Cambridge University Press.
Howell, D. (2002). Increasing earnings inequality and unemployment in developed countries: Markets, institutions and the "unified theory" (Working Paper No. 1). New York: Center for Economic Policy Analysis.
Ichino, P. (2000). *Il contratto di lavoro. 1, Fonti e principi generali, autonomia individuale e collettiva, disciplina del mercato, tipi legali, decentramento produttivo, differenziazione dei trattamenti e inquadramento*. Milan: Giuffré.
ILO. (2005). *Yearbook of labor statistics*. Geneva: Author.
International Monetary Fund. (2003). *World economic outlook*. Washington, DC: Author.
Iversen, T., & Cusack, T. R. (2000). The causes of welfare state expansion: Deindustrialization or globalization? *World Politics*, 52, 313–49.
Jones, E. L. (1974). *Agriculture and the Industrial Revolution*. Oxford, UK: Oxford University Press.
Jones, G., & Zeitlin, J. (Eds.). (2007). *Handbook of business history*. Oxford, UK: Oxford University Press.
Joseph Rowntree Foundation. (1999). *Job insecurity and work intensification: Flexibility and the changing boundaries of work*. Cambridge: Cambridge University Press.
Kaelble, H. (Ed.). (1978). *Probleme der Modernisierung in Deutschland. Sozialhistorische Studien zum 19. und 20. Jahrhundert*. Opladen, Germany: Westdeutscher Verlag.
Katz, H., & Darbishire, O. R. (2000). *Converging divergencies: World-wide changes in employment systems*. Ithaca, NY: Cornell University Press.
Kern, H., & Schumann, M. (1994). *Das Ende der Arbeitsteilung? Rationalisierung in der industriellen Produktion*. Munich: Beck.

Kilpatrick, C. (2003). Has new labor reconfigured employment legislation? *Industrial Law Journal*, 32, 135-63.

Kochan, T. A., Lansbury, R. D., & MacDuffie, J. P. (Eds.). (1997). *After lean production: Evolving employment practices in the world auto industry*. Ithaca, NY: ILR Press.

Liechtenstein, N. (Ed.). (2006). *Wal-Mart: Template for 21st century capitalism*. New York: New Press.

MacDuffie, J. P. (1991). *Beyond mass production: Flexible production systems and manufacturing performance, in the world auto industry*. Cambridge MA: MIT Press.

MacDuffie, J. P. (1995). Human resources bundles and manufacturing performance: Organizational logics and flexible production systems in the world auto industry. *Industrial and Labor Relations Review*, 48(2), 197-221.

Maier, C. S. (1975). *Recasting bourgeois Europe*. Princeton, NJ: Princeton University Press.

Majid, N. (2005). *On the evolution of employment structure in developing countries* (Working Paper No. 18). Geneva: Employment Analysis Unit, Employment Strategy Department, ILO.

Manwaring, T. (1984). The internal extended labor market. *Cambridge Journal of Economics*, 8, 161-87.

Marchington, M., Grimshaw, D., Rubery, J., & Willmott, H. (2005). *Fragmenting work, blurring organisational boundaries, and disordering hierarchies*. Oxford, UK: Oxford University Press.

Massey, A., & Pyper, R. (2005). *Public management and modernisation in Britain*. Basingstoke, UK: Palgrave Macmillan.

Milward, N., Bryson, A., & Forth, J. (2000). *All change at work? British employment relations 1980-98*. London: Routledge.

Musso, S. (2004). *Le regole e l'elusione. Il governo del mercato del lavoro nell'industrializzazione Italiana (1898-2003)*. Torino, Italy: Rosenberg & Sellier.

O'Connor, J. (1973). *The fiscal crisis of the state*. New York: St. Martin's Press.

Osborne, D., & Gaebler, T. (1992). *Reinventing government: How the entrepreneurial spirit is transforming the public sector*. Reading, MA: Addison Wesley.

OECD. (1999). *Employment outlook*. Paris: Author.

Offe, C., & Heinze, R. G. (1992). *Beyond employment : Time work and the informal economy*. Cambridge: Polity Press.

Ohno, T. (1988). *Toyota production system: Beyond large-scale production*. Cambridge, MA: Productivity Press.

Osterman, P. (2000). Work organization in an era of restructuring: Trends in diffusion and impacts on employees welfare. *Industrial and Labor Relations Review*, 52, 2, 180-96.

Osterman, P. (2001). *Flexibility and commitment in the United States labor market* (Employment Paper No. 18). Geneva: ILO.

Piore, M. J., & Safford, S. (2006). *Changing regimes of workplace governance, shifting axes of social mobilization and the challenge to industrial relations theory* (Mimeo). Cambridge MA: MIT.

Pyke, F., & Sengenberger, W. (1992). *Industrial districts and local economic regeneration*. Geneva: International Institute for Labor Studies.

Pyke, F., Becattini, G., & Sengenberger, W. (1990). *Industrial districts and inter-firm cooperation in Italy*. Geneva: International Institute for Labor Studies.

Regini, M., & Sabel, C. S. (Eds.). (1989). *Strategie di riaggiustamento industriale*, Bologna: Il Mulino.

Rodgers, G. (Ed.). (1994). *Workers, institutions and economic growth in Asia*. Geneva: IILS.

Rorty, R. (1998). *Achieving our country: Leftist thought in twentieth century America*. Cambridge, MA: Harvard University Press.

Rorty, R., Nystrom, D., & Puckett, K. (1998). *Against bosses, against oligarchies: A conversation with Richard Rorty*. Charlottesville, VA: Prickly Pear Pamphlets.

Sassen, S. (1997). *Informalization in advanced market economies* (Discussion Paper on Issues in Development, No. 20). Geneva: Development Policies Department, ILO.

Semenza, R. (2004). *Le trasformazioni del lavoro. Flessibilità, disuguaglianze, responsabilità dell'impresa*. Rome: Carocci.

Sennet, R. (1998). *The corrosion of character. The personal consequences of work in the new capitalism*. New York: Norton.

Sennet, R. (2006). *The culture of the new capitalism*. New Haven, CT: Yale University Press.

Sloan, A. P. (1964). *My years with General Motors*. Garden City, NY: Doubleday.

Smith, P. (2006). Neoliberalism and employer regulation in the United Kingdom, 1979–2006. Paper presented to the working group for the project "State and Work Relations in the Twentieth-Century," Paris.

Snower, D., & de la Teresa, G. (Eds.). (1997). *Unemployment policy: Government options for the labor market*. Cambridge: Cambridge University Press.

Visser, J. (2001). Industrial relations and social dialogue. In Auer, P. (Ed.)., *Changing labor markets in Europe: The role of institutions and policies*. Geneva: ILO.

Volkmann, H. (1978). Modernisierung des Arbeitskampfes? Zum Formwandel von Streik und Aussperrung in Deutschland 1864-1975. In Kaelble, H. (Ed.), *Probleme der Modernisierung in Deutschland. Sozialhistorische Studien zum 19. und 20. Jahrhundert*. Opladen, Germany: Westdeutscher Verlag.

Voss, K., & Sherman, R. (2000). Breaking the iron law of oligarchy: Revitalization in the American labor movement. *American Journal of Sociology*, 106, 303-49.

A Tentative Conclusion

LOUIS GALAMBOS

Can we talk with confidence about a third industrial revolution in global business in the late twentieth and twenty-first centuries? Is this theory in concert with what we know about the changes taking place in business organizations and practices in this era? The preceding chapters provide substantial evidence of a wave of change in business systems, in the governmental context for business activity, in labor relations, and in the financial markets that sustained entrepreneurship. Accustomed as most historians are to anecdotal evidence and eager as most historians are to embrace general concepts that give clear meaning to the past, we could easily leap to a positive conclusion. Yes, the authors are telling us, business systems and the surrounding political economy have been transformed for the third time in the history of industrial capitalism. The information age involves, we could conclude, just as dramatic a trans-formation for business as did the factory systems of the first industrial revolution and the bureaucratized, corporate economy of the second.

Before we leap, we need to think again about the evidence and conclu-sions offered by Giovanni Dosi, Alfonso Gambardella, Marco Grazzi, and Luigi Orsenigo. Their "bird's-eye statistical" perspective creates prob-lems for the historian satisfied that he or she would not be writing on a computer if there had not been a revolutionary change. Dosi et al. estab-lish that the balance between business activities oriented to the market and those encompassed within organizations (hence their emphasis on "the relative stability of size distributions") has not changed very much in the information age. Within that relatively stable framework, they find little evidence of organizational transitions of the magnitude of the structural changes that accompanied the second industrial revolution in the developed economies. Yes, they tell us, revolutionary technological breakthroughs took place in the recent past, but the organizational perspective "is rather more blurred."

Their quantitative map guides us, I believe, to a deeper understanding of the process of industrial change, particularly during the second industrial revolution and the transition into our current information age. Dosi et al. portray a business system experiencing substantial change within a broader political economy in which there were and still are large elements of institutional continuity. Thus we can see various degrees of change from sector to sector, various organizational adaptations in and outside of business, and various political accommodations to the new techno-economic setting. However, there was also a considerable amount of economic activity remaining stable while "the processes of creative destruction–creative accumulation" and "the new techno-economic paradigm" were making themselves felt.

This, I would suggest, was true as well in the second industrial revolution. In Europe, in the United States, and in Asia, for instance, family enterprises were still common long after the modern corporation had emerged in industry. Most commercial and agricultural activity continued to be conducted along traditional lines, and we now know that various forms of batch production persisted in an era that we usually associate with the assembly line, mass production, and mass distribution. The borderline between modern corporate enterprise and older institutional forms was shifting, but the change was scalar and far from complete, even in the later stages of the second industrial revolution.

Dosi et al. thus guide us toward a history written in search of the sequences of scalar change and mindful of important economic continuities. As Pamela Adams, Stefano Brusoni, and Franco Malerba conclude, the boundaries of knowledge essential to business have experienced a dramatic expansion, as has the division of labor in the application of that knowledge. However, the governance of that knowledge has remained concentrated in the hands of "large firms, system integrators, and network firms." In this and other ways, the information age builds upon the previous revolution, and it is historically unique because the second industrial revolution was part of its historical context. All of these authors guide us toward narrower fronts in order to find decisive, revolutionary changes in global business.

Looking deeper into the electronic age, we do indeed find remarkable change in the electronic industries analyzed by Richard Langlois. These are the newest of the new producers, present where the digital age was unfolding with amazing speed. Here, the old models of U-form and M-form frequently – but not always – gave way to specialized organizations coordinating production over several continents. Globalization, a political phenomenon with a technological element, enabled network organizations to thrive. The consequences of global competition in this new technical setting appeared very decisively among the top 100 employers in the leading developed economies. No longer did first-movers enjoy the type of stability that Alfred D. Chandler emphasized. Now the "boundaries of knowledge," that is, the knowledge relevant to firms, experienced a rapid expansion and fostered "interaction and exchange across organizations"; hence the network phenomenon identified by Manuel Castells as the signature characteristic of the new age.

The new technology and its organizational and political institutions thus began to change some sectors, some industries, and some firms. The picture that emerges is one of concentric circles of change rippling through the developed world and then into the developing societies. The means of financing entrepreneurial activities changed as a result of innovations in the stock markets and in the venture capital industry in the United States. Meanwhile, many aspects of the aircraft industry were, for instance, altered dramatically by electronic innovations. A batch-production industry, aircraft design, construction, and operation were all changed by "electronic-based innovations such as avionic systems." New IT-based reservations systems were accompanied by new business strategies that altered competition in Europe and the United States.

Even a commodity like aluminum felt the direct and indirect impacts of the new age. Computer control, modulation, and digital communications eased the industry toward a truly global scale of operations. The new electronic technology, Margaret Graham says, "has enabled a spread of enterprises around the globe, a certain expansion of the span of control of any one enterprise, an increase in scale, an ability to automate processes and dramatically reduce direct employment, and possibly an increase in employee mobility, especially managerial employee mobility."

Certainly, new patterns of labor relations emerged, creating important opportunities for those with appropriate skills and important problems for those who lacked skills and found their lives changed by the pressures of the electronic transformation. For the most part, Stefano Musso explains, jobs themselves remained relatively stable. But the demands for flexibility, cost-cutting, and the declines in union strength in many societies left workers rightly fearful of the future and looking to their governments for protection. There were many different models of employer-employee relations, with a general tendency for power to shift from the workers and their organizations to management. The emergence of the service industries was a crucial part of what happened: the boundaries between manufacturing and services were vanishing. The "dominant paradigmatic public discourse" was no longer focused on "economic growth and social progress in terms of security as a human need. . . . Now, the paradigm has shifted to one of change, risk, mobility, and individual adaptability." This is a harsh world indeed.

The newest elements in the modern economy began to press changes on the administrative state in most societies. There was, as you might expect, a high degree of continuity in governmental institutions. The promotional state was well developed long before the twentieth century; hence, the relevance of Adam Smith's assault in *The Wealth of Nations* (1776) on mercantilism and state privileges. But the demands in the twentieth century were more indirect, more expensive, and far more complex. Creating a professional setting that would encourage the development of solid-state physics or microbiology was a new challenge that called for new institutional responses in the developed nations. The pressure to change was impossible for most to resist, especially when their leaders or the media realized that they were falling behind in the race to develop sciences and technologies relevant to innovation in the private sector. Now, the effort "to preserve . . . vitality, in terms of entrepreneurial effervescence above all, was probably the most important and delicate task of new public policies at the turn of the new millennium."

The various chapters in this volume indicate quite clearly that we are in the first stages of a new industrial era with evolutionary and revolutionary as well as some very stable characteristics. While the balance between market-oriented and bureaucratically organized activities demonstrates considerable overall stability, supporting an analysis framed in terms of coevolution, the perspective within and between sectors is characterized by a stunning array of changes. The science and technology base has shifted in a dramatic fashion, requiring a new orientation to networks, new leaders, and a new culture characterized by one of its leaders as a functional brand of paranoia. The administrative state has responded with new patterns of direct and indirect promotion of innovation. Stabilizing institutions – especially those serving labor – have come under great pressure as societies turned toward innovation and efficiency and away from security and equity as their primary, long-range goals. On the science-based frontiers of the public, private, and nonprofit sectors, there is a stark realization that progress in the information age is creative for some, destructive for others, and challenging for all.

Index

Printed in the United States
By Bookmasters